A Word in Season

A Word in Season

Isaiah's Reception in the Book of Mormon

JOSEPH M. SPENCER

© 2023 by the Board of Trustees
of the University of Illinois
All rights reserved
1 2 3 4 5 C P 5 4 3 2 1
♾ This book is printed on acid-free paper.

Library of Congress Cataloging-in-Publication Data
Names: Spencer, Joseph M., author.
Title: A word in season : Isaiah's reception in the Book
    of Mormon / Joseph M. Spencer.
Description: Urbana : University of Illinois Press,
    [2023] | Includes bibliographical references and
    index.
Identifiers: LCCN 2023017487 (print) | LCCN 2023017488
    (ebook) | ISBN 9780252045523 (cloth) | ISBN
    9780252087639 (paperback) | ISBN 9780252055157
    (ebook)
Subjects: LCSH: Book of Mormon—Relation to the
    Bible. | Bible. Isaiah—Criticism, interpretation,
    etc. | Book of Mormon—Criticism, interpretation,
    etc.
Classification: LCC BX8627.S73 2023 (print) | LCC
    BX8627 (ebook) | DDC 289.3/22—dc23/eng/
    20230512
LC record available at https://lccn.loc.gov/2023017487
LC ebook record available at https://lccn.loc.gov/
    2023017488

Contents

Acknowledgments   vii
Introduction   xi

1   Preliminaries   1

PART I. MORMON'S ISAIAH   25

2   Controversy in a Nephite Colony   29
3   Tradition and Innovation   53
4   A New Direction at the Meridian of Time   77
5   A Radical Hermeneutic in Outline   100

PART II. NEPHI'S ISAIAH   123

6   Nursing Fathers and Nursing Mothers   127
7   The Structure of Nephi's Record   151
8   He Shall Set His Hand Again the Second Time   175
9   As One That Hath a Familiar Spirit   197

Notes   223
Works Cited   265
Index   285
Scripture Index   293

Acknowledgments

This book has taken shape over many years, and so it has incurred—as such projects do—a great many debts.

I have been privileged to present my research and findings on Isaiah in the Book of Mormon on many occasions and in many settings. Aspects of the arguments in this book came out in talks at the American Academy of Religion, the Society of Biblical Literature, the American Historical Association, the Latter-day Saint Theology Seminar, the Summer Seminar on Mormon Culture, the Society for Mormon Philosophy and Theology, the Mormon Scholars Foundation, the Friday Faculty Forum in Religious Education at Brigham Young University, and the Neal A. Maxwell Institute Seminar. In addition, I have given somewhat less formal presentations of some of these findings at the Institute of Religion at Southern Virginia University, Writ and Vision Rare Books and Fine Art (in Provo, Utah), Pioneer Book (also in Provo), Brigham Young University's Education Week, the Claremont Mormon Studies Council, and Latter-day Saint congregations in Albuquerque, New Mexico; Seattle, Washington; Thousand Oaks, California; and Provo, Utah. All these speaking opportunities have been deeply enriching, and they have sharpened the argument in the book substantially.

I am grateful also to the Department of Ancient Scripture at Brigham Young University—my academic home—for granting me a leave from teaching for the first half of 2021. Without that breathing space to focus on this project, I could not have completed it.

Much more than institutions, however, I wish to thank individuals. I owe deep gratitude to Adam Miller, Kim Matheson, Nephi Henry, Robert Couch, Sharon Harris, Edje Jeter, and Jenny Webb, my most consistent interlocutors and the best friends a person can have. Jim Faulconer has long been my most important mentor, and this book owes much to his wisdom and unswerving support. Jana Riess edited the entire manuscript, taking on the task of cutting tens of thousands of words from a longer version of the book. In the process, she has made me sound like a more coherent and succinct writer than I will ever be. Alison Syring, my editor at the University of Illinois Press, has been a tireless champion of this project since I first brought it to her. She has helped me to make the book far better than it would have been while nimbly maneuvering the sometimes complicated politics in the field of Mormon studies. I owe my thanks to her—and, through her, to several anonymous reviewers (and one nonanonymous reviewer: Mark Thomas).

I owe gratitude also to Loyd Ericson, Deane Galbraith, Brian Hauglid, and Thom Wayment, all of whom encouraged me to publish preliminary findings in journals they edited or presses they managed. Chad Brady, Stan Hall, Jeremiah John, Brad Kramer, Travis Patten, Jacob Rennaker, and Duane Winden all created opportunities for me to present my findings to lay audiences, for which I am grateful. Brian Hauglid (already mentioned) and Jerry Bradford (whom I deeply miss) have been encouraging supporters, and their generous financial support for early parts of my research through the Laura F. Willes Center for Book of Mormon Studies (housed at the Neal A. Maxwell Institute for Religious Scholarship) proved indispensable.

There are many others who have encouraged me in this project and been willing to engage critically with it over many years: Jacob Baker, Chris Blythe, Don Bradley, Sam Brown, Richard Bushman, Jason Combs, Luke Drake, Amy Easton-Flake, James Egan, Rob Fergus, Julie Frederick, Nick Frederick, Terryl Givens, Clark Goble, Alan Goff, Deidre Green, Matt Grey, George Handley, Grant Hardy, Heather Hardy, Kristian Heal, Jared Hickman, John Hilton, Blair Hodges, Shon Hopkin, Brad Kramer, Michelle Lee, Sue Mangelson, Mike MacKay, Brock Mason, Taylor Petrey, Andy Reed, Noel Reynolds, Andrew Smith, Chris Smith, Jonathan Stapley, Chris Thomas, Rosalynde Welch, Miranda Wilcox, and anyone who has attended the study group my wife and I have occasionally hosted on Friday evenings. Thanks to you all (and to those I am sure I have forgotten to mention).

Interactions with students in my Book of Mormon courses at Brigham Young University have also helped me to sharpen the arguments in this book.

These students' intense interest in Latter-day Saint scripture always encourages me greatly, and their healthy pushback consistently makes me a better reader. Among them, two student research assistants have done especially important work for this project. Cole Rolfson gathered numerous resources from the nineteenth-century American frontier, deepening the picture I sketch in this study. And Alice Judd gave her attention to a variety of tasks that, so ably fulfilled, have helped make the book more readable. She has also become one of my best friends and a favorite interlocutor.

Beyond any of these people, however, I wish to thank Karen, my wife, and our delightful children. Their patience is immeasurable, and this book is one of the products of their patience. It was Karen who, on the first Christmas we spent together, gave me the Hebrew Bible in which I first began to study Isaiah seriously. She has been my best conversation partner, and I often steal her ideas. This work owes much to her mind, her spirit, and her love. Dedicating this book to her is the tiniest way to demonstrate my appreciation for her profound partnership. It does nothing, though, to pay the debt I am thrilled to continue owing her.

Introduction

In one important sense, a book is no more than the set of interpretations it proves capable of prompting. The half-century of literary theory that has unfolded since the late 1960s has made forcefully clear that a written work is, in its very being, irreducibly intertwined with the worlds of its readers. No literary product can be made to mean just anything, of course; the warp and the woof of its words exert pressure on anyone who comes honestly to the task of reading. In the words of philosopher Adam Miller, a book is *resistant* to whoever encounters it in the materiality of its syntax and semantics. At the same time, a book is what it is only to the extent that it is simultaneously *available* to its readers, again evoking Miller.[1] The measure of a work therefore might ultimately be just the *resistant availability* it offers to anyone who takes it up, or even might take it up.

All this is true of sacred literature as of other kinds of writing. Indeed, those who reflect on the idea of sacred literature argue that what constitutes scripture *as* scripture is the way a community of believing readers invest it with authority.[2] For these reasons, reception history has come to a position of some prominence in the study of the Christian Bible. The Bible *is* its reception. It *is* whatever interpretive possibilities it makes available to its readers, even as it resists them with the force of its networked words. To grasp the range of the Bible's interpretive possibilities, it has proven helpful to investigate the history of its reception, to consider past moments when this or that scriptural text has served for a time as what one biblical passage calls "a word in season"

(Isaiah 50:4). Investigating actual but unfamiliar interpretations of biblical texts, one comes to see better the versatility or the virtuality of the scripture, the whole range of its resistant availability.

Naturally, the tangled history of human interests shapes the history of biblical interpretation. The reading of sacred texts is as affected by structures of power as anything else in history, providing scholars with one reason for considering the reception history of the Bible: to unveil the workings of human investments in what has mostly been presented as the outworking of the divine spirit. This motivation has its merits but has a tendency toward positivism and naïveté about how texts mean. The temptation is to pretend that texts have only one scientifically responsible meaning and then to insist that all interpretations that have failed to agree with it are impositions on the text. A less ideological way of investigating reception history, however, is to ask how each interpreter's project or program with a text probes its resistance and reveals its availability. How does each historical interaction with a text help to deepen, rather than to distract from, its meaning? Put another way, how might what the Bible *has meant* reveal what it *might mean*, or in fact what it *will have meant* when all is said and done?

Because of its length and historical importance, reconstructing the Bible's reception history in its entirety is impossible. Even tracing the basic contours of the reception of this or that book within the Bible is the work of an entire career. We nonetheless stand to learn much from investigating with care any particular moment—and especially any poignant moment—in the Bible's reception history. Wherever some foray into the Bible's meaning has been particularly influential, it deserves attention. It should tell us something about both the resistance and the availability of the biblical text to its readers and therefore something about how this book means. Just as often, though, instructive work on the Bible's meaning comes from unlikely sources, from things influential in their own right but not at all within the mainstream of interpretation. That is, instructive work on the Bible's meaning occasionally and importantly happens to appear in, say, a book that is not "universally considered by its critics as one of those books that must be read in order to have an opinion of it."[3]

In 1838, Joseph Smith decided the time had come to take control of his story. From the time, eight years earlier, when he had organized his church and published the first edition of the Book of Mormon, Smith had faced a steady stream of public criticism in print. Citing "many reports . . . put in circulation by evil-disposed and designing persons," he stated as his aim in writing his history "to disabuse the public mind, and put all inquirers after truth in possession of the facts."[4] The largest of the branches of the religious movement Smith launched would eventually canonize part of his attempt to tell his own story. Consequently, it remains a major source for understanding the popular view of Smith's early career. And at the heart of the story he had to tell in 1838 lie the words of the biblical prophet Isaiah.

According to Smith, the new religious tradition he shepherded into existence had its beginnings in two visionary experiences. The first occurred in 1820 in a small grove of trees behind the Smith family farm. There the young Smith saw both God the Father and Jesus Christ, who appeared in response to the young man's question about "which of all the sects was right."[5] Although Smith (along with others among his followers) reported different details about this experience each time it was narrated, the official account from 1838 provides only a few short lines of description of what God had to say during his appearance.[6] Smith was told that he "must join none" of the various churches of his day, "for they were all wrong"; "all their creeds were an abomination in [God's] sight," and their "professors were all corrupt."[7] This dire situation God then summarized, according to Smith's account, by invoking a passage from the twenty-ninth chapter of Isaiah: "They draw near to me with their lips, but their hearts are far from me, they teach for doctrines the commandments of men, having a form of godliness, but they deny the power thereof."[8] Looking back on his earliest spiritual experiences almost two decades after the event, Smith reported that his prophetic mission had begun with the God of heaven using the words of Isaiah to explain his purposes.

Three years after his first encounter with the divine, Smith had a second vision—this time of an angel, rather than of God himself. Again, there are various early accounts of the angel's visit, some remarkably elaborate.[9] Smith's 1838 account is again strikingly spare in the details it provides. The angel's purpose was to alert Smith to the fact that buried in a nearby hill was a set of gold plates, on which an unknown book of scripture written in an unknown ancient language was to be found. Smith would have the responsibility to translate the plates by the gift and power of God. But, according to the 1838 history, in order to provide context for the calling he was extending to Smith, the angel went on to quote passages of scripture to the young man—some apparently "with a little variation" from standard renderings.[10] Smith identified four passages quoted by the angel, three of them shorter texts excerpted from their biblical contexts. Only one passage of scripture mentioned by Smith was of substantial length; the angel "quoted the eleventh chapter of Isaiah, saying that it was about to be fulfilled."[11] As in his 1820 encounter with God, Smith's 1823 encounter with an angel found the divine being turning to the words of Isaiah to communicate with the budding nineteenth-century prophet.

Four years after his encounter with the angel, Smith's history reports, he finally received the gold plates and haltingly began to work on translating them. Another year and a half would pass before he would begin to translate in earnest.[12] But when Smith finally undertook to dictate the contents of the Book of Mormon to a scribe in a burst of inspiration in the spring and summer of 1829, he heard falling from his own lips the themes of his earliest visionary experiences as he would later describe them. The Book of Mormon is, among other things, a sustained engagement with the writings of Isaiah. And, important to note, two of the chapters of Isaiah that receive the most focused and consistent attention in the Book of Mormon are chapters 11 and 29, precisely those Smith said God and the angel quoted to him. As Smith saw things when he began to write his history in 1838, dictating the text of the Book of Mormon apparently brought to a climax ten years of revelatory communications about the relevance and meaning of Isaiah's writings.

Despite this focus on Isaiah in the founding stories and documents of the religious movement begun by Joseph Smith, relatively little attention has been given to the ways Smith's prophetic oeuvre interprets the biblical Book of Isaiah.[13] Recent years have seen a drastic increase in interest in the history of Isaiah interpretation, but scholars involved in that conversation have largely ignored the persistent engagement with Isaiah in the foundational documents and early history of the various religious groups that trace their origins to Smith.[14] In part, the reason seems to be that the Book of Mormon, the most remarkable among the texts made public by Smith, has itself only recently begun to receive serious attention in the academy. Careful and illuminating work on the basic meaning and message of the Book of Mormon remains preliminary, making detailed analysis of its extensive engagement with the Isaian corpus look like a project best left for later.[15] But, as I hope to show in the course of the present work, it is necessary to consider the Book of Mormon's treatment of Isaiah to make real sense of this unique volume of scripture. Isaiah is a key—perhaps *the* key—to the Book of Mormon's meaning, and certainly to how the volume understands its own significance. It is for this reason that it might be appropriate to talk of a *program* within the Book of Mormon with respect to the use of Isaiah.

I therefore take as my double task in this study to provide a close analysis of how Isaian writings function in the Book of Mormon and of how the Book of Mormon functions as an interpretation of Isaian writings. I aim, that is, both to elucidate the basic program of the Book of Mormon in terms of its systematic treatment of Isaiah and to place the Book of Mormon within the larger network of approaches to the Book of Isaiah on offer in Judeo-Christian history. Details about my larger argument and several conclusions appear in chapter 1 and unfold over the remainder of the book, but it might be useful to state right up front what this study aims to achieve. Above all, I argue that the Book of Mormon intentionally—even programmatically—makes the interpretation of Isaiah a central and sustained concern in order to raise questions about and then to defend vigorously the modern relevance of the ancient institution of prophecy. In this way, the Book of Mormon forestalls in advance two centuries of criticism of its own relationship to history because it insists on the priority of faith over knowledge and of the prophetic over the historical. If the Book of Mormon really treats Isaiah so centrally and even uniquely, it deserves a vital place in the study of Isaiah's reception, and the interpretation of Isaiah deserves recognition as the organizing force for the materials making up the Book of Mormon. What should make the Book of Mormon of real interest to students of the history of Isaiah's reception is the exceptional way it goes about the work of interpreting the prophet. Like so much of the tradition, it offers interpretations of and commentaries on important passages from Isaiah. Nonetheless, it does a good deal more than that, and in what eventually shows itself to be a remarkably inventive way.

The Book of Mormon presents itself as the history of an ancient Israelite people transplanted to the New World from Jerusalem some six centuries before Christ. Telling a story that covers a thousand years of history, it traces major changes in the religious institutions of the people whose history it recounts: divisions between believers and unbelievers, struggles among rival religious sects, tensions between governmentally sponsored and ideally independent religious institutions, developments in theological commitments, changes in how religious rituals of various sorts were practiced and understood, wars driven by ideological views of a variety of religious phenomena, and transformations effected by the eventual visit of Jesus Christ to the New World after his resurrection. But of peculiar importance to the tortured history told in the Book of Mormon is a prolonged debate about the relevance and meaning of Isaiah's prophecies. Stretched across the whole narrative arc of the book, its debate makes the question of Isaian interpretation an explicit focus, and the volume offers a variety of often mutually exclusive interpretations of Isaiah's writings without definitively deciding among them.[16] At the same time, there is a discernible telos for the book's interactions with Isaiah, a climactic experiment with the Isaian text that arguably constitutes its key contribution. The unresolved debate within the Book of Mormon ultimately yields a novel Isaian hermeneutic with a sharp theological edge, deserving close reading and theoretical reflection. Isaiah in fact becomes the medium through which the Book of Mormon reflects on its own status as scripture.

It is remarkable enough that the Book of Mormon presents its sustained and programmatic reflection on the interpretation of the Book of Isaiah in the form of a centuries-long debate over the subject, but it is more remarkable still that it does so by audaciously presenting that debate as having taken place in relatively close proximity to the historical Isaiah. Because the Book of Mormon presents itself as having its origins in Jerusalem just before the destruction of Solomon's temple and the deportation of Jerusalem's inhabitants to Babylon, it offers its quotations of extensive selections of Isaiah's writings as if they provided glimpses of an extremely early form of what Hugh Williamson nicely refers to as "the book called Isaiah."[17] Rather than slavishly reproducing a well-known version of the Isaian text, the Book of Mormon's Isaiah quotations contain a host of variants both minor and major, ranging from the deeply intriguing to the suggestively suspicious.[18] In many places as well, it is clear that contributors to the Book of Mormon are to be understood as themselves directly adapting Isaiah's texts for their own peculiar purposes, sometimes briefly and in relatively obvious ways and sometimes—in particular when the Book of Mormon's programmatic interaction with Isaiah reaches its climax—in extensive midrashic appropriations that explore the potentialities of the Isaian text in virtuosic ways. Thus, not only does the Book of Mormon present in its pages a lively and often inconclusive debate over the meaning of Isaiah's writings, it also claims to do so while having more immediate access than most sources to what Isaiah himself actually said.

At the same time, the Book of Mormon never traps itself in the ancient world. Even as it claims to reach into antiquity, it presents itself as a divinely ordained communication directed to the modern world. The book emphatically presents itself as a translation, undertaken in the nineteenth century and with a prophetic eye on the American experiment. The prophets whose stories appear in the Book of Mormon consistently turn to Isaiah when they wish to say something about the "latter days," the era of the Book of Mormon's eventual coming forth. The volume's debate about the meaning of Isaiah's writings ultimately amounts to a debate about their relevance to a world rapidly falling under the sway of widespread secularism. Further, the textual variants in the Book of Mormon's lengthy quotations of Isaiah are presented as variants in the King James Version of Isaiah—that is, as variants in the most popular translation of Isaiah available in Joseph Smith's era. The Book of Mormon thus presents itself both as a purported window onto the most ancient reception of Isaiah's writings and as a forceful articulation of the relevance of Isaiah's prophecies to the modern world.[19]

Whether one believes the Book of Mormon's claims to antiquity or prefers to regard it as a strictly modern production, the volume is striking for the unique way it goes about engaging with the biblical Book of Isaiah. It deserves close and careful analysis for what it contributes to the interpretation of the prophet whose writings have historically been regarded as providing "the theological high water mark" of the Hebrew Bible.[20] And the role played by Isaiah in the Book of Mormon deserves close and careful analysis for what it might contribute to an understanding of the book. I hope, therefore, that the following pages begin to do justice to the richness of the Book of Mormon's treatment of Isaiah.

1

Preliminaries

In a delightful memoir, Avi Steinberg records his experience as a largely secular Jew wandering about Jerusalem looking for a copy of the Book of Mormon. His search grows frustrating and finally proves fruitless (he can find only a secondhand copy in Samoan), and so he reflects on why the book is so hard to find in the sacred city. His answer is insightful. He does not point to politics surrounding Christian missionizing in Israel, as do others who comment on the Book of Mormon's unwelcome status in Jerusalem.[1] Instead, he outlines a theological explanation. The city of Jerusalem, he points out, "desires to be singular, set apart as the dwelling of the One True, the creator of all, that violently monogamous god of gods." Further, according to the prophets of the Hebrew Bible, Jerusalem "is indeed the place where the world will end, the destination point of history." The Book of Mormon, however, makes Jerusalem not a destination but, "sacrilegiously," a "point of departure. It's a story about *leaving* Jerusalem—and not returning."[2] The sacred geography of the Book of Mormon works against that of the Bible. Its heroes leave Jerusalem to settle in a *different* "promised land," one located in the ancient Americas, where a "new Jerusalem" is eventually to be built.[3] Thus Thomas O'Dea called the Book of Mormon, "in content as well as origin," "an American document."[4]

The Book of Mormon surely contests the sacred geography of the Bible, but it affirms it as well. Steinberg rightly notes that "Jerusalem is what binds *The Book of Mormon* with the Bible."[5] To be sure, those in the volume who leave Jerusalem continue thinking about the city and its destiny, and they occasionally mourn their geographical distance from Jerusalem. For instance, one of the Book of Mormon's early prophets describes his people's experience in the ancient Americas as a kind of exile; they were "wanderers cast out from Jerusalem" for whom life "passed away like as it were . . . a dream" (Jacob 7:26). The Book of Mormon indeed tells a story about leaving Jerusalem and not returning, but it also pines for the land left behind. It retains an abiding connection to Jerusalem and to the prophetic stories told about it. In fact, the strongest connection the volume's characters maintain with Jerusalem is with the prophets quite precisely. At crucial points in their history, Book of Mormon peoples obsessively read and reflect on the writings gathered under the name of Isaiah of Jerusalem. Although the book says that those in the New World did not much dwell on "the things of the Jews," at least some of them found "delight in the words of Isaiah" (2 Nephi 25:5). The Isaian traces found throughout the Book of Mormon form something like its navel, the persistent trace of its primordial dependence on a world left behind.

The present study is therefore an experiment in navel-gazing. Its central question is the Book of Mormon's obvious rootedness in the Bible. Research has made it increasingly clear that the Book of Mormon is no "tedious plagiarism" of the Bible, as Mark Twain once said of it.[6] Nor is it any longer right to say, as Fawn Brodie once flippantly claimed, that whenever Joseph Smith's "literary reservoir . . . ran dry," he gave himself a break and "arranged for his Nephite prophets to quote from the Bible."[7] The Book of Mormon, quite to the contrary, consistently probes the meaning of biblical texts in inventive ways.[8] My purpose here is to ask about this probing in terms of the biblical source the Book of Mormon cites and discusses most frequently. In light of the book's irrepressible interest in Isaiah and the way Isaiah serves to organize the volume's relationship to the Bible in a particularly explicit way, how might a study of Isaiah in the Book of Mormon clarify the nature of this unique volume of world scripture? In light of the intense investment in biblical prophecy alive among the Book of Mormon's first readers—antebellum American Christians—what did the volume's interactions with Isaian texts mean to contribute to its message?

I attempt to answer these questions over the course of the chapters to follow. In this first chapter, however, I outline some preliminary points by way of preparation. Three things need attention before work can begin. First, then, I address the rather general question of just what parts of the Bible's Book of Isaiah show up in the Book of Mormon, showing the latter's unexpected selectivity about the former. Second, I take up the question of where the Book of Isaiah makes its various appearances in the Book of Mormon, clarifying the basic trajectory of Isaian quotations and commentaries as it stretches across the volume. Third, I explain and defend the order in which the following chapters take up the Book of Mormon's several interactions with the Book of Isaiah, namely the order of Joseph Smith's original dictation of the volume rather than the order of the volume's final, published form. As part of this last preparatory point, moreover, I state for the first time what I hope to have shown by the end of the present study and preliminarily clarify the stakes of my intervention. Along the way of these preparatory discussions, I also introduce a host of details anyone seriously interested in Isaiah in the Book of Mormon needs to know.

A Selective Approach to Isaiah

What does a good reader find if she reads the Book of Mormon looking for what it has to say about Isaiah? Certainly, what she finds first is simply that the book privileges Isaiah over other biblical texts. Hundreds—if not in fact thousands—of biblical passages find their way in various forms into the Book of Mormon, but none so persistently, overtly, and provocatively as those originating from the Book of Isaiah. No comprehensive list of biblical passages occurring in the Book of Mormon has yet appeared in order to provide full comparative data,[9] but studies of the Book of Mormon's use of at least some (non-Isaian) biblical texts help to show how distinct the use of Isaiah is.

One study of how the Book of Mormon uses the Book of Psalms, for example, shows how the volume generally interacts with the books of the Hebrew Bible, or the Old Testament.[10] Forty-three uncontroversial allusions to the biblical psalms appear in the Book of Mormon, all of them brief and most of them within just two psalmlike texts native to the New World scripture.[11] The allusions are to texts from throughout the Book of Psalms, not just from certain privileged sequences of the text, and no extended quotation of any biblical psalm appears in the Book of Mormon.[12] Significantly, no allusion to Psalms identifies its biblical source but rather expects the reader to know the source or at least to appreciate the allusiveness without knowing the exact source text. These same patterns of usage within the Book of Mormon hold for most books from the Old Testament. The obvious and only sustained exception is the Book of Isaiah. Unlike Psalms, for example, Isaiah appears in the Book of Mormon strikingly often and in texts representing a variety of literary genres. There are, moreover, clear preferences in the Book of Mormon for certain Isaian texts over others, which appear primarily in lengthy, acknowledged quotations and alongside elaborate adaptations. Point by point, Isaiah is unique among Old Testament books when it comes to their presence in the Book of Mormon. What, though, of the Book of Mormon's interactions with the New Testament? Apart from the mere question of frequency, the Book of Mormon generally treats New Testament texts as it does Old Testament texts, borrowing from them in similar literary contexts and without apparent preference for specific authors and sources. Here, too, allusions are usually brief and do not make their biblical sources clear.[13] Again, then, the style of the Book of Mormon's dependence on the New Testament dramatically differs from its interest in Isaiah. Where Isaiah is an object of investigation for the Book of Mormon, the New Testament—specifically in the King James (or KJV) rendering—functions more as a source of vocabulary and style for the Book of Mormon.[14]

Of course, general patterns have exceptions. The Book of Mormon unquestionably gives greater attention to some non-Isaian biblical texts than to others. At one point in the narrative, the resurrected Jesus quotes Malachi 3–4 and explores two extended passages from the Book of Micah (4:12–13 and 5:8–15). He also reproduces the entire Sermon on the Mount from Matthew 5–7 (with variants) and makes especially significant references and allusions to the Gospel of John.[15] Elsewhere in the Book of Mormon, one finds a full quotation of the Ten Commandments from Exodus 20:1–17, explicit references to the New Testament's Book of Revelation, and a reproduction of Paul's list of the gifts of the Spirit.[16] Further, recent scholarship has shown that the Book of Mormon engages in an especially complex conversation with the prologue from the Gospel of John.[17] Thus, there are other longer texts from the Bible with which the Book of Mormon interacts—texts in addition to Isaiah. How do the volume's exceptional interactions with them compare with its interactions with Isaiah?

Although a few extended biblical texts apart from Isaiah appear in the Book of Mormon, Isaiah's place of honor remains untouched. The two chapters quoted from Malachi are among "other scriptures" that Book of Mormon peoples had no access to, but which Jesus wished them to know (3 Nephi 23:6). Apart from being quoted in full by Jesus, however, they play only a small role in the volume and are in this way quite distinct from Isaiah.[18] The two passages drawn in turn from Micah appear alongside quotations from Isaiah and seem to make their way into the text only because of their thematic proximity to Isaian texts. It certainly appears significant that Jesus never cites Micah by name as he does Isaiah, perhaps even leaving less biblically literate readers with the impression that Isaiah was the author of the quoted Micah passages.[19] As for the Sermon on the Mount, Jesus quotes it in the Book of Mormon primarily so that disciples in both the Old World and the New World will have heard the same doctrines (3 Nephi 15:1), and Krister Stendahl has shown that variants in the Book of Mormon's version of the sermon are part of an implicit conversation specifically with the Gospel of John and its unique Christology.[20] It serves a function in the volume quite different from that served by the long passages quoted from Isaiah. The Ten Commandments are, for their part, used solely as a legal text, self-evident in its meaning and implications, quite distinct from the uses of Isaiah. Further, most of the volume's extended engagements with New Testament texts (allusions to the Gospel of John, interactions with Pauline passages, and so on) are presented as confirming parallels rather than (like the Isaiah texts) attempts at interpreting texts known directly to Book of Mormon peoples.[21] Finally, the Book of Mormon's several references to the New Testament's Book of Revelation are never accompanied by extensive quotations of or commentaries on it—in the earlier part of the volume because it is there assumed that Revelation has not yet been written (1 Nephi 14:18–28), and in the later part of the volume because it seems to be known that Revelation would be available to the Book of Mormon's readers (Ether 4:13–17). Where the Book of Isaiah serves as a kind of foundation for the Book of Mormon, the Book of Revelation serves as its projected horizon.[22]

It thus seems perfectly clear that, although certain other extended biblical texts are quoted or engaged in the Book of Mormon, none approximates the Book of Isaiah; none receives the intense treatment the volume gives to this particular prophet.[23] The Book of Mormon is unmistakably a biblically flavored book, but it treats its biblical sources unequally, addressing the Book of Isaiah not only more extensively than any other biblical text (quoting nearly a third of it!) but also in a unique way. This one prophetic source alone becomes the site of an extensive conversation about the nature of textual interpretation. The Book of Mormon asks its audience to reread Isaiah conscious of the difficulties involved in interpreting the most celebrated of Israel's prophets. And it gives hundreds of pages to explicating what it might mean to interpret Isaiah's writings in a certain way.

Having gleaned Isaiah's unique role among biblical books in the Book of Mormon, what else might a careful reader note as she reads the volume with an eye to Isaiah? I mentioned in passing earlier that part of what differentiates the Book of Mormon's uses of Isaiah from its uses of other biblical books is the fact that it privileges certain portions of Isaiah over others. The Book of

Mormon, it might be said, is a discerning reader of Isaiah, expressing particular interest in certain portions of the book without exhibiting much interest at all in others. This is something a careful reader watching for Isaiah in the Book of Mormon will immediately recognize. It is, moreover, a point that deserves some preliminary unpacking.

Interpreters today commonly distinguish among several parts of the Book of Isaiah. The general consensus is that the book divides into three parts: First Isaiah, made up of chapters 1–39; Second Isaiah, made up of chapters 40–55; and Third Isaiah, made up of chapters 56–66. Decades ago, scholars largely treated these divisions as independent works from distinct historical periods, works that, although produced by three discernibly different authors, were misleadingly and maybe even unethically placed at some point under a single name.[24] Today, these same divisions in the text are usually understood to be primarily *literary* divisions, seams in an otherwise literarily coherent whole.[25] Of course, the vast majority of scholars working on Isaiah still understand it to have been assembled from prophecies originating with at least two or three distinct historical figures or from within at least two or three distinct historical periods, but greater emphasis is laid today on the *processes* through which the book seems to have approached its final shape. These processes and the larger literary unity now remarked in the text make it difficult to isolate particular passages of Isaiah from their places in the book as a whole.[26]

Despite these developments, scholars still routinely refer to First, Second, and Third Isaiah as larger divisions within the Book of Isaiah because each exhibits unique thematic and literary features that distinguish it from the others. First Isaiah focuses more consistently on prophecies of judgment than do Second and Third Isaiah, while Second and Third Isaiah feature promises of redemption and restoration far more frequently than First Isaiah. Prophecies gathered in First Isaiah tend to exhibit qualities and themes that lead researchers to date them to the eighth century BCE, at the time of the Assyrian campaign that passed through the lands of Israel and Judah, while prophecies gathered in Second and Third Isaiah consistently suggest to historians that they had their origins in or after the sixth century, just before and then after the Persians conquered the Neo-Babylonian Empire. Certain relationships of apparent literary dependence—of passages in Second Isaiah on passages in First Isaiah, and of passages in Third Isaiah on both First and Second Isaiah—further suggest the wisdom of discerning distinct parts within the larger Book of Isaiah. And indications of different sociopolitical and cultural conditions in Second and Third Isaiah support the idea that, despite many points of proximity between these portions of the text, they should be regarded as distinct in certain ways.[27]

These basic literary divisions within the Book of Isaiah—regardless of what should be concluded about their implications for authorship or dating—are useful for classifying or categorizing Isaiah passages that appear in the Book of Mormon. Setting aside for the moment isolated allusions and shorter quotations,[28] the Book of Mormon draws almost exclusively from two major stretches of the Book of Isaiah, one from First Isaiah and one from Second Isaiah. The more apparent of the two is Isaiah 2–14, quoted in one solid block early in the Book of Mormon. The other, somewhat less apparent, is Isaiah 48–54, major portions of which are quoted over the course of the whole volume.[29] Thus, rather than drawing indiscriminately from throughout Isaiah, the Book of Mormon turns its focused or programmatic interest to just certain portions of the text. Further, the specific portions of Isaiah that function in the Isaian program in the Book of Mormon appear only at certain places in the volume; they are not distributed evenly throughout the text. In fact, the vast majority of Isaian material appears just within the writings attributed in the Book of Mormon to Nephi, the son of Lehi. After Nephi's death, which occurs just a few decades into the thousand-year history recounted in the volume, only three chapters of Isaiah receive any kind of serious treatment. That these latter are all from Second Isaiah and that they do not (apart from passing allusions) play a significant role in Nephi's writings seems noteworthy. The Isaiah-soaked record of Nephi draws on a lengthy stretch of First Isaiah (Isaiah 2–14) and a considerable stretch of Second Isaiah (Isaiah 48–51), but then it leaves to the remainder of the Book of Mormon to add a few substantial interpretive interventions into another considerable stretch of Second Isaiah (Isaiah 52–54).

What might a careful reader say, in a general vein, about the Book of Mormon's predilection for these particular portions of the Book of Isaiah? And what might she wish to say, also, about its apparent lack of programmatic interest in much of the rest of Isaiah? Certainly, the Book of Mormon's general failure to draw on Third Isaiah is striking. Only a very few possible (and in my view unlikely) allusions to—and no clear quotations of—Third Isaiah appear in the Book of Mormon.[30] In that the resurrected Jesus who appears at the climax of the volume quotes at length from the prophecies of Malachi, glossing them as predictions of apocalyptic events, it seems somewhat surprising that he never draws also on the similarly apocalyptic scenes described at the close of Third Isaiah. Still more striking, the Book of Mormon's Nephi draws often on Isaiah 49:22–23, a key passage from Second Isaiah, to articulate his prophetic vision of latter-day events, but he never once draws on the obvious expansion of and commentary on Isaiah 49:22–23 that appears at the heart of Third Isaiah (Isaiah 60).[31] Further, major passages from Third Isaiah that feature prominently in the New Testament—most famously, Isaiah 61:1–3, the prediction of the anointed figure quoted by Jesus in the synagogue in Luke 4:16–23—never make an appearance, even by way of allusion, in the Book of Mormon. Other Isaian texts privileged in the Gospels, by contrast, certainly do appear in the Book of Mormon.[32] Thus, while there are relatively obvious reasons to expect the Book of Mormon to quote from and comment on key passages from Third Isaiah, it never does so.

As for Second Isaiah, the Book of Mormon's Isaian program ignores most of its first half. It quotes all of Isaiah 48–54 but quotes none of and gently alludes to only a passage or two from Isaiah 40–47. It therefore ignores passages where Second Isaiah is most explicit about the historical determinations of its prophecies—those passages, for instance, where the text explicitly mentions Cyrus, the Persian king who would return Judah from exile in Babylon (Isaiah 44:28; 45:1). Thus, the Book of Mormon's preference for the second half of Second Isaiah allows it to draw on prophecies that address the situation of Israel in exile without much investment in the historical particularities of Judah's sixth-century sojourn in Babylon. Further, by avoiding the first half of Second Isaiah, the Book of Mormon leaves out Second Isaiah's polemics against idolatry, never a major theme in the Book of Mormon. Finally, since Isaiah 40–48 famously focuses on the role of Israel as God's servant, while Isaiah 49–55 shifts to a focus on "an individual figure" rather than a whole people as God's servant,[33] the Book of Mormon seems to privilege that singular servant—traditionally understood in Christian circles to be Jesus Christ—over the collective servant of the omitted texts. (There is even evidence that the Book of Mormon introduces variants into the only chapter it does quote from the first half of Second Isaiah—Isaiah 48—in order to refocus it on a singular servant.) All these details together suggest a near-programmatic relationship between the Book of Mormon and Second Isaiah.

The Book of Mormon's relationship to First Isaiah is more complicated. Most interpreters divide First Isaiah into four discernible literary subsections: a first (Isaiah 1–12) that introduces the prophet's life and themes; a second (Isaiah 13–27) that collects oracles directed against various nations and then the whole world; a third (Isaiah 28–35) mostly made up of prophecies stemming from the same historical setting as those in the first sequence;[34] and a fourth (Isaiah 36–39) made up of narratives about Isaiah's relationship to King

Hezekiah late in the prophet's life.[35] From among these possible sources, the Book of Mormon draws primarily on the first subsection (and a related chapter from the third subsection: Isaiah 29), adding to it just the first two chapters of the second subsection (focused on Babylon's fall). Most of the prophecies grouped together late in First Isaiah (that is, most of Isaiah 28–35) and nearly all the oracles against the nations (all of Isaiah 15–27) are ignored, along with the whole of the fourth subsection and, peculiarly, Isaiah 1 from the first subsection. The portions of First Isaiah privileged by the Book of Mormon therefore suggest a lack of interest in prophecies against Israel's neighbors (such as Edom and Moab) and a preference for prophecies directed against major imperial powers (Assyria and Babylon). This seems to be rooted in the fact that major imperial powers readily serve as types for satanic forces. And the selective attention paid just to Isaiah 29 from Isaiah 28–39 helps to clarify the fact that quite specific themes draw notice from the Book of Mormon; the twin themes of sealed books and familiar spirits, which appear in Isaiah 29 and also in Isaiah 8 (both quoted in the Book of Mormon), are apparently of more interest than many others. Finally, the absence of Isaiah 1 from the Book of Mormon suggests preference for the vision of Isaiah 2 (the conversion of the nations) over the vision of Isaiah 1 (Israel's wartime desolation) as an introduction to the Book of Isaiah.[36]

From all these details, it becomes perfectly clear that the Book of Mormon is no haphazard interpreter of Isaiah. It reliably focuses through its programmatic lens on just one longer block of text from First Isaiah and another from Second Isaiah, and there are consistent patterns in what it ignores in its longer and more systematic investigations of the biblical book. Where one might naturally expect an even distribution of Isaian allusions—as one finds, for example, in the Pauline literature in the New Testament[37] or in nineteenth-century speculations about Isaiah's importance for understanding America's destiny[38]—what one actually finds in the Book of Mormon is instead a focused set of selective textual interests. The Book of Mormon shows itself, again, to be a choosy interpreter of Isaiah. In all that follows, it will be the *program* of the Book of Mormon's interaction with Isaiah—rather than, exhaustively, every borrowing and allusion to Isaiah at all—that is the focus of the present study.

Patterns of Where Isaiah Appears

The foregoing provides a few points of general orientation for a reading of Isaiah in the Book of Mormon, but it remains fundamentally quantitative when what is needed is a genuinely qualitative analysis of the Book of Mormon's programmatic uses of Isaiah. That is, while it is helpful to see that the book grants Isaiah more substantial attention than other biblical texts and that certain portions of Isaiah receive analysis rather than others and are complexly distributed throughout the Book of Mormon, these first points really just motivate closer study. It must be asked, then, what a careful reader of the book finds as she investigates the details of its programmatic uses of Isaiah more carefully.

It might prove helpful to sharpen the lens focused on the distribution of Isaiah texts within the sprawling narrative of the Book of Mormon. Again setting aside shorter, nonprogrammatic allusions and borrowings, there are three places in the Book of Mormon where Isaiah makes an appearance. This is uncontroversial.[39] First, as already noted above, Isaiah forms the principal focus in the writings the volume presents as coming from its first contributor: Nephi, son of Lehi. Nephi devotes his writings almost exclusively to the task of expounding Isaiah's meaning, quoting, adapting, or discussing eighteen full chapters of Isaiah.[40] Second, some centuries after Nephi's death, a conflict arises within a group of Nephi's descendants (unsurprisingly called the Nephites) settled in a colony situated among their enemies (the racially otherized Lamanites, descendants of Nephi's brother Laman). The conflict arises when a prophet, Abinadi, rails against the colony's depraved and idolatrous leaders. Hauled before the colony's leading priests in a show trial, Abinadi finds himself in a controversy over the interpretation of Isaiah. The situation ends poorly for Abinadi, but one of the priests rallies to his cause and defects to establish a church based on Abinadi's preaching. Several hundred pages of text then separate the Abinadi story (which follows rather quickly after Nephi's record) from the third cluster of texts focused on Isaiah, a gap that strikes the careful reader as strange. At any rate, the third particularly Isaian moment in the Book of Mormon comes at the volume's narrative climax, when, shortly after his resurrection in the Old World, Jesus Christ visits the New World Israelite peoples whose history the book recounts.[41] After establishing his identity and laying the foundation for a fully Christian church, the Book of Mormon's Christ spends his time quoting from and providing expositions of the writings of Isaiah, weaving Isaian themes into passages drawn from elsewhere in the Bible.

How does the larger arc of Isaian interest within the Book of Mormon unfold as the reader works from Nephi's writings through the Abinadi episode and eventually to Jesus Christ's own contribution? This is, of course, the order in which the Book of Mormon, in every major edition in its publication history, unfolds—the order in which every reader of the published book has encountered Isaiah's presence in the book. But do all three characters who express interest in Isaiah and Isaian interpretation approach the Hebrew prophet in the same fashion? The perhaps surprising fact is that Nephi, Abinadi, and Jesus all approach Isaiah in substantially different ways. The result is that the trajectory from Nephi through Abinadi to Jesus traces a kind of debate about the meaning of the Book of Isaiah. This deserves preliminary development here.[42]

Coming at the outset of the Book of Mormon, Nephi's extensive engagement with Isaiah clearly serves as a foundation for the whole volume's treatment of the prophet. Nephi quotes many chapters from the Book of Isaiah, heavily adapts other Isaian texts, and weaves into his own prophecies a host of further allusions to Isaiah. By contrast, as has been noted already, the remainder of the Book of Mormon quotes the larger part of just three chapters of Isaiah and contains only a small handful of other allusions to the prophet. Thus, the Book of Mormon exhibits far more interest in Isaiah in its opening sequence than ever again afterward. It is thus that Nephi's treatment of Isaiah effectively establishes—if not *over*establishes—the first major position in the debate that unfolds over the course of the book. Further, Nephi's record uniquely dedicates the necessary space to establish a complex hermeneutical program. In fact, as I argue in a later chapter, there is abundant evidence that Nephi's record is meant to be read as principally if not solely dedicated to outlining an interpretive approach to Isaiah's prophecies. Without Nephi, the Book of Mormon would, in a suggestive but largely uncommitted way, just flirt with Isaian prophecy. But thanks to Nephi's contribution, it irreversibly weds itself to Isaiah from the outset.

It is important that Nephi's record nowhere indicates awareness of the debate over Isaiah that organizes the larger narrative of the Book of Mormon. Rather, the reader finds in Nephi a quite confident interpreter of Isaiah, someone largely unaware—or simply uninterested in the possibility—that Isaiah might be read in any way substantially different from his own (except, maybe, that Isaiah might be read naïvely). Nephi simply uses and explains (at great length) his interpretive approach, authoritatively and forcefully. Because Nephi's record works out an interpretation of Isaiah without having to look over its shoulder—or at least because the reader never feels that Nephi has to worry about whether other Book of Mormon voices agree with him—the first sequence of the volume exhibits a kind of freedom. Nephi pursues his work on Isaiah without hindrance. There is, nonetheless, something almost obsessive about Nephi's attachment to Isaiah. He speaks of little else, and he gives enough space and attention to Isaiah to frustrate many readers of the Book of Mormon.[43] Rather than succinctly or directly outlining an interpretive approach to Isaiah, Nephi provides narrative accounts of the provenance of his copy of Isaiah and of his resources for Isaian interpretation (1 Nephi 1–9), develops his resources for interpretation at length while preliminarily introducing their relevance to Isaiah (1 Nephi 10–15), initiates his readers into his interpretive project with a first illustration (1 Nephi 19–22), provides distinct examples of his approach as modeled by both himself and his brother Jacob (2 Nephi 6–10, 25–30), and includes a thirteen-chapter block of Isaiah text at the heart of his record (2 Nephi 11–24). The immense labor Nephi's record undertakes to lay out a hermeneutic program makes it unmistakably clear that the Book of Mormon opens with its most extensive and detailed investigation of Isaiah.

It therefore strikes the reader as passing strange that Isaiah nearly disappears from the Book of Mormon after Nephi's record. Only chapters after Nephi's death occurs, the narrative reports the centuries-later confrontation between Abinadi and the wicked priests of the disastrous Nephite king Noah, whose love of riches leads his people to ruin. This section, as noted above, also focuses on Isaiah. But thereafter, for hundreds of pages, more or less all talk related to Isaiah fades from the volume. To put these observations in perspective, one might consider the 1830 (first) edition of the Book of Mormon, which presented the text of the book in straightforward prose, without any apparatus. In the pagination of that stripped-down edition, programmatic uses of Isaiah disappear from the record on page 190 and do not reappear until after page 485. The text's profound interest, if not symptomatic obsession, thus gives way quickly to an apparent lack of interest in—if not total ignorance of—Isaiah (even nonprogrammatic allusions largely disappear). Whatever else the Book of Mormon means to accomplish with the story it tells, it clearly narrates a rapid decline in programmatic Nephite investment in Isaiah.

Readers generally feel this shift in the Book of Mormon, although it is seldom described in the terms I have used here. Lay readers often describe Nephi's writings—especially the more explicitly Isaian writings—as alienating or boring: chapter after chapter of abstruse discussion of Israel's history, both ancient and modern.[44] Most therefore experience the transition that occurs after Nephi's writings as a welcome change, since the text begins to focus on familiar doctrines and stories illustrative of everyday Christian living. The Book of Mosiah, for instance, opens with a lengthy sermon on service and grace, on atonement and submission to God, on care for the needy and Christian community, and on the importance and meaning of covenant making (Mosiah 1–6). All this is a far cry from Nephi's detailed prophecies on Jewish history, his lengthy quotations from Isaiah, and his open fretting about the destiny of Israel's remnant. Readers naturally feel this larger thematic change, and they especially make note of the retreat from Isaiah's prophecies.

The natural reaction of lay readers to the shift away from Isaiah in the Book of Mormon, then, is one of relief. But this shift gives the careful reader pause. Why such a change? Is there any obvious reason for Isaiah's removal from his privileged position in Nephi? Does the narrative itself explain the withdrawal? It arguably does. Abinadi's confrontation with Noah's priests grows at first out of a situation of simple social and political oppression. King Noah is not one to "keep the commandments of God" (Mosiah 11:2), and so his reign is marked by sexual and financial oppression. He obtains "many wives and concubines" (11:2) just as he imposes "a tax" on his people to finance his lavish lifestyle (11:3). Further, he leads his people to become collectively "idolatrous" (11:7), and they also grow proud and bloodthirsty, inspired by "the wickedness of their king and priests" (11:19). Abinadi initially appears in the Book of Mormon's narrative in direct response to this social and political situation. And his prophecy is at first unconcerned with Isaiah; he simply rails against Noah and his people. For "their abominations and their wickedness and their whoredoms," they are to face bondage and eventually destruction unless they repent (11:20). At the outset, then, Abinadi seems more reminiscent of Jeremiah than interested in Isaiah.

Isaiah enters the Abinadi narrative only when Noah's people take the prophet captive and the king forces him to take part in a show trial. Hoping to "cross him, that thereby they might have wherewith to accuse him" (Mosiah 12:19), Noah's priests ask Abinadi about the interpretation of Isaiah. "What meaneth the words which are written and which have been taught by our fathers?" they ask (12:20). They go on to quote, in full, Isaiah 52:7–10. It is thus Noah's priests rather than Abinadi himself who first bring up Isaiah. And, significantly, the priests' implicit interpretation of the passage from Isaiah finds its methodological precedent in Nephi's writings. The narrative provides too little detail to indicate that Noah's priests were as obsessively concerned with Isaiah as Nephi, but they nonetheless share with him a broadly similar hermeneutical program. To a certain extent at least, the priests ask Abinadi to contest Nephi's approach to Isaiah, since they seem to believe that Nephi's approach to the prophet allows them to mobilize Isaiah's prophecies in defense of their king's (oppressive) regime. In response, Abinadi indeed outlines a rather different, non-Nephi-like hermeneutic, making possible a substantially distinct appropriation of Isaiah. For Abinadi, Isaiah's prophecies are all about the (then-still-future) coming of Jesus Christ. And this arguably serves to explain the transition away from Isaiah in the larger narrative arc of the Book of Mormon. Abinadi's approach to the prophet eliminates the need, for those in his wake, to read Isaiah carefully, since they have other, plainer prophecy to draw on in their worshipful anticipation of Christ's coming.

Thus, after the Abinadi story, the several hundreds of pages bereft of Isaiah follow, but then the Isaian focus of the Book of Mormon suddenly and intensely returns. As already noted, this forceful return to Isaiah occurs in connection with the climactic visit of Jesus Christ, newly resurrected, to the peoples whose story the Book of Mormon recounts. At this point, nearly two centuries after Abinadi's prophetic interventions, the Book of Mormon's Jesus revisits the very passage on which the Abinadi story is founded: Isaiah 52:7–10. The interpretation of the passage offered by the resurrected Jesus, however, differs dramatically from that offered either implicitly by Noah's priests or explicitly by Abinadi. As if in direct conversation with Abinadi and Noah's priests, then, Jesus outlines yet another hermeneutic approach to the writings of Isaiah.

Jesus's approach to Isaiah is in some ways reminiscent of Nephi's. Like Nephi and unlike Abinadi, Jesus views Isaiah's message as profoundly centered on Israelite history, and he also, again like Nephi and unlike Abinadi, readily applies Isaiah's words to the circumstances of the remnant of Israel—which the Book of Mormon identifies with the latter-day descendants of Nephi's brother Laman.[45] But, in broadest terms, what matters more than Jesus's approach to Isaiah is the bare fact that his preaching at the climax of the Book of Mormon marks an unmistakable return to an intense focus on Isaiah. It overcomes three hundred pages and two hundred years of relative silence about the prophet. Something like Nephi's near-obsessive relationship to Isaiah recurs in the narrative recounting Jesus's visit, and the frequency of allusions and references to Isaiah through the remainder of the Book of Mormon is substantially higher than in the stretch between the stories of Abinadi and Jesus.

The whole of the Book of Mormon thus traces a definite arc with regard to Isaiah. Not only are there particularly important moments in the text where Isaiah is a chief focus—in the writings of Nephi, in the confrontation between Abinadi and Noah's priests, and in the sermonizing of the resurrected Christ—but there is a larger pattern of surprising withdrawal and eventual return. It is this larger arc that requires attention from readers of the Book of Mormon if they wish to make sense of what the book does with Isaiah. Whatever the several positions on Isaian interpretation ultimately are (and this is the subject of the chapters that follow in the present study), they collectively trace a kind of narrative of inaugural, then waning, and then resurging interest in the question of Isaian prophecy.

It may well be that the Book of Mormon itself wishes to draw attention to debates about Isaian interpretation and its larger narrative arc. It is striking that the narrative has Jesus signal at the volume's climax that Nephi's people had been involved in debates over theology and ritual before his arrival. Despite general recognition of the centrality of Jesus's visit in the Book of Mormon, few readers give serious attention to Jesus's claim about this point: "There hath hitherto been," he says to some newly called disciples, "disputations among you" (3 Nephi 11:28).[46] The disputations in question, according to Jesus, are of two sorts. First, Book of Mormon peoples have apparently debated certain aspects of ritual and practice, principally the manner of baptism (3 Nephi 11:22). Second, debate has focused on doctrine and theology, principally on the nature of the triune God and the basic outline of the gospel message (3 Nephi 11:28). The Book of Mormon apparently expects its readers here to cast a retrospective eye on what they have read so far, viewing it now as the story of a long debate. It is true, of course, that this debate might seem at first to have little to do with Isaiah, but closer investigation suggests otherwise.

The debates to which the Book of Mormon's Jesus refers might appear obscure and underemphasized, but they can be reasonably reconstructed. It is in reconstructing them that the relevance to Isaiah begins to appear, at the very least because the debate concerns, as with Isaian interpretation, Nephi and Abinadi. Early in the book, Nephi outlines what he calls "the doctrine of Christ"—"the only and true doctrine of the Father and of the Son and of the Holy Ghost" (2 Nephi 31:21)—in connection with a detailed exposition of Christian baptism (2 Nephi 31:4–21). Later, however, Abinadi articulates the nature of the Godhead in a way fundamentally distinct from that of Nephi (Mosiah 15:1–9), and Abinadi's discourse on the subject becomes the foundational document for the Nephite church that develops shortly after his death. That church, moreover, is officially launched through the institution of a Christian baptism that seems to be at odds in certain ways with the one articulated by Nephi (Mosiah 18:1–17). Although the Book of Mormon provides little direct evidence for an actual debate between these two theological and practical perspectives, it seems relatively obvious that Jesus's words at the climax of the book are meant to encourage readers to imagine such a debate as having occurred.[47] Significantly, if it is true that the Book of Mormon's Jesus decides between these two rival views, he unquestionably sides with the views of the prophet Nephi rather than with the views of the prophet Abinadi.

Now, as has already been noted, nowhere in Christ's brief discussion of historical "disputations" over ritual and doctrine is it made explicit that these concerned factions aligned themselves with Nephi and Abinadi, respectively. Further, nowhere before Christ's appearance is there any overt description of disputations over baptism and its associated theology. The data gathered and analyzed in the preceding paragraph have to be reconstructed retroactively beginning from the vague claims made by Christ during his visit at the Book of Mormon's climax. It may be profoundly significant, however, that the Book of Mormon in fact does narrate a larger theological debate over the course of the book, one it presents as closely connected to the apparent tensions between Nephi's and Abinadi's approaches to Christianity. As I have already made clear, the debate that does receive explicit and sustained attention in the Book of Mormon is over the interpretation of Isaiah. Far more attention is given in Nephi's writings, in Abinadi's sermon, and in Jesus's ministry to matters of Isaian interpretation than is ever given to questions of Christian theory and practice. Only one of Nephi's fifty-five chapters pays sustained attention to the form of baptism or the nature of God, but Nephi dedicates dozens of chapters to the work of interpreting Isaiah. Just four or five verses from Abinadi's chapters-long preaching focus on the nature of God, and it is his convert Alma rather than he himself who outlines an Abinadite practice of baptism. In contrast, two whole chapters (and a handful of other verses) from the Abinadi story focus on quoting from and interpreting Isaiah's words. Finally, Jesus's ministry in Third Nephi focuses only half of a chapter on the form of baptism and the nature of God but fully eight chapters on the larger project of interpreting Isaiah.

The visit of Jesus to the New World culminates with him reading from and interpreting Isaiah for his listeners. Then, after several chapters of such interpretive work, Jesus tells them, "And now, behold, I say unto you that ye had ought to search these things. Yea, a commandment I give unto you that ye search these things diligently. For great is the words of Isaiah" (3 Nephi 23:1). This endorsement serves as an obvious anchor to the whole volume, indicating that the status of Isaiah is among its chiefest concerns. Further, later in the Book of Mormon, the volume's final editor, Moroni, expresses his frustrated desire to say something about "the intent" of the whole book (Mormon 8:5), as well as to "make all things known" to his readers (Mormon 8:12). Apparently because he finds it impossible to do either of these—"I have not," he says, "room upon the [gold] plates" (Mormon 8:5)—he contents himself just with telling his readers to "search the prophecies of Isaiah" (Mormon 8:23). Thus, according to the testimony of the Book of Mormon itself, it would seem that its main "intent" is rooted in what it communicates about Isaiah's prophecies. The book appears to assume that readers will learn "all things" if they turn their attention to the writings of Isaiah.

The preliminary conclusions reached so far might well surprise. Not only does the Book of Mormon carefully sift its biblical sources to lay particular emphasis on select portions of the Book of Isaiah, it organizes its interactions with Isaiah into a volume-long investigation and debate that presents a variety of distinct hermeneutic positions. Further still, it sometimes subtly and sometimes conspicuously draws attention to this complex set of interactions with Isaiah. The Book of Mormon, it seems, has something like a conscious program to execute with respect to this biblical book.

Ideal Reading and the Ideal Reader

The arc of obsession-withdrawal-return makes sense of the Book of Mormon's narrative in final form. That is, it makes sense of the book as it has appeared for the reading public since 1830, when the first edition issued from E. B. Grandin's bookshop in Palmyra, New York. It is abundantly worth considering the way the Isaian program within the Book of Mormon unfolds in this most familiar form.[48] It is crucial to note, however, that this is not how the Book of Mormon's *very first* reader experienced the volume. Joseph Smith, according to his own account, was the book's first reader, reciting the contents of the volume to a scribe as he saw words appear in a sacred stone.[49] What Smith read out to his scribe over the busy summer of 1829 began not with Nephi's writings and their systematic exposition of Isaiah but with the non-Isaian story of King Benjamin, a narrative just prior to the Abinadi story. Summarily put, the final form of the Book of Mormon does not match that of the original dictation. The overall content is (almost exactly) the same,[50] but the order of the materials was different when Smith originally dictated it than when he published it a few months later. The change in order has implications for how one makes sense of the role Isaiah plays in the Book of Mormon.

The reason for the difference between the order of dictation and the final published form of the Book of Mormon is no mystery. After dictating more than a hundred manuscript pages of text (popularly known as the Book of Lehi), the prophet allowed his scribe at the time, Martin Harris, to keep the manuscript while Smith attended to his wife, Emma, who was near term in a difficult pregnancy. Harris returned with the manuscript from Pennsylvania, where he was helping with the translation, to New York, where he lived. Smith prolonged his time with his wife, whose baby died shortly after birth and who herself hovered near death for a while. When she recovered enough to allow for it, Smith traveled to New York only to discover that the manuscript had been stolen from Harris. When Smith eventually began to translate again (wisely, with a new scribe), he began where he and Harris had left off, *in medias res*. Only as he finished dictating the remainder of the book—now the stretch from the Book of Mosiah to the Book of Moroni—did he raise the question of what to do about the earliest part of the text, the manuscript that had been lost. At that point, however, Smith said he was directed by God not to reproduce the already translated material (the Book of Lehi itself). Instead, he was to dictate a different, parallel account of early Nephite history. What Smith had dictated before (and then lost) was just a summary or abridgment of Nephi's and his royal successors' annalistic writings.[51] Now, though, he would be given to dictate directly Nephi's and his spiritual successors' unabridged prophetic and ministerial writings. The dictation of Nephi's writings and the short books following them therefore concluded Smith's dictation of the Book of Mormon.[52] Thus, however most readers experience the Book of Mormon, in its final, published form, the very first reader of the volume (and its first hearers) experienced it differently. For Smith and his scribes, the Isaian interests of the Book of Mormon would have had a rather different cast.

Naturally, Smith had good reasons to publish the book in an order different from that of the actual dictation. Nephi's writings (and the short books following them) serve as a replacement for the lost narrative, filling a gap and making the larger history told in the published book sequential. Readers easily follow the history recounted in the Book of Mormon in its final published form (despite the lost manuscript), but arguably many would have trouble following the narrative if the book opened in the middle of an incomplete history and included Nephi's writings only as a kind of appendix. It is nonetheless worth asking what impressions Smith and his scribes would likely have had about Isaiah as Smith dictated the text of the book out of sequential order. This might seem at first inconsequential, but the answer suggests that it is not an idle question. If one reads the Book of Mormon in order of dictation, a remarkable pattern emerges about Isaiah. First, because Nephi's obsession with Isaiah is displaced to the end of the reading experience, the controversy involving Abinadi becomes the book's opening salvo about Isaiah—immediately followed by three hundred pages of silence on the prophet. Second, the preaching of the resurrected Christ here does not mark a return to Nephi's original obsession with Isaiah, but instead moves in a new and unprecedented direction—especially considering that Christ begins with the very passage from Isaiah discussed by Abinadi. Third, Nephi's writings here serve to complete rather than to inaugurate the volume, radicalizing and deepening the turn begun in Christ's sermons—as if the point was, at the end of the reading experience, to unpack fully what the volume's climax only introduces. The final form of the Book of Mormon presents its Isaian elements like the movement from one peak of a wave to another (from obsession through withdrawal to climactic return). The Book of Mormon in order of dictation, by contrast, begins with an Isaian blast (in the Abinadi story) and then a long silence, only eventually reintroducing an Isaian chorus (through Christ's visit) in a crescendo that becomes deafening (with Nephi's writings) just prior to the volume's end.

Minimally, setting final form and order of dictation side by side shows that the content of the Book of Mormon ultimately divides into two movable parts. On the one hand are the writings of Nephi and the short books that follow it (Jacob, Enos, Jarom, and Omni), which make up the replacement text for the lost manuscript. These are all first-person texts presented as the original works of Nephite authors living during the first four or five centuries of Book of Mormon history. On the other hand is the remainder of the Book of Mormon, which mostly tells the rest of Nephite history (the Books of Mosiah, Alma, Helaman, Third Nephi, Fourth Nephi, Mormon, Ether, and Moroni). Most of the books making up this remainder are summary works recounting an abridged history of the Nephites, presented as the work of Mormon, a redactor and editor (*and* prophet and war captain!) born more than nine hundred years after Nephi. The question of final form or dictation order thus amounts just to a question about which of these two larger parts of the Book of Mormon is ideally read before the other. Although a reading of the Book of Mormon in final form allows the historical debate traced by the volume to emerge with full force, there are compelling reasons to ignore the final form for the purposes of close study of how the Book of Mormon interacts with Isaiah.[53] The Isaian intensity of Nephi's writings is so much greater than in the remainder of the book that a sequential reading of any substance too easily makes the contributions of Abinadi and Jesus seem like inconsequential aftershocks of Nephi's Isaian earthquake.[54] To begin instead with Abinadi and

Jesus, however, is to establish the basic framework for the Book of Mormon's larger debate, introducing through them (and Abinadi's priestly interlocutors) a range of interpretive options before turning to Nephi's more substantial contribution. Further, the similarities between Jesus's and Nephi's interpretive styles allow Jesus's climactic contribution to remain final and definitive. That is, on such a reading, Nephi's writings serve as a detailed exposition of the climactic interpretive approach that would otherwise be limited to just the largely truncated presentation of Jesus's visit in the Book of Mormon. Finally, as already noted, this approach might help reproduce the experience of the very first person to have read the book, Joseph Smith.

For all these reasons, the following chapters are divided into two larger sections that follow the order of dictation: a first on Mormon's abridgment of Nephite history, and then a second on Nephi's writings.[55] Each pair of chapters in part 1 focuses first on providing a detailed exposition of what its focal Book of Mormon figure—Abinadi, Jesus—does with the Book of Isaiah (chapter 2, chapter 4) and second on exploring the relationship of the Isaian hermeneutic in question with the larger history of Isaiah interpretation, along with its place in Mormon's larger editorial project (chapter 3, chapter 5). Part 2, focused in turn on Nephi's systematically Isaian writings, approaches matters rather differently. A first chapter considers the place of Nephi's first substantial interaction with Isaiah (chapter 6), but this then motivates closer study of how the overall structure of Nephi's writings reveals the intentional centrality of Isaian hermeneutics to Nephi's project, the subject of a separate chapter (chapter 7). There then follow studies of the most detailed and most surprising elements of Nephi's approach to interpreting Isaiah—a first one about the Book of Mormon's longest quotation of Isaiah (chapter 8), and a second one about the Book of Mormon's most experimental and virtuosic reworking of an Isaian text (chapter 9).

A concluding discussion here of method might help to clarify more fully where this study ends up, as well as how it gets there. The scholarly literature on the Book of Mormon has traditionally been divided in tone and content. At one end of the spectrum, much of what believing scholars have written about the book has focused on gathering evidence for its ancient historicity—primarily by showing that, despite being addressed to the modern period and deliberately translated for a modern audience, the Book of Mormon bears traces of ancient themes and practices of which Joseph Smith should have known nothing, with his limited education.[56] Much of this literature, as is no surprise, has been spurred by learned dismissals of the Book of Mormon that justify their contempt for the book's claims to ancient historicity by pointing to unmistakably modern elements in the book. At the other end of the spectrum, then, are critics of the book's claims to ancient origins, those who dedicate their intellectual attention to gathering evidence that the book fits more comfortably in the nineteenth century than in the ancient world.[57] Much of this literature focuses on apparent anachronisms in the Book of Mormon, elements that might not be explained by the text's focus on and rendering for the modern world. Caught between these two camps, those who write on the Book of Mormon for a more strictly academic audience often lament that the vast majority of the available literature is unnecessarily antagonistic—half of it uncharitably critical, half of it reactionarily defensive.[58]

An occasional—but in many ways central—focus of these debates over the historicity of the Book of Mormon is Isaiah's presence in it.[59] As interesting as the question of and the debates about Book of Mormon historicity might be, though, they do not concern me here. I am, for my part, a believer in the Book of Mormon, convicted at the religious and existential level of its spiritual value and its historical truth, but I have no interest in staging a defense of the book's historicity in this study. It very much seems to me that there are questions about Isaiah and the Book of Mormon worth asking on which matters of historicity have little or no bearing, however fundamental they might be in other contexts. More important, it seems that the Book of Mormon is itself convinced that there are questions about Isaiah and the Book of Mormon worth asking on which matters of historicity have little or no bearing. As the Book of Mormon, read in order of dictation, slowly moves toward its most remarkable interaction with Isaiah late in Nephi's record, it also slowly works out a theological argument—presented eventually through a direct interaction with Isaiah 29—for why questions of the Book of Mormon's historicity must come only after certain other questions are answered.[60] That is, over the course of the dictated text of the Book of Mormon, there emerges through its interactions with Isaiah a case against every prioritizing of historical over theological questions. A major burden of the present study—borne throughout the chapters that follow—is to develop this argument within the text of the Book of Mormon, moment by moment. At the end of the dictated text, when the Isaian project is at fever pitch, one finds not only the volume's richest treatment of its favored biblical resource but also its fullest argument that logical proofs, scientific evidences, and historical questions are essential only *in the last instance*. It is remarkable that the Book of Mormon makes this case, and that it makes it using specifically Isaian resources. Further, though, it seems to me deeply ironic that the Book of Mormon's labors expended in making this case become invisible when the only question being asked about Isaiah in the volume is whether it supports or problematizes the book's ancient historicity.

For all these reasons, it is crucial to keep questions of historicity at bay while trying to discern what the Book of Mormon actually sets out to do with the Book of Isaiah. How, though, might one earnestly pursue such a task? Here I would like to borrow the idea of creating an imagined reader from the Isaiah scholar Katheryn Pfisterer Darr. In her book *Isaiah's Vision and the Family of God*, Darr creates an imaginary reader from among "post-exilic Israel's cognoscenti, a scribe or religious leader and educator enjoying such legal rights and social standing as were possible at the beginning of the fourth-century BCE."[61] Further, Darr pictures the experience of a first-time but well-informed reader "engaging a text sequentially in a dialogical process," such that it is part of the process of reading to "continually reassess earlier expectations and judgments, forming fresh ones as new insights and data emerge."[62] Finally and most provocatively, though, she imagines this reader coming to the text with questions—for whatever reasons—about how the Book of Isaiah speaks of and refers to women and children.[63] This literary conceit allows Darr to track the development of certain themes across the whole of the Book of Isaiah, building consistency and coherence in a text that might otherwise seem to lack it. Something very real about the text makes itself available to a well-imagined reader, something that might never be glimpsed beginning from other readerly positions.

Throughout the following chapters, I develop my interpretation of the Book of Mormon by looking at the text through the eyes of such an imagined reader—one I do not hesitate to call ideal, in fact. I say "reader," but it might be just as well to say "listener." My ideal reader is, here, an imagined person who sits in the room with Joseph Smith and his scribes all through the dictation of (the extant portions of) the Book of Mormon, listening intently. This ideal listener thus hears the text unfold, over the course of months, in the order of its dictation. Let us imagine, moreover, that such an ideal listener goes on to have access to the Book of Mormon text in readable form, with leisure time (and motivating interest) to revisit salient passages for closer examination and, especially, comparison with various biblical texts. So far, of course, this ideal listener/reader does not seem to be an *imagined* one, since it well describes several historical persons in Smith's circle in 1829 and after. But there is more to an ideal listener/reader's required qualifications that Smith's sympathetic acquaintances lacked: an ideal listener/reader would additionally be more than passingly familiar with—would in fact be seriously interested in—the general history of Isaiah's interpretation (up through 1830 or so).[64] Such an ideal listener/reader would be particularly interested in understanding how Isaiah fits into the Book of Mormon's project and would be fully capacitated to see how the Book of Mormon departs from or aligns with the tradition in specific ways. Such an imagined listener/reader would be attuned to all the things I hope to discern in the course of this study but also would be untouched by scholarly debates about the Book of Isaiah's authorship (the root of questions about Isaiah's relevance to the Book of Mormon's historicity).

Thus, the question I ask repeatedly in this study is this: *How would someone living in the United States of America in 1829–1830 react to the Book of Mormon if she were (1) familiar with the general history of Isaiah's interpretation and (2) a particularly close and generous interpreter of the Book of Mormon?* An ideal listener, attentively sitting with Joseph Smith and his colleagues as he dictated the text for transcription—especially one who then became an ideal reader, sitting down with plenty of time and a printed copy of the Book of Mormon after its publication—should have been able to see much in the volume's treatment of Isaiah that goes unnoticed by most. Listening to the book in dictation order and then following up with the printed volume in final form, a sympathetic person familiar with the history of Isaiah's reception up through the early nineteenth century could teach others much about the volume's Isaian meaning. In many ways, it is precisely that kind of reader that the Book of Mormon as a text seems to hope for, if not to imagine.

Now, the use of imagined readers might naturally worry some readers. What prevents a scholar from crafting an imagined reader so that it conveniently confirms whatever position she wishes to defend? Would it not in fact be best to avoid imaginary readers and privilege instead the recoverable interpretations of actual historical readers of the Book of Mormon? Do the facts of history not impose crucial limits on the potentially dangerous freedom of the unrestrained imagination? Of course, the problem with the actual historical readers of the Book of Mormon in its first years of circulation is twofold. They were either too unsympathetic to the Book of Mormon's project to ask after its meaning earnestly (the moral imperative to denounce it was too strong to give it a serious hearing)[65] or too unfamiliar with the history of Isaiah's interpretation to discern the Book of Mormon's Isaian project responsibly.[66] And, further, using an ideal listener/reader allows for an appropriate bracketing of the accidents of history, such that the text's shape and meaning become fully visible.

All this is to say, in a way, that the following study—even as it draws often on historical sources—is not ultimately historical in orientation. Rather, it is primarily literary and theological. The aim is to use resources from the history of Isaiah's interpretation—to insert the Book of Mormon into the flow of Isaiah's reception history—in order to see how Isaiah informs the volume's theological project. It is true that one product of this study is a contribution to reception history. To the extent that the Book of Mormon's own engagement with Isaiah becomes clear, a deeply interesting moment in the larger history of Isaiah's reception comes into focus. Yet the work undertaken here to yield that reception-historical data point is literary and theological. It requires bracketing the historically incidental so that what is literarily and theologically essential about the Book of Mormon's Isaian project becomes apparent. The deployment of an imagined and ideal listener/reader seems to me the best way to make this happen—especially without falling into the trap of making the Book of Mormon's historicity the only or the most important issue in investigating its uses of Isaiah. This listener/reader will be with us all through the pages that follow.

At the end of this study, I hope that I will have shown—or perhaps that an ideal listener/reader will have shown *for* me—at least that the Book of Mormon is more interesting than the questions usually asked about it, and that what it does with the biblical Book of Isaiah helps to make its interest particularly clear. It is not enough to say just that the Book of Mormon makes a real contribution to the history of Isaiah interpretation and that the Book of Isaiah makes a real contribution to the constitution and nature of this unique volume of world scripture. The Book of Mormon's contribution on this question goes right to the heart of key theological issues surrounding what it means for scripture to remain relevant—if indeed it can—in the modern age. If Isaiah has a life to live still in and beyond the twenty-first century, the Book of Mormon puts itself forward as having something to say about it.

Part I
Mormon's Isaiah

According to the Book of Mormon, the volume's chief authorial voice is that of a fourth-century prophet and war captain named Mormon. Mormon took up the task of writing, the text reports, because God gave him a responsibility to sift through and then to summarize the written records of nearly a thousand years of his people's history. What remains of his writings today focuses primarily on just two hundred years of history—from around 150 BCE to around 50 CE. His abridgment of the history prior to that period, after it was dictated by Joseph Smith to scribes in 1828, was lost by one of those scribes (and then replaced with a text not written by Mormon). Further, his abridgment of the history after those two dominant centuries is so astonishingly short that it serves as little more than an epilogue. What Mormon offers to readers within the volume that bears his name thus primarily investigates just the years leading up to and immediately following the birth of Jesus Christ—albeit focused on events in the New World.

The two-century period that absorbs Mormon's attention divides into four sequential phases, each the subject of a distinct book within the larger volume: the Book of Mosiah, the Book of Alma, the Book of Helaman, and the Book of Nephi (often called the Third Book of Nephi). What distinguishes these several subperiods or the associated books from each other is the fact that each tells the history of a unique political formation among the people of Nephi. The Book of Mosiah recounts the era of a revitalized Nephite monarchy, while the Book of Alma narrates the subsequent period when a system of hierarchized judges replaces the Nephite kings. The Book of Helaman tells of a time when a shadow government usurps the power of the Nephite judges, and the Third Book of Nephi reports the collapse of Nephite government just before Jesus Christ arrives to establish a theocratic era of peace. Intricate and fascinating as this periodized political history is in itself, however, it serves the Book of Mormon primarily as a contextual backdrop for a more central drama, one that is ecclesiastical in nature. The Book of Mosiah places at its narrative center the rise of a Nephite proto-Christian church: a body of believers anticipating the still-coming Jesus Christ. The Third Book of Nephi later reports the fulfillment of the church's expectations with Christ's arrival, as well as the church's replacement with a new Christian organization sponsored by the visiting Christ himself. Between these two historical extremes, the Books of Alma and Helaman trace the ebb and flow of the church's progress from its full establishment and stabilization to its culmination and replacement.

The four chapters making up part 1 of this study focus on the role the biblical Book of Isaiah plays in Mormon's political-cum-ecclesiastical history just described. The point is to show how Isaiah is central to the whole of Mormon's narrative, despite the fact that it goes more or less unmentioned in the Books of Alma and Helaman. The fact is that Mormon's interest in Isaiah appears only at the framing extremes of his narrative. The Book of Mosiah places Isaiah and the question of its interpretation at its heart, where Abinadi's prophetic intervention lays the foundation for the rise of the Nephite Christian church. Similarly, the Third Book of Nephi gives a place of privilege to Isaiah, making the biblical book the chief focus of the sermons offered by the resurrected Christ as he fulfills and replaces the earlier church. In sum, Mormon's story moves from an Isaian beginning to an Isaian conclusion, despite the loud Isaian silence that sounds between these textual extremes.

To take the measure of the role played by Isaiah in Mormon's writings, it will thus be necessary to focus almost exclusively on Mosiah and Third Nephi. The first two chapters in this part of the present study therefore consider Mosiah, with an eye to how Abinadi's story raises and answers questions about the interpretation of key passages from Second Isaiah. The last two chapters then address Third Nephi, asking about its distinctive approach to key passages from Second Isaiah. The aim is, by the end of these four chapters, to discern what Mormon's record—the first-dictated portion of the extant Book of Mormon—suggests about the meaning and relevance of the Book of Isaiah. What would a well-informed and charitable American reader in 1830 have seen the thrust of Mormon's uses of Isaiah to be? What happens in the progression from Abinadi to Jesus Christ, and what do the differences between their respective interpretive styles suggest? And how might answers to these questions help an imagined ideal reader be prepared to offer an equally incisive reading of Nephi's contribution, which is the focus of part 2 of the present study?

2
Controversy in a Nephite Colony

In Mormon's project as it is known in the text today, Isaiah first appears in connection with the prophet Abinadi. Mormon presents the latter figure as having been active a hundred and fifty years before the birth of Jesus Christ, albeit in the Book of Mormon's setting in the New World. For all the reasons established in the preceding chapter, it is best to begin serious study of what the Book of Mormon does with Isaiah by looking carefully at this prophet. What would our ideal listener/reader, sitting with Joseph Smith during the Book of Mormon's dictation and then revisiting the text thoughtfully after its completion, find Isaiah doing in the Abinadi story?

Abinadi appears in many ways to be the Book of Mormon's most traditional prophetic figure, cut from the same cloth as the prophets of the Old Testament's histories.[1] As in the Old Testament's narrative style, Abinadi is introduced first simply as "a man" (Mosiah 11:20), and his initial message concerns the excesses of monarchical power in a time of economic prosperity. Noah—the Nephite king in Abinadi's historical period and geographical location—collects "many wives and concubines" (11:2), exacts "a tax of one fifth part" of his people's possessions (11:3), deposes the established priesthood to garner support for his regime (11:4–5), pursues and encourages "idolatrous" worship (11:7), undertakes an ostentatious building program (11:8–13), and invites his people to trust solely in their military might (11:16–19). The Lord raises up Abinadi—as if out of nowhere—in direct response to these moral and social injustices. Abinadi's preaching therefore begins as a straightforward call to repentance, a warning that Noah's people will end up in "bondage" and "afflicted by the hand of their enemies" if they do not turn to God (11:21). When the people fail to repent, the prophet's message grows more serious. Not only does Abinadi then claim that the bondage previously predicted has become sure, he now adds that utter destruction will be the consequence of further refusal to repent. Further, "the life of king Noah," according to Abinadi, is now forfeit; it "shall be valued even as a garment in a hot furnace" (12:3) or will "be as a stalk—even as a dry stalk of the field—which is ran over by the beasts and trodden under foot" (12:11).

Abinadi's attempt to speak truth to power predictably lands him in a dangerous situation, much like other representatives of the prophetic tradition he embodies. Taken captive, he finds himself forced to perform in a show trial for Noah and his corrupt priests. Curiously, in his chapters-long response to the priests' interrogation, Abinadi's style of speech changes drastically. Before he comes to the court of Noah and his priests, Abinadi's prophetic words suggest nothing of Christian commitment, fitting comfortably within the scope and concerns of the Jewish scriptures. Thus, until Abinadi has to defend himself to Noah's corrupt regime, he largely imitates the prophet Isaiah as portrayed in Old Testament narrative, inveighing against corrupt institutions of power and using stock prophetic imagery to predict doom. But once Abinadi opens his mouth in the presence of the king and his priests, he instead reflects on the text of Isaiah, finding in the Judean prophet's words a host of direct anticipations of God's self-revelation in Jesus Christ. This transformation of Abinadi from Hebrew prophet to Christian interpreter—or, perhaps better, this exchange of Hebrew prophecy for Christian interpretation—is so striking that it cannot but appear deliberate to the careful reader.[2] Quite early in the Book of Mormon as Joseph Smith first dictated it, a complex fusion of Old and New Testaments is effectively woven into the Abinadi narrative.[3]

What seems to spur the transformation in Abinadi's prophetic status is, as already noted, a question about the writings of Isaiah. Noah's priests have Abinadi brought before them so they can "question him that they might cross him, that thereby they might have wherewith to accuse him" (Mosiah 12:19). The only question the narrative reports on—perhaps the only question the priests actually ask before Abinadi takes control of the conversation—concerns the meaning of scripture: "What meaneth the words which are written, and which have been taught by our fathers?" (12:20). The specific "words" to which the priests refer with this question are found in Isaiah 52:7–10, a passage they quote for Abinadi in its entirety. The question about this passage's meaning spurs Abinadi to leave off *being* a Hebrew prophet in order to *interpret* Hebrew prophecy, and he quickly assumes a Christian hermeneutic position, guided by what he calls "the spirit of prophesying" (Mosiah 12:25). In this light, it appears significant that Abinadi's priestly interlocutors defend what the text presents as a (locally inflected) Jewish perspective. Not only do they insist that they "teach the law of Moses" (12:28), they also appear to espouse an interpretation of Isaiah's prophecy focused on the political context of their own circumstances, rather than on the Christian idea of the coming of God in human form. When Noah later brings an official accusation against Abinadi, it is in fact for having said "that God himself should come down among the children of men" (17:8).[4]

Such is the complex setting in which the Book of Mormon's first interaction with Isaiah appears. In the course of this chapter and its sequel, it will be necessary to clarify this founding Book of Mormon story devoted to Isaiah's meaning. In this chapter, I will focus solely on exegetical matters, excavating the respective interpretive approaches to Isaiah represented respectively by Noah's priests and by Abinadi. In the following chapter, I will explore the larger significance of Abinadi's Christian appropriation of the Book of Isaiah, in both the external context of the history of Isaiah's interpretation and the internal context of the Book of Mormon as a unified project. That is, the present chapter asks how a charitable and careful reader can make sense of the role played by Isaiah in the Abinadi narrative, and the next chapter explores how a well-informed reader in the early nineteenth century could make sense of the role played by the Abinadi narrative in the history of Isaian interpretation.

Noah's Priests

As our ideal reader would recognize with some study especially of the published Book of Mormon, the Abinadi narrative does not appear in a contextual vacuum in the Book of Mormon. The setting in the larger flow of the volume's history is complex, and it proves to be of real interpretive significance for understanding the controversy over Isaiah that lies at the story's heart. Noah rules as king not in the largely secure capital city of the Nephite lands, but instead in a small Nephite colony settled in the midst of lands occupied by the Nephites' enemies, the Lamanites. More than a generation before Noah's accession to the throne, the Nephites were driven from the land of Nephi, the land of their "first inheritance" (Mosiah 9:1), resettling in a location "called the land of Zarahemla" (Omni 1:13). Zarahemla was already peopled, but the newly arrived Nephites soon rose to power, and their leader, Mosiah, was "appointed" to be "king" over an unstably unified people (1:19). Within a generation, Mosiah and his successor, Benjamin, secured some measure of "peace in the land" of Zarahemla (Words of Mormon 1:18), but not before "a certain number" of Nephites began to express their desire "to possess the land of their inheritance" anew (Omni 1:27). After some serious setbacks, those hoping to return to the land of Nephi proved successful in establishing a treaty with Lamanite occupiers settled in their former lands, and they thus established a colony in the midst of what had become Lamanite territory. Noah's "overzealous" but God-fearing father, Zeniff, headed this effort and stabilized the colony before handing the throne to his son (Mosiah 9:1). Noah, sadly, "did not walk in the ways of his father" (11:1).

Noah's corruption, which galvanizes Abinadi's prophetic intervention, thus unfolds in a peculiar context. He is king over a remote Nephite colony, at some distance from and uncommunicative with the central Nephite power established in Zarahemla. The text reports that the Nephites in Zarahemla have heard nothing from the colony for decades (Mosiah 7:1), and a search party sent from the colony a generation later ends up "lost" because they are unsure of Zarahemla's location (8:7–8). Moreover, the isolated colony's population includes those who risked their lives to reclaim the lands of their inheritance from their enemies, and who actually succeeded in doing so. The confrontation between Abinadi and Noah's priests therefore occurs within a strongly political context, and the narrative explicitly ties this political context to the question of interpreting Isaiah. It is not Abinadi but Noah's priests who bring up Isaiah in the course of their interrogation, and in doing so they note that the passage they cite from Isaiah has been "taught by [their] fathers" (Mosiah 12:20). Isaiah enters the controversy between Abinadi and Noah's priests with direct reference to the ideological bearings of the Nephite colony over which Noah reigns. As early as Zeniff's time, readers are clearly meant to assume, certain Isaiah texts have been used to justify the colony's self-understanding. Zeniff himself seems to have at least entertained a specific interpretation of Isaiah that has come to play a major role in the way Noah's people in the Nephite colony make sense of their successes.

That the Isaiah passage in question is to be understood as serving such a role in the colony is clear from the fact that the priests bother to question Abinadi about it at all. The text emphasizes that if their aim were simply to rid themselves of Abinadi, they could do so without further ado. In fact, when Abinadi allows himself to be captured and brought before Noah, his captors explicitly give the king permission to kill him with impunity. "Behold, here is the man," they say, "we deliver him into thy hands. Thou mayest do with him as seemeth thee good" (Mosiah 12:16). Further, at one point during Abinadi's trial—specifically, when Noah begins to realize that his priests' plan of verbal attack has completely failed—the king tries unsuccessfully to interrupt the legal proceedings to have Abinadi summarily executed: "Away with this fellow and slay him!" (Mosiah 13:1). These details indicate that, within the economy of the story, Noah *can* simply have had Abinadi killed as an insubordinate rebel. Yet, after consulting with his priests, the king allows them to stage a trial, asking Abinadi to interpret Isaiah's words. The reasonable explanation for this failure to use available executive power is that something more important than being rid of an enemy is at stake. By having a trial in which Abinadi might himself make clear to the public the danger he poses to the prevailing ideology, the priests can fully secure the ideological foundation on which their power—along with their king's power—rests. Because Noah's priests position a passage of Isaiah at the center of their interrogation of Abinadi, the narrative asks its readers to see that passage as playing a central role in the self-understanding of Noah's entire people. Only so could Noah's priests assume either that Abinadi would naturally agree with their interpretation or that any alternative he might offer would be unconvincing, allowing them to drum up something "wherewith to accuse him" (Mosiah 12:19).[5]

It is significant that the Book of Mormon never bothers to clarify directly the actual details of the priests' or the people's interpretation of Isaiah. Yet it is not difficult to reconstruct.[6] The passage put to Abinadi by the priests is Isaiah 52:7–10, which reads as follows:

> How beautiful upon the mountains are the feet of him that bringeth good tidings, that publisheth peace, that bringeth good tidings of good, that publisheth salvation, that saith unto Zion, "Thy God reigneth!" Thy watchmen shall lift up the voice; with the voice together shall they sing, for they shall see eye to eye when the Lord shall bring again Zion. Break forth into joy! Sing together, ye waste places of Jerusalem! For the Lord hath comforted his people. He hath redeemed Jerusalem. The Lord hath made bare his holy arm in the eyes of all the nations, and all the ends of the earth shall see the salvation of our God. (Isaiah 52:7–10; quoted in Mosiah 12:21–24)

Point by point, the several elements of this passage can be explained as proof texts for a particular self-understanding promulgated among members of Zeniff's colony in the land of Nephi. To make such an interpretation clear, it is useful to provide a line-by-line analysis of the passage with an eye to the circumstances of the Nephite colony. With each line of the text, I provide both an analysis of the priests' understanding of the text and an outline of the text's meaning in its original Isaian context (as reconstructed by recent critical scholarship).

How beautiful upon the mountains. In the Book of Isaiah, this phrase draws on traditional imagery, such as that of Song of Songs 2:8: "The voice of my beloved! Behold, he cometh leaping upon the mountains, skipping upon the hills!" Even closer literarily to the Isaian text, however, is Nahum 1:15: "Behold upon the mountains the feet of him that bringeth good tidings, that publisheth peace!" The standard interpretation of the Nahum passage is that "the mountains are the hills of Judah that surround the city of Jerusalem," since the prophecy seems to have had its origins in Jerusalem at the time of Assyria's collapse in the second half of the seventh century before Christ.[7] Assyria's demise is good news that a herald brings to Jerusalem as he bounds over the surrounding hills. Many interpreters today understand Isaiah 52:7 to draw on this language from Nahum in order to say to its readers: "That prophecy in Nahum: its time has now come"—albeit reapplied to Babylon's collapse in the sixth century.[8]

The reference to mountains in this passage would seem to have a different significance for Zeniff's people and Noah's priests. The Book of Mormon consistently presents the land of Nephi as substantially higher in elevation than the land of Zarahemla.[9] In returning to the land of Nephi to reclaim his people's former lands of inheritance, Zeniff removes his followers from the plains and the valleys to resettle in the mountains. The good tidings the Nephites in Zeniff's colony anticipate receiving come bounding across the mountains of the land of Nephi. Not unlike those before them who anticipated Jerusalem's deliverance from Babylon's oppression, they anticipate good news being brought to them in their mountain retreat.

Are the feet of him that bringeth good tidings, that publisheth peace, that bringeth good tidings of good, that publisheth salvation, that saith unto Zion, "Thy God reigneth!" The news brought to Jerusalem in the Isaian text is good, announcing both peace and deliverance.[10] More significantly, the messenger of good news makes known that Zion's God reigns. John Goldingay points out that this particular announcement in Isaiah directly echoes a number of Israel's psalms, verses uttered originally in the context of sacred worship. Consequently, because the declaration emphasizes a decisive event in actual history—the collapse of Babylon, Judah's ancient conqueror—"Second Isaiah declares that [God's kingship] is not only a matter of religious conviction but of imminent historical reality."[11] Further, in light of the way that this verse recapitulates the whole of Second Isaiah,[12] it lays clear emphasis on a decisive change in the Lord's attitude toward exiled Judah. The latter has, as an earlier passage makes clear, "received of the LORD's hand double for all her sins," and now God wishes only to "speak ... comfortably to Jerusalem" (Isaiah 40:2).

In the context of Zeniff's recolonization of the land of Nephi, it seems Noah's priests find in these verses a categorical statement that every divine message delivered to the victorious colony will be peaceful and edifying. In other words, because they believe that the recolonization of Nephi marks a certain fulfillment of Isaiah's prophecies, it follows that the only possible prophetic word that could be delivered to Noah's people should be a celebratory one, happy news along the lines of Second Isaiah's general message. This interpretation, of course, excludes Abinadi's preaching, since he has come only with a First-Isaiah-like message of doom and destruction. Instead of speaking of peace and deliverance, Abinadi has spoken of conflict and bondage. Perhaps still more egregiously, he has questioned the king's righteousness, reflecting a lack of faith in the divine institution of the monarchy.

Thy watchmen shall lift up the voice; with the voice together shall they sing, for they shall see eye to eye when the Lord shall bring again Zion. In the Isaiah passage, it is not only messengers coming to the city, but the city's own watchmen, who witness and announce the Lord's intervention on Judah's behalf. "Like the heralds," Goldingay notes, "the lookouts are thus testifying to what they have themselves seen."[13] The text depicts them at their observation posts, eagerly watching for any messengers from the north who might come to report what happened in the conflict between Israel's God and Babylon. When they receive word, "they start shouting the news to the waiting inhabitants of ruined Jerusalem."[14] On this interpretation, the watchmen see eye to eye with the arriving messenger. Either way, the messenger's "voice of good news" is "joined by a larger group of heralds."[15]

Because "prophets are also known [in the Hebrew scriptures] as lookouts or sentinels," Noah's priests may understand the implications of this verse as largely equivalent to those of the preceding verse.[16] Here again the prophets are understood as exulting figures, celebrating God's mighty acts among his people, mighty acts Zeniff likely sees in the successful recolonization of the land of Nephi (and Noah's priests likely see in their own military victories against the Lamanites; Mosiah 11:18–19). But it seems more likely, in the end, that Noah's priests understand themselves to be Zion's watchmen, plural witnesses to the singular messenger who should arrive with good news. The priests and any supposed prophet should see eye to eye—should be in perfect agreement—about the nature of God's relationship with the blessed colony. Not only does Abinadi come to the land of Nephi with the wrong sort of news, then, but he also fails to get on well with the priests, the appointed watchmen of the restored city.

Break forth into joy! Sing together, ye waste places of Jerusalem! For the Lord hath comforted his people. He hath redeemed Jerusalem. In the Isaian context, the good news brought by the messenger and received or recognized by Jerusalem's own sentinels provides the city's inhabitants with good reason to rejoice. It is a sign that the Lord indeed comforts his people and has removed Jerusalem from a compromised situation. But what draws commentators' attention most frequently in connection with this verse is the fact that it addresses Jerusalem's inhabitants metaphorically through the city's "waste places." Strictly speaking, that is, it is not the *people* of Jerusalem but its *ruins* that the prophet commands to sing. In Walter Brueggemann's words, "the very stones of the city cry out in joy for the restoration that is assured by the coming of Yahweh."[17] With Judah returning from exile, the city's ruins are to be rebuilt, and this is reason for the ruins themselves to rejoice.

It is relatively obvious how Zeniff's and Noah's people are supposed to understand this particular verse. When Zeniff's people resettle in the land of Nephi, they find it in ruins, despite the relatively short period since it has left their control. Long before Noah's reign, with its massive building program, Zeniff reports that he and his people have to dedicate their first efforts at settlement to "build[ing] buildings" and "repair[ing] the walls of the city" (Mosiah 9:8).[18] This specific mention of the need to rebuild the city's walls directly echoes the many biblical texts focused on the rebuilding of Jerusalem's walls after exile in Babylon. These Judah-like developments continue with Noah's building program, especially with its emphasis on the need to restore the temple's former glory (Mosiah 11:10). The Zeniffite colony and postexilic Judah run in parallel. Just as Jerusalem's ruins were to rejoice at the prospect of the city's restoration, so are the land of Nephi's ruins to rejoice at the prospect of the colony's success. Once again, Abinadi's gloomy message is at odds with the apparent spirit of the times.

The Lord hath made bare his holy arm in the eyes of all the nations, and all the ends of the earth shall see the salvation of our God. In the Isaian context, the meaning of this verse is perfectly clear. A central theme in Second Isaiah is the revelation of God's power to all the gentile nations—something to be accomplished through Judah's miraculous and unexpected return from exile. As one commentator puts it, "everyone from all the ends of the earth will observe [God's] revelation of his power; thus his name and glory will be known throughout the world."[19] This unveiled power has a rather specific shape, moreover, since it is God's *arm* that is revealed. "Yahweh has bared his holy arm like a warrior rolling up his sleeve so that all nations can see the powerful military muscle that assures Israel and intimidates the nations."[20] Further, the redemption of Jerusalem takes the form of redemption from among gentile peoples—Babylonians, Persians, Medes—precisely so that those gentile peoples have an opportunity to see the workings of the true God, the God of Israel. That in turn provides gentiles with the possibility of joining the effort to redeem Judah. As another passage from Second Isaiah has it, a passage also central to the Book of Mormon, gentiles can carry Judah's "sons in their arms" and Judah's "daughters . . . upon their shoulders" (Isaiah 49:22).

The circumstances described in the record of Zeniff suggest how he and his people are supposed to have interpreted this last part of the passage from Isaiah. Zeniff twice led his colony to battle against the Lamanites, both times "in the strength of the Lord" or "putting their trust in the Lord," as Zeniff claims (Mosiah 9:17; 10:19). They believe that the Lord's arm has been manifested in Nephite military might, and that "all the nations" surrounding the Nephite colony—all of them Lamanite tribes, of course—have witnessed God's supposed preference for the restored Nephites. This theoretical military superiority, already on display during Zeniff's reign, has been confirmed during Noah's reign, when Noah's armies drive Lamanite marauders from their lands. The priests' interpretation of Isaiah 52:10 thus seems to be on display in the narrative's report of how Noah's people react to this (actually rather minor) victory. "And now because of this great victory, they were lifted up in the pride of their hearts. They did boast in their own strength, saying that their fifty could stand against thousands of the Lamanites. And thus they did boast and did delight in blood and the shedding of the blood of their brethren, and this because of the wickedness of their king and priests" (Mosiah 11:19).[21]

Such, I argue, is the basic interpretation of Isaiah 52:7–10 that the Book of Mormon assumes its readers will attribute to Noah and his priests, if not in fact to all of Noah's people. And such, therefore, is the basic interpretation of the passage that Noah's priests assume Abinadi could not possibly disagree with. For them, Isaiah's words can be likened to their own situation of restoration and supposed redemption, triumphalistically interpreted, and so they believe they have scriptural or prophetic confirmation of their right to oppressive and apostate rule. If Abinadi were to concede the validity of their understanding of Isaiah's words—an understanding apparently already operative in their society for decades—they could dispense with him rather easily, at the same time securing the respect and trust of their constituents. The priests anticipate Abinadi seeing that God himself has assisted in founding their regime, confirming his approval by giving them victory in battle against the Lamanites. From their perspective, Abinadi must come to recognize that his prophetic interventions conflict with Isaiah's description of messengers bringing "good tidings" and publishing "peace" and "salvation." From there, it should be possible to have the supposed prophet condemned for his dispiriting message—and the priests can even have him executed with Mosaic impunity, since they will have shown him to be a false prophet, one not sent by the Lord.[22]

The Book of Isaiah thus finds its way into the Book of Mormon project first as a resource for those who would reject the uncomfortable message of a prophet. Before any of the volume's protagonists says a word about the positive meaning of Isaiah's prophecies, those prophecies are already being used negatively and ideologically to justify sloth and corruption. Right from the moment Isaian texts begin to appear in the Book of Mormon, the volume presents the task of its real heroes as partially that of *re*interpreting Isaiah, of recovering Isaiah's words for genuinely *just* purposes. As Abinadi narratively leaves off imitating the prophets to begin interpreting the prophets, he bears responsibility for outlining a novel approach to Isaiah. How can this privileged prophet from the Bible be reclaimed for righteous ends?

The Song of the Suffering Servant

In posing their question about the interpretation of Isaiah, Noah's priests present Abinadi with Isaiah 52:7–10 as a proof text: a few lines drawn from an authoritative source that derive their interpretive force in part from the fact that the interpreters ignore original context. Abinadi responds to the priests in large part by calling into question their proof-texting approach. That is, instead of using Isaiah 52:7–10 as a proof text of his own, Abinadi's response attempts to place the passage within its larger scriptural setting, based on a motif from Isaiah 52–53 that Abinadi subtly identifies. The final verse of Isaiah 52:7–10 focuses on the Lord's making his arm bare before all nations. Abinadi challenges the apparently obvious meaning of this claim by connecting it to the poem of Isaiah 53, which opens with the double rhetorical question: "Who hath believed our report, and to whom is the arm of the Lord revealed?" (Isaiah 53:1; quoted in Mosiah 14:1). Abinadi apparently sees Isaiah 53 as complicating the too-quick interpretation of Isaiah 52:7–10 offered by the priests.[23] The arm of the Lord *is* to be made bare in the eyes of all the nations, but there is some question of when and how that is to be accomplished, as Isaiah's own questions suggest. Only with Abinadi's full elaboration of the meaning of Isaiah 53 in hand, then, is it possible to see clearly what he does with Isaiah 52:7–10.

Isaiah 53 contains (most of) a poem, often called the song of the suffering servant.[24] It recounts the fate of an unfortunate figure, variously interpreted (as our ideal listener/reader would remind us) over the centuries as a rejected prophet, the mistreated people of Israel, and the promised Messiah. It tells of someone plain—without "form" or "comeliness" or "beauty" (Mosiah 14:2)—who falls afoul of the masses and so ends up being "despised and rejected of men" (14:3). People regard the figure as "smitten of God" (14:4) despite the fact he "was wounded for [their] transgressions" (14:5): "the Lord hath laid on him the iniquities of [them] all" (14:6). Eventually, the suffering servant is "brought as a lamb to the slaughter" (14:7) and is "cut off out of the land of the living" (14:8). Buried with "the wicked" despite having "done no evil" (14:9), he is made "an offering for sin" (14:10). Suddenly, in a predicted reversal, the poem states that the sufferer "shall prolong his days" (14:10), triumphing over his adversity and gaining the ability to "justify many" (14:11). In the end, he is to receive "a portion with the great" and to share "the spoil with the strong" (14:12), all this as a reward for his willingness to suffer. The arc of the poem thus traces a pathway from a time when the servant is "humiliated and abused" to a time when he is "exalted"; as Joseph Blenkinsopp nicely summarizes, the servant, "once counted among criminals, will be in the company of the great and powerful."[25] Abinadi quotes this poem—or as much of it as appears in Isaiah 53—in full, basically without alteration.[26] How, though, does he interpret it?

Abinadi presents Isaiah 53 as telling the straightforward story of Jesus Christ's suffering, death, and resurrection. Within the context of his defense before Noah's priests, this interpretation appears radical and novel. The priests would presumably interpret the song of the suffering servant as a rich description of their misfortunes prior to divinely granted victory.[27] Abinadi, however, inventively sees in it a messianic anticipation of a Christ still to come. Of course, from the perspective of any Christian reader of the Book of Mormon in the nineteenth century or today, Abinadi's interpretation appears, on the whole, profoundly traditional. Nearly eighteen hundred years of Christological interpretation of Isaiah 53 preceded the appearance of the Book of Mormon in English. This point is of more concern in the next chapter of this study, but it is worth noting it already because it is of real interest that the Book of Mormon presents Abinadi's traditional Christological approach to Isaiah 53 in a peculiar narrative context. It is presented here as a radically *novel* interpretation offered in the context of a *pre-Christian* debate over the prophet's meaning. It is true enough that Abinadi presents a classically Christological approach to the song of the suffering servant, but the Book of Mormon presents him as doing so at least two centuries before Christ—at least two centuries, therefore, before anyone else in any extant historical record attempted a similar hermeneutic. The odd status of Abinadi's pre-Christian Christological interpretation will have to receive fuller attention. In the meanwhile, it is necessary to ask about the particulars of Abinadi's interpretation of Isaiah 53.

Actually, Abinadi does not turn immediately from the priests' leading question on Isaiah 52:7–10 to his complicating investigation of Isaiah 53. Rather, he first undermines the priestly authority of his interrogators. Questioning their motives for asking their interpretive question, Abinadi forcefully replies with the following: "Are you priests, and pretend to teach this people and to understand the spirit of prophesying—and yet desireth to know of me what these things mean?" (Mosiah 12:25). Demanding to know what they themselves "teach," Abinadi provokes Noah's priests into stating the grounds of their own hermeneutical position; they "teach the law of Moses" (12:27–28). From there Abinadi begins to weave his way toward a messianic interpretation of the prophets, justified by his insistence that "salvation doth not come by the law alone," but also and especially thanks to "the atonement which God himself shall make for the sins and iniquities of his people" (13:28). Abinadi finds prophetic anticipation of "the coming of the Messiah" in Moses-the-Lawgiver himself, but he claims also that "all the prophets which have prophesied ever since the world began" have "spoken more or less concerning these things" (13:33). Among "all the prophets," however, is one who especially draws Abinadi's attention for obvious reasons in the course of his debate with the priests: Isaiah. Only three verses after claiming that Moses anticipated the coming of the Messiah, Abinadi begins quoting Isaiah 53.

As already noted, Abinadi quotes Isaiah 53 in its entirety. Although he never interrupts his recitation with commentary, he in no way leaves the interpretation of this key text to his resistant audience. Rather, he prefaces his quotation with a paragraph or so that frames his approach to the text and then follows it with a few paragraphs of direct commentary. The preface of sorts presents itself as a summary of what Abinadi takes to be the basic message of "all the prophets" (Mosiah 13:33): "Have they not said that God himself should come down among the children of men, and take upon him the form of man, and go forth in mighty power upon the face of the earth? Yea, and have they not said also that he should bring to pass the resurrection of the dead, and that he himself should be oppressed and afflicted?" (13:34–35). All the claims made in these two sentences appear again—most of them in roughly the same words—in the paragraphs of commentary Abinadi provides after quoting Isaiah 53.[28] The last of these several claims uses words drawn directly from Isaiah 53—"He was oppressed, and he was afflicted, yet he opened not his mouth" (Isaiah 53:7; quoted in Mosiah 14:7)—making clear that Abinadi's summary of "all the prophets" is meant to preface his long quotation of the poem.[29] For him, then, the song of the suffering servant makes the following five claims: (1) God himself will come down among his people; (2) God will assume a fleshy human form; (3) God will exhibit mighty power or miracles; (4) God will effect the general resurrection; and (5) God in flesh will be oppressed and afflicted.

Where does Abinadi find each of these claims illustrated in Isaiah 53? It is, of course, in no way difficult to see how Christians have found the story of Jesus there—maybe the aspect of Isaiah's reception history most familiar to our ideal listener/reader (to *any* reader). An apparently mortal figure suffers, but in a way that ultimately serves to redeem the sufferer's persecutors. As early as the second century, Christians found in this poem a description of how forgiveness comes in response, in Justin Martyr's words, to "faith through the blood and the death of Christ, who suffered death for this precise purpose."[30] Despite this consistent tradition, aspects of Abinadi's prefatory interpretation of the poem seem odd. He claims to find in Isaiah 53 not merely a description of Christ's being "oppressed and afflicted," but also a description of divine condescension, a doctrine of incarnation, a narration of Jesus's miracles, and a claim about the general resurrection. These Christological points of interpretation are harder to defend at the level of the text. The poem never identifies the sufferer as a divine being, says anything about the incarnation, or discusses God taking "the form of man" (13:34). Moreover, although one might see a reference to Jesus's resurrection in Isaiah 53's cryptic claim that the sufferer "shall prolong his days" (53:10), it seems difficult to find there any reference to a general "resurrection of the dead" (Mosiah 13:35). Is there any hermeneutical justification for Abinadi's claim to find these Christological principles in the text of Isaiah 53?

With the possible exception of the reference to Jesus's miracles, Abinadi's postquotation commentary attempts to root these less-than-obvious points of interpretation directly in the text of Isaiah 53.[31] Yet it does so in unexpected ways. In essence, Abinadi justifies his claims concerning Christology by outlining an *esoteric* reading of the Isaiah text. He never claims to find Isaiah 53 overtly outlining a theology of incarnation or straightforwardly referring to a general resurrection. But he does indicate that these two theological points can be found darkly present in the poem, hiding in two short lines that are clear only to those who "understand the spirit of prophesying" (Mosiah 13:25). These two lines and Abinadi's esoteric interpretation of them deserve close attention. They appear in Isaiah 53:8 and 53:10. The first is a question that interpreters have understood in a wide variety of ways: "Who shall declare his generation?" (Isaiah 53:8).[32] The second line in question is a brief statement that also raises questions about interpretation: "He shall see his seed" (Isaiah 53:10). Abinadi brings these two lines together in his commentary, despite the fact that they are two verses apart in the text of Isaiah 53. "And now I say unto you," he announces to Noah's priests in the middle of his commentary, "who shall declare his generation? Behold, I say unto you that when his soul has been made an offering for sin, he shall see his seed" (Mosiah 15:10). This close linking of the two lines from Isaiah 53 suggests that Abinadi means to interpret the second of them as providing an answer to the question posed in the first. "Who shall declare his generation? His seed."

Although the Hebrew word translated as "generation" is ambiguous at best,[33] it is not difficult to see a potential link between *generation* and *seed*. Both terms concern progeny.[34] Abinadi nonetheless does not seem to take the two terms to be equivalent, as if what is "generated" is, precisely, the Messiah's "seed"; rather, it seems it is the task of the Messiah's seed to declare the Messiah's generation. Thus, while "seed" seems for Abinadi to concern the progeny of the Messiah, *his children*, "generation" concerns the Messiah's own status as progeny, his own status *as child*. God in the flesh is in some paradoxical sense a child (the Son), and the only people who could possibly understand that in such a way that they might declare it are those who in turn become the children of God enfleshed.

What makes all this clear is Abinadi's full commentary on Isaiah 53. In the verses following his quotation of the poem and leading up to his restatement of the question about declaring the Messiah's generation, Abinadi provides a detailed exposition of the idea that God, dwelling in the flesh, must be regarded as his own son in some paradoxical sense. His restatement of the question from Isaiah 53:8 seems straightforwardly intended to summarize this whole exposition with the word *generation* and then to ask who is supposed to "declare" such difficult doctrine. And then, after Abinadi uses the statement from Isaiah 53:10 to give an answer to his question, he provides a detailed exposition of the Messiah's seed, clarifying quite directly what he believes it means to say, that certain human beings "are heirs of the kingdom of God" (Mosiah 15:11). In short, about half of Abinadi's commentary on Isaiah 53 means just to clarify the sense of Isaiah's word *generation* (Mosiah 15:1–9), while the other half or so means just to clarify the sense of Isaiah's word *seed* (15:11–20). And, at the center of the commentary, marking the transition from the exposition of *generation* to the exposition of *seed*, is a simple statement of the relationship between these two expositions (15:10). The Messiah's seed has the unique task of announcing the Messiah's generation to the world.

How, then, does Abinadi understand each of these terms, *seed* and *generation*? His exposition of the Messiah's generation may be the most notorious passage in the Book of Mormon.[35] The passage has drawn attention because, as Melodie Moench Charles puts it, there seems to be "no good way to reconcile Abinadi's words with the current Latter-day Saint belief that God and his son Jesus Christ are separate and distinct beings."[36] As is well known, Joseph Smith eventually developed a robustly tritheist view of the Godhead, arguing that the Father, the Son, and the Holy Ghost are three distinct beings. But, earlier in Smith's life, he published relatively orthodox conceptions of God,[37] leaving his followers to reconcile those statements with his clearly heterodox tritheism later.[38] Setting aside debates about the apparent orthodoxy or heterodoxy of Abinadi's exposition, however, it must be asked simply how Mosiah 15:1–9 understands the word *generation* from Isaiah 53:8.

The point of Abinadi's exposition of the Messiah's generation seems largely to be to outline the mystery of incarnation, the mystery of how God could possibly generate himself in the flesh. "I would that ye should understand," Abinadi begins (Mosiah 15:1), and with these words he harks back to his first words of criticism directed at Noah's priests: "Are you priests—and pretend to teach this people and to *understand* the spirit of prophesying—and yet desireth to know of me what these things mean? . . . For if ye *understand* these things, ye have not taught them. . . . Ye have not applied your hearts to *understanding*" (12:25–27, italics added). Abinadi thus seems fully to recognize, at the outset of his exposition, that he has the task of making a profound mystery clear to an uncomprehending audience. He employs the metaphor of paternity. God is God's own father and God's own son, and so the process through which God becomes an enfleshed human being can be described as generation, as the production of progeny. Of course, this particular production of progeny is paradoxical, because the father in question *is* the son in question. Yet the relationship between a father and a son is supposed to help explain the dual nature of God in the flesh, who is at once the Father "because he was conceived by the power of God" and the Son "because he dwelleth in flesh" (15:2–3). The subjection of "the flesh . . . to the spirit" is, according to Abinadi, equivalent to the subjection of "the son to the father" (15:5). Just as "the will of the son" is "swallowed up in the will of the father," in Christ "the flesh" becomes "subject" to the spirit "even unto death" (15:7).[39] It is only in this way that "God breaketh the bands of death" (15:8).

Because the priests fail to comprehend—or at least to teach—all this, Abinadi focuses next on the question of who will declare the Messiah's mysterious generation. This he explains in terms of Isaiah's talk of the servant's seed, and again he strikes an esoteric note. The Messiah's seed, he explains, includes two distinct sorts of people. First, it consists of all those who have "heard the words of the prophets . . . and believed that the Lord would redeem his people and have looked forward to that day for a remission of their sins" (Mosiah 15:11).[40] Second, the Messiah's seed includes "the prophets" themselves, "every one that has opened his mouth to prophesy, that has not fallen into transgression" (15:13). Thus, pre-Christian prophets who predict the Messiah's coming, along with those who believe and live in light of their words, together make up the Messiah's seed. But why should these be called his seed? A few verses later, Abinadi explains that these two sorts of people—"all the prophets, and all those that have believed in their words"—make up those who will "come forth in the first resurrection" or who simply "are the first resurrection" (15:22). The pre-Christian prophets and their disciples are, in effect, regenerated thanks to the Messiah's generation, and so Christ's paradoxical status as his own progeny makes it possible for those who have looked forward to his coming to become his progeny as well—his seed.

Abinadi's teachings on the Messiah's seed end up having a towering influence over the subsequent narrative in the Book of Mormon. Noah and his priests ultimately have Abinadi executed, but not before one of Noah's priests defects because Abinadi's words convict him. This priest, Alma by name, goes into hiding, "write[s] all the words" of Abinadi (Mosiah 17:4), and then goes about secretly teaching Abinadi's words until he develops a serious following. He then organizes all those who believe Abinadi's—that is, the pre-Christian prophet's—teachings into what he calls a "church" (the first in the Book of Mormon's narrative).[41] Alma explicitly states that the purpose of the church is to keep those who believe in Abinadi's words faithful so that they might "be numbered with those of the first resurrection" (18:9). A generation later, Alma's successor (and son, also named Alma) outlines his understanding of the church's nature, and it remains focused on gathering all those who "believe in the words which was delivered by the mouth of Abinadi" (Alma 5:11). The Nephite Christian church that exists through the longest stretch of the Book of Mormon's narrative is thus meant to gather and to keep faithful those Nephites who hope to be a part of the Messiah's seed, who hope to rise with him in the first resurrection.

Abinadi's interpretation of Isaiah 53's talk of seed, then, is clear. Some people are given to know, long before the event occurs, that God will take on flesh through a mysterious process of *generation*. And because these people announce this good news to any who will hear, such prophets and their disciples become anticipatory heirs to the kingdom of God and receive the promise that they will rise, themselves *re*generated, with the Messiah at his resurrection. This is what it means, for Abinadi, to speak of the Messiah's *seed*. Once the Messiah's "soul" has been made "an offering for sin, he shall see his seed"—and this at the same time that, because he has himself risen from the dead, "he shall prolong his days" (Isaiah 53:10). With such an esoteric reading, Abinadi can justify to his own satisfaction his initially outlandish claim, namely, that he finds in the text of Isaiah 53 robust Christological doctrines like the idea that "God himself should come down among the children of men and take upon him the form of man" (Mosiah 13:34) or like the idea that Christ "should bring to pass the resurrection of the dead" (13:35). For anyone who has "the spirit of prophesying," the truth of such an esoteric interpretation is supposed to be apparent. Abinadi makes clear his assumption that Noah's priests either *should* have access to such a spirit of prophesying or at least that they *pretend* to have access to it (12:25), although it is clear that they are actually ignorant of it.

And thus it is awkwardly apparent that the arm of the Lord has in fact *not* been made bare in everyone's eyes, since even the priests in the Nephite colony have not yet seen it. Isaiah 52:7–10 cannot yet be completely fulfilled from Abinadi's perspective. And so, the opening question from Isaiah 53, which Abinadi asks of the priests impertinently, is in fact profoundly pertinent. "Who hath believed our report, and to whom is the arm of the Lord revealed?" (Mosiah 15:1). The proper answer to this question is, for Abinadi, clearly that almost no one has yet witnessed the baring of the Lord's arm. Only a few prophets and their few but faithful followers—those making up the Messiah's forthcoming seed—escape being indicted by the prophet's question. Certainly Noah's priests would do well to "fear and tremble before God" and learn from Abinadi's interpretation (15:26). For the moment, they are numbered among those who have neither believed the prophets' report nor had the Lord's holy arm revealed to them, despite the fact that they "pretend . . . to understand the spirit of prophesying" (12:25).

Upon completing his commentary on Isaiah 53, Abinadi has already unsettled the priests' interpretation of Isaiah 52:7–10, to which he now turns. And if Abinadi can extract a complex Christology from just a couple of stray lines in Isaiah 53, readers might rightly expect him to do something equally impressive with Isaiah 52:7–10, certainly something as interesting as what Noah's priests find in the passage.

The Baring of the Lord's Arm

Abinadi moves seamlessly from his direct commentary on Isaiah 53 to the beginnings of his interpretation of Isaiah 52:7–10, focusing initially just on the first verse, which praises the beautiful feet of those who bring good tidings and publish peace. Abinadi connects this work of publishing peace to what he has developed out of Isaiah 53:8 and 53:10. The prophetic portion of the Messiah's seed "shall declare [Christ's] generation" (Mosiah 15:10), and that same prophetic portion of his seed is therefore the same that, in Isaiah's words, "hath published peace, that hath brought good tidings of good, that hath published salvation, that saith unto Zion, 'Thy God reigneth!'" (15:14). Abinadi establishes this identity between the Messiah's generation-declaring seed and the peace-publishing messengers of Isaiah 52:7 with three simple words: "these are they" (15:14). After asserting this hermeneutic link, Abinadi continues by borrowing Isaiah 52:7's words of praise, which he turns into a repeating refrain about those who publish peace in the past, present, and future. Prophets before Abinadi, prophets during his own time, and prophets still to come after him—all these publish peace and bring good tidings, speak of salvation, and announce the sovereignty of Zion's God. They are the roaming messengers who bring comfort to the world by speaking of the coming Christ.

It should be noted that Abinadi's interpretation of Isaiah 52:7 continues but also expands the temporal or historical determinations of his interpretation of Isaiah 53:10. For Abinadi, the Messiah's seed spoken of in Isaiah 53 is made up *only* of pre-Christian prophets and their pre-Christian disciples (along with pre-Christian individuals ignorant of God's law). All these, having died before Christ's advent, can expect to rise with the Messiah at the time of his resurrection. The same pre-Christian prophets "are they which hath published peace," according to Abinadi (Mosiah 15:14), but their beautiful feet are praised along with the feet of those who, from Abinadi's pre-Christian perspective, "shall hereafter publish peace—yea, from this time henceforth and forever!" (15:17). Within Isaiah 52:7, then, Abinadi finds a slightly looser referent than he does in Isaiah 53:10. In the latter, *only* the pre-Christian prophets are at issue, but in the former, *both* pre-Christian prophets and those who preach of Christ's redemption after his resurrection receive praise. The work of the pre-Christian prophets, who speak "of things to come as though they had already come" (Mosiah 16:6), continues into the Christian era with what other Book of Mormon voices do not fail to call "the apostles."[42] Thus, the declaratory work of the prophetic portion of the Messiah's seed does not exhaust the meaning of Isaiah 52:7. It seems, for Abinadi, that the pre-Christian prophets are the primary referent of the passage ("these are they"), but they are not its sole referent. This expansion of scope in Isaiah 52:7, when compared to Abinadi's narrower interpretation of Isaiah 53, is of some importance for the remainder of his reading of the passage the priests have given him to explain.

Beyond prophets and apostles, Abinadi applies the words of praise from Isaiah 52:7 to one other figure: the coming Christ (Mosiah 15:18). This accomplishes two things simultaneously. First and obviously, it makes clear that any praise offered to the messengers who announce Christ's victory ultimately amounts to praise for the Victor. Second, however, it allows Abinadi to turn directly to "the redemption which [Christ] hath made for his people" (15:19) in order to clarify the meaning of the "first resurrection" already discussed (15:21). It seems important that this focus on the events surrounding Christ's death and resurrection—especially on those who rise with Christ in the first resurrection (his "seed")—interrupts Abinadi's belated exposition of Isaiah 52:7–10. Before he provides any clarification of verses 8–10 but after he has offered his full explanation of verse 7, he describes the time of "restoration" for all those from before Christ's era who are the first to receive the benefits of his redemption (Mosiah 15:24). Further, before turning from the first resurrection to the exposition of Isaiah 52:8–10, Abinadi also offers a direct word of warning to his priestly interlocutors, saying they "had ought to tremble" because those who rebel against the Lord will die in their sins (Mosiah 15:26). All this allows Abinadi to clarify the stakes of the pre-Christian context he has derived from Isaiah 53:10 and applied most directly to Isaiah 52:7 before he turns to Isaiah 52:8–10, the fulfillment of which he projects into the Christian (rather than the pre-Christian) era.

When he finally comes to it, Abinadi's exposition of Isaiah 52:8–10 unfolds quickly. He predicts simply that "the time shall come that the salvation of the

Lord shall be declared to every nation, kindred, tongue, and people" (Mosiah 15:28). It becomes apparent eventually that Abinadi here has reference to the Christian era, to the apostolic work of taking the good news of Christ's victory over death to the whole world. With Christ will arise all those who "have died before Christ came, in their ignorance, not having salvation declared unto them" (15:24). Beyond that event, it is possible for the message of Christ's victory to spread across the whole earth. Further, a few verses later, Abinadi begins to apply the language of Isaiah 52:8–10 specifically to the event of the final judgment, long after the Christian era begins (Mosiah 16:1). This makes retrospectively clear that Abinadi understands Isaiah 52:8–10 to have its primary fulfillment in and toward the end of the Christian era, rather than, as with Isaiah 53:10, squarely in the pre-Christian era. Thus, immediately after predicting the time when the Lord's salvation will begin to spread throughout the whole world, Abinadi simply reproduces Isaiah 52:8–10 in its entirety in Mosiah 15:29–31. Most of the interpretive work Abinadi does here he accomplishes just by providing a context in which to quote the passage, rather than in any direct exposition on the passage. A detailed examination of the text provides a fuller picture of the implicit details of the interpretation Abinadi offers, both of Isaiah 52:8–10 and of Isaiah 52:7, already exposited.

How beautiful upon the mountains are the feet of him that bringeth good tidings, that publisheth peace, that bringeth good tidings of good, that publisheth salvation, that saith unto Zion, "Thy God reigneth!" As has been made clear, Abinadi finds in these lines from Isaiah 52:7 an exclamation focused on the "seed" mentioned later in Isaiah 53:10. That seed he esoterically interprets as being made up of pre-Christian prophets and their disciples, those who believe in the Messiah's mysterious "generation" referred to in Isaiah 53:8. Further, though, he takes clear issue with the priests' flat understanding of "good tidings." Where they see Isaiah's words as referring simply to words of comfort and affirmation for a once-embattled colony, Abinadi hears in them a nearly technical reference to *the* good news, the gospel. In a similar vein, where Noah's priests apparently understand Isaiah's talk of salvation to have reference simply to temporal deliverance from threatening enemies, Abinadi esoterically understands such talk to indicate spiritual redemption, salvation from death and from sin. These are pieces of news the pre-Christian prophets announce in advance (to be followed later by Christian apostles, of course) and so can be described as messengers with beautiful feet. Abinadi, of course, is himself one of the pre-Christian prophets in question, and so the priests are wrong to imply that he performatively contradicts Isaiah's words; rather, he embodies them precisely, and, uniquely within the colony, he announces the Lord's eternal reign—being "the very eternal Father of heaven and of earth" as much as "the Son because of the flesh" (Mosiah 15:3–4).

Thy watchmen shall lift up the voice; with the voice together shall they sing, for they shall see eye to eye when the Lord shall bring again Zion. Abinadi relatively straightforwardly interprets Isaiah's talk of watchmen in terms of the classic image from the Hebrew Bible—and, in fact, from elsewhere within the Book of Isaiah. The watchmen are the prophets, or at least, in Abinadi's usage, their Christian-era heirs.[43] That Abinadi interprets the text this way is clear from the context in which he finally quotes Isaiah 52:8. Immediately before quoting the passage, he announces the time when "the salvation of the Lord shall be declared to every nation, kindred, tongue, and people" (Mosiah 15:28). He follows this announcement with a confirming "yea" and then quotes the verse. The watchmen from the Isaiah text Abinadi therefore clearly understands to be those who declare the Lord's salvation to all peoples, apparently accomplishing their work primarily during the Christian era (in light of its universal spread). Further confirming Abinadi's interpretation here is his insertion of the vocative "Lord" between the confirming "yea" and the quotation of the verse: "Yea, Lord, thy watchmen shall lift up their voice," he begins. By addressing Isaiah 52:8 directly to God—rather than to the ruined city of Jerusalem (as in the original) or the rebuilt land of Nephi (as in the priests' use)—Abinadi indicates his understanding of Isaiah's "watchmen" as God's vocal representatives, declaring good news to the whole world. He clearly disregards the idea that the watchmen are some city's guards or caretakers, and so he clearly disregards the basic interpretation espoused by Noah's priests.

Further, Abinadi interprets Isaiah 52:8's talk of seeing "eye to eye" in an unexpected way. At first, it seems as if he refers to classic Isaian anticipations of all nations coming to peace by giving up war and aggression.[44] When Abinadi continues his statement, however, he clarifies his meaning, stating that all nations "shall confess before God that his judgments are just" (Mosiah 16:1). It would seem, at the very least, that he understands the event of people's seeing eye to eye as taking the specific shape of confession, a formal gesture of self-resignation to God's final judgment. For Abinadi, the Lord will bring again Zion only at the final judgment, and it is all nations rather than just the watchmen who see eye to eye—with each other, perhaps, but certainly with God.

Break forth into joy! Sing together, ye waste places of Jerusalem! For the Lord hath comforted his people. He hath redeemed Jerusalem. Unlike Noah's priests, who see in these words a command to celebrate the Nephite settlement's rebuilding of the walls and the temple of its own "Jerusalem" (the city of Lehi-Nephi), Abinadi's understanding of this verse seems to be rooted in his constant talk of God's work in redeeming "his people." Indeed, Abinadi seems to draw the short phrase "his people" directly from Isaiah's words and then make it a constant refrain in his response to the priests.[45] Significantly, Abinadi usually couples the verb "to redeem" with "his people," rather than the verb "to comfort," and he never speaks of "Jerusalem" except in his direct quotation of this verse. It therefore appears as if Abinadi fuses two parallel clauses—"the Lord hath comforted his people" and "he hath redeemed Jerusalem"—to produce his own central theological claim, that "God himself shall come down among the children of men and shall redeem his people" (Mosiah 15:1). Here Abinadi either deliberately displaces Isaiah's geographical specifications or, more likely, takes Jerusalem to serve as a useful symbol for God's people more generally. It is not an actual city in ruins that so much concerns Abinadi as the fallen state of human beings: "Thus all mankind were lost, and behold, they would have been endlessly lost were it not that God redeemed his people from their lost and fallen state" (16:4). Jerusalem's waste places serve for Abinadi as apt images for understanding human beings, who are desperately in need of deliverance from death. The good news—reason for the wasted human race to celebrate—is that "Jerusalem" has been redeemed, or will be in Christ's resurrection. The mere rebuilding of a ruined colony is little reason to celebrate.

The Lord hath made bare his holy arm in the eyes of all the nations, and all the ends of the earth shall see the salvation of our God. Abinadi makes his interpretation of this last verse particularly clear: the revelation of the Lord's arm develops in stages. At first, it seems, the Lord's real strength is hidden from the world, which Abinadi signals by opening his quotation of the song of the suffering servant with Isaiah 53:1. "To whom is the arm of the Lord revealed?" Isaiah asks, answering his own question by noting that "he hath no form nor comeliness" (Mosiah 14:1–2). The Lord's mysterious generation *is*, however, declared in advance by the pre-Christian prophets and then by the apostles (and their heirs) in the Christian period.[46] When the once-largely-unknown message has been fully disseminated, a nondeclarative baring of the Lord's arm is to occur. All will at that point *see* the salvation of the Lord in an event of climactic final judgment, a time when everyone will confess God's righteousness. This is the progressive story of the Lord's self-revelation, of the Lord's slowly but surely baring his arm in the eyes of all the nations. Obviously, from Abinadi's grand perspective, Noah's priests, with their trust in minor military victories in their far-flung colony, exhibit badly misplaced faith. Their self-application of Isaiah's words is yet again startlingly narrow.

These, then, are the basic contours of Abinadi's interpretation of Isaiah 52:7–10, the passage put to him by the priests at the outset of his trial. His understanding of the passage differs drastically from the reconstructed meaning assumed in modern scholarship, to be sure. It differs also at every point from the interpretation assumed by his priestly accusers. His is a deliberately and consistently Christian interpretation of the text, focused on the spread of the good news of Christ's victory over death. The preaching of this good news begins, for Abinadi, already in the pre-Christian era, but it continues and broadens drastically in the Christian period before coming to a kind of fruition in the final judgment. All this Abinadi finds in Isaiah 52:7–10. Of course, as I have shown, what allows him to read the text in this way is an esoteric interpretation of Isaiah 53. In that poem's references to both the "generation" (verse 8) and the "seed" (verse 10) of the servant whose suffering it recounts, Abinadi finds the mystery of the Christian gospel and the prophetic and apostolic task of preaching the Christian gospel. Because the passage offered by the priests and the song of the suffering servant complexly connect by referring in contrasting ways to the baring of the Lord's arm, Abinadi sees the two canonically proximate texts of Isaiah 52:7–10 and Isaiah 53:1–12 as interpretively intertwined. The esoteric interpretation of the one grounds the esoteric interpretation of the other.

How then, in the end, do the prophetic and the priestly models of Isaian hermeneutics compare within the Abinadi narrative? It is significant that both Noah's priests and Abinadi locate the interpretive center of gravity for Isaiah 52:7–10 outside the passage itself. But where the priests situate the passage in their own immediate historical and geographical circumstances, Abinadi finds his center of gravity in the prophetic spirit that points toward the Messiah, as articulated in Isaiah 53:1–12. Both the prophetic and the priestly approaches to Isaiah put on display in the Abinadi narrative exhibit textual sensitivity, each attempting to address all relevant details within the text. Noah's priests, as much as Abinadi, have an identifiable methodology. The two approaches differ substantially in that one takes the meaning of Isaiah's prophecies to be immediately obvious and publicly available, while the other takes their meaning to be hermeneutically complex and singularly obscure.

Our always present ideal listener/reader would thus conclude that the Book of Mormon dedicates its first serious encounter with the Book of Isaiah—following the order of dictation—to a nuanced comparison between these first two approaches to the Hebrew prophet. Because the text presents Abinadi as a protagonist, it clearly means to privilege the esoteric or prophetic reading he represents over that of the priests. Yet, as will be seen, Abinadi's interpretation of Isaiah 52:7–10 is emphatically *not* the only understanding of the passage offered by a Book of Mormon protagonist. It is therefore necessary to ask about the ultimate significance for the Book of Mormon of the debate between Abinadi and Noah's priests. What does it mean for the Book of Mormon as dictated text to open with a debate between these two particular positions on Isaiah's meaning if the text will eventually go on to offer still other interpretive options? To ask this question is actually to ask at least two questions, which I will explore in the next chapter. First, it must be seen whether the interpretations of Abinadi and of Noah's priests find clear echoes in the history of Isaian hermeneutics, especially as it leads up to the early nineteenth century, when our ideal listener/reader would have encountered the Book of Mormon. Where connections with the tradition exist, careful study might help to clarify the bearings of the Book of Mormon's early deployment of the debate between the prophetic and the priestly. Second, it must be asked whether the place occupied by the Abinadi narrative within the larger Book of Mormon—both as dictated text and as published work in final form—says something about the purposes and significance of the confrontation between Abinadi and Noah's priests.

3

Tradition and Innovation

Abinadi's confrontation with Noah's priests, in a tale from early in the dictation of the Book of Mormon, establishes the basic stakes for the larger project's involvement with biblical Isaiah. From the outset, Isaiah is a subject of controversy, a matter of dispute rather than settled opinion. Abinadi defends a normative approach to the Hebrew prophet, but only in the context of a larger marketplace of models for interpreting Isaiah. To take the full measure of the stakes, it is necessary not only to see—as in the previous chapter—what basic interpretive approaches are debated in the Abinadi narrative but also to investigate each approach's potential connections with other hermeneutic models, both inside and outside the Book of Mormon. This is what our ideal listener/reader, familiar with the interpretive tradition surrounding Isaiah, would insist on. Having seen that the Nephites find themselves from the beginning of the dictated text of the Book of Mormon in a marketplace of models for interpreting Isaiah, our listener/reader would want to reflect on how the Nephite marketplace compares with the larger Judeo-Christian one.

Although the particulars of interpretation complicate matters, Abinadi's general approach to Isaiah—or at least Isaiah 52–53—fits well with the Christian tradition. Despite the fact that the Book of Mormon presents his interpretation as something novel, something at odds with the established priestly understanding of the prophet, the earliest readers of the Book of Mormon unquestionably found in Abinadi's expositions something familiar. When the Book of Mormon first appeared, Christological interpretation of Isaiah represented an eighteen-hundred-year tradition. Already within the New Testament itself, Saint Paul used Isaiah 52:7 to make sense of the preaching of the Christian gospel,[1] and Paul and other New Testament authors often used Isaian texts to outline their understanding of Christianity's meaning.[2] From early in Christian history, then, interpreters have often seen Isaiah as a "fifth gospel,"[3] such that Brevard Childs speaks of the long "struggle to understand Isaiah as Christian scripture."[4] By the first decade of the fifth century, Saint Jerome could undertake a systematic Christian exposition of Isaiah, aimed to "show him not only as a prophet, but as an evangelist and apostle." To justify his strategy, Jerome cited the very passage debated by Abinadi and Noah's priests: "For [Isaiah] himself says of himself and of other evangelists, 'How beautiful are the feet of those who evangelize, [announcing] good things, who preach peace.'"[5] The same basic Christological interpretation of Isaiah's prophecies—Isaiah 53 in particular—continued through the medieval era into the present.[6] Today, continuing efforts by some Christians to convert Jews to belief in the messiahship of Jesus tend to focus on the prophecies of Isaiah.[7]

Upon its appearance in the nineteenth century, then, the Book of Mormon's presentation of Abinadi's approach to Isaiah would have appeared to most—and certainly to our informed ideal listener/reader—as largely conservative and traditional. The (implicit but reconstructable) interpretation espoused by Noah's priests and the whole Zeniffite colony, moreover, resembles what American Christians might have expected from a roughly caricatured Jewish interpretation: an application of the prophet's words to their own historical and political circumstances, instead of a deliberately Christian reading focused on the coming of God in Christ. At first glance, then, the Book of Mormon's uses of Isaiah in the Abinadi narrative would have met the earliest readers' expectations. In the Christian United States prior to the Civil War, interpreters generally understood Isaiah as filled with focused prophecies about Jesus Christ.[8] As our *ideal* listener/reader would insist after spending some time with the Book of Mormon, however, a closer look at the details complicates and enriches this picture. There are peculiarities of Abinadi's interpretation that deserve closer attention. For example, he includes elements that our ideal listener/reader, familiar with the history of Isaiah interpretation, would have described as quaintly and even surprisingly traditional in 1829 or 1830, even if other elements would have been unsurprising. Further, beyond the traditional, there are in Abinadi's exposition certain entirely nontraditional elements, fully at odds with typical Christian commentary. Despite a veneer of familiarity with the Christian tradition, Abinadi's exposition of Isaiah holds it at arm's length in crucial ways.

Complicating matters further is the fact that Abinadi and Noah's priests are not the only figures in the Book of Mormon to interpret Isaiah 52:7–10. A few hundred pages separate the Abinadi narrative from the next interpreter of Isaiah, but when that next interpreter appears and takes up the same passage, something fundamentally non-Abinadite emerges. And still further along in Joseph Smith's dictation of the Book of Mormon would come other voices corroborating the non-Abinadite approach to Isaiah. That these several non-Abinadite voices are positioned on either side of the Abinadi narrative in the Book of Mormon's final form (one major voice prior to the Abinadi narrative, and one major voice subsequent to it) suggests that Abinadi's approach to Isaiah eventually occupies an even more contested space than in the immediate setting of the controversy with Noah's priests. It is therefore necessary not only to ask how Abinadi's interpretation of Isaiah fits in the context of antebellum Christian America, but also to investigate preliminarily how Abinadi's Christological approach to Isaiah is challenged within the Book of Mormon itself, in final form. The task of this chapter is to assess these two points in turn.

Echoes of the Patristics

In comparing Abinadi's Christological interpretation to that of the Christian tradition, it seems best to begin with the quaintly or the surprisingly traditional—those aspects of Abinadi's reading that were consonant with an era long before the Book of Mormon's appearance in the 1830s. Put simply, Abinadi's interpretation shares a crucial feature with the hermeneutics of the early Christian fathers, but not—generally speaking—with Christian interpreters of the nineteenth century, whether in America or elsewhere.[9]

As discussed in the previous chapter, Abinadi proffers a strikingly esoteric interpretation of Isaiah 53:8 in the course of his defense before Noah's priests. According to this interpretation, the prophet's talk of the suffering servant's "generation" refers to the mysterious process through which the one God of Israel, coming into the flesh, assumes a dual nature. For Abinadi, one best understands this mystery by seeing how Christ is both Father and Son, Father of himself and Son of himself. But, as John Sawyer notes in a summary treatment, the early Christian fathers also sometimes referred to "the ineffable mystery of the incarnation" by citing "the words of [Isaiah] 53:8: *Generationem eius quis enarrabit*? Who will be able to explain his generation (that is, how he was 'generated')?" Summarizing a common early Christian interpretation of the verse, Sawyer explains, "Human language cannot describe how both 'substances' or 'natures,' divine and human, came together in one person: it is a matter of faith."[10] Even without further exposition, it is easy to see a parallel between this common early Christian interpretation of Isaiah 53:8 and the interpretation set forth by Abinadi. To grasp the significance of this connection, however, it is necessary to explore briefly both just how central this interpretation was in the first several centuries of Christian history and how the same interpretation eventually came nonetheless to fall out of popularity.

One Christmas early in the fifth century, Saint Augustine stepped into the pulpit to give a celebratory sermon. In the course of his remarks, he beautifully represented the standard approach among the patristics:

> The Son of God, who is also the Son of man, our Lord Jesus Christ, born of the Father without mother, created every single day; born of his mother without father, he consecrated this particular day; invisible in his divine birth, visible in his human one, in each of them wonderful. Thus it is difficult to judge about which of the two the prophet is more likely to have prophesied, "Who shall tell the tale of his begetting?"—whether of that one in which, never not born, he has the Father co-eternal with himself; or of this one in which, born at a particular time, he had already made the mother of whom he would be made; whether of that one where he was always born, since he always was.[11]

Augustine well illustrates the common early Christian approach to Isaiah 53:8 extant in available records. On this score, he was no innovator. The interpretation appears as early as the second century—in, for example, Justin Martyr's *First Apology* and his *Dialogue with Trypho*[12]—and had become standard by Augustine's time two and a half centuries later. Thus Jerome, Augustine's exact contemporary, reproduced in his influential commentary the same interpretation (albeit in the stilted prose of the learned): "*Who has declared his generation* (*generationem*)*?* This is understood in two ways: one should either interpret it concerning his deity, that it is impossible to know the mysteries of the divine generation (*nativitatis*) . . . ; or it should be understood concerning his birth from a virgin, that it could scarcely be explained."[13]

Despite its apparent popularity in the early church, this interpretation was neither uncontroversial nor uncomplicated. Between Justin and Augustine it appeared in the early writings of Athanasius, in a work (*On the Incarnation*) written just before the rise of the Arian controversy, in which Athanasius would play a central role.[14] Unfortunately for Athanasius, however, adherents of the Arian opposition would soon use this same text and interpretation as a weapon against his supposed orthodoxy.[15] This controversy, which raged for the better part of a century and ultimately settled the basic Christian conception of God, concerned a theological debate over Christ's nature. From early in the debate, Arians cited Isaiah 53:8 in support of their position, interpreted in the by-then-standard fashion.[16] Arians used this Isaian proof text with such frequency, however, that eventually defenders of Athanasian orthodoxy found it necessary to address its meaning in their own polemics.[17] Although Athanasius himself apparently did not appeal to Isaiah 53:8 in his interventions in the Arian controversy,[18] his followers certainly did, eventually developing an Athanasian interpretation of the passage, directly opposed to the Arian interpretation.[19]

Even as the Arian and Athanasian interpretations of Isaiah 53:8 opposed each other at one level, however, they shared at another level what had become by the fourth century the standard reading of the passage. For both parties, Isaiah's question referred to the divine mystery of Christ's birth and the divine incarnation, whatever one might understand to be the theological implications of that mystery. When the controversy settled down or fell into the background, what each party shared by way of assumptions about the verse's meaning continued to inform Christian interpretation.[20] Consequently, this particular Christological understanding of Isaiah 53:8's question, "Who shall declare his generation?" continued as normative in medieval Christianity and was really displaced only with the rise of modern critical hermeneutics.

The shape of the general Christian approach to Isaiah 53:8 began to change especially with the interpretive work of the major Reformers in the sixteenth century.[21] They assumed—like so many Christians before them—that the song of the suffering servant predicts Christ's life, death, and resurrection. They nonetheless found a rather different meaning in the word "generation" than did their medieval Christian predecessors. Taking the context in the passage to predict Christ's glorification in resurrection, Martin Luther writes:

> *As for His generation, who will tell it?* Who can relate its duration, since His life and duration is eternal? Note the two contrary statements: Someone dying and yet enduring forever. *Generation* properly means age, era, a lifetime. . . . Here, then, the prophet established Christ in an eternal age, something that cannot be expressed, namely, that He has been transposed into eternal life. Peter

expounds this passage in Acts, where he says (Acts 2:24): "God raised Him up, having loosed the pangs of death, because it was not possible for Him to be held by it," and led Him into generation, that is, into length of life and eternity."[22]

John Calvin wrote in a similar vein.[23]

Luther's and Calvin's basic interpretation soon became standard in Protestantism.[24] It thus appeared in the widely influential Latin scholarly commentaries in the seventeenth and early eighteenth centuries,[25] as well as in popular commentaries produced in vernacular languages, such as those of the Non-Conformist English divines, Matthew Poole and Matthew Henry, written in English in the seventeenth century and widely available into the twentieth. Both Poole and Henry—shaping the conversations in the world of Joseph Smith and our ideal listener/reader as well—offered two interpretations of Isaiah 53:8's reference to the servant's "generation." The passage might refer to Christ's "age, or the continuance of his life," with the sense "that he shall not only be delivered from death, and all his punishment, but also shall be restored to an inexpressible or endless life, and to an everlasting kingdom"; or it might refer to Christ's "posterity," with the sense "that Christ's death shall not be unfruitful, and that when he is raised from the dead, he shall have a spiritual seed, as is promised ver. 10."[26] In John Wesley's well-traveled *Explanatory Notes*, written in the eighteenth century and particularly influential in the Methodist tradition with which Joseph Smith felt some affinity,[27] the interpretation favors just one of Poole's two options: "His generation—His posterity. For his death shall not be unfruitful; when he is raised from the dead, he shall have a spiritual seed, a numberless multitude of those who shall believe in him."[28]

The eighteenth century saw an important development in English-speaking approaches to Isaiah. The Anglican bishop Robert Lowth produced a new English translation of Isaiah's prophecy, rendering it in poetic form for the first time in modernity. Lowth, moreover, added to his edition extensive scholarly interpretive notes. For much of the English-speaking world, for more than a century, Bishop Lowth's Isaiah—rendered in English and widely printed—was the correct Isaiah.[29] Lowth's interpretations of Isaiah appear in both scholarly and popular treatments of the prophet throughout the eighteenth and nineteenth centuries. As regards Isaiah 53:8, Lowth simply rendered the Isaian question as "And his manner of life who would declare?" Noting that the underlying Hebrew for "generation" simply "signifies age, duration, the time, which one man or many together pass in this world," Lowth understood the question just to be asking who would stand up in defense of the suffering servant described in the Isaian poem.[30] The importance of this commentary for subsequent interpretation can be glimpsed by noting that Adam Clarke, a dramatically influential Methodist commentator writing during Joseph Smith's early life (contemporary with our ideal listener/reader), simply reproduced Lowth's comments on this passage, adding nothing of his own.[31] But Lowth influenced not only scholarly interpretation like Clarke's; in the very popular edition of the Bible produced by the conservative scholar Thomas Scott, the interpretation of Lowth is reproduced as well, albeit with the added note, "If so, [the word *generation*] has, 'in this place' a signification, which it bears in no other text of the Hebrew Bible."[32]

This evolution did not mean that the patristic interpretation had entirely disappeared from the hermeneutic tradition. Indeed, opinions found in scholarly commentaries seldom represent patterns of interpretation among lay readers of the biblical text, or even among pastoral patterns of interpretation. Some sources suggest that the pre-Reformation approach to Isaiah 53:8 persisted in certain contexts or among certain readers. Thus, in a work of systematic theology from late in the eighteenth century—a work that explicitly states its debt to the opinions of the early Christian fathers—one finds the following: "The manner of the operation whereby the Holy Ghost effected the human generation of our Lord is difficult for us to comprehend. . . . For as the prophet says, who shall declare his generation: a performance so wonderfully sublime cannot be clearly comprehended or minutely described by man."[33] Similar in spirit to this work's interpretation of Isaiah 53:8 is an excerpt from a lecture series given in London in the first years of the nineteenth century (and, significantly, published in three American editions shortly thereafter): "'Who shall declare his generation?' Incapable thou art, O man, to trace back the short and slender thread of thy own existence and descent. . . . Canst thou declare the generation of this insect, to day a butterfly, yesterday a moth, the third day a mere lifeless incrustation, and presumest thou to explain the great mystery of godliness, 'God made manifest in the flesh'?"[34] The early Christian interpretation of "generation" can also be found in some still more popular Protestant sources as well. It appears, for instance, in the October 1804 issue of the *Connecticut Evangelical Magazine* (drawn in turn from an 1803 issue of *The Religious Monitor or Scots Presbyterian Magazine*), where Isaiah 53:8 is cited by way of demonstrating that "the eternity of Christ's generation and Sonship seems . . . to be fairly implied in many Scriptures of the Old Testament."[35]

But even as it is *possible* to find occasional popular Protestant sources in the eighteenth and nineteenth centuries deploying the patristic interpretation of

Isaiah 53:8, it is far *easier* to find in popular Evangelical periodicals of the era evidence of a general shift away from that approach. Thus, the editor of the *Evangelical Magazine* in 1802 quoted then-standard Protestant scholarly commentaries (especially that of Bishop Lowth) to respond to a question about the meaning of Isaiah 53:8.[36] Still more telling, the *Missionary Magazine* in the same year featured a letter to the editor that meant to correct an earlier editorial on the passage by working through various possible interpretations and settling on what had become the scholarly consensus.[37] Further evidence of the shift toward a standardization of the Protestant interpretation perhaps appears in notes added to a posthumous edition of Jonathan Edwards's *History of the Work of Redemption*. In a 1788 edition of the book supplied with what Edwards's editors supposed "probably the Author would for the most part have inserted in the body of the work" if he were still alive,[38] there is an interpretation of Isaiah 53:8 closer to the Reformers than to the patristics: "As [Christ's] Lordship has largely and satisfactorily proved, 'Who would declare his manner of life?' who shall witness the purity of his conduct and character?"[39] Overall, J. P. Dabney puts the general trend well in an 1829 comment: "*Who shall declare his generation?* This rendering is approved by few."[40] Such a line could of course have been written by our ideal listener/reader.

The approach to Isaiah 53:8 exemplified in Abinadi's defense before Noah's priests therefore echoes principally precritical and premodern interpretations of the text, approaches that had already fallen out of favor by the time of the Book of Mormon's publication in 1830. To be sure, many aspects of Abinadi's interpretation fit comfortably into the larger Christian interpretive tradition still thriving at the time of Joseph Smith. But a Protestant in 1829 or 1830 who was generally familiar with the tradition would have regarded one major pillar of Abinadi's approach to Isaiah as quaint, if not in fact pathetically traditional. Even an informed Catholic in the same context would likely have regarded this aspect of Abinadi's interpretation as a bit passé. Abinadi, reading Isaiah esoterically, as if there were woven into the prophet's words obscure but theologically freighted allusions to the divine mystery of incarnation, fits better in early than in modern Christianity.

At issue here is, of course, precisely the esoteric nature of Abinadi's interpretive approach. Confronting his priestly opponents with a prophetic reading of the prophets, Abinadi emphasizes his own relationship to "the spirit of prophesying," as I have emphasized (Mosiah 12:25). And so the scandal of Abinadi's interpretation, in the nineteenth-century context, lies primarily in what it claims about the prophetic spirit. It arguably proposes, in a polemical way, a return to what would have seemed to many of its readers a bygone era. Similar polemical moments can be found throughout the Book of Mormon, places where the importance of spiritual gifts receives particular emphasis (see especially 2 Nephi 28–29; Mormon 8–9). Abinadi's story thus essentially proposes a return to early Christian trust in the prophetic spirit, and so would have appeared to a knowledgeable reader at the time of the Book of Mormon's publication as a deliberate provocation, an intentional form of resistance to an increasingly secular interpretation of Isaiah.

Our informed and charitable listener/reader, sitting in the room as Joseph Smith dictated the text of the Abinadi narrative to his scribe and then returning to it in written form, would therefore likely have heard in the Abinadi story a bit of deliberately countercultural polemic. Why give up on the idea that God spoke esoterically of Jesus Christ through ancient Jewish prophets? Why trap all of scripture in the secular confines of absolute history, cutting the word off from God? In view of the interpretation offered in the Abinadi narrative by Noah's priests, in fact, such a polemic might well have been felt to have a rather sharp edge. Ignoring apparently Jewish elements of the priests' interpretation, someone in the nineteenth century might have seen there an embodiment of a popular American use of Old Testament language, imagery, and ideas in their own context. In oral sermons and printed sources, Americans in the early republic consistently used the Old Testament as a mirror in which to see themselves—justifying their political self-understanding through divinely given scripture.[41] Further, as Eran Shalev has shown, the early republic produced much "pseudobiblical literature" that wove biblical and Elizabethan language into presentations of American political self-understanding. The resulting "republicanization of the Bible" set out "to make America relevant to the Bible, to biblicize America."[42] Although Shalev aligns the Book of Mormon with such literature, it would have been easy for our ideal listener/reader to see a caricature of such literature and American self-understanding in Noah's priests—and therefore to see in Abinadi's charismatic defense a polemic against such literature.[43] Why should American Christians allow the texts of the Old Testament to serve just as so many divine words that one can apply to one's own political circumstances however one sees fit?

Where Abinadi's approach to Isaiah mirrors that of the early Christian fathers, then, he would most naturally have suggested to informed nineteenth-century readers like our ideal one that he was calling for a return to an earlier era of faith. But this is only one way—and perhaps the lesser way—in which Abinadi's interpretation diverges from the spirit of the times of the Book of

Mormon's publication. Not only are there elements in his Isaian hermeneutic that seem to hark back polemically to a then-past era but features of his interpretive approach appear entirely at odds with the whole Christian interpretive tradition. Abinadi's interpretation of Isaiah is thus not only quaint but sometimes emphatically heterodox. The point deserves close attention.

The Traditional and the Nontraditional

As I have shown, much of what Abinadi says about both Isaiah 52–53 fits well in the mainstream of English-speaking Christian interpretation in the nineteenth century. It is also consonant with early Protestant interpretation and, before that, with medieval Catholic interpretation, both early and late. Abinadi's Christological reading of Isaiah 53 and his insistence on finding allusions to the preaching of the gospel in Isaiah 52:7–10 would thus likely have appeared obvious to readers, ideal ones or not, in the nineteenth century—even if in the one aspect just discussed (on Isaiah 53:8), Abinadi's approach would have appeared uncritical and quaint, if not outright polemical against creeping historicism.[44] There is, however, one key aspect of Abinadi's interpretation of Isaiah 52–53 that does not manifest any degree of conventionality, the kind of thing we need our particularly informed and hermeneutically savvy ideal listener/reader to see. Where Abinadi breaks with the tradition—both with the medieval tradition and with the modern tradition still current in the nineteenth century—is in his esoteric interpretation of Isaiah 53:10, along with the way that it shapes his further interpretation of Isaiah 52:7. In the reference to the suffering servant's promised "seed" in Isaiah 53:10, Abinadi finds a cipher for the shared faith of pre-Christian prophets and their disciples, all of them looking forward anachronistically to redemption in Christ. And then Abinadi extends this interpretation to find in Isaiah 52:7, with its talk of publishing peace and salvation, a further description of the pre-Christian prophets, anticipating the Christian era in startling detail. It is here that Abinadi articulates a fundamentally heterodox reading of Isaiah.

Our ideal listener/reader could see the tension between Abinadi and the Christian tradition preliminarily by considering standard patristic interpretations of Isaiah 53:10. These interpretations often connected the verse to the New Testament's parable of the sower, which they interpreted in terms of the early Christian missionary effort rather than the pre-Christian era indicated by Abinadi.[45] For the fathers, then, the "seed" referred to in Isaiah 53:10 is the promise of resurrected life that Jesus Christ offered and his apostles announced. Abinadi's interpretation thus parallels that of the early Christian tradition only in that each saw in the text an indication of Christ's gift of resurrection. What clearly distinguishes the two approaches is the historical era to which each assigns the events it reads in the text. For Abinadi, the "seed" of Isaiah 53:10 refers to pre-Christian prophets and their followers, all looking forward from the pre-Christian era to the coming advent of Christ and receiving anticipatory promises of rising with him at his resurrection. For the early Christian fathers—as for most everyone writing in their wake in the larger Christian tradition—Christ's seed is made up of Christians who, only *after* his death and resurrection, discover they have received a promise of immortality and eternal life.

Later mainstream Christian commentators also did not advance Abinadi-like applications of Isaiah 53:10 to the pre-Christian era. Luther interpreted the passage in terms of the spiritual offspring of the messianic king, won through Christ's suffering: "A king of the world does not see his offspring for long. In fact, when he dies, he leaves them behind. Here you see what the will of the Lord is. He placed all our iniquities upon Him, freeing us from death and giving us eternal life."[46] For his part, Calvin, like Abinadi, laid emphasis on how the Messiah's seed constitutes a community, but he differed from Abinadi in interpreting Isaiah's words to refer to the people of God constituted only after the resurrection of Jesus. "Isaiah means that the death of Christ not only can be no hindrance to his having a seed, but will be the cause of his having offspring; that is, because, by quickening the dead, he will procure a people for himself, whom he will afterwards multiply more and more."[47] As so often happened, Luther and Calvin's interpretations of Isaiah 53:10 long remained standard in Protestantism.[48] Thus the Methodist Adam Clarke, writing during the lifetime of Joseph Smith and our own ideal listener/reader, commented simply, "*seed*—True converts—genuine Christians."[49] Apparently, by the early nineteenth century, there was little reason to bother with niceties of interpretation, since the going approach to the text's meaning had become standard.[50]

Such standard interpretations—standard as much among Catholics as among Protestants into the nineteenth century—ruled out the kind of reading Abinadi offers. This is clear, for instance, in one widely read English-language commentary, Matthew Henry's. Writing in the first decade of the eighteenth century, Henry provided an analysis of "seed" that emphatically distinguished it from anything pre-Christian by establishing a typological relationship between the corruptible seed of Abraham and the incorruptible seed of Christ.[51] Using (or abusing) Saint Paul's discussion in Romans 9–11,[52]

Henry distinguishes the literal or physical seed of Abraham from the symbolic or spiritual seed of Christ, understanding the covenant of grace to bind only the latter. For an interpreter like Henry, quite in line with the larger Christian tradition, Christ's seed is unquestionably *not* pre-Christian.

As far as I have been able to discover, then, Abinadi's interpretation of Isaiah 53:10 is unprecedented, unique in its application of the verse's talk of "seed" to the pre-Christian prophets and their disciples.[53] The whole tradition seems to agree with Abinadi that the passage concerns preachers and listeners, people who form a kind of church or community. But the church in question for Abinadi must be a pre-Christian church—a "church of anticipation"—while the church in question for the whole Christian tradition has a history that unfolds only in the wake of Christ's life, death, and resurrection.[54] And this same tension between Abinadi and the Christian interpretive tradition on the interpretation of Isaiah 53:10 holds also in the case of Isaiah 52:7, where Isaiah speaks of beautiful feet and glad tidings. Abinadi directly connects the latter passage to his interpretation of the servant's seed, such that it is precisely Christ's seed that proclaims peace to ruined humanity. Christian interpreters, however, from the beginning down to the nineteenth century, consistently interpreted Isaiah 52:7 and the verses following it in terms of Christian (rather than pre-Christian) history.

It is noteworthy that verse 7 is the only part of this passage from Isaiah 52 in which Abinadi diverges substantially from the larger Christian tradition; his reading of verses 8–10 is standard by comparison. It is in realizing this that the sheer oddity of Abinadi's approach to Isaiah 52–53 makes itself manifest.[55] Abinadi largely concedes the standard Christian interpretation of Isaiah 52:7–10 *except* that he holds that the first verse of the passage finds its primary fulfillment in anachronistic pre-Christian prophetic anticipation of the Christ event. Agreeing on so much, so to speak, Abinadi's disagreement about the interpretation of just one verse reverberates all the more loudly for readers such as our ideal one, familiar with the interpretive tradition.

Here again, then, Abinadi's approach to Isaiah 52–53 is out of sync with the spirit of nineteenth-century English-speaking Christians, for whom the Book of Mormon was first made available. But where Abinadi's interpretation of Isaiah 53:8 would have appeared to the informed Protestant reader of the Book of Mormon in the nineteenth century as either quaint or polemically traditional, his interpretations of Isaiah 53:10 and 52:7 would have come across as either wrong or wildly innovative. It is one thing to make heard an appeal in a nineteenth-century American context to the traditional "spirit of

Tradition and Innovation 65

prophesying," largely out of fashion by that time. It is another thing entirely, though, to hear someone insist in the same context that the "spirit of prophesying" working on a pre-Christian prophet could have made the esoteric interpretation binding for pre-Christian hearers. In effect, Abinadi's treatment of Isaiah 52–53 weaves certain surprising elements into a theologically inoffensive (that is, standard) understanding of the prophet's meaning. First, there are in Abinadi's treatment indications of profound conservatism, manifesting a lack of interest in historically informed critical interpretation. And, second, Abinadi's interpretation exhibits heterodox—if not in fact heretical—commitments, expounding the idea of a pre-Christian form of interpretation that fully anticipates hermeneutic models from the later Christian era.

At issue here is the notion of typological hermeneutics. But although Abinadi mentions typology in the course of his defense before Noah's priests (Mosiah 13:30–31), it is no traditional notion of the typological that he defends in his interpretation of Isaiah.[56] If, as Blaise Pascal explains, typological interpretation offers itself as the means to avoid two parallel errors—"to take everything literally" and "to take everything spiritually"—then Abinadi seems to commit both errors at once, because he takes the *literal* and uniquely correct meaning of Isaiah's prophecies to be the *spiritual* (or esoteric) meaning that points to the Christ event.[57] Further, Abinadi cannot have reference to the usual typological idea that "the Old Testament is a cipher" that the New Testament alone deciphers,[58] since he himself predates the New Testament. In the last analysis, traditional typology depends on a key paradox that Abinadi simply ignores: that prophecy must be "simultaneously obscure in the time of its pronunciation, and retroactively clear once the Christ-event, interpreted by faithful preaching, establishes its truth."[59] For Abinadi, typology is not a solution to a problem generated by the idea that history has been (or, from his perspective, would be) interrupted by a divisive event. It is, rather, a way of acknowledging the straightforwardly anticipatory meaning of pre-Christian prophecies of Christ.

In Abinadi's insistence on the existence of detailed pre-Christian prophecy focused on the coming of God in Christ, then, one might well wish to see another interpretive polemic, another deliberate attempt to correct the Christian interpretive tradition. Because Abinadi concedes *most* of the story told by Christians in connection with Isaiah 52–53 throughout the Christian era, the subtle points where he tells the story *differently* suggest subversive intention. As N. T. Wright notes, stories are "particularly good at modifying or subverting other stories and their worldviews. Where head-on attack would certainly fail, the parable hides the wisdom of the serpent behind the innocence of the dove, gaining entrance and favor which can then be used to change assumptions which the hearer would otherwise keep hidden away for safety."[60] So much of Abinadi's story about Isaiah 52–53 is familiar to Christians, with the consequence that points of severe difference subtly but forcefully contest the traditional Christian story. For Abinadi, God gives clear anticipatory knowledge of the Christian era to some pre-Christian prophets, and they and their followers form a community (Christ's "seed") that expects to rise with their Savior in a "first resurrection." In this way, this Book of Mormon prophet's approach to the Old Testament's prophet drastically expands the scope of the Christian narrative. As Terryl Givens says, "Instead of a cardinal eruption of the divine into the human, spawning a spate of mythic reverberations, we have [in the Book of Mormon] a proliferation of historical iterations, which themselves collectively become the ongoing substance rather than the shadow of God's past dealings in the universe."[61] Christianity does not begin with Christ's advent for Abinadi; rather, it begins *before* that crucial event, with prophets very much like Abinadi himself.

In this regard, Abinadi's hermeneutics would seem to be rooted in a major theological aspect of the Book of Mormon, one that outstrips Abinadi's speech. The book consistently presents the pre-Christian Nephites (and eventually the Lamanites) as having had, from early in their history, detailed prophetic foreknowledge of the Christian gospel. Nephi, more than five centuries before Christ, wrestles with his responsibility to "keep" the Mosaic law despite his knowledge that the law would "be fulfilled." In a key passage, he confesses, "The law hath become dead unto us, and we are made alive in Christ because of our faith—yet we keep the law because of the commandments" (2 Nephi 25:24–25). Nephi's brother Jacob claims that he and his brother write up their thoughts so that their readers "may know that we knew of Christ," having "a hope of his glory many hundred years before his coming" (Jacob 4:4). Two generations after Jacob, the prophet Jarom claims that the prophets and priests and teachers of his day "did labor diligently, . . . teaching the law of Moses and the intent for which it was given, persuading [the people] to look forward unto the Messiah and believe in him to come as though he already was" (Jarom 1:11). Abinadi himself, like his near contemporary, King Benjamin, deliberately "speak[s] of things to come as though they had already come" (Mosiah 16:6).[62] At one point, a Book of Mormon character explicitly worries about this pre-Christian knowledge, about "why these things should be known so long beforehand" (Alma 39:17), making clear the volume's awareness of its own theological novelty on the point.[63] Throughout the pre-Christian portion of the history recounted by the Book of Mormon, the volume lays emphasis on its pre-Christian Christianity.[64] It naturally appears, therefore, that Abinadi's approach to Isaiah takes its orientation from this general aspect of the Book of Mormon.

The Book of Mormon's earliest interaction with Isaiah thus apparently aims in major part at marshaling the prophet into defending the pre-Christian availability of the Christian gospel. Our ideal listener/reader from 1829–30 might therefore see Abinadi as mobilizing Isaiah to address what has often been called "the scandal of particularity": the worry that Christianity's exclusivist tendencies leave the majority of human beings out of heaven.[65] According to Abinadi, Isaiah's prophecies offered the Christian gospel to pre-Christian people. Even if the Christian gospel were only esoterically signaled in Isaiah's words, strictly speaking, those worked on by the prophetic spirit, even in the pre-Christian context, could understand their plain meaning perfectly. Abinadi certainly feels he can explain all this to recalcitrant and apostate priests—and he even intimates that the very responsibility of pre-Christian Mosaic priests just *is* to lay out the clear Christian meaning of Isaiah's prophecies (Mosiah 12:25; 16:14–15). That this understanding ran against prevalent Christian ideas in the early nineteenth century is clear from the very first pamphlet written against the Book of Mormon, published by the famous preacher of the Disciples movement in 1832, Alexander Campbell. In his list of "internal evidences" against the Book of Mormon, Campbell says that "the twelve Apostles of the Lamb, are said by Paul, to have developed certain secrets, which were hid for ages and generations, which Paul says were ordained before the world to their glory, that they should have the honor of announcing them." The Book of Mormon, however, makes the whole Christian gospel available in plainness in the pre-Christian, pre-apostolic era.[66]

Here, though, a peculiarity deserves notice. If Isaiah 52–53 were in fact such a ready tool for battling exclusivist Christian theologies or for making clear the need for a pre-Christian community of believers, one would expect to find echoes throughout the remainder of the Book of Mormon not only of Abinadi's pre-Christian Christianity, but also of Abinadi's particular interpretive uses of Isaiah 52–53. Readers certainly do encounter echoes of pre-Christian Christianity elsewhere in the Book of Mormon, but no one in the Book of Mormon apart from Abinadi ever outlines an Abinadi-like hermeneutic of Isaiah's prophecies, for defending pre-Christian Christianity or for any other purpose. Further, at least one Isaiah passage that Abinadi interprets Christologically receives an entirely *non*-Christological interpretation from a later voice within the bounds of Mormon's project. If, therefore, as seems likely, one purpose of the Abinadi narrative is to reinforce the Book of Mormon's general theological commitment to blurring the boundaries between pre-Christian Judaism and post-Jewish Christianity, the use of Isaiah in the Abinadi narrative to accomplish this purpose remains nevertheless singular.

It must be conceded that the Book of Mormon marshals the Abinadi narrative into its volume-wide defense of a heterodox—if not heretical—idea: that the Christian gospel was as much a feature of the pre-Christian era as of the Christian era. At the same time, however, it is a peculiar fact that Abinadi's use of this theological notion as an interpretive lens for reading Isaiah is unique within the Book of Mormon. And anyway, the Abinadi narrative in no way presents its protagonist as defending the idea of pre-Christian Christian prophecy against Christian-era defenders of exclusivist Christianity—in the nineteenth century or at any other time. Although Mormon directs himself to later readers, Abinadi addresses himself not to post-Jewish Christians but to pre-Christian Jews who defend the law of Moses. It is to Noah's priests and their Isaian form of self-justification that Abinadi defends the Christological interpretation of Isaiah. Where Noah and his priests see themselves as the beneficiaries of a successful eschatological struggle predicted by Isaiah, Abinadi insists that the prophet's words remain unfulfilled, and so that the ideal (pre-Christian) community is one that looks forward in longing for redemption. Good news requires announcement in Abinadi's present, to be sure, but all genuinely good news concerns things still to come, according to Abinadi.[67] Thus the pre-Christian Christianity that Abinadi reads into Isaiah is a weapon mostly used against ideologically driven appropriations of the prophet.

Why is this last point worth making? In the end, what Abinadi's confrontation with Noah's priests accomplishes is to set up the Book of Mormon's encounter with Isaiah as a problem to be worked on, not as an answer to a clear question of interpretation. The priests, with their consistent and even intriguing understanding of the text, are not straw men set up as Abinadi's punching bags. And Abinadi, for his part, develops a commentary on Isaiah woven of the conventional and the novel, a commentary attributed to the traditional spirit of prophetic interpretation that Abinadi nonetheless receives and promulgates in a pre-Christian era. Further, there follow in Mormon's project quite distinct interpretations of some of the same texts addressed by Abinadi. The Abinadi narrative poses at the foundation of the Book of Mormon a question about how best to read Isaiah. Although the Abinadi narrative incontestably privileges one

Tradition and Innovation

party's solution to the problem, Mormon's larger project implicitly questions this privilege in an essential way; Abinadi's interpretations make up only one set of interpretations on offer, as I will show.

Abinadi and the Nephite Tradition

The preceding discussion considers the Abinadi narrative largely as a standalone story, extractable without real loss of meaning from its context in the Book of Mormon. The sheer fact that Jesus Christ himself, a few hundred pages later in the volume, directly comments on the same text that forms the focus of the Abinadi narrative should already make clear that this approach is problematic. Of course, if it were the case that Christ offered more or less the same interpretation as Abinadi, then perhaps the latter's interpretive approach to Isaiah could be regarded as relatively stable and without need for further comment. But the fact that Christ's interpretation of Isaiah 52:7–10 and contiguous passages strikingly differs from Abinadi's makes indelibly plain that Abinadi's hermeneutic must not be treated in isolation. It is necessary to read Abinadi's Isaian intervention—as well as that of Noah's priests—within the larger context of the Book of Mormon as a whole. And, of course, our ideal listener/reader would become aware of this point in the course of listening to the dictation or rereading the text, perhaps with a bit of surprise. Consequently, while leaving for the next two chapters the task of looking carefully at Christ's uses of Isaiah in Third Nephi, it might be useful here to look at how Abinadi fits into the Book of Mormon narrative up until the arrival of Christ. Even before Christ comes to offer a non-Abinadite approach to Isaiah, there are literary features of the volume that destabilize Abinadi's Isaian hermeneutic in important ways.

A first point, already mentioned in chapter 1, deserves careful attention, namely that quotations of, comments on, and even allusions to Isaian texts disappear more or less entirely from the Book of Mormon for several hundred pages after the Abinadi narrative. The few exceptions to this rule prove instructive. First, only a few chapters after the Abinadi narrative, the text describes the work of a few Christian preachers, representatives of the church founded on Abinadi's preaching. These preachers the text calls blessed because "they did publish peace. They did publish good tidings of good, and they did declare unto the people that the Lord reigneth" (Mosiah 27:37). This passage clearly draws on Isaiah 52:7 and harks back to Abinadi's interpretation of the passage, focused on pre-Christian announcements of Christ's coming. Second, one of these same Christian preachers, a decade or two later, makes an apparent reference to Isaiah 53:4 in a sermon. After predicting Christ's "pains and afflictions and temptations," this preacher states that Christ will experience them "that the word might be fulfilled, which saith, 'He will take upon him the pains and the sicknesses of his people'" (Alma 7:11). The wording here differs from the King James rendering of Isaiah 53:4, but it appears strikingly like a direct quotation of that passage in the New Testament, where Matthew speaks of Jesus's miracles as fulfilling what "was spoken by Esaias [Isaiah] the prophet, saying, Himself took our infirmities, and bare our sicknesses" (Matthew 8:17).[68] Here again, then, the Isaian borrowing is unmistakably Abinadite in orientation. Third and finally, a much-later Nephite prophet passingly mentions Isaiah in a list of pre-Christian prophets who spoke of "the Son of God" (Helaman 8:20). In this case, no particular passage from Isaiah receives attention, but the reference points in the direction of clearly Christological interpretation, once again suggesting an Abinadite view of Isaiah.

These three passing references to Isaiah—the only references in nearly three hundred pages of text—indicate, however minimally, that Abinadi's approach to Isaiah has three major effects on Nephite hermeneutics after his death. First, it seems clear that his approach to Isaiah is supposed to have definitively dislodged the sort of use to which the Zeniffite colony was supposedly putting Isaiah's prophecies. Abinadi's Christological approach strikes the reader as having become the only Isaian hermeneutic on offer among the Nephites, since every Isaian reference in Abinadi's wake—seldom as they occur—employs his same approach. Second, it seems striking that the two clear references to Isaiah come directly (or indirectly) out of the very texts discussed by Abinadi: Isaiah 52:7 and Isaiah 53:4. It thus appears that Abinadi's very choice of Isaian texts is to be understood as having determined the shape of subsequent Nephite readings of Isaiah. Third, it seems that Abinadi's intervention is *so* decisive that subsequent generations are supposed to have felt little need to say much about Isaiah, perhaps concluding that everything necessary had been said by Abinadi. Certainly, in a book otherwise so consistently involved in questions of Isaian interpretation, the general absence of Isaian allusions between Abinadi and Christ suggests something like waning interest in the wake of Abinadi's definitive interpretations.

None of this surprises, however. The immediate consequence of Abinadi's preaching—apart from its resulting in martyrdom—is the sole conversion of one of Noah's priests, Alma, who directly goes about the task of creating an Abinadite church. That church of anticipation, founded on "the words of

Abinadi" (Mosiah 18:1) and aimed at embodying the messianic "seed" from Abinadi's teachings, is the dominant spiritual force in the Book of Mormon between the time of Abinadi's death and the arrival of Christ. The priests assigned the task of preaching in Alma's church, the narrative reports, are even instructed to "teach nothing" but Abinadi's words, along with whatever "had been spoken by the mouth of the holy prophets" (Mosiah 18:19; see also 18:1–2). Alma's Abinadite church, then, is presented as bearing the responsibility precisely of keeping the Abinadite interpretive tradition alive.

At the same time, the matter is complicated by the larger literary structure and flow of the book within which the Abinadi narrative appears—not the Book of Mormon as a whole, but the shorter Book of Mosiah that serves as the immediate context of the Abinadi story. The title of Mosiah puzzles the careful reader. The titles of the Book of Mormon's several books name either purported authors of portions of the volume (the Book of Jacob, for instance, or the Book of Moroni) or characters whose stories are told within the volume (the Book of Helaman, for instance, or the Book of Ether).[69] It is curious therefore that Abinadi's story occurs in a book named not for him, but for a king he seems never to have met. But, in the last analysis, it seems appropriate that the Book of Mosiah bears the name of a king rather than a prophet, since it plainly aims to investigate both the virtues and the limitations, from a religious perspective, of monarchical systems of government.[70] It is true that the Abinadi narrative, along with the sheer existence of the Abinadite church, serves in Mosiah to reveal the potential dangers of monarchy. Yet the Abinadi narrative runs parallel to (or perhaps interrupts) another narrative in the book that suggests that monarchy may in fact be the *ideal* institution for the success of the Christian religion. In the end, the question of the monarchy's virtues is complex, and the Book of Mosiah ends with King Mosiah's uneasy decision to rescind the monarchy in order to replace it with a "reign of the judges." Some development of these points helps to clarify the role played by Abinadi's story in the Book of Mosiah's narrative, in addition to the role it plays in the larger Book of Mormon.

Turning to details, then, one finds that the Book of Mosiah tells the story of two concurrent Nephite dynasties, one established at the center of the Nephite lands (that is, in the land of Zarahemla) and the other established in a Nephite colony located in Lamanite territory (in the land of Nephi). Through literary echoes and other structural features, the book sets the two dynasties side by side, clearly in order to highlight crucial points of contrast between them—and in particular between the second king of each dynasty.[71] Similarities that help to highlight real differences are striking. Both dynasties last for only three generations, and each is founded by a man who moves his followers into an already-peopled land and then, thanks to the kindness of the inhabitants, rises to a position of royal power. Upon the death of each dynasty's founder, rule passes to a king who faces difficulties of disunity among his people; one successfully replaces disunity with unity thanks to his attention to the words of a heavenly messenger, and the other unfortunately allows disunity to supplant unity by rejecting a parallel heavenly message sent to him.[72] Finally, each of the two dynasties ends when its founder's royal grandson decides, in major part in response to the rise of the Abinadite church, to give up the monarchy. Point by point, then, the two dynasties run parallel, which allows for a comparison that reveals striking contrasts between the two regimes, already suggested in the preceding.

The Nephite colony and its monarchy appear negative from the outset by contrast with the monarchy established in the Nephite capital of Zarahemla. A man named Mosiah (the grandfather of the Mosiah for whom the Book of Mosiah is presumably named) founds the latter, moving his people from the once-Nephite land of Nephi after being "warned of the Lord that he should flee out of the land" (Omni 1:12). Leading his people "by many preachings and prophesyings," as well as "continually by the word of the Lord" (1:13), Mosiah establishes a righteous royal dynasty at Zarahemla where he rules as spiritual leader. By contrast, the Nephite colony in the land of Nephi is settled by a group of Nephite zealots from Zarahemla who develop a desire "to possess the land of their [former] inheritance," abandoned by Mosiah (1:27). That group is led at first by "an austere and bloodthirsty man" with martial intentions (Mosiah 9:2) and then (in a more diplomatic, second attempt at recovering the land) by an "overzealous" but sensitive individual named Zeniff, who will later become the father of King Noah (9:3).[73] Zeniff succeeds in peacefully securing for his colony land that the Lamanites have claimed in the meanwhile, and he establishes a strongly ideological monarchy that justifies its successes and power through the use of Isaiah's prophecies, as discussed in chapter 2. From the very beginning, then, the text presents Mosiah and Zeniff's parallel dynasties as respectively divinely sanctioned and problematically lucky.[74]

Of further interest, the Book of Mormon in final form (rather than in order of dictation) presents both dynasties' founders as echoes of the volume's first hero, Nephi (the subject of chapters 6–9). But, along the lines just traced, Mosiah is presented as a good and proper echo of Nephi, while Zeniff is arguably presented as a problematic and ironic echo of Nephi. Mosiah, like

Nephi, is directly warned by God to move his followers to a new settlement if they would escape destruction at the hands of the Lamanites (Omni 1:12–13; 2 Nephi 5:5–8).[75] His people's "many preachings and prophesyings" suggest that Mosiah, as he moves his people to a place of safety, makes him Nephi's direct spiritual heir (Omni 1:13). Zeniff, in turn, presents himself as Nephi *redivivus* by opening his history (which the Book of Mormon includes as an "embedded document")[76] with an unmistakable imitation of the opening of Nephi's first-person narrative (Mosiah 9:1–2; 1 Nephi 1:1).[77] In the end, however, Zeniff's record appears more a parody than a new embodiment of Nephi's account. Where Nephi speaks of having "a great knowledge of the goodness and the mysteries of God" (1 Nephi 1:1), for instance, Zeniff can boast in distant echo only of "a knowledge of the land of Nephi" (Mosiah 9:1). Thus, although Zeniff returns a Nephite people to the land once settled by their eponymous ancestor, the text presents him as a pale shadow of the hero. Significantly, it is not he, the king in the land of Nephi, who wields Nephi's ceremonial sword in defense of the Nephites, but the rival Nephite monarch in the land of Zarahemla.[78]

Placing a capstone on all these points of (dis)continuity between Nephi and Zeniff is the latter's apparent use of Isaiah's prophecies to justify his colonizing resettlement of the land of Nephi—a use of Isaiah then inherited by Noah and marshaled against Abinadi. As will become fully clear later, Nephi is the Book of Mormon's voice most concerned with Isaiah, and this makes for another important point of contact between Nephi and Zeniff. But, as with all other points of contact, this one shows Zeniff to be more a parody than a reincarnation of Nephi. I will show in later chapters that Nephi's record outlines a complex Isaian hermeneutic based on the notion of "likening." With this word, it seems Nephi means to recommend to his people the task of searching for parallels between the written text of Isaiah and the visionary experiences Nephi himself has in the course of his life, using such parallels to allow the written text of Isaian prophecy and the oral tradition of Nephi's own prophetic experiences to illuminate one another. Because Nephi's prophecies concern the far-distant future of his own people, there is a kind of self-application at the heart of the program of likening. In light of all this, it appears that Zeniff and his heirs a generation later in Noah's regime adhere to a Nephi-like hermeneutic in reading Isaiah's prophecies. They do so, however, with a self-serving twist. Rather than looking to a prophesied and far-distant future, when their descendants are to be redeemed in a way that brings the attention of the whole world to the faithfulness of Israel's God, Zeniff applies Isaiah's prophecies directly to his own immediate historical circumstances, seeing his people's resettlement of the land of Nephi as the likened fulfillment of Isaiah's prophecies. Thus, it is apparent to readers of the Book of Mormon in final form that Zeniff effectively misunderstands (if not in fact deliberately corrupts) Nephi's hermeneutic program—or at least that he oddly and quite wrongly sees his own people as the latter-day branch of Israel predicted by Nephi.

The final form of the Book of Mormon thus complicates the context in which Abinadi outlines his Christological interpretation of Isaian prophecy. It is not simply that he has to provide an alternative to the self-satisfied interpretation of Isaiah 52:7–10 assumed by Noah's priests. Because the larger text presents that interpretation as continuous with—albeit a corruption of—Nephi's earlier hermeneutic program, he has the task of setting the entirety of Nephite hermeneutics on a new footing. Not only does the priests' question about the meaning of Isaiah 52:7–10 threaten to reveal that Abinadi opposes the whole of the Nephite colony in the land of Nephi, it threatens to expose that Abinadi opposes the very founder of the entire Nephite nation. As will be seen later, Nephi *never* privileges Christological interpretation of Isaiah in the way Abinadi does. Further, unlike Abinadi, Nephi emphatically *does* liken the text to his own people (even if he refuses to apply it directly to his own historical circumstances in the corrupt fashion of Noah's people). As Nephite history unfolds in the Book of Mormon's published order, it seems Abinadi finds it necessary to move the people away from Nephi's interpretive style as much as from that of Noah's priests. The stakes of Abinadi's intervention are thus higher than they might seem in the immediate context of the Abinadi narrative.[79]

All this complicates—or perhaps enriches—the fact that references to Isaiah largely disappear from the Book of Mormon for several hundred pages after the Abinadi narrative. The effective withdrawal of interest in Isaiah from the Book of Mormon for the reader of the volume in final form suggests not only that Abinadi's interpretation is to be regarded as in some sense definitive for the Nephite church founded by his prophet. It suggests also that Abinadi's purposes in contesting the interpretation of Isaiah 52:7–10 set forth by Noah's priests include a *deliberate* dampening of interest in Isaiah. The final form of the volume suggests that Abinadi sees in the priests' corrupt use of Isaiah—or in Zeniff's already-problematic use of Isaiah before them—a certain inherent danger in Nephi's hermeneutic program. Instead of defending Nephi against the Zeniffite interpretation, specifying the exact points where the earlier hermeneutic program has been corrupted, Abinadi points in an entirely novel interpretive direction, one as much at odds with Nephi's as with Jesus Christ's interpretive style later in the volume. From the perspective of the volume in final form, it inevitably appears as if Abinadi *wants* to draw Nephite Christianity away from the difficult task of interpreting Isaiah.

What makes this last point particularly clear is a curious detail, never commented on in the literature on Isaiah in the Book of Mormon. A remarkable host of parallel phrases and theological concepts makes perfectly clear that the core of the Book of Mosiah's opening sermon by King Benjamin (the second king in the Zarahemla dynasty) is connected in a fundamental way to Abinadi's words of defense before Noah's priests. The portion of Benjamin's sermon he attributes directly to an angelic visitor (specifically to be found in Mosiah 3) outlines the same theological picture sketched in Abinadi's defense, and Benjamin's angel uses unmistakably Abinadite phrasing to present the relevant ideas.[80] The only major difference between the content of Abinadi's sustained defense before Noah's priests and the words Benjamin attributes to his angelic visitor is, strikingly, the former's heavy investment in Isaiah. Not once in Benjamin's whole sermon, let alone in the angelic portion of it that parallels Abinadi's teachings, does Isaian phrasing make an appearance. In Benjamin's sermon, then, which appears a few chapters before Abinadi's (chronologically earlier) story is told, the text outlines the possibility of an entirely *non*-Isaian presentation of Abinadi's theology. The Book of Mosiah, that is, opens with an anticipation of Abinadi's teachings, but it presents them at that point as if Isaiah were in no way relevant to Abinadite theology. In the Zarahemla dynasty, then, the theological picture the Book of Mormon wishes to present is allowed to unfold without complicated Isaian entanglements. It is only in the land of Nephi, thanks to the self-justifying Isaian hermeneutic of the dynasty established there, that Abinadi finds it necessary to weave his interpretation into the words of Isaiah.

All the foregoing plainly suggests that Abinadi's Christological interpretation of Isaiah is less the outline of a recommended hermeneutic program than an attempt to force the work of interpreting the prophet into a larger set of theological commitments that the Book of Mosiah recommends to its readers. It would seem as if Abinadi deliberately aims at doing away with Isaian interpretation because of the dangers associated with (speculative) likenings of the text. The definitiveness of Abinadi's interpretation of Isaiah for the Nephite church founded after his martyrdom serves primarily just to make Isaiah's prophecies into a set of arcane confirmations of Benjamin's and Abinadi's far-plainer predictions of the Christ event and its aftermath. The prophets have, as Abinadi says, only "more or less" spoken concerning Christ

(Mosiah 13:33), but Abinadi prophesies so plainly that he speaks "of things to come as though they had already come" (16:6). After Abinadi but before the visit of Christ to the New World, there is no *need* to look seriously at Isaiah.

In the end, then, Abinadi represents an effectively *deflationary* interpretation of Isaiah. Where his interpretations of specific verses match up with the Christian tradition, they trade on the obvious in order to indicate the nonnecessity of getting involved in the niceties of Isaian interpretation. And where his interpretations of specific verses part ways with the larger Christian tradition, they deliberately reinforce Abinadi's theological insistence on Christian prophecy before Christianity, such as he himself (along with other Nephite prophets) practice it. Here again, the non-necessity of getting involved in Isaian obscurities is front and center. What Abinadi aims at above all else is solely the task of giving center stage to Christian theology.

In this, however, Abinadi differs substantially from the actual Christ who comes among Lehi's children later in Mormon's contribution to the Book of Mormon. It seems that Abinadi is just the first plank in a larger Isaian platform, which requires a careful look at Third Nephi. This is the task of the following two chapters.

4

A New Direction at the Meridian of Time

The previous two chapters make a case that one of Abinadi's roles in the Book of Mormon's narrative is to steer the Nephites away from the textual obscurities and interpretive dangers of Isaiah. Noah's priests model misuse of the prophet, while Abinadi pushes for a partially traditional (but also crucially innovative) Christological approach. Like many in the Christian tradition, Abinadi finds in Isaiah 53 an esoteric prediction of Christ's birth. But, unlike the tradition, as the ideal listener/reader we always have with us would especially point out, Abinadi finds in the song of the suffering servant and in Isaiah 52:7–10 with it a unique theology of pre-Christian Christianity, spurring the creation of a community set on rising with Christ at his resurrection. These revisionary features of Abinadi's interpretation complicate matters, but they draw on a perspective so pervasive in the Book of Mormon that no Nephite would need Isaiah to understand them. Consequently, the effect of Abinadi's handling of Isaiah is to decrease or even eliminate Nephite interest in the prophet. In the three hundred pages following Abinadi's story, one finds only three passing allusions to Isaiah. But then, quite suddenly after the hiatus, Isaiah returns to center stage. And the new Book of Mormon voice that addresses Isaiah recommends careful study of the prophet. "Great is the words of Isaiah!" this new voice proclaims, issuing "a commandment" to "search these things diligently" (3 Nephi 23:1). What should make every reader of the Book of Mormon sit up is the fact that the one issuing this command is the resurrected Jesus Christ.

Readers routinely point out that Mormon's project reaches its apex with the visit of Christ to the ancient Americas. The book reporting this visit—Third

Nephi—has therefore often been called "the fifth gospel," a nickname it shares with Isaiah.[1] It presents Nephite and Lamanite history from the time of Jesus's Old World birth through his post-resurrection visit to the New World remnant of Israel. Eleven of Third Nephi's original fourteen chapters focus exclusively on events surrounding Christ's visit.[2] As Grant Hardy says, "it seems obvious that the climax of the Book of Mormon is Christ's three-day visit to the Nephites."[3] Hardy, however, goes on to describe how the text might naturally disappoint readers of Third Nephi. It first describes a host of New World disasters concurrent with Christ's death: "storms, whirlwinds, lightning fires, earthquakes, landslides, and flooding, as well as three terrifying days of total darkness"—all these interrupted by "a voice from heaven." This spectacular "buildup," as Hardy calls it, encourages expectation of "novelty and fresh insight" from the sermons that follow when Christ appears.[4] What one finds, though, is "a lightly revised version of the Sermon on the Mount to the Nephites, followed by extended quotations from Isaiah, Micah, and Malachi." For nonbelievers, Hardy notes, "it may seem as if Joseph Smith's scripture-creating hubris reached its limit when it came to writing lines for the Lord himself, and instead he fell back into plagiarism and filler."[5] Perhaps more startling is how little Christ says in Third Nephi about traditional Christian theology: "The word *atonement* is never used and [Christ] nowhere mentions Adam, Gethsemane, Golgotha, or the empty tomb. He never even explains how he received the wounds he invites the multitude to examine" upon his arrival.[6] After hundreds of pages of traditional Christian preaching (albeit oddly before Christ's birth), the subject of Christ's own preaching in the Book of Mormon hardly seems climactic. It unsettles rather than fulfills expectations.

Hardy suggests that "if Third Nephi seems disappointing or frustrating, it may be that our expectations are at odds with Mormon's own objectives."[7] This is insightful, and it seems right that "Mormon's own objectives" include marking a strong contrast between the Christological focus after Abinadi (sermon after sermon on human depravity, Christ's mercy, a saving atonement) and the starkly non-Christological focus of Christ's own teachings in Third Nephi. To take the measure of Third Nephi's role in Mormon's project, one must feel the jarring redirection of theological matters occurring with Christ's arrival in the New World. Mormon's narrative reaches its climax with fulfillments of prophetic predictions from earlier Nephite generations, but also and especially with a new theological tradition and a return to Isaian interpretation.

What needs immediate unpacking, therefore, is the theological intention that guides the use of Isaiah in Third Nephi. What are Third Nephi's bearings? How do those bearings shape Christ's uses of Isaiah, especially for our ideal listener, listening in on the dictation of the Book of Mormon in 1829, or our ideal reader, returning to the Book of Mormon in printed form afterward to study the text more closely? In short, if Christ strongly recommends that readers of the Book of Mormon take Isaiah seriously, how does he himself read Isaiah within the narrative? After answering these questions, we can ask in the next chapter how Christ's interpretations of Isaiah fit into the larger framework of the volume's treatment of the prophet, as well as into the larger Judeo-Christian interpretive tradition.

The Covenant Given to Israel

Third Nephi's redirection of the Book of Mormon's theological concerns actually begins before Christ's arrival. Third Nephi opens in the year of Jesus's birth, and the first part of the book traces the thirty-four years of New World history leading up to Christ's post-resurrection visit. In that sketch, one finds the first glimmerings of the new theological focus that will become central later in Third Nephi. Twenty-five years after Jesus's birth and a few years before his death, the narrative breaks off suddenly, and Mormon addresses his readers directly about the new theological theme. "I have reason to bless my God and my Savior," Mormon says, "that he brought our fathers out of the land of Jerusalem. . . . Surely he hath blessed the house of Jacob and hath been merciful unto the seed of Joseph" (3 Nephi 5:20–21). There is in these words an unprecedented focus within Mormon's extant project on "the house of Jacob" and "the seed of Joseph." (Only once before has there been mention of such traditional Old Testament themes, and that reference is nothing like what appears in the rest of Third Nephi.)[8] Although Mormon introduces this theme by speaking of God's mercy in delivering his people from Jerusalem, he quickly turns from the past to the eschatological future:

> Yea, and surely shall he again bring a remnant of the seed of Joseph to the knowledge of the Lord their God. And as surely as the Lord liveth will he gather in from the four quarters of the earth all the remnant of the seed of Jacob, which are scattered abroad upon all the face of the earth, . . . unto the restoring all the house of Jacob unto the knowledge of the covenant. (5:23–25)

Mormon focuses here on eschatological events that mark God's long-term fidelity to Israel's covenants, promises for the last days.

The focus of Mormon's hopes and confidence at this point is the key theme of the Hebrew prophets, and those interpreted literally. Mormon does not adopt the classically Christian approach of spiritualizing the prophets' national hopes. He never claims here or later that the prophets' predictions find their real fulfillment in the rise of Christianity, as if the Christian Church were—as Christians from the second century to the present have often claimed—"the true Israel."[9] A second and subtler anticipation of later theological emphases confirms this. After the above-mentioned natural disasters at Jesus's death, a "thick darkness" blankets the New World, thick enough to be felt (3 Nephi 8:20). A voice sounds in the darkness, speaking of divine punishment and calling for repentance. The voice identifies itself as that of "Jesus Christ, the Son of God" (9:15), not yet risen, and then it briefly refers also to the gathering of literal Israel.[10] Drawing on language from Matthew 23:37–38, the soon-to-rise Christ describes past, present, and future failed attempts at gathering Israel. "O ye people of the house of Israel," he cries, "ye that dwell at Jerusalem as ye that have fallen, yea, how oft would I have gathered you, as a hen gathereth her chickens, and ye would not! O ye house of Israel whom I have spared, how oft will I gather you, as a hen gathereth her chickens under her wings, if ye will repent and return unto me with full purpose of heart! But if not, O house of Israel, the places of your dwellings shall become desolate" (3 Nephi 10:5–7). Israel's past is desperate, but its distant future promises reversal. Christ predicts desolation for Israel only "until the time of the fulfilling of the covenant" to their "fathers" (10:7). Again the text anticipates a literal fulfillment of the prophets.

Not only, then, does Mormon interrupt his narrative to prepare readers for Christ's sermons, so also does Jesus Christ interrupt Mormon's narrative to speak of Israel's covenant. By the time Christ arrives in person, readers should be fully prepared to receive his teachings. It takes time for a vessel as large as the Book of Mormon to change directions, but the narrative's gentle guidance makes the transition smoother than it might otherwise be. Perhaps more important, such signposting confirms that the theological transition in Third Nephi is deliberate, something the author recognizes as a radical departure that needs finessing.[11] It fits the narrative that, once Christ actually appears among the Nephites and the Lamanites, he finds they struggle to make sense of his covenant teachings. Immediately after he first quotes Isaiah to his hearers (3 Nephi 16:16–20), he recognizes their weakness, noting that they "cannot understand" (17:2).

Turning from anticipations to then actual sermons about Israel's covenant, one finds that Mormon's account of Christ's visit divides into three major sequences. During a first day, Christ offers instructions addressed alternately to the gathered multitude and to just twelve newly called disciples (3 Nephi

11–16). During a second day and with a larger audience, a second series of instructions appears, addressed to the whole assembly (20:10–26:5). Finally, suspended between the two days of instruction is a series of transitional events (17:1–20:9).[12] Each of Christ's two days of ministry features instruction on covenantal history and prophecy, in 3 Nephi 15–16 on the first day and in 3 Nephi 20:10–23:5 on the second day. The first of these two covenant sermons is rather obviously preparatory to the second, signaled by the already noted fact that Christ interrupts it when he recognizes that his audience "cannot understand" his teachings (17:2). The transitional material that leads from the first covenant sermon to the second seems in fact meant to prepare Christ's hearers to understand the covenantal theme as fully as possible. It thus appears that Christ's first covenant sermon provides only a first approximation, while the second delves more deeply into the subject. Important to note is that the first covenant sermon ends with only a first (and brief) quotation of Isaiah, while the second is saturated with Isaian content and commentary.

This is not the place to work through Third Nephi's covenant sermons in detail, but a summary might prove useful.[13] The briefer, preliminary sermon in 3 Nephi 15–16 opens by distinguishing between the Law, "fulfilled" in Christ (3 Nephi 15:4), and the Prophets, at least part of whose predictions have "not been fulfilled" (15:6). Christ explains that, "Because I said unto you that old things hath passed away, I do not destroy that which hath been spoken concerning things which is to come—for behold, the covenant which I have made with my people is not all fulfilled" (15:7–8). Here, the text presents Christ himself as interrogating Christianity's traditional equation of the Mosaic law with Israel's covenant.[14] The covenants associated with Abraham, Isaac, and Jacob bind Israel's God to a work that remains incomplete after Jesus's messianic triumph. Thus, Christ next addresses the topic of "this people" in the New World, "this people which are a remnant of the house of Joseph" (15:12). In a gloss on John 10:16 (Jesus's "other sheep" saying), he explains that his visit to the New World is just one of *several* post-resurrection visits around the world, since Israelite "sheep" in various places await his arrival (3 Nephi 15:11–16:3). Having explained this, he then adds a commandment that the Lehites "write these sayings," so that their witness might eventually supplement the biblical record (16:4). He fully anticipates the Bible being incomplete because his Old-World disciples may not "ask the Father . . . that they may receive a knowledge of [the Nephites] by the Holy Ghost, and also of the other tribes which they know not of" (16:4). Within the Book of Mormon, Christ presents the Book of Mormon itself as a necessary fix for the problematic Christian Bible.

After outlining various latter-day events, including the coming forth of the Book of Mormon and warnings about unrepentant gentiles (3 Nephi 16:5–15), Christ turns at last to what most interests our ideal listener/reader, "the words of the prophet Isaiah," and announces a time "when" they "shall be fulfilled" (16:17). He identifies the specific Isaian words he has in mind, and they are three of the four verses at the heart of the Abinadi story. Christ quotes Isaiah 52:8–10, exactly as it stands in the King James Version (and exactly, therefore, as it stands in the quotation by Noah's priests). Even before he offers a word of interpretation, the context in which Christ quotes Isaiah's words signals that they will here bear a new meaning, irreducible to either the self-serving interpretation of Noah's priests or the Christological hermeneutic of the martyr Abinadi. That is, by having Christ quote Isaiah 52:8–10 at the conclusion of a preliminary sermon on the literal fulfillment of God's ancient covenants to Israel, the text indicates that watchmen lift up their voices and see eye to eye when the Lord *literally* "bring[s] again Zion" (16:18). For Mormon's Christ in Third Nephi, the Lord makes his arm bare before all nations neither by giving Nephites victory over Lamanites nor by rising from the grave to gain victory over death; instead, he does so by gathering and restoring Israel.

The quotation of Isaiah 52:8–10 at the conclusion of the preliminary covenant sermon is peculiarly open-ended in the earliest text. Recent editions of the Book of Mormon make Christ's final words in 3 Nephi 16 a prediction of the fulfillment of Isaiah's prophecy. "And *then*," such editions read, apparently referring to the time when God will restore to the New-World remnant of Israel its lands of inheritance, "the words of the prophet Isaiah shall be fulfilled, which say . . ." (3 Nephi 16:17). Manuscript sources, however, along with earlier editions of the book (like any our ideal listener/reader would encounter), read differently, opening an unfinished thought with the Isaiah quotation: "And *when* the words of the prophet Isaiah shall be fulfilled, which saith . . . ," Christ says immediately before he quotes Isaiah 52:8–10, apparently never finishing the thought.[15] After the quotation, Mormon interrupts the unfinished thought with a chapter break and then has Christ look around on his listeners and recognize, as mentioned before, that they "cannot understand" his words (3 Nephi 17:2). Thus, while it is clear from the original text that Christ means to present Isaiah's words as relevant to covenantal history, he at first presents them as marking the limit of the intelligible. He recognizes that his hearers—and perhaps Mormon's readers too—are unprepared to make sense of Isaiah and are therefore unprepared to make real sense of covenantal history. He thus temporarily turns from sermonizing and undertakes a series of transitional preparations before taking up a new covenant sermon at the beginning of a second day of ministry.

Although Christ's second covenant sermon is more developed, its conception of covenantal history echoes the first. Christ speaks again of gathering "from the east and from the west and from the south and from the north," as well as of the Israelites obtaining "the knowledge of the Lord their God who hath redeemed them" (3 Nephi 20:13; compare 16:4–5). All this, as before, is set in motion by the coming forth of the Book of Mormon "from the gentiles unto [the Nephites' and Lamanites'] seed" (21:5; compare 16:6–7, 11). Further, Christ warns again that "a remnant of the house of Jacob" will rise up among unrepentant gentiles; "if [this remnant] goeth through," Christ says, it "both treadeth down and teareth in pieces, and none can deliver" (20:16; compare 16:13–15). To be sure, there are new details in the second sequence, such as talk of "a New Jerusalem" to be built in the last days in the New World, thanks to the assistance of repentant gentiles settled there (21:22–25). But what primarily distinguishes the second discourse from the first functions at the level of *presentation style* rather than *content* or *concept*. The style of the second sequence is one of weaving into its largely repeated outline of covenantal history a host of borrowed biblical texts, drawn principally from three prophetic books: Isaiah, Micah, and Malachi. Christ quotes two full (albeit rather short) chapters of Malachi (Malachi 3–4, in 3 Nephi 24–25) and two substantial blocks of text from Micah (Micah 4:12–13; 5:8–15 in 3 Nephi 20:16–19; 21:12–21).[16] All but a couple of verses of Isaiah 52 find their way into Christ's second-day sermon as well (3 Nephi 20:32–45), along with the whole of Isaiah 54 (3 Nephi 22). In addition, there are significant quotations from Genesis and Deuteronomy (Genesis 22:18 and Deuteronomy 18:15, 18–19 in 3 Nephi 20:23–27; 21:11).[17] While just one major Old Testament text, Isaiah 52:8–10, makes any appearance in the covenant sermon of Christ's first day of ministry, a veritable handbook of Old Testament texts emerges in the second day. The basic conceptual and historical schema from day one becomes the template for interpreting the whole of the Old Testament on day two. This makes the textual progression of Third Nephi into a march toward and then through the work of Old Testament hermeneutics.

As it turns out, however, a less obvious but perhaps more pervasive question of biblical interaction in Third Nephi also requires attention. Not only does Christ directly and explicitly put his outline of covenantal history into conversation with canonical Old Testament texts in his second-day sermon he *also* exhibits a thoroughgoing interest in the New Testament's Gospel of

John. It is somewhat peculiar that this Johannine aspect of Christ's ministry in Third Nephi, despite its saturation of the text, never directly announces itself, waiting to be discovered by careful readers. It deserves attention here, however, because the Johannine interests of Third Nephi entangle themselves inextricably with what Mormon has Christ do with Isaiah.

A Johannine Lens

The discovery of John's centrality to Third Nephi should be credited to New Testament scholar Krister Stendahl. Stendahl takes his orientation in Third Nephi from the slight but significant textual differences between the famous Sermon on the Mount from Matthew 5–7 and its parallel in Third Nephi, found in 3 Nephi 12–14.[18] This New World repetition of the Old World sermon appears as prefatory to the covenant sermons at issue here. Thus, the Sermon on the Mount introduces in Third Nephi the idea of the Mosaic law's fulfillment, allowing Christ then to distinguish the total fulfillment of the Law from the partial fulfillment of the Prophets in Christ's messianic work (3 Nephi 15:1–9).

Stendahl shows that analysis of differences between the New Testament and Book of Mormon versions of the sermon—the sermons are *mostly* identical—collectively "point in the direction toward that which we shall call a Johannine Jesus, the revealed revealer who points to himself and to faith in and obedience to him as the message. In the Matthean Sermon on the Mount," Stendahl explains, "Jesus is pictured rather as a teacher of righteousness, basing his teaching on the law and prophets, scolding the superficiality and foibles of the religionists of his time, proclaiming the will of God and not the glories of himself."[19] Stendahl finds Johannine resonances elsewhere in Third Nephi as well. He notes the exposition, during the preliminary covenant sermon, of John 10:16, which offers direct commentary on a passage from John. He mentions also "the style of John 4" in part of 3 Nephi 18 and "the style and terms of John 17" in 3 Nephi 19, points to which I will return.[20] He further observes that Third Nephi mirrors John by offering primarily "revelatory speeches or revelatory discourses" rather than narrative events. Similarly, in Third Nephi as in John, "everything" recounted in the synoptic Gospels of Matthew, Mark, and Luke "gets a little more miraculous."[21] Still more stark, as Stendahl points out, is that "the real analogy between the Johannine Jesus and the Jesus of 3 Nephi is found in the style of discourse": the constant use of statements beginning with "I am" or otherwise presented as self-referential, the emphasis on faith, and the associated use of "verily" and "behold," and so on.[22] Woven into an otherwise conservative re-presentation of Matthew's Sermon on the Mount, this makes Third Nephi a "transposition" of Matthew (and Mark and Luke) "into Johannine style."[23]

Stendahl's analysis is remarkable and his argument convincing. Third Nephi represents, generally, a kind of "Johannization" of the synoptic Gospels. In fact, closer study of Third Nephi reveals that Stendahl discerns only a few of the Johannine elements of Mormon's presentation of Jesus, and only a few of the ways he transposes elements of the synoptic Gospels into Johannine style. Examining the saturation of Third Nephi by Johannine themes is essential to understanding the Johannine entanglements that eventually show up in connection with Isaiah there. Already in Christ's previsit speech, addressed to Nephites and Lamanites in the dark after Jesus's death, the text underscores John's importance for Mormon's Christ. Identifying himself as "the Son of God," he gives an unmistakably Johannine speech:

> I created the heavens and the earth, and all things that in them is. I was with the Father from the beginning. I am in the Father and the Father in me, and in me hath the Father glorified his name. I came unto my own, and my own received me not, and the scriptures concerning my coming are fulfilled. And as many as have received me, to them have I given to become the sons of God—and even so will I, to as many as shall believe on my name. For behold, by me redemption cometh, and in me is the law of Moses fulfilled. I am the light and the life of the world. I am Alpha and Omega, the beginning and the end. (3 Nephi 9:15–18)

As Nicholas Frederick, a student of Book of Mormon intertextuality, has shown in detail, this brief speech reworks the famed prologue to the Gospel of John, weaving into it a few other well-known Johannine lines.[24]

The speech, offered before Christ even appears, thus sets up the Johannine interest of Third Nephi. But the way that this interest trumps—and in fact calls for a revision of—synoptic themes and sayings becomes fully clear only when Christ first descends among New World Israel. When he descends from heaven in glory, the voice of the Father is heard, announcing the Son's arrival, and the Father's words give a Johannine twist to a classic Matthean text: "Behold my Beloved Son, in whom I am well pleased, in whom I have glorified my name! Hear ye him!" (3 Nephi 11:7). This reproduces and revises the "voice from heaven" reported in Matthew's account of Jesus's baptism: "This is my beloved Son, in whom I am well pleased" (Matthew 3:17).[25] Perhaps more accurately, it reproduces and revises the "voice out of the cloud" in Matthew's account of Jesus's mountaintop transfiguration: "This is my beloved Son, in whom I am well pleased; hear ye him" (Matthew 17:1). The replacement of "this is" with "behold" is already Johannine in flavor, as Stendahl's study suggests, but more striking is the coupling of "in whom I am well pleased" with "in whom I have glorified my name." This echoes John 12:28, which also reports "a voice from heaven." There, in response to Jesus's petition to the "Father" to "glorify [God's] name,"[26] John reports a voice "saying, I have both glorified it, and will glorify it again." The Third Nephi presentation of the Son by the Father takes the Matthean "voice from heaven" or "voice out of the cloud" and revises it in a Johannine direction, drawing on John's own voice-from-heaven scene. Without the same gesture of transposition, Christ's self-introduction a few verses later draws on John as well.[27] And the same Johannine self-presentation continues when Christ offers his first invitation to his hearers: "Arise and come forth unto me," he says, "that ye may thrust your hands into my side, and also that ye may feel the prints of the nails in my hands and in my feet" (3 Nephi 11:14). This invitation obviously echoes the scene where doubting Thomas, coming face to face with the risen Christ, hears this: "Reach hither thy finger, and behold my hands; and reach hither thy hand, and thrust it into my side" (John 20:27). In Third Nephi, a whole multitude has the experience John in the New Testament offers just to Thomas.

Right from his first appearances in Mormon's narrative, then, the Christ of Third Nephi is Johannine. His disembodied voice ringing out in the dark of New World destruction, his presentation by the Father as he descends from heaven, and even his initial self-presentation to his New World audience—all this makes clear his identity with the Jesus of John's Gospel. It is *this* Jesus who will weave Johannine language and themes into his quotations of Isaiah. In the meanwhile, the pattern continues.[28] An exposition of just a single verse from John follows the Johannized Sermon on the Mount—the "other sheep" passage of John 10:16. But then, after this and the associated preliminary covenant sermon just reviewed, there follow the transitional events that pave the way from the first covenant sermon to its sequel on the second day. It is perhaps unsurprising at this point, though, that even this series of transitional events—especially Christ's prayers and Eucharistic performances—strikingly deploys the same pattern of synoptic-Gospels-transposed-into-a-Johannine-key. These are *particularly* worthy of attention here, because they suggest that the Johannization of synoptic scenarios, themes, and texts paves the way from the more preliminary to the more developed of Christ's two covenant sermons, where Isaiah stands at center stage. Further, the treatment of Isaiah in the covenant sermon of the second day centrally concerns Johannine theology.

Shortly after concluding his preliminary covenant sermon (but still during the first day of his visit), Christ asks the multitude to bring "their little children" to him (3 Nephi 17:11), and the children encircle him with their parents and the rest of the multitude standing without. Christ groans and offers a prayer: "Father, I am troubled because of the wickedness of the people of the house of Israel" (17:14). Having spoken these words, he kneels and continues his prayer, but "the things which he prayed cannot be written," and "tongue cannot speak" them (17:15, 17). He then blesses the children thronging him while angels come down from heaven to form a larger circle around "those little ones" (17:24). The formal geometric features of this event, as the text describes it, will prove crucial: Christ both stands and kneels at the center of a circle of children, who are in turn encircled by heavenly angels, who are in turn encircled themselves by the larger multitude. At the heart of this concentrically circular scene, Christ suffers under the weight of Israel's "wickedness" (17:14) and prays for the remnant of Israel gathered about him.

Here again the contrast between John's Gospel and the synoptics is relevant. The scene just described echoes the New Testament event of Jesus's suffering in Gethsemane as reported in the Gospel of Luke (Luke 22:29–46). Significantly, no scene of suffering in Gethsemane appears in John. The scene in Luke lacks the formal geometric features of the scene in Third Nephi,[29] but other clear parallels link it together. Only in Luke's Gethsemane scene is Jesus described as having "kneeled down," just as it is only in 3 Nephi 17:15 in the Book of Mormon that Christ kneels. Also, the Christ of 3 Nephi 17 groans and describes himself as "troubled" (3 Nephi 17:14), just as Jesus in Luke is "in an agony" and therefore prays "earnestly" (Luke 22:44). Still further, in both narratives, Christ's prayer yields angelic visitation: a whole group of angels in Third Nephi but just one angel "from heaven" in Luke (22:43). These connections and parallels signal that 3 Nephi 17 contains the Lukan Gethsemane story.[30]

While Luke does not contain the formal geometric features of the 3 Nephi 17 story, they progressively reappear in the scene that opens the second day of Christ's ministry, just prior to the second covenant sermon. Christ withdraws overnight, and, in his absence, twelve disciples teach his words from the previous day to the larger multitude. With Christ's authority, they then begin baptizing. As they emerge from the water "filled with the Holy Ghost" (3 Nephi 19:13), angels again "come down out of heaven" and encircle them (19:14). The concentric circles of the previous day thus reappear, with the multitude again outermost and angels forming a circle around the central scene.

In the place of the previous day's children are the newly called disciples.[31] As soon as these circles take complete shape, reproducing the formal geometric features of the previous day's event, Christ himself arrives (19:15), completing the formal reproduction of the preceding day.[32] As soon as this occurs, Christ proceeds to do as he has done previously; he offers a prayer whose words, again, are "so great and marvelous . . . that they cannot be written, neither can they be uttered by man" (19:34). This time, however, the prayer unfolds in three sequences, not one, and the record produces the full text of the first two sequences of Christ's prayer.

Like the parallel scene from the previous day, this event bears relation to the New Testament's stories about Jesus's visit to Gethsemane. But where the first day's event parallels just Luke's account of that visit, the second day's event mirrors the stories told by Mark and Matthew, such that all three synoptic Gospels come to supply Third Nephi with features for its own Gethsemane scenes. As in Mark and Matthew's story about Gethsemane, Christ in 3 Nephi 19 offers three prayers while commanding his disciples to pray, and each time he offers his own prayer only after "depart[ing] out of the midst of them" and going "a little way off" (3 Nephi 19:19; see 19:27, 31). These parallels are notably clearer than those between the Lukan Gethsemane story and 3 Nephi 17.[33] Nonetheless, significant points distinguish the Gethsemane events of Matthew and Mark from Christ's prayers in 3 Nephi 19, points clearly meant to draw the reader's attention. As Douglas Davies notes, these differences emerge in the disciples' behavior: in Third Nephi, they "remain awake, pray intensely, and share in Jesus's alert attitude," while the New Testament disciples fall asleep and are "seemingly unable to watch with their needy master, despite requests to do so."[34] The result is that the Nephite disciples are "purified" (19:28) and take on the appearance of "the countenance . . . of Jesus" (19:25). Further, as Christ himself declares, the difference between the New World and Old World disciples results in a distinction between what each group witnesses: "I could not shew unto [my Old World disciples] so great miracles," Christ explains, "because of their unbelief" (19:35).

A crucial point is that the second day of Christ's New World ministry reaches its pinnacle by weaving into its reenactment of Gethsemane the non-Gethsemane prayer of John 17. As Stendahl notes (along with most Latter-day Saint commentators), the two recorded prayers of Christ in 3 Nephi 19 echo the famous intercessory prayer that concludes Christ's long evening with his disciples before his betrayal in John.[35] As in John 17, the focus in Christ's Third

Nephi prayers is on how the Father has given the Son disciples from out of the world, and Christ pleads for a relationship of mutual indwelling with them similar to what he has with the Father. Here again, the careful reader discovers a Johannization of synoptic materials. In this case, however, Mormon's story couples its Johannine elements with a contrast between the *success* of Christ's intentions with his New World disciples and the *failure* of Christ's similar intentions with his Old World disciples. In both the New Testament and Third Nephi, Christ wishes to involve his disciples in his prayerful relationship to the Father when it grows most intense and intimate. In the New Testament—because "the spirit indeed is willing, but the flesh is weak" (Matthew 26:41)—the disciples miss out, and so too do readers. In Third Nephi, however, the disciples are purified as they join Christ in prayer. And what they hear is the prayer from John.

The point is that John's Gospel not only serves as the locus of a high Christology here, but as the container of esoteric theology revealed only to the initiated. A similar pattern appears in two other narrative sequences in the transitional portion of Third Nephi, each following the respective Gethsemane events of 3 Nephi 17 and 3 Nephi 19. After the prayer of 3 Nephi 17, Christ concludes the first day of his New World ministry by introducing the sacrament of the Lord's Supper. Blessing, breaking, and distributing bread, he explains the rite in language from the synoptic Gospels: "This shall ye do in remembrance of my body, which I have shewn unto you. And it shall be a testimony unto the Father that ye do always remember me—and if ye do always remember me, ye shall have my spirit to be with you" (3 Nephi 18:7). Similar in spirit is his explanation of the wine: "Ye shall [drink] it in remembrance of my blood, which I have shed for you" (18:11). These expositions might be compared with the one that appears especially in the Gospel of Luke: "This is my body which is given for you: this do in remembrance of me," Jesus says; "this cup is the new testament in my blood, which is shed for you" (Luke 22:19–20).[36] Third Nephi's first Gethsemane experience is thus, like the Gethsemane experiences of the synoptic Gospels, associated with the Last Supper. And the Last Supper in question is indelibly synoptic.

The second of Third Nephi's Gethsemane experiences also associates itself with the Lord's Supper, but, following the now well-established pattern, the presentation of the sacramental elements is not synoptic but Johannine. First, Christ provides a New World parallel to the Old World miracle of the loaves and fishes—the occasion when Jesus feeds a great multitude with a meal just large enough to feed a family.[37] This miracle appears in all four Gospels, not only in the synoptics but also in John, and from among those options the Third Nephi story mirrors the account from John. This is clear from the fact that the Gospel of John couples the miracle with the so-called "Bread of Life Sermon," in which Christ uses the imagery of the miracle to present himself as bread to eat and wine to drink. Similarly, the sacramental scene that follows Third Nephi's second Gethsemane experience couples the miraculous feeding of the New World multitude with an explanation of the rite drawing on the Bread of Life Sermon from John 6. As before, the connection with John is among the Johannine points Stendahl notes in Third Nephi, even if he does not explicitly recognize the larger logic I hope to draw out here.[38] This logic is built on a contrast. Where on day one Christ speaks of bread and wine as tokens of remembrance, he now refers to the emblems as his actual flesh and blood. "He that eateth this bread eateth of my body to their soul, and he that drinketh of this wine drinketh of my blood to their soul—and their soul shall never hunger, nor thirst, but shall be filled" (3 Nephi 20:8). This language comes directly from John 6. Here, once more, what begins as a synoptic presentation—the Lord's Supper as presented especially in the Gospel of Luke—is ultimately transposed into a Johannine key. Again and again, the basic theological commitments of the Gospel of John constitute the telos of Third Nephi's narrative logic. When Christ is victorious and his disciples are one with him, the result is Johannine rather than synoptic. John provides the theological picture that only the fully initiated can enjoy in the right way, preparatory to their learning about Isaiah's prophecies.

This discussion belabors the articulation of the Johannine thematic in Third Nephi, giving it more space than might seem warranted for a study of the role played in the text by Isaiah. Our ideal listener/reader, ever at hand, might raise an eyebrow at what at first seems a tangential discussion. Of course, to some extent, the theme deserves attention just because it has gone largely unnoticed in previous literature. But what makes it important in the present context—and thus even for our ideal listener/reader—is that the culminating instance of Johannization in Third Nephi concerns passages drawn from the Old Testament, and one key passage from Isaiah in particular. The Johannizing pattern and its consistency are worth developing at such length because they play a major role in shaping the presentation of Isaiah in Third Nephi, especially where this presentation contrasts with the presentation of Isaiah in and around Abinadi's defense before Noah's priests.

Isaiah in Third Nephi

The last few examples of Johannizing logic clarify the relationship between Christ's two sermons in Third Nephi. At one level, what distinguishes them is just depth of interaction with prophetic texts. On day one, Christ makes Isaiah 52:8–10 the (incomprehensible) endpoint of his preliminary sermon; on day two, the same passage is one among many biblical allusions. But at another level, what differentiates the two days is the multitude's preparation. On day one, they "cannot understand" his teachings (3 Nephi 17:2) but, on day two, they clearly can. What makes the difference between the two situations is that Christ brings his hearers from a merely synoptic to a fully Johannine understanding, initiating them into the full esoteric theology of John's Gospel. Only after the Johannine Gethsemane in 3 Nephi 19 and the Johannine Eucharist in 3 Nephi 20 does Christ attempt to "finish the commandment" to explain Israel's destiny and its relevance to New World Israel (20:10). Only then does he ask his hearers to "remember" what he had left unsaid about Isaiah 52:8–10.

The first word of the second-day sermon concerns the Isaiah quotation that open-endedly concludes the first-day sermon. "Ye remember," Christ begins, "that I spake unto you and said that when the words of Isaiah should be fulfilled, then is the fulfilling of the covenant which the Father hath made unto his people, O house of Israel" (3 Nephi 20:11–12). This clearly refers to 3 Nephi 16:17–20, the unfinished thought that incorporates Isaiah 52:8–10 and exhausts the audience's comprehension on day one. With this thought finally completed, Christ reviews themes from the first covenant sermon, deepened with borrowings from other biblical texts. Non-Isaian texts receive attention first: Micah 4–5, Deuteronomy 18, and Genesis 22. Christ comes back to Isaiah 52:8–10 only after these other passages receive attention. Micah, Deuteronomy, and Genesis provide the language for enriching the story of the covenant.[39] It is significant, though, that it is only with Isaiah that the Johannine thematic begins to play a role in the second-day sermon on Israel's covenants.

When he finally comes to it, Christ's fuller exposition of Isaiah 52:8–10 on day two presents the passage as describing "the time" when, in the last days, Jews "shall believe in . . . Jesus Christ" (3 Nephi 20:31). It is "then," when the Father will gather Jews and restore Jerusalem to them, that Isaiah's prophecy is to be fulfilled (20:33). Christ quotes the passage anew to mark the occasion of its fulfillment but, without warning, alters it as he quotes it. The alterations might be taken in at a single glance by setting the two passages side by side, with clear points of distinction underlined:

ISAIAH 52:8–10	3 NEPHI 20:32–35
<u>Thy</u> watchmen <u>shall</u> lift up <u>the</u> voice;	<u>Then shall their</u> watchmen lift up <u>their</u> voice,
with the voice together shall they sing:	<u>and</u> with the voice together shall they sing—
for they shall see eye to eye,	for they shall see eye to eye.
<u>when the LORD shall bring again Zion.</u>	<u>Then will the Father gather them together</u>
	<u>again and give unto them Jerusalem for the</u>
	<u>land of their inheritance.</u>
Break forth into joy,	<u>Then shall they</u> break forth into joy.
sing together, ye waste places of Jerusalem:	Sing together, ye waste places of Jerusalem,
for the <u>LORD</u> hath comforted his people, he	for the <u>Father</u> hath comforted his people! He
hath redeemed Jerusalem. The <u>LORD</u> hath	hath redeemed Jerusalem! The <u>Father</u> hath
made bare his holy arm in the eyes of all the	made bare his holy arm in the eyes of all the
nations; and all the ends of the earth shall	nations, and all the ends of the earth shall
see the salvation of <u>[our]</u>[40] God.	see the salvation of <u>the Father</u>.
<u>And the Father and I are one.</u>	

Some of the differences here are minor and contextual—the replacement of "thy" with "their," or the addition of "then" to clarify sequence. Even the expansion of "when the Lord shall bring again Zion" (making the text describe gathering and restoration for Jews) is largely self-explanatory. Other differences, however, require close analysis.

Two preliminary points deserve notice. First, Mormon's Christ in no way means to restore an "original" Isaiah text. Because certain Isaiah passages in the Book of Mormon contain variants, distinguishing them from their biblical counterparts, many readers conclude that the Book of Mormon provides an original or at least earlier version of Isaiah.[41] That is clearly *not* appropriate at this point in Third Nephi. Christ first quotes Isaiah 52:8–10 as it stands in the Bible, just as Noah's priests quote the passage in its biblical form. Mormon assumes this text to be correct in the Bible. Readers are meant to understand that Christ *deliberately* alters the text of Isaiah in 3 Nephi 20. Second, Christ deliberately manipulates the text rather than commenting on or pedantically explaining it. Having quoted the passage during day one, Christ *could* simply provide an expository commentary on Isaiah's meaning, an explanation of how it applies to his last-days predictions. Instead, though, he alters the text to bring out its latent possibilities of meaning. Especially after the handling of the same Isaiah passage in the Abinadi narrative, Christ's approach should strike Mormon's readers as novel.[42]

Turning to the actual content of Christ's alterations to Isaiah 52:8–10, we might note the Johannine flavor of the changes. Three times Christ replaces the word "Lord" with the word "Father." Once, he similarly replaces "God" with "Father." These alterations might not initially appear Johannine, since, although Jesus speaks much about his relationship to the Father in John, John has no monopoly on scripture's use of that title. What clinches the Johannine character of such talk, though, is the addition at the end of the Isaiah passage: "And the Father and I are one" (3 Nephi 20:35). This borrows straightforwardly from John 10:30: "I and my Father are one." And the borrowed passage is anything but obscure. It is rather, as Raymond Brown says, "perhaps the best commentary on Jesus' attitude [in John] toward the question of whether or not he is the Messiah"; and it provides "an answer that is affirmative in tone but not phrased in traditional terminology."[43] John's Jesus in fact offers this formula in response to a key question: "How long dost thou make us to doubt? If thou be the Christ, tell us plainly" (10:24). Jesus's bald reply, affirming his oneness with the Father, yields dangerous consequences, an attempted stoning (10:31). For Mormon's Christ to use this line highlights the text's increasingly overt commitment to Johannine theology.

The insertion from John 10:30 into the quotation of Isaiah 52:8–10 retroactively confirms that the replacement of "the Lord" and "God" with "the Father" in 3 Nephi 20:32–35 is also Johannine. The oneness of Father and Son has been presented from the very beginning of Christ's visit to the New World in strictly Johannine terms, a matter of mutual witness and indwelling. Thus, the direct manipulation of Isaiah 52:8–10 in Christ's second Third Nephi sermon not only focuses the passage's meaning on the theme and history of Israel's covenant it also casts the passage in the mold of Johannine theology—or perhaps better, in the mold of Johannizing non-Johannine biblical texts. To understand Christ's interest in Isaiah in Third Nephi, one must view it through a Johannine lens. Only then can the meaning of Isaiah become manifest for Mormon's Christ—and for Mormon's readers.

What work does the supplement about the oneness of Father and Son do? A similar formula appears earlier in Third Nephi, as just noted, with a determinate function. Introducing the rite of Christian baptism, Christ in 3 Nephi 11 at first speaks in an apparently contradictory fashion. Citing "disputations" about baptism (3 Nephi 11:22), Christ instructs that all are to "be baptized in my name" (11:23). But then, in providing the words to be used in the rite, he explains that all are to be baptized "in the name of the Father, and of the Son, and of the Holy Ghost" (11:25). This surely seems at odds with baptizing in Christ's name. But then, after providing the threefold formula for the rite, Christ says that it is precisely "after this manner" that one should "baptize in my name" (11:27). Baptism is to be in the name of Christ, but that apparently means that one should baptize in the name of the Father, the Son, and the Holy Ghost. How are these equivalent? Christ explains: "For behold, verily I say unto you that the Father, and the Son, and the Holy Ghost are one; and I am in the Father, and the Father in me, and the Father and I are one" (11:27). The oneness of the Father, the Son, and the Holy Ghost makes baptism "in the name of the Father, and of the Son, and of the Holy Ghost" equivalent to baptism in Christ's name.[44]

A brief Johannine epilogue of sorts is added later to a series of quotations from Isaiah 52. "Verily, verily I say unto you," Christ says after quoting so much Isaiah text, "all these things shall surely come, even as the Father hath commanded me. And then shall this covenant, which the Father hath covenanted with his people, be fulfilled" (3 Nephi 20:46). Here Christ retroactively casts the whole concatenation of Isaiah texts as tied to a larger Johannine picture. The events they describe, Christ explains, will occur according to the Father's commandments to the Son. This is also a classically Johannine formulation. Jesus explains several times in John that he receives his commandments from the Father and executes them faithfully (John 10:18; 12:49; 14:31; 15:10). In addition, Jesus says in John that "the Son can do nothing of himself, but what he seeth the Father do: for what things soever he doeth, these also doeth the Son likewise" (John 5:19; see also 8:28). In Third Nephi, Mormon's Christ places *the whole of world history* within this same Johannine framework of the Son's execution of the Father's commandments. Isaiah's prophecies are fulfilled "even as the Father hath commanded." Then, beyond such prophetic fulfillment, the Father can pursue the fulfillment of his covenant "with his people." In the end, the lack of direct Johannine revision in the quotation of Isaiah 52:1–3, 6–7, 11–15 in 3 Nephi 20 does not break with the pattern established in the Johannine revision of Isaiah 52:8–10. Rather, the latter, coupled with the epilogue of sorts that concludes the series of quotations, inscribes the whole series within a Johannine theological frame.

This last point suggests that a latent Johannine significance permeates the predictive gestures that introduce the several elements in the quotations from Isaiah 52: "and then shall be brought to pass that which is written" (3 Nephi 20:36), "and then shall they say" (20:40), and "and then shall a cry go forth" (20:41). These formulas, added to the Isaiah texts to mark the role played in the predicted future by each element in the series, collectively look forward to the Johannine epilogue: "all these things shall surely come, even as the Father hath commanded me" (20:46). Even where specific Johannine alterations have *not* been made to Isaiah 52 in 3 Nephi 20, the larger framing makes clear that they are meant to fit into the Johannine theology predominating in Mormon's text. The covenant history Christ predicts again has a Johannine cast, something viewed properly only in light of the sovereign work of the Father and the Son, mutual witnesses and one in each other.

More, though, needs saying about Isaiah 52 in 3 Nephi 20. Mormon's Christ does the work of sifting that particular chapter of Isaiah.[45] He selects one passage as particularly salient, placing it, out of order, before the others (otherwise arranged sequentially). He then apparently chooses among remaining passages those most relevant to his predictions, leaving two verses from Isaiah 52 out of the series. The remainder of Isaiah 52 appears in order, then, but interspersed with transitional interjections assigning each passage a place in the history of covenant fulfillment. The several divisions in Third Nephi's serial quotation of Isaiah 52, coupled with interjections, might be presented formally as in table 4.1.

This table clarifies how Mormon's Christ uses Isaiah 52. Verses 8–10 receive a kind of privilege, not only because Christ weaves Johannine elements into them, but also because he extracts them to position them at the chapter's head. He uses these verses, it seems, to encapsulate the larger fulfillment of events from Isaiah 52. Verses 1–3, 6, 7, and 11–12 then follow with interjections that signal each passage's place within the buildup identified by verses 8–10. After Zion's redemption and a Jewish turn toward Jesus, the content of verses 1–3 "shall be brought to pass." Because verses 1–3 contain a series of commands, the implication seems to be that Israel will fulfill these commands, waking up to recognize its royal status. Verse 6 seems meant to confirm Israel's response to the commands, affirming that "in that day" Israel "shall know [Christ's] name."[46] Verse 7 predicts Israel's subsequent retrospective affirmation of those who have proclaimed salvation; understanding their relationship

Table 4.1. Serial quotations of Isaiah 52 in 3 Nephi 20

Text from Isaiah 52	Is it directly Johannized?	Transitional interjection	Content of the Isaiah text
Verses 8–10	Yes, heavily (see the text).	"And it shall come to pass that the time cometh when the fullness of my gospel shall be preached unto [the Jews], and they shall believe in me—that I am Jesus Christ the Son of God—and shall pray unto the Father in my name."	"Then shall their watchmen lift up their voice, and with the voice together shall they sing, for they shall see eye to eye. Then will the Father gather them together again and give unto them Jerusalem for the land of their inheritance. Then shall they break forth into joy. Sing together, ye waste places of Jerusalem—for the Lord hath comforted his people! He hath redeemed Jerusalem!"
Verses 1–3	No.	"And then shall be brought to pass that which is written"	"Awake! Awake again, and put on thy strength, O Zion! Put on thy beautiful garments, O Jerusalem, the holy city—for henceforth there shall no more come into thee the uncircumcised and the unclean! Shake thyself from the dust! Arise! Sit down, O Jerusalem! Loose thyself from the bands of thy neck, O captive daughter of Zion! For thus saith the Lord: 'Ye have sold yourselves for naught, and ye shall be redeemed without money.'"
Verse 6	Yes, but minimally (an addition of "verily, verily I say unto you")	"yea, in that day"	"Verily, verily I say unto you that my people shall know my name—yea, in that day they shall know that I am he that doth speak."
Verse 7	No.	"And then shall they say"	"How beautiful upon the mountains are the feet of him that bringeth good tidings unto them, that publisheth peace, that bringeth good tidings unto them of good, that publisheth salvation, that saith unto Zion, 'Thy God reigneth!'"
Verses 11–12	No.	"And then shall a cry go forth"	"Depart ye! Depart ye! Go ye out from thence! Touch not that which is unclean. Go ye out of the midst of her. Be ye clean that bear the vessels of the Lord. For ye shall not go out with haste, nor go by flight—for the Lord will go before you, and the God of Israel shall be your rearward."
Verses 13–15	No.	"Behold"	"My servant shall deal prudently. He shall be exalted and extolled and be very high. As many were astonished at thee—his visage was so marred, more than any man, and his form more than the sons of men—so shall he sprinkle many nations. The kings shall shut their mouths at him, for that which had not been told them shall they see, and that which they had not heard shall they consider."

to God, Israelites praise those who brought them to understanding. Finally, verses 11–12 constitute a concluding cry for Israel to remove itself from exile to its own lands of inheritance. With conversion complete, geographical movement becomes the focus, and Israel begins moving to its promised land.

The remarkably natural flow of this sequence, outlined using just Isaiah's words, comes to a halt with the quotation of Isaiah 52:13–15, appearing without any interruption or break in the text. Most Isaiah scholars today regard these verses about a disfigured servant who rises to glory less as part of Isaiah 52 than as the opening stanza of the poem in Isaiah 53.[47] Indeed, Isaiah 52:13–15 transparently parallels the final stanza of Isaiah 53 (its verses 10–12), describing the suffering servant's exaltation despite his abasement in the poem.[48] The quotation of Isaiah 52:13–15 thus seems out of place in 3 Nephi 20, as the particularly weak transitional interjection that opens it—a mere "behold"—seems to confirm. The sudden reference to an unidentified "servant," the apparently irrelevant talk of the suffering and exaltation of some individual not obviously identical to Israel, and the rather obscure phrasing combine to make the final passage Christ draws from Isaiah 52 seem inappropriate. While the arrangement of everything else from Isaiah 52 in 3 Nephi 20 seems careful, it seems at first as if the last verses from Isaiah 52 are included in the text without any intention, sloppily and distractingly.

Yet it is only these peculiar last lines from Isaiah 52 that *reappear* as Christ continues the second-day covenant sermon.[49] The events Christ associates with Isaiah 52:1–12 are clearly sequenced in 3 Nephi 20, but the events he associates with Isaiah 52:13–15 are obscure and apparently out of sequence there. In 3 Nephi 21, however, Christ returns to the latter passage to give it clarity and a place in the sequence of eschatological events. As Gaye Strathearn and Jacob Moody have argued convincingly, Christ in Third Nephi identifies the servant of Isaiah 52:13–15 as, of all things, the Book of Mormon itself, whose latter-day emergence is described in the opening of 3 Nephi 21.[50] It is the Book of Mormon that—through the loss of part of the original manuscript[51]—is "marred," as Isaiah 52:14 says. Christ explains, though, that "the life of my servant shall be in my hand" and "therefore they shall not hurt him, although he shall be marred because of them. Yet I will heal him, for I will show unto them that my wisdom is greater than the cunning of the devil" (3 Nephi 21:10). The healing described here seems straightforwardly to be the (anticipated) use of Nephi's record to replace the manuscript lost during Joseph Smith's dictation project.[52] Language from an 1829 revelation to Smith confirms this reading, describing the divine response to the lost manuscript and its replacement with words identical to those in 3 Nephi 21. "I will not suffer that they [whoever stole the manuscript] shall destroy my work," God tells Smith; "yea, I will show unto them that my wisdom is greater than the cunning of the devil."[53] It thus appears that the final verses of Isaiah 52 appear in Third Nephi as an excerpt from Isaiah's suffering servant song, meant to introduce the coming forth of the Book of Mormon into the prophesied sequence of latter-day events. It is apparently the Book of Mormon itself that will cause "kings" to "shut their mouths" as they "see" what "had not been told them" (3 Nephi 21:8).

In the end, then, all the excerpts from Isaiah 52 included in 3 Nephi 20 play a specifiable role in the sequence of eschatological events. The Book of Mormon itself, the Lord's marred but then healed servant, is to spur all this salvation history. And the Johannine style runs throughout Christ's uses of Isaiah 52. Even in using Isaiah 52:13–15 to describe Smith's troubles, Christ deploys the Johannine entanglements of Father and Son (3 Nephi 21:8–11). But far more consistent is the persistent focus of Isaian interpretation throughout Third Nephi on the theme of Israel's covenant. The Johannine lens focuses the reader's attention theologically, but it focuses it squarely on Israel's final redemption.

Further quotation of Isaiah slightly later confirms this. After fresh quotations of Micah in 3 Nephi 21, Christ again promises the day when "the work of the Father" is to "commence among all the dispersed" of Israel (3 Nephi 21:26). This work is to make possible a gathering of all Israel to Christ, "that they may call on the Father in my name . . . and then shall the work commence with the Father among all nations in preparing the way" for gathering (21:27–28). "And then," Christ continues, "shall that which is written come to pass" (22:1). Here Christ leaves off Isaiah 52 to quote Isaiah 54, in one uninterrupted and unaltered block of text.[54] Where Abinadi quotes Isaiah 53—so apparently messianic in nature—to clarify the meaning of Isaiah 52, Christ instead quotes Isaiah 54—unmistakably focused on Israel's promised restoration—to clarify the meaning of the same text. In this case, however, Christ offers no substantive commentary or clarifying discussion. All that introduces the lengthy quotation of Isaiah 54 is the line already quoted ("and then," at the time of Israel's redemption, "shall that which is written come to pass"). And Christ follows his full quotation of Isaiah 54 with a recommendation to "search these things diligently" (3 Nephi 23:1), since Isaiah's prophecies concern "the house of Israel" and also "the gentiles" (23:2). Isaiah 54 serves essentially to *confirm*, rather than to *clarify*, Christ's general interpretive strategy in Third Nephi.[55]

The discussion of Isaiah 52 just concluded thus provides a clear sense of Christ's Isaian hermeneutic in the Book of Mormon. Addressing himself to the very text central to the Abinadi narrative, Christ offers an approach radically distinct both from the self-serving interpretation of Noah's priests (who read the text as typologically descriptive of their own political ascendency) and from the half-traditional, half-nontraditional interpretation of the prophet Abinadi (who reads the same passage as esoterically predicting Christ and a pre-Christian community ready to rise with him at his resurrection). For Christ, Isaiah 52—like, it appears, Isaiah more generally—primarily outlines the eschatological destiny of Israel. As throughout Third Nephi, the Christ of the Book of Mormon focuses intensely on the history of Israel's covenant, and on the meaning and possibilities of that covenant's fulfillment. For that reason, he finds in Isaiah's words something to be fulfilled when eschatological events bring Jews and other Israelites scattered throughout the world to a believing understanding of Jesus's work as Christ. Further, in outlining this Isaian hermeneutic, the Christ of Third Nephi subtly but indelibly sifts the various theological commitments on offer in the New Testament. He neither dismisses nor dispenses with the synoptic Gospels, with their relatively lower Christology and their emphasis on what Jesus does vicariously for human beings. But he gives pride of place to the Gospel of John, with its astonishingly high Christology and its consistent desire to invite all potential Christian disciples into the sort of mutual relationship of indwelling had by the Father and the Son. John becomes a Christological frame for making sense of the covenantal interpretation Christ offers of Isaian prophecy.

Through Mormon's story of Jesus Christ's visit, in short, the Book of Mormon sets forth a third approach to the same Isaian text. Within the larger framework of Mormon's editorial project, this clearly constitutes a culmination, the end of Isaian interpretation. The hermeneutic debate between Abinadi and Noah's priests is revealed as limited in scope—or at least as less resolved than the Abinadi narrative suggests. Hundreds of pages after the Abinadi story seems to have decided the question of Isaian interpretation, Jesus Christ opens the question afresh. This question prompts questions I will consider in the next chapter. How does Christ's rather different approach to Isaiah resonate within that larger history of Isaiah's reception that so interests our ideal listener/reader, and within the American nineteenth century particularly, when our ideal listener/reader lived? And what does the trajectory of the Isaiah question in Mormon's project—moving from apparently settled debate, through hundreds of pages of neglect, to renewal of the question and a novel answer—indicate about the volume's intended audience in the nineteenth century?

5
A Radical Hermeneutic in Outline

As we have seen along with or through the eyes of our imagined ideal listener to and reader of the Book of Mormon, the narrative climax of Mormon's project in Third Nephi depicts a resurrected Jesus Christ presenting a fresh interpretation of Isaiah, one irreducible to the positions of either Abinadi or Noah's priests. Our ideal listener/reader, remember, has not only sat with Joseph Smith and his scribes during the dictation of the Book of Mormon and soaked in the flow of the text's argument; such a listener/reader is also broadly familiar with the history of Isaiah's interpretation, right up to the moment of the Book of Mormon's publication. To feel with such a listener/reader the full force of Christ's interventions within Mormon's larger literary project, then, it is necessary to move beyond general analysis of the interpretive approaches from Christ's two days of sermonizing and so to investigate how Christ's handling of Isaiah stands with respect to other models of Isaian interpretation, both within and outside the Book of Mormon.

It seems peculiar that Mormon presents Christ as departing from Abinadi's approach to Isaiah. When a Book of Mormon prophet anticipating Christ reads Isaiah, he sees there many foreshadowings of and preparations for the Messiah still to come. But then the Messiah himself, having come within the Book of Mormon, apparently sees little of himself in Isaiah; he anticipates other events and foreshadowings of a different nature. With one set of eschatological expectations fully realized, Mormon's Christ outlines another.[1] This peculiar facet of Christ's interpretation of Isaiah within the Book of Mormon, moreover, suggests a literalism running against the grain of the broad history of Christian interpretation of Isaiah. Those features of Abinadi's approach that align him comfortably with the larger Christian tradition (despite certain essential peculiarities that distance him from it) disappear entirely when the Book of Mormon's Christ begins to interpret. In dispensing with Christological hermeneutics, Christ in Mormon's project moves from near the center of the hermeneutic tradition to the margins, where literalism about Israel's ultimate destiny becomes nearly obsessive. Already from the outset, thanks to the peculiarities of Abinadi's approach, Mormon's project suggests an attraction to the margins of the interpretive tradition. With Christ's arrival, however, Mormon leaves all pretense of centrism behind to occupy a permanent place on those margins. Thus, Mormon's project—the first major portion of the Book of Mormon manuscript dictated by Smith—seems to move its readers *deliberately* from the center to the fringe through its handling of Isaiah.

How the difference between Abinadi's and Christ's respective approaches to Isaiah would have struck our particularly informed and exemplarily charitable listener/reader in 1829–30 deserves emphasis. I have shown that Abinadi's Christological approach to Isaiah earlier in the Book of Mormon would have looked stubbornly quaint or even polemically traditional to such a person. Beyond that, Abinadi's interpretation exhibits other theological peculiarities that distance it from the mainstream—especially its commitment to the idea of a pre-Christian Christianity, a plain form of anticipatory Christian prophecy. This latter difference from the theological tradition would have been apparent to readers precisely because so much in Abinadi's exposition of Isaiah indicates deliberate interpretive conservativism—adherence to the greater Christian interpretive tradition despite developments in biblical hermeneutics after the Reformation. Abinadi's Isaian hermeneutic would thus have struck our ideal listener/reader as intentionally polemical because it was staking out a novel theological position *within* a well-known tradition. By contrast, the approach Mormon attributes directly to Jesus Christ would have looked to that ideal listener/reader as less informedly polemical than simply naïve, like something from the margins of Christian society—crass, literalistic, and millenarian.[2] Generally speaking, the Isaiah of Third Nephi would have struck such a reader as largely *outside* the tradition, smacking of the fanatical. In short, it would most likely have appeared as the product of enthusiastic speculation, a provincial notion uninformed by or unacquainted with the mainstream.

What would strike our especially reflective listener/reader is the peculiar fact that Abinadi *and* Christ appear within the same project attributed to

Mormon. There is enough cohesion between the two stories to make Third Nephi's flight to the margins appear as a continuation of, rather than a break with, the polemic already developed in the context of the Abinadi narrative. Although Third Nephi would, taken alone, appear nonpolemical and provincial, the same text, taken as part of the history begun by Abinadi's explorations of Isaiah, might have instead symbolized what Nathan Hatch calls "the right to think for oneself" among democratizing Christian movements: "*self-consciously provincial, fiercely independent, and culturally marginal*."[3] Our informed and charitable listener/reader in the early nineteenth century would have read Third Nephi as an intentionally provocative flight to the margins.[4]

These are points that need full exposition. It is thus necessary to ask how the approach to Isaiah in Third Nephi would have been situated in antebellum Christian America, as well as within the larger project of the Book of Mormon. Where and how does Christ's interpretation of Isaiah within the Book of Mormon differ from the mainstream in the Christian interpretive tradition—and in what ways does it still maintain its independence even among marginal interpretive approaches? Further, what does the placement of this interpretation of Isaiah within the Book of Mormon suggest about Christ's approach to the prophet? The present chapter will address these points in turn.

Apocalyptic Isaiah in the Mainstream

James Moorhead nicely sums up the general situation for apocalyptic expectation among mainstream American Protestants before the Civil War by alluding to Sherlock Holmes's "curious incident of the dog in the nighttime." "In mainstream Protestantism," he writes, "apocalypticism was the dog that did not bark."[5] Already by the end of the eighteenth century, mainline Protestant clergy were largely giving themselves to a postmillennial conception of salvation history—that is, one that looked to political and scientific developments as the key (but not sole) resource for moving toward the era of peace promised in Christian scripture. Thus, mainline Protestants were focused during this era on creating earthly institutions—colleges, temperance societies, missions, abolition lobbies—aimed at ameliorating the human condition and inviting heaven to come to an earth better prepared for it. By the time the Book of Mormon appeared in 1830, this view "dominated the popular denominational magazines as well as the weighty theological quarterlies; it commanded allegiance in leading seminaries and pulpits alike."[6] Consequently, as Stephen Stein says, "the widespread interest in apocalyptic in the United States has often reached its fullest and most radical expressions" primarily in "religious communities situated on the margins of American life."[7] The kind of sharp expectation fully on display in Third Nephi's sermons of Christ was thus unquestionably a marginal view when the Book of Mormon first began to circulate. It was not without traditional elements, to be sure. Stein elsewhere points out, for instance, that "it was a time-honored Christian view that the conversion of the Jews to Christianity would occur shortly before the end time," and "the Mormons accepted that traditional view" thanks in part to the way Christ in the Book of Mormon himself embraces and expounds that view.[8] But there is more of the nontraditional and the marginal than of the conventional and the mainstream in Third Nephi's approach to biblical prophecy.[9]

Of course, occasional bursts of widespread apocalypticism have punctuated Christian history. But Whitney Cross, establishing context for the emergence of Adventism in the 1840s (a decade after the publication of the Book of Mormon), points out that "no recent belief had specified so dramatic an [apocalyptic] event" as at that time, "nor had any sizable group of folk adopted such [apocalyptic] ideas so wholeheartedly since the early days of the Roman Empire."[10] Groups who explicitly claim that history fast approaches its final and definitive crisis have consistently found themselves occupying the fringes of the Christian world. The center and the margins of Christianity, in short, differ crucially in that the former is most consistently drawn to *abstract* belief in an overarching historical schema whose apocalyptic end lies in *the distant future*, while the latter is most consistently drawn to *concrete* insistence that the apocalyptic end of the traditional historical schema is *near*. And, therefore, early Latter-day Saints—who, as Grant Underwood has shown, officially emphasized Christ's Isaian discourses of Third Nephi over all else in the Book of Mormon[11]—found themselves very much on the margins of American Christianity.

This does not mean that every interpretation of Isaiah in Third Nephi would have been unrecognizable to the Christian mainstream in early nineteenth-century America—far from it. The centuries leading up to the Book of Mormon's appearance in fact witnessed a gradual increase in apocalyptic interpretation of certain Isaian prophecies among mainstream commentators. Apocalyptic interpretation of Isaiah is worth tracking carefully in order to see what it means to place the Book of Mormon's presentation of Jesus Christ's Isaiah on the margins in the nineteenth-century context.

Chapter 3 discussed how the mainstream Christian tradition has interpreted Isaiah 52:7–10. Beginning already with Saint Paul and stretching into the modern period, Christians have generally understood that text to refer to the preaching of Jesus's apostles and their evangelical heirs. In the ancient Christian context already, then, Justin Martyr could quote Isaiah 52:10 as describing the Christ event preached by the apostles,[12] Eusebius of Caesarea could predictably take Isaiah 52:8's reference to Zion to denote "the church established by Christ in every part of the world,"[13] and Jerome could insist that "the deserts of Jerusalem were refreshed" only when God "dwelled among us and became flesh."[14] At the other end of the historical spectrum, in the widely circulated English-language commentaries with which our ideal listener/reader would be especially familiar, there is a stronger historicist sense, but there is equal emphasis nonetheless on interpreting Isaiah as pointing to the Christian era. The Anglican divine William Lowth, for example, calls Isaiah 52:7 "a poetical description of the messengers who first brought the good news of Cyrus's decree for the people's return home" but adds that the text "is very fitly applied by St. Paul to the first preachers of the gospel."[15] Writing within the very lifetime of Joseph Smith, in fact, the Methodist Adam Clarke spoke of "the *literal* sense" of the text but concluded that "from the use made of [the passage] by our Lord, and the apostles, we may rest assured that the preachers of the gospel are particularly intended."[16] Clarke's comment is perhaps unsurprising in light of the importance of itinerant preaching in his tradition. Itinerant Methodist preacher Francis Asbury reported reflexively sermonizing on Isaiah 52:7, explaining its talk of "spreading" God's work through preaching, the feet of missionaries beautiful "because of their message; their holy walk; their treading the mountains, enduring hardship."[17]

Similar patterns of interpretation occur in connection with the rest of Isaiah 52:1–12. Jerome exemplifies the standard early Christian interpretation, directly contesting literal readings of Isaiah 52: "It is not as the Jews dream, that everything that is promised to Zion and Jerusalem is being said to its stones, ashes, and embers, that it will be restored to its pristine condition."[18] Rather, Jerome avers, the passage is exclusively about "the chorus of apostles and all the saints."[19] In the modern period, however, one sees a greater range of interpretations that result from the rising historicist sensibility. The Nonconformist Matthew Henry is representative of learned interpretations when he assigns each detail from Isaiah 52:1–6 to aspects of postexilic Jewish history and explains verses 11–12 in terms of the historical return from Babylonian exile.[20] More popular interpretations were generally less historicist in nature, as a Baptist missionary report from 1818 makes clear, calling Isaiah 52:8–10 "the rapture of Isaiah" when looking to much later Christian missionary successes.[21] Only one of the most widely circulated and well-respected commentaries so much as hints at an eschatological interpretation akin to that of Third Nephi: the Anglican Thomas Scott's commentary, particularly popular in antebellum America.[22]

Scott's commentary shows that the general sort of interpretation of Isaiah 52 offered in 3 Nephi 20–21 finds traces—on rare occasions and with a bit of special pleading—within the mainstream of traditional Christian interpretation, perhaps a reflection of Scott's traditionalism. Even then, however, crucial differences separate Scott's understanding of Isaiah 52 from that of Mormon's Christ. Scott interprets verses 1–3 as intending "the New Testament church . . . , and probably with especial reference to its last and purest ages"—at or even after "the restoration of the Jews, and the bringing in of the fulness of the Gentiles."[23] By contrast, Christ in Third Nephi interprets these verses as applying directly to Jews and (presumably) directly to the literal city of Jerusalem, which is to be restored (3 Nephi 20:36). Both Scott and Mormon's Christ understand verse 6 to speak of Jewish restoration, but then they differ drastically over the meaning of verse 7. For Scott, the exclamation about beautiful feet on the mountains straightforwardly finds fulfillment in "the preaching of the gospel to the nations of the earth."[24] For Mormon's Christ, however, the words of verse 7 are shouted by Jews in celebration of God's faithfulness as Jerusalem is built anew and prepared for their return (3 Nephi 20:40). Finally, verses 11–12 point toward Jewish restoration for both Scott and the Christ of the Book of Mormon, but the latter is far more explicit on this point. Scott only vaguely notes that "greater things are evidently prefigured" in Isaiah's words,[25] while Mormon's Christ makes clear that verses 11–12 describe "a cry" issued to Jews who prepare to leave for the restored Jerusalem (3 Nephi 20:41). Thus, even where someone in the mainstream approaches the sort of eschatological interpretation of Isaiah 52 offered in Third Nephi, the details differ in significant ways.

Do things change at all if one turns one's attention from Isaiah 52 to Isaiah 54, since Christ in the Book of Mormon quotes the whole of the latter chapter, stating that it will "come to pass" (3 Nephi 22:1) at the time that Jews and the lost tribes of Israel are "gathered home to the land of their inheritance" (21:28)? Our ideal listener/reader might well ask how the mainstream tradition understands Isaiah 54 and whether Mormon's Christ occupies a similarly marginal position on that text.

The history of mainstream Christian interpretation of Isaiah 54 has been deeply influenced by the apostle Paul's use of it in Galatians 4 (in the context of a mystifying allegory about gentile Christians).[26] Under that influence, the tradition has generally understood Isaiah 54 as being about the gentile church, figured as a heavenly Jerusalem. It is used this way already though in somewhat vague fashion in the second century in the Apostolic Fathers,[27] in the apocryphal "Epistle of the Apostles,"[28] in Justin Martyr's "First Apology,"[29] and in Irenaeus's *Against Heresies*.[30] By the third and fourth centuries, this reading was fully established and had taken a strongly supersessionist turn.[31] By the early fifth century, when the lineaments of Christian orthodoxy took definitive shape, the kind of interpretation embraced directly by Jesus Christ in the Book of Mormon had been relegated to the margins—the approach of Jews and Judaizers reducible to "a frivolous quarrel of the Hebrews."[32]

Leaping once more to the centuries immediately prior to the appearance of the Book of Mormon (and the activities of our ideal listener/reader), one finds recognizable patterns. Learned commentators from the seventeenth through the nineteenth century exhibit a stronger historicist sense for the Isaiah text, recognizing that it has, in Matthew Henry's words, "a primary reference to the welfare and prosperity of the Jewish church after their return out of Babylon."[33] At the same time, they all cite Galatians 4 and so express the need to argue that Isaiah 54 "has a further and principal reference to the gospel-church, into which the Gentiles were to be admitted."[34] Popular interpretations from the time confirm the picture.[35] Despite these convictions, one notes occasional nods to an eschatological interpretation of the chapter. William Lowth, for instance, assigns the meaning of the chapter to "the increase and glory of the church which should follow upon [Christ's] sufferings,"[36] while the Methodist Adam Clarke—writing during Joseph Smith's own childhood—sees Isaiah 54's "most obvious import" as referring "to the future conversion of the Jews, and to the increase and prosperity of that nation, when reconciled to God after their long rejection."[37] Clarke echoes certain popular interpretations as well, such as that reflected by a Baptist missionary writing in 1810 about witnessing the conversion of a handful of Jews to Christianity. "I have no other words to express either the feelings of my heart or the sentiments of my mind but in those of the prophet," he writes, quoting Isaiah 54:1–3.[38]

There is thus some evidence that the interpretation of Isaiah 54 that Christian authorities of the fourth and fifth centuries had polemically relegated to the margins as Jewish or Judaizing was newly on the rise among Christian authorities in the modern period. Of course, this fresh interest in a half-literal, half-eschatological interpretation of Isaiah 54 was, even then, only presented in general terms, without sharp textual specificity. It was elsewhere in Isaiah that modern (but precritical) commentators found clearer eschatological predictions of Jewish restoration—especially in Isaiah 11. William Lowth saw that chapter, from verse 10 onward, as foretelling the restoration of the Jews "to their own country from the several dispersions where they are scattered"[39]—a reading echoed by Adam Clarke and Thomas Scott.[40] Thanks to these tendencies among certain English-speaking early modern commentators—and especially among those most popular in eighteenth- and nineteenth-century America—those who approached the apocalyptic fringes of nineteenth-century American Christianity could appeal to centrist authorities to shore up apocalyptic and eschatological interpretations of Isaiah 11.[41] Those who insisted on detailed apocalyptic expositions of texts like Isaiah 54 remained, however, at the interpretive margins.

This point must be understood carefully. What was unique in the Book of Mormon at the time of its publication was not—for the most part—its basic outline of eschatological or apocalyptic history. That outline it shared in general terms with the rest of Christianity. Rather, two developments distanced the Book of Mormon from the mainstream. First, Mormon's Christ insists that the eschaton was *near* at the time of the Book of Mormon's publication, which moved the book's adherents from the center to the margins of Christianity. Second and more specifically, the Book of Mormon finds traces of this eschatological picture and its nearness in texts like Isaiah 52 and Isaiah 54. The position was more marginal than mainstream, despite then-recent developments in that direction in commentaries by Lowth, Clarke, and others. The Book of Mormon's Christ would thus have spoken far more readily to the fringes of American Christianity when the volume first appeared than to the mainstream interpretive tradition. It should thus prove instructive to leave behind the mainstream interpreters of texts like Isaiah 52 and Isaiah 54 to look directly at those interpreting them (and other Isaiah texts) from the Christian fringe in the early nineteenth century. How does Third Nephi and its Christ look when set side by side with figures writing and speaking at the margins of the interpretive tradition?

Apocalyptic Isaiah at the Margins

It is difficult, naturally, to develop a comprehensive picture of marginal interpretation of Isaiah in American Christianity in the early nineteenth century. Frankly, one would have to speak at length with a flesh-and-blood version of our ideal listener/reader to develop such a picture. The world of print privileges the centrist perspectives of the learned, and scholarship has tended to focus on the mainstream rather than on fringe movements and developments. Further, it is difficult to know, from today's perspective, exactly what constitutes marginality. When the Dartmouth-trained Congregationalist clergyman Ethan Smith produced in 1823 a scholarly defense of an entirely nonstandard interpretation of Isaiah 18, weaving it into a controversial (but not exactly marginal) theory about the Israelite identity of Native Americans, did he produce something at the center or at the margins of antebellum American Christianity?[42] Smith in many ways reproduced (without citing it) the slightly earlier interpretation of Isaiah 18 published in 1814 by John McDonald, a respected Presbyterian minister in Albany, New York.[43] Is McDonald's treatment of Isaiah 18—which in no way attempts to link Native Americans to Israel but certainly differs from most commentaries at the time—marginal, despite his obvious erudition and attempt to speak within the mainstream? And then, for his part, McDonald draws on the interpretation of Isaiah 18 from Samuel Horsley and George Stanley Faber—the former a Cambridge-trained and the latter an Oxford-trained clergyman, both respected figures in theology in (respectively) the late eighteenth and early nineteenth centuries.[44] Are these unmistakably centrist figures, because of their somewhat unconventional views on this or that chapter of Isaiah, to be relegated to the margins of the tradition? At least one mainstream nineteenth-century commentary—that of Thomas Scott—saw it needful to acknowledge Horsley and Faber in addressing the meaning of Isaiah 18, acknowledging the "entirely new" character of their interpretation and claiming to be "by no means satisfied" with it.[45] While it is relatively clear where the center of the tradition is at any given point, it is difficult to know exactly how far one can move from it before arriving at the margins.

What makes interpreters like Ethan Smith more centrist than marginal is a largely untroubled relationship with establishment branches of Protestantism—Anglicanism (or Episcopalianism), Presbyterianism, and Congregationalism. Nonstandard interpretations of Isaiah from within the established churches are more unconventional than marginal. Rather than attempts to speak from the fringe, they represent new interpretive suggestions that simply did not succeed in the marketplace of ideas. They aimed to revise mildly, rather than contest outright, the American Christian establishment. Hence, to move more strictly to the margins, where our ideal listener/reader would likely have located the interpretations of Mormon's Christ, it is necessary to look to those who existed entirely outside the boundaries of establishment Christianity. That there was no shortage of such individuals and religious groups was due to the growing "impotence of Congregational, Presbyterian, and Episcopalian churches" in the early nineteenth century.[46] A weakening of the center allowed for proliferation on the margins, which in turn allowed the margins to become wider and eventually graded. That is, between the American Revolution and the Civil War, a range of noncentrist options emerged at various distances from the long-established center. Unquestionably contesting the religious traditions at the center, but nonetheless without moving terribly far from the center, were flourishing sects such as Baptists, Methodists, and Disciples. All these remained, at least as regards biblical interpretation, largely close to the mainstream interpretive tradition.[47] But beyond the sectarians, more obviously occupying the extreme margins, were groups like the Latter-day Saints.[48] Thus, while Baptists largely spent the first decades of the nineteenth century clamoring for acceptance from the establishment,[49] and a Methodist like Adam Clarke could in the same years write an influential commentary on Isaiah largely by reproducing an Anglican bishop's notes for his readers, Latter-day Saints looked to the Book of Mormon's drastically nonmainstream interpretations and uses of Isaiah as normative.[50] What kind of comparative data might be used, then, to situate the meaning of Mormon's Christ in the antebellum context?

Some have suggested that early Latter-day Saints are best approached alongside the Millerites, millenarian Christians who rallied in anticipation of a calculated date for Christ's second coming (in 1843–44). Mark Noll groups together "Millerites and Mormons" as definitive and illustrative "outsiders" in his history of North American Christianity,[51] and Grant Underwood dramatically presents the two movements as "apocalyptic adversaries" in a classic treatment.[52] It is an apt pairing (one that would certainly have occurred to our ideal reader a few years after the publication of the Book of Mormon). William Miller worked out his unique interpretation of biblical prophecy between 1818 and 1823, while Joseph Smith received his first vision in 1820; Miller began lecturing and writing in 1833–34, just a few years after Smith published the Book of Mormon and organized his Church of Christ in 1830; Miller first published his *Evidences from Scripture and History of the Second Coming of Christ* in 1836, the year Smith dedicated his first temple and the year after Smith published his *Doctrine and Covenants* for the first time; and Miller's movement nearly disbanded after the Great Disappointment of 1844, more or less at the very moment Smith was killed by an angry mob in Illinois. As this comparison demonstrates, the proto-Adventist William Miller and the Latter-day Saint prophet Joseph Smith were, as far as their *religious* careers went, strict contemporaries,[53] and Millerites and Latter-day Saints certainly found themselves together on the fringe of American Christianity.[54] At the same time, Noll points out that even these two groups were not equidistant from the center of the Christian establishment. "If the Millerites lived on the border between evangelical Protestant insiders and sectarian Protestant outsiders, the Mormons under Joseph Smith went even further toward the outside."[55] The Millerites nonetheless provide a helpful data point in establishing the basic status of Isaiah on the fringes of American Christianity in the antebellum period. Especially useful here is Miller's *Evidence from Scripture and History*.

The aim of the lectures that became *Evidence from Scripture and History* was to outline a biblical hermeneutic that would specify the date of Jesus Christ's promised second coming, and it was this specificity that would eventually attract wide interest and a following. William Miller had developed his interpretation of biblical prophecy in the decade after the War of 1812—a period of rabid optimism, rooted in "material improvements, political democratization, and moral reform," which "all provided encouraging signs that history was moving in the right direction."[56] Miller's biblical hermeneutic contrasted in being rooted in a kind of pessimism.[57] As Ruth Alden Doan puts it, "Miller quickly concluded" from his own observations that a straightforward interpretation of the Bible did not support the idea that the Jews would return to Israel before the coming of Christ, or that "the millennium might be expected before the end of the existing world."[58] Although such pessimism was out of step in the 1820s while Miller was working out his ideas, it would fit the mood of the country after his lectures' 1836 publication: the panic of 1837 and the consequent economic depression may have prompted Americans to doubt popular narratives of progress.[59] The lectures focus primarily on interpreting passages from the Books of Daniel and Revelation, seen through the lens of the "rapture" passage of Paul's first letter to the Thessalonians. As Miller makes clear in his introduction, however, his view of biblical prophecy had a wider scope than just the emphatically apocalyptic books of the Bible. "God in his wisdom has so interwoven the several prophecies," Miller explains, "that the events foretold are not all told by one prophet, and although they lived and prophesied in different ages of the world, yet they tell us the same things." Consequently, he continues, "a Bible reader may almost with propriety suppose, let him read in what prophecy he may, that he is reading the same prophet, the same author."[60] Alongside Daniel and John the Revelator, then, Miller gives frequent attention to Isaiah, whom he names in a short list of particularly important prophetic figures in his introduction.[61]

Of course, frequency of reference does not make Isaiah central to *Evidence from Scripture and History*.[62] Isaiah's role in the project is a supporting one, but it is nonetheless revealing. First, the Book of Isaiah is for Miller what it had already long been for the Christian tradition: the fifth gospel, a collection of prophecies anticipating the *first* (rather than the *second*) advent of Christ. Thus, already in the introduction to the lectures, Miller gathers a few scraps from Isaiah (as well as from other Old Testament books) to demonstrate that Christ's "first coming was literally according to the prophecies" (which allows Miller to "safely infer" that Christ's "second appearance" will also be "according to the Scriptures").[63] Similarly, in the very last lecture in the collection, he uses these and other Isaiah passages in a list of twenty-one "signs which the Jews had . . . as evidences of Jesus being the true Messiah."[64] Thus, Miller definitely understood Isaiah first as one who foresaw Christianity's beginnings. But of course he uses Isaiah in other ways in the lectures, more obviously in concert with his innovative interpretations of Daniel and Revelation. He thus takes a handful of Isaian texts to be straightforward predictions of events surrounding the *second* coming of Christ. All of them, it is interesting to note, derive from Isaiah 40–66.[65] Miller takes passages scattered across Second and Third Isaiah to describe relatively traditional aspects of Christ's second coming: glory revealed (Isaiah 60:18), the burning of the wicked (Isaiah 66:15–16), and the marriage of God to his people (Isaiah 54:5).[66]

More interesting is Miller's treatment of two passages from Isaiah (Isaiah 35:1–2; Isaiah 49:22–23) that he treats as connected to the theme of the church in the wilderness, a famous image from Revelation 12. This image played an important role in the early development of Latter-day Saint theology, even if it does not make an obvious appearance in the Book of Mormon,[67] and the two Isaian passages Miller connects to the image play significant roles either within the Book of Mormon itself (Isaiah 49:22–23) or in close connection to the early reception of the Book of Mormon (Isaiah 35:1–2).[68] The latter passage, with its talk of the desert blossoming as the rose and its inhabitants witnessing the glory of the Lord, Miller takes to describe Isaiah's own "vision of the church in the wilderness," of those "true servants of God" who "fled into the north-east part of Europe," hoping to escape the influence of Roman Catholicism in the sixth or seventh century after Christ.[69] According to Miller, Isaiah thus helps to clarify God's intentions in allowing the church to be driven into the wilderness. But further, Isaiah also describes the emergence of the church from the wilderness, a time when the church "enjoys possessions, privileges, and laws among the kingdoms and political nations of the earth."

Isaiah speaks in chapter 49 of kings and queens attending to God's people, bowing to them and licking the dust from their feet. Miller interprets thus: "That is, the church, when in this situation, receives the courtly smiles of the great, and the sycophantic cringing of the political demagogue. But let the church remember, although kings, queens, and great men of the world may bow down, court, and idolize her, and may descend to lick the dust from her feet, yet it is only to flatter and to betray; for their '*faces*' are not Zion-ward, but to the '*earth*'."[70] In these passages, Miller finds significant points on the general outline of history leading up to the second coming of Christ.

What Isaiah does *most* often according to Miller's lectures, however, is something other than offer prophetic predictions. Although Miller sees in Isaiah prophecies of Christ's two comings—sometimes the one, sometimes the other—what most interests him is how Isaiah's imagery and language help to confirm his esoteric interpretative style more generally. Hoping to show that the word *blessed* used in Revelation 20:6 often points to the resurrection, for example, Miller calls on passages in Isaiah where such a connection is "either expressed or implied": Isaiah 62:11–12 and Isaiah 30:18.[71] To prove that the word *sanctuary* in Daniel 8:13–14 refers to the Jewish temple, he cites Isaiah 63:18 alongside other biblical texts.[72] Isaiah 28:17 and Isaiah 30:30 help Miller show that the talk of hail in Revelation 16:21 is unlikely to be merely metaphorical.[73] Perhaps most important for Miller's purposes, passages in Isaiah 22:10 and Isaiah 65:12 (along with Daniel 5:25–26 and, later, other biblical texts) help him decide what to "understand by numbering anything . . . in Scripture."[74] This is especially important, since so much of Miller's purposes are taken up with the task of showing how to calculate the date of Christ's second coming as exactly as possible.[75]

Ultimately, then, much more than serving to predict Christ's first or second comings, Isaiah functions as a resource Miller uses to confirm and clarify the nature of biblical prophecy. This allows Miller to develop his confidence and that of his reader that his interpretations of passages in Daniel and Revelation are correct. Miller's Isaiah thus plays a secondary role to apocalyptic prophecy. The interpretation of Isaiah is—despite Miller's occasionally unorthodox readings—assumed to be straightforward and relatively obvious rather than controversial, and Isaiah can thus be called as a reliable witness to decide thorny issues in the more obviously controversial prophecies of Daniel and Revelation. In this regard, Miller's uses of Isaiah in *Evidence from Scripture and History* differ drastically from those in the Book of Mormon, where Isaiah is an object of clear controversy and the direct focus of interpretation. Further, for Miller, by contrast with the Christ of Third Nephi, Isaiah's prophecies have nothing to do with the eschatological gathering of Israel.[76] At the same time, nevertheless, the uses of Isaiah by Mormon's Christ in Third Nephi very much find a place on the margins of nineteenth-century American Christianity alongside Miller's lectures. Certainly, Miller shares with Mormon's Christ the enthusiastic conviction that Isaiah deals with events set to occur soon in the nineteenth century, even if Miller sees rather different events beginning at that point in time.

These same margins might be further illuminated by reviewing briefly another example of Isaian interpretation after the Second Great Awakening: the "Shaker Bible" of 1843. Unlike William Miller's followers, the Shakers had difficulty commanding a widespread following—in part because of their belief in strict celibacy—and so occupied a place further still into the margins of American Christianity. Further, where Miller's *Evidence from Scripture and History* was a series of informative lectures, the Shaker Bible was presented as a revelation from God (specifically a series of revelations to New York Shaker Philemon Stewart), thus looking much more akin to the Book of Mormon than Miller's work. Confirming the relevance of this volume to understanding the Book of Mormon, David Holland couples the two books in his study of canonical restraint in the antebellum period,[77] and other historians have examined the socioreligious proximity of the two religious traditions.[78] And still more important is the fact that Isaiah is central to the Shaker scripture, although the latter has no genetic relationship with the Book of Mormon.[79] For these reasons alone, the Shaker Bible, properly titled *A Holy, Sacred and Divine Roll and Book*, should also provide a helpful point of comparison for making sense of how Isaiah was read or understood far outside the mainstream Christian tradition at the time of the Book of Mormon's appearance. What would happen were our ideal listener/reader to pick up *Sacred and Divine Roll* a few years after reflecting closely on the Book of Mormon?

Occasional lists of biblical texts that allegedly confirm the sacred history embraced by the Shakers punctuate the more than two hundred published pages of *Sacred and Divine Roll*—texts interpreted as referring to Christ's first coming, the life he enjoins people to live, the rise of the antichrist, Christ's second coming, Christ's coming a second time as a woman, the general resurrection, the peaceable kingdom at the eschaton, and the stirring of the Shakers themselves to action and religion making. Some of these lists include texts from Isaiah, but *Sacred and Divine Roll* provides little commentary on the quoted texts, apparently largely satisfied to allow them to speak for themselves, in this way approaching the hermeneutic uses of William Miller in *Evidence from Scripture and History*. The distribution of quoted Isaiah texts within *Sacred and Divine Roll* is instructive, in some ways again approximating Miller's uses of Isaiah. Two passages (Isaiah 7:14 and Isaiah 53:1–3),[80] both traditionally interpreted, predict the first coming of Christ, but no Isaiah passages are cited as predicting the second coming of Christ—either in a straightforward Christian formulation or in uniquely Shaker terms (that is, with Christ returning as a woman). By contrast, though, a dramatically long list of passages from Isaiah appears in the list of scriptures "relative to the peaceable kingdom of Christ."[81] Similarly, another substantial set of passages from Isaiah (although not as long as the one just mentioned) is interpreted as "referring to the present work of inspiration in Zion"—that is, to the Shaker awakening.[82] Here, as with Christ in Third Nephi and as with Miller in *Evidence from Scripture and History*, the meaning of Isaiah is understood to focus in crucial ways on events in the last days, especially those beginning in the middle (or so) of the nineteenth century: a fresh, latter-day intervention on God's part in history, with the promise of ancient prophecies fulfilled at long last. But, where Christ in Third Nephi focuses the interpretation of Isaiah on a fresh gathering of literal Israel through the instrumentality of the gentiles, and where William Miller uses Isaiah to specify events surrounding the second advent of Christ at a specifiable date, *Sacred and Divine Roll* focuses on Shaker revivalism and on the Shakers' responsibilities in Zion and throughout the world. As does Miller, *Sacred and Divine Roll* consistently presents Jews as superseded by the Christian gospel and never speaks of a restoration of Israel or a gathering of the scattered covenant people.

The lists of Isaiah passages appearing in *Sacred and Divine Roll* are of less interest, however, than the final part of the volume, "A Prophecy from the Spirit of the Ancient Prophet Isaiah," which is "communicated through his [Isaiah's] archers, in six parts."[83] These Isaian archers, whose identity or significance *Sacred and Divine Roll* never fully clarifies,[84] sound "the watch," warning of coming judgment. Four speak the prophet's word but two must "withhold, and speak not, until the time shall be fulfilled."[85] The last two archers' words appear in the published text as well, however. In all these complex and fascinating communications, *Sacred and Divine Roll* affirms the relevance of Isaiah to the modern world not solely through an interpretive approach to the prophet's biblical book, as earlier in the text, but more audaciously through a *new* Isaian word, communicated—however strangely—through his archers. Still more striking, between the words of the fourth and fifth archers, new "words of the prophet Isaiah" himself appear, words apparently unmediated by the prophet's archers.

The task of Isaiah's archers becomes clear as one reads. Each weaves recognizable biblical language into general exhortation to produce warnings that are then addressed to the "watchmen" placed to protect the Shakers' Zion. The responsibility of the watchmen is stated clearly: "Hath not man, by his own disobedience, made this a world of sorrow?" asks the second archer in an exemplary passage. "And shall he cease to watch where his own safety is engaged, and his life at stake? Nay, but let him watch and pray without ceasing, and the ransom of his own soul shall be full compensation."[86] As for the biblical passages borrowed from and alluded to by the archers, they derive from both the Old and New Testaments—occasionally, but only occasionally, deriving directly from the Book of Isaiah.[87] This makes clear that the archers' words are Isaian not in that they draw on the known Book of Isaiah (although they occasionally do that), but rather in that the actual person of Isaiah commands them to speak. But this very aspect of the text makes it all the more striking that the archers' words are eventually interrupted with two pages of the "words of the prophet Isaiah" himself, unmediated by the archers. And it is fascinating that, when Isaiah speaks in his own voice, he begins by effectively apologizing for the "strange and singular" manner in which his message has been delivered.[88] Nevertheless, Isaiah explains, "archers are used, when sent of God for that purpose, to draw the bow, and let swiftly fly the arrows of destruction."[89] Because understanding requires time and effort, an intervening angelic voice recommends patience, "as the different states of Zion therein represented may be some hundreds of years apart."[90]

The Shaker community published *Holy, Sacred and Divine Roll and Book* in 1843, appending to it a whole volume of testimonies about its divinity. Many of these testimonies appear under the names of leading members of the Shaker community. Others, however, although received through various members of the community (who employ the epithet "Inspired Writer"), are actually attributed to biblical prophets, patriarchs, and apostles (as well as to various angels). It is significant that among those offering testimonies in this fashion is "the holy prophet Isaiah" himself, in a communication "copied by inspiration at Enfield, New Hampshire, August 11, 1843."[91] The testimony concludes with an explanation of why the long-dead Isaiah would bother to write anew in a modern context: "As a friend to the lost children of men, and in love to the Father of light, have I written at this time; that it may be known that we, the Prophets, foresaw this very work, long ere this time; and now we do make it manifest to those who dwell on the earth, and in a way of God's own choosing."[92] Although Isaiah's testimony on the Shaker scripture technically falls outside the bounds of *Sacred and Divine Roll* itself, it confirms the basic role he plays within the volume. Isaiah has a message directly relevant to antebellum Christianity, one that he delivers by stepping out of the pages of his biblical book. Isaiah *returns*, so to speak, in (and around) *Sacred and Divine Roll*, offering a *new* Isaian word.[93]

Isaiah's place in *Sacred and Divine Roll* largely confirms the general sketch already presented of Isaian interpretation on the margins of American Christianity in the first decades of the nineteenth century. Some of Isaiah's prophecies are traditionally understood to refer to the events of Christ's birth, life, and death. Others—against the grain of mainstream interpretation—are taken to focus in specifiable ways on events set to occur in the nineteenth century. In other ways, *Sacred and Divine Roll* takes this last application further than other movements relegated to the margins, in that Isaiah himself is willing to speak from among the dead with a new prophetic word addressed directly to the Shaker community. While for William Miller the Bible remains a closed book that requires interpretation to show its continuing relevance, *Sacred and Divine Roll* reopens the Bible by giving the actual person of Isaiah a chance to add entirely new prophetic words to the canon. Isaiah himself, and not only the book he once wrote, continues to speak.

Somewhere between the quasi-respectability of the Millerite Isaiah and the definitively heterodox Isaiah of the Shakers is the Isaiah presented by the Book of Mormon's Christ. It might arguably have found little sympathy from anyone positioned comfortably within establishment American Christianity early in the nineteenth century. At the same time, it is important to underscore that the presentation of Isaiah in Third Nephi is in no way irrational, even if it was unconventional. Steven Harper has shown not only that the Book of Mormon's earliest converts approached the religion in strikingly rational fashion but also that "many early converts contrasted the rationalism of the Book of Mormon to the revivalism of the day, in which they found little thought-provoking theology"—something other students of the Latter-day Saint tradition have pointed out as well.[94] As Thomas O'Dea tellingly puts it, "the *Book of Mormon* is millennial, but it is calm in its hopes, and neither it nor the movement to which it gave rise ever suggested anything like Millerite enthusiasm. Yet it has held that in the last days the Jews will be gathered, as will their descendants on the new continents, the American Indians."[95] When the reader of Mormon's project comes to Third Nephi, she encounters something definitively outside the mainstream in its hermeneutic moves and its concrete expectations. But she comes also to something that presents its case in rational terms and through sustained interpretive argument. Christ's Isaiah in Third Nephi would have been for our always present ideal listener/

reader something like—to use an Isaian image—a voice crying in the wilderness, but in relatively calm and rational tones.

The rational appeal of Third Nephi's treatment of Isaiah is, moreover, profoundly confirmed by the fact that Mormon presents Third Nephi as being in conversation with Abinadi's more obviously mainstream and nonfanatical treatment of Isaiah before Noah's priests. The continuity between Third Nephi and Mosiah, again, implicitly insists that even the more marginal—or marginalized—theological interpretations offered in the volume deserve a hearing from those situated within established Christianity. Abinadi, as it were, anchors Mormon's Christ in the interpretive tradition so that its polemical and hermeneutical force might really be felt, rather than simply dismissed with a wave of the hand. It thus seems best to conclude these particular considerations by reflecting on how Mormon places Abinadi and Christ in a kind of conversation, and on what that means for Isaiah in the Book of Mormon.

Christ and Abinadi

Before concluding both this chapter and the larger study of Mormon's treatment of Isaiah that makes up part 1 of the present study, two things deserve attention. First, drawing on this chapter and the preceding, it is worth laying out in detail some specific points of contrast between Abinadi and Christ within Mormon's project. Second, drawing on such a summation of things, it seems proper to outline a set of conclusions about the role played by Isaiah within the portion of the Book of Mormon attributed to Mormon himself, the long historical account that Joseph Smith dictated to his scribes first.

What most obviously distinguishes Christ's uses of Isaiah in the Book of Mormon from Abinadi's concerns salvation history. Despite the fact that both figures address the same Isaian passage, they associate it with strikingly different visions of sacred history. For Abinadi, the whole of salvation history turns on the Christ event. Everything before that event—even key moments in Israel's sacred history[96]—looks forward to it, and everything after that event, including the final judgment, looks back to it. For the Christ of Third Nephi, on the other hand, salvation history focuses first and foremost on covenants anciently granted to Israel. Isaiah 52:7–10 makes the contrast clear: for Abinadi, it is a strictly Christological text, a prophetic exploration of Christian preaching before and after the advent of Jesus Christ. For the Book of Mormon's Christ, the same passage is a covenantal text, a prophetic explanation of what things look like when God finally restores Israel to its promised lands through the assistance of the gentiles. Even the basic context within which each figure quotes the passage makes clear their drastically different presuppositions about the meaning or applicability of Isaian prophecy. Abinadi looks forward to a time when "the Lord shall bring again Zion" (Mosiah 15:29) by having "every nation, kindred, tongue, and people" finally "see eye to eye" and "confess before God that his judgments are just" (16:1). Mormon's Christ predicts instead a time when "the Father" will "gather [Jews] together again and give unto them Jerusalem for the land of their inheritance" (3 Nephi 20:33).

This first difference between Christ and Abinadi is a stark one, theologically.[97] Somewhat less apparent but equally important is the difference between the Christological assumptions of each figure and what that difference means for the immediate *presentation* of Isaiah's words (if not for their actual *interpretation*). Both Abinadi and Christ work out relatively full Christological pictures, but they differ in substantial ways. For Abinadi and those following after him in the Book of Mormon's pre-Christian story, the focus of Christology is the paradoxical nature of God in the flesh—at once spirit and flesh, father and son, sovereign and subject. This theological conception predominates in the Book of Mormon right up until the beginning of Third Nephi, where the barely premortal Christ speaks to a prophet and confirms the Abinadite theology in a crucial way (3 Nephi 1:14). But, as I have shown in the course of the present discussion, Christ's own Christology in Third Nephi concerns less the nature of God enfleshed than the nature of God risen from the dead. At issue in Christ's sermons is a relationship of mutual indwelling between two distinct persons, the Father and the Son, who bear witness to each other in different ways. This difference between Christologies matters because each provides a lens through which to understand Hebrew scripture. Abinadi situates the meaning of Isaiah 52:7–10, along with Isaiah 53, within his Christological picture. When Isaiah speaks of generation, he refers to the paradoxical duality of Christ. When he speaks of good news and its announcement, he describes the promulgation of the message of Christ's duality and what it makes possible. When he discusses seed, he points to those who rise from the dead through their belief in the dual Christ.[98] Mormon's Christ, on the other hand, situates the meaning of Isaiah 52:7–10 within his own, distinct Christological picture, strikingly Johannine in orientation. Despite the fact that John is regarded as the New Testament Gospel least interested in historical Israel,[99] the Christ of Third Nephi unites a basically Johannine conception of God and Christ to an entirely non-Johannine interest in Isaiah.

The differences between Abinadi and Christ within Mormon's project are real. And yet it is necessary to speak at the same time of continuity—continuity that serves primarily to make real differences more apparent. Certainly, there is continuity in that Abinadi and Christ give their attention to Isaiah starting from the very same passage from Isaiah 52. After three hundred pages of silence on the Hebrew prophet in the Book of Mormon, our ideal listener/reader can only be startled to hear Christ turn his attention to the prophet by taking up afresh exactly the same passage that lies at the heart of the Abinadi narrative. There is also continuity in that Abinadi and Christ both focus their interpretations of Isaiah on questions of salvation history and both refract their presentations of Isaiah through a Christological prism, even if they reach different conclusions. The general strategy for reading Isaiah remains constant within Mormon's larger project, even if the specifics about salvation history or Christology change drastically.

Why should both continuity and stark difference join and separate Abinadi and Christ across a gulf of three hundred pages and nearly two hundred years? Why should Jesus Christ himself make an appearance within the Book of Mormon and offer a reflection on Isaiah that questions not only the interpretive assumptions of a certain wicked priestly tradition within the narrative, but also that of a righteous prophetic tradition? What might our ideal listener/reader—thoughtful and charitable, yet deeply informed about the history of Isaian interpretation—conclude about Mormon's project after finishing Third Nephi?

Because of the privilege readers would be expected to grant to Jesus Christ over any priest or even prophet, it seems obvious that the Isaian interpretations of Third Nephi are those Mormon implicitly recommends.[100] Does it not, though, seem wrong to assume that Christ's interpretations simply trump those of Abinadi, as if the prophet were misguided? It seems crucial that, just a few chapters before he comes in person to speak about Isaiah, the barely premortal Christ speaks in a strictly Abinadite style (see, once again, 3 Nephi 1:14). Perhaps, then, Christ does not contest Abinadi's theology and hermeneutics so much as he sublates them, incorporating a narrower salvation history and a temporary Christological picture into a broader salvation history and the accompanying Christology of perfect messianic fulfillment. Yet what definitely keeps Abinadi's and Christ's theological perspectives at some distance is the fact that they root their noncoinciding theological perspectives in unquestionably distinct interpretations of the very same (and relatively short) passage from the Book of Isaiah. Even if Abinadi and Christ could be reconciled or harmonized—Abinadi's attraction to the fringe and Christ's settlement on the fringe—still it would be necessary to confront the fact that each pole of Mormon's literary project offers an irreducibly distinct interpretation of Isaiah 52:7–10. However close Abinadi's and Christ's respective teachings might be to each other, Isaiah 52:7–10 names the point of their unmistakable noncoincidence and irreconcilability.

It is therefore the interpretation of Isaiah that forces the reader to feel as if something substantial has changed over the course of Mormon's project. And it is not only *differences* between interpretations of Isaiah that suggest substantial change. It is also the sheer fact *that* Third Nephi marks a return to interpreting Isaiah *at all*. Whatever Abinadi's actual readings of particular Isaiah texts might say, it seems best to conclude that the overall effect of Abinadi's Isaian intervention is *deflationary*, as I argued at the end of chapter 3. Third Nephi presents Jesus Christ himself as effectively *reflationary* about Isaiah, since Mormon's Christ reverses the effect of Abinadi's interpretation by revitalizing Isaiah's relevance. And wherever Christ's interpretive approach to specific Isaiah passages differs substantially from Abinadi's, Isaiah's meaning is taken to outstrip the standard Nephite theological point of view. For Christ in Third Nephi, the message of Isaiah cannot be reduced to tracing the contours of a pre-Christian community of anticipation. Instead, Isaiah's words point to something in the distant future, events far beyond the centuries leading up to or immediately after the advent of Jesus Christ. For Mormon's Christ, Isaiah deserves attention precisely to the extent that he speaks of an eschatology to be realized long after the realized eschatology of the Gospel of John.

Our ideal listener from 1829, working through Mormon's project without awareness yet of the record of Nephi to be considered in part 2, would thus most likely have concluded that Mormon's endgame was to outline an epoch-changing transition from Abinadi's pre-Christian interpretation of Isaiah, deflationary in nature, to Christ's covenantal interpretation of Isaiah, which is then reflationary. Christ's reinvestment in Isaian prophecy marks a major reversal, along with a novel interpretive program. Priestly *and* prophetic commentaries are left behind as a fully divine interpretation comes to center stage. With the spotlight focused intensely on Isaiah again, Mormon brings his project to a climax by having Jesus Christ outline in his own voice an Isaian hermeneutic that would have appeared distant from the mainstream at the time of the Book of Mormon's publication. Mormon's project, through its uses of Isaiah, goes somewhere definite, however slowly it gets there. Mormon essentially asks the reader to move, one step at a time, from the long-established tradition to embrace the interpretive (and existential) possibilities that remain alive outside the orthodox tradition.

The remainder of Mormon's project—and what his son, Moroni, adds after Mormon's death—arguably draws down the intensity of Third Nephi, but it is worth underscoring the fact that the interpretive approach introduced there remains consistent to the end. This is clearest in the final paragraphs of the volume as published. Bidding farewell to his readers as he closes the book, Moroni issues eight exhortations. The last of them draws heavily on Isaiah 52 and Isaiah 54. "And again," Moroni says, "I would exhort you that ye would come unto Christ and lay hold upon every good gift, and touch not the evil gift nor the unclean thing" (Moroni 10:30). Already in these words, Moroni obliquely gestures toward Isaiah 52:11, which commands Jews leaving Babylon to "touch no unclean thing." But then the Isaian resonance becomes especially clear: "And awake! And arise from the dust, O Jerusalem! Yea, and put on thy beautiful garments, O daughter of Zion! And strengthen thy stakes, and enlarge thy borders forever—that thou mayest no more be confounded, that the covenants of the Eternal Father, which he hath made unto thee, O house of Israel, may be fulfilled!" (Moroni 10:31). The first part of this series of commands draws rather obviously on Isaiah 52:1–2: "Awake, awake; put on thy strength, O Zion; put on thy beautiful garments, O Jerusalem, the holy city. . . . Shake thyself from the dust; arise, and sit down, O Jerusalem." As the passage continues, however, it weaves into these borrowings from Isaiah 52 allusions to Isaiah 54, especially verses 2 and 4: "Enlarge the place of thy tent, . . . lengthen thy cords, and strengthen thy stakes; . . . fear not; for thou shalt not be ashamed: neither be thou confounded."[101] In the Book of Mormon's concluding farewell, then, Moroni confirms Christ's linking of Isaiah 52 and Isaiah 54 in an injunction to take seriously "the covenants of the Eternal Father" made with the "house of Israel." From Third Nephi to the end of the volume, the hermeneutic program introduced into the Book of Mormon by Mormon's Christ remains constant: the focus is on the culmination of God's covenants with Israel.

What Mormon accomplishes with Isaiah over the course of his project is thus clear. And what he introduces in Third Nephi continues strong to the very end of the project, reappearing in the appended writings of his son, and not only in Mormon's own writings. Where the Abinadi narrative outlines and defends a style of interpretation that reads Isaiah in only slightly unorthodox (but definitely polemical) ways, the Christ narrative forces onto the reader an approach to Isaiah that works outside the boundaries of traditional or orthodox interpretation, settling the controversy by moving to the margins of the interpretive tradition. The consistent presentation of covenantal theology through to the end of Moroni's farewell makes clear that this is deliberate, a sustained call to all Christian readers to move beyond the confines of the tradition to recognize other possible meanings lurking within their own sacred texts.[102]

What might be even more striking than the fact that Christ's hermeneutic continues to the end of the volume once it is introduced, however, is the fact that roughly the same hermeneutic continues to the end of the dictated text once it is introduced. Mormon never reverts to Abinadi's pre-Christian interpretive approach to Isaiah, and his son Moroni makes clear that Christ's covenantal interpretive approach remains relevant as the Book of Mormon ends. But, of course, Joseph Smith had more text to dictate even after he had completed dictating Mormon's and Moroni's words. As discussed in chapter 1 of the present volume, he continued by dictating the text of the record of Nephi, which would eventually find its canonical place as the first part of the printed volume. And, in Nephi's record, something far more like Christ's hermeneutics than like Abinadi's appears. Further, Nephi's treatment of Isaiah is far more developed, far more thorough, and far longer than what appears in Third Nephi. Someone listening attentively and charitably to the dictation of the text of the Book of Mormon in the summer of 1829 would most naturally have felt as if Mormon's project were really a long preface to the record of Nephi. Mormon delicately and dutifully prepares his readers for the brief (but complex) outline of Christ's hermeneutical project in Third Nephi. Nephi then seems to feel free to explore much the same hermeneutical project with reckless abandon, largely assuming that his readers are fully prepared to receive his readings of Isaiah. While the Book of Mormon in final form often loses readers somewhere in Nephi's long quotations of Isaiah, the Book of Mormon as originally dictated arguably gives ample time and attention to the difficult task of preparing readers for a nonstandard approach to Isaiah. Mormon's slow and deliberate development of the context for Christ's hermeneutic—an approach that would almost certainly be marginalized in the context of the Book of Mormon's first appearance—therefore helps in crucial ways to soften the impact of Nephi's record. But it is unmistakably within Nephi's record that the Book of Mormon's Isaian project reaches its peak.

It is necessary now, therefore, to leave Mormon, allowing him to have served as a kind of preparer of the way, in order to engage Nephi directly, whose record provides a full exposition of the most developed Isaian hermeneutic.

Part II

Nephi's Isaiah

Readers of the Book of Mormon today first encounter not Mormon but Nephi, whose record serves effectively as a replacement for the (lost) first part of Mormon's writings. Where Mormon abridges the long history of a nation whose end he witnesses, Nephi writes in his own voice about his own experiences and revelations. He reports that he was born in Jerusalem in the last decades of the seventh century before Christ, although God led his family—he was still a youth at the time—away from Jerusalem and so delivered them from the impending destruction of the city. According to Nephi's narrative, a protracted period of hiding in and then traveling through the desert brought the group (augmented through marriages and growing families) to the ocean to the east of the Arabian Peninsula. Crucial to Nephi's account is the fact that they carried with them from Jerusalem an Israelite record containing the biblical books of Moses, a history of the Jewish nation, and a host of prophetic writings—most notably, writings of Isaiah. These Nephi says he took with his family across the ocean to the New World.

Arrival in the New World apparently turned Nephi's attention to writing, since he reports in one breath the family's first explorations in their new land and the divine commandment to begin producing a record, the start of a nation's ever-growing annals. Like Mormon, Nephi understands his writerly activities to fulfill a responsibility given him by God. Also as with Mormon, only some of Nephi's writings are available in the Book of Mormon, although Joseph Smith never translated or lost Nephi's unavailable writings. Instead, these writings went into the massive set of records Mormon would later abridge. One of Joseph Smith's scribes would lose after its dictation the portion of Mormon's abridgment that pertained to Nephi. But, as Nephi explains to his readers, God commanded him to produce a second record some decades later, and Joseph Smith translated this at the end of the dictation process. What opens the Book of Mormon in final, printed form is Nephi's later record, which Nephi divides into two successive books, each with the simple title "The Book of Nephi," although it has become customary to call these, respectively, "The First Book of Nephi" (or just "First Nephi") and "The Second Book of Nephi" (or just "Second Nephi"). Nephi describes these two books as particularly focused on prophecy. And they certainly do focus principally on prophetic matters. Although the record opens with the story of how Nephi's family came from Jerusalem to the New World, detailing also the family's eventual division into rival factions that gave rise to two warring nations, it dwells most consistently and certainly climactically on Nephi's prophetic anticipations regarding the last days. And these Nephi ties to the writings of Isaiah.

The four chapters making up this second part of the present study naturally focus on the role the biblical Book of Isaiah plays in Nephi's later, prophetic record. It is obvious to any reader of Nephi's record that he has a fondness for Isaiah, since he quotes more or less in full eighteen chapters from Isaiah over the course of his two books. The point here, though, is to make clear just how much more central to Nephi's project Isaiah is than most readers recognize. Readers tend to see Isaiah as a mild distraction from what is most interesting in Nephi's record, a kind of diversion that might have its own importance but that should not receive undue attention. It is, however, possible to show that Nephi organizes his whole record around questions of Isaian interpretation. Further, one can show that Nephi develops his reading of Isaiah toward a climactic theological appropriation that theorizes what it means to read and to receive the Book of Mormon itself. Taken together, then, First and Second Nephi work to extend the Isaian project of Mormon's record much, much further.

To take the measure of the role Isaiah plays in Nephi's record, it will thus be necessary to begin with the question of how Nephi's treatment of Isaiah is continuous with or departs from Mormon's. The first chapter in this part of the present study therefore considers the selection of Isaiah texts in First Nephi and the interpretive strategies used in making sense of them. The apparent systematicity of Nephi's interpretations in his first book, however, motivate a closer study of the larger plan of the two books, of how the whole of Nephi's project takes an Isaian focus. This is the subject of the second chapter in this part. With clarity about how central Isaiah really is to Nephi's climactic writings, a third chapter takes up the longest and most sustained interaction with Isaiah in the whole of the Book of Mormon, the so-called Isaiah chapters proper that appear at the heart of Second Nephi. A fourth and final chapter then addresses itself to Nephi's last—and most virtuosic—interaction with Isaiah, his theological recasting of Isaiah in a full theorization of what it means to read the Book of Mormon.

Throughout these investigations, questions that have guided the preceding part of this study remain live and require further elaboration. Especially important to keep in mind is our well-informed and charitable listener/reader from 1829–30. From the outset, we have had with us this imagined figure, first privileged to sit with Joseph Smith and his scribes during the dictation of the Book of Mormon and then graced with the leisure time necessary to revisit the readable text of the Book of Mormon carefully. We have imagined this ideal listener/reader as being not only curiously sympathetic to the Book of Mormon as a project, but also genuinely informed with the broad contours of Isaiah's history of interpretation, up through 1830. What would such a listener have seen in Nephi's uses of Isaiah? How does Nephi's more fully elaborated hermeneutic program look to such a reader?

I have insisted from the outset on at least one major thing such an ideal listener/reader would see in Nephi's project right away: that it constitutes (when the Book of Mormon is listened to or read in order of dictation) a culmination of the Book of Mormon's Isaiah project. For such a listener/reader, it is when the Book of Mormon comes to Nephi's writings that its Isaian investments receive a kind of systematic exposition. Readers of the volume following its final form, familiar from published editions, find in it an initial obsession with Isaiah that then enters briefly into a period of controversy before disappearing for hundreds of pages, only to return seriously but not necessarily decisively at the volume's narrative climax. By contrast, the ideal listener/reader imagined throughout this study finds in the Book of Mormon's climactic account of Jesus Christ's visit the beginnings of a prolonged investigation, one continued into the particularly carefully wrought record of Nephi.

And so, a key question drives all that remains in this study: How does Nephi's continuation of certain interpretive moves made by Mormon's Christ in Third Nephi give shape to the whole Book of Mormon project? How does the volume's interest in Isaiah look when it comes fully into its own?

6

Nursing Fathers and Nursing Mothers

Three passages from Isaiah receive the heaviest emphasis in Nephi's record, with references and allusions to them appearing throughout his two books. One, Isaiah 29:11–14, comes from the undisputed core of First Isaiah, although it emphasizes verses often regarded as a later gloss.[1] Another, Isaiah 11:11–12, also derives from First Isaiah, but many scholars view it as an interpolation as well.[2] The last, Isaiah 49:22–23, comes from the largely seamless second half of Second Isaiah. Despite their dispersion within the canonical Book of Isaiah, Nephi repeatedly draws these three passages into a single theological constellation, giving sustained attention to each and probing their mutual relevance.[3] Each illuminates Nephi's relationship to Isaiah, but one in particular suggests strong continuity between Mormon's and Nephi's Isaian projects. For our ideal listener sitting with Joseph Smith and his scribes during the Book of Mormon's dictation, the treatment of Isaiah 49 would have linked the two halves of the dictation—the chronologically-later-but-dictated-earlier and the chronologically-earlier-but-dictated-later. Significantly, Isaiah 49 forms the peculiar focus of Nephi's first book, the first swelling Isaian chorus of this second half of the Book of Mormon symphony. It will be necessary to consider all three of Nephi's privileged Isaiah passages eventually, but this first plays a key role that paves the road to the others' accessibility.

Part of what suggests continuity between Mormon's and Nephi's projects is that Nephi's first chosen verses come from Second Isaiah's prophecies of redemption, the focus of Mormon's project. Moreover, among the resources Nephi uses to explain Isaiah 49 is a verse from the most privileged passage from

Mormon's Isaian project: Isaiah 52:10: the same passage debated by Abinadi and Noah's priests and set forth in Christ's sermonizing is among Nephi's key tools for making sense of other Second-Isaian prophecies. Thus, interpreting Isaiah 49, Nephi says, "And I would, my brethren, that ye should know that all the kindreds of the earth cannot be blessed unless 'he shall make bare his arm in the eyes of the nations'—wherefore, the Lord God *will* proceed to make bare his arm in the eyes of all the nations, in bringing about his covenants and his gospel unto they which are of the house of Israel" (1 Nephi 22:10–11, emphasis added).[4] The words of Isaiah 52:10 are unmistakable here. Nephi evokes a passage linking Abinadi's Isaian interests to those of Mormon's Christ, creating continuity through all the Book of Mormon. As always, though, with repetition comes difference. Just as Mormon's Christ takes up the passage from Abinadi but interprets it distinctly, Nephi addresses the same passage in his own fashion.

Nephi's handling of Isaiah 49 marks the newness of his approach to the text in two ways, despite clear continuity with Mormon's project. Obviously, one of these concerns just the fact that Nephi dramatically expands the scope of the Book of Mormon's Isaian investment. Where Mormon's long history draws on just three chapters of Isaiah, Nephi reproduces eighteen. The second way concerns a method Nephi uniquely develops within the Book of Mormon, an appropriating interpretive style he calls "likening" (introduced briefly in chapter 3 of the present volume). Unlike Mormon's Christ, Nephi extends his uses of Isaiah beyond the prophet's (assumed) literal meaning, likening his prophecies to events Isaiah never directly predicts. If Mormon's Christ pushes the Book of Mormon's approach to Isaiah from the Christian mainstream to the millenarian margins, Nephi pushes it further into the fringes. Taking in eschatological prophecies unavailable to Jewish and Christian interpreters— unavailable because they are Nephi's own—he forges the Book of Mormon's final hermeneutic contribution, diverging with other parts of the book despite points of continuity.

In the present chapter, the task is to clarify Nephi's interpretation of Isaiah 49:22–23. What does this passage mean for him, in itself but also through the likening that allows him to relate Isaiah to his own prophetic visions? How exactly do Nephi's interpretations of this passage mark his continuity with and distance from the interpretive styles exhibited in Mormon's project? And of course there is the question our insistent ideal listener/reader would ask: How does Nephi's handling of this specific Isaiah text sound in the context of the Book of Mormon's publication and circulation in nineteenth-century America?

Jews, Israelites, and Gentiles

Readers generally appreciate First Nephi as a collection of didactic narratives. With vivid portrayal of dark days in a doomed city, romantic stories about the underdog son who rises above his abusive older brothers, evocative sketches of desert and seafaring life, and accounts of symbol-rich dreams from an aging patriarch, the book is a favorite for Latter-day Saint children and adults alike. After its many narratives, however, this relatively short book concludes with an extended reflection on the prophecies of Isaiah. For many making their way through Nephi's record, the Isaian telos of his first book feels out of place[5] and serves as a first hint that still rougher Isaian terrain lies ahead.

Of course, attentive readers cannot be terribly surprised when they come to the Isaiah material at the end of First Nephi. The opening story of the book concerns the adventurous acquisition, by Nephi and his brothers, of a set of brass plates from Jerusalem, a sacred Old-Testament-like record that contains at least some of Isaiah's writings (see especially 1 Nephi 5:10–16). Later in First Nephi, but chapters before long quotations from Isaiah appear, Nephi tells of his father prophesying of Jesus Christ with language reminiscent of Isaiah 40:3 (1 Nephi 10:4–10). Further along but still shy of the first serious engagement with Isaiah, Nephi describes himself as answering his brothers' theological questions by rehearsing "the words of Isaiah," although he provides his readers with no quotations in this report (15:20). Thus, when First Nephi ends with two full chapters of Isaiah in quotation and a full chapter of explanation, it should not be wholly unexpected. Indeed, it might well be that readers are intended to experience the Isaian conclusion of First Nephi as a natural one, the sort of place the book must end up.

The first unmissable interaction with Isaiah in Nephi's record, at any rate, happens at the end of First Nephi, where Nephi quotes the whole of Isaiah 48–49 before offering a few words of commentary. The placement is significant. By dividing his record into two successive books and making the first substantial quotation of Isaiah the threshold between them, Nephi makes the reading of Isaiah both something that requires preparation and something that sets the stage for further developments. Carefully listening to and genuinely understanding the Isaian sermon of sorts that concludes First Nephi is thus like a coming-of-age ritual.

Nephi's brief introduction to this first substantial quotation from Isaiah deserves notice. His editorial comments introduce the idea of likening Isaiah's prophecies to something other than their literal referents—of hearing in Isaiah's prophecies not only predictions about Jewish redemption (their immediate and intentional subject) but also predictions about the redemption of other branches of Israel, separated out from the main body of the covenant people. The context or setting for the quotation within Nephi's narrative makes the question of other Israelite branches pressing. He and his family have just journeyed from Jerusalem to the New World, definitively "a branch which has been broken off" (1 Nephi 19:24) or "driven out" (21:1) from the house of Israel. It therefore becomes necessary and natural to ask about whether and how this scattered branch of Israel—proto-Nephites and proto-Lamanites—might "have hope" for their distant descendants' redemption, trusting in Isaiah's promises much like those back in Jerusalem "from whom [they] have been broken off" (19:24). Nephi thus announces that Isaiah's writings might "persuade" his family "to believe in the Lord their Redeemer," the God of Isaiah who watches over Israel's destiny (19:23).

One might ask why it is specifically Isaiah 48–49 that Nephi quotes and comments on at the culmination of his first book. Isaiah's interpreters today usually regard Isaiah 48 as the concluding chapter of the first half of Second Isaiah (of Isaiah 40–48) and Isaiah 49 as the introductory chapter of the second half of Second Isaiah (of Isaiah 49–55).[6] Nephi thus seems to extract from Second Isaiah what functions in its biblical context as a hinge between the two halves of a longer prophetic message. What is puzzling, though, is that these two chapters at first glance have little to do with each other. Both affirm "the certainty of restoration" for Israel, but Isaiah 48, very much unlike Isaiah 49, "lays equal emphasis on Jacob-Israel's resistance to Yhwh."[7] In fact, Isaiah 48 is unique within all of Second Isaiah for its harsh words toward Israel. It may be, though, that the coupling of these two chapters makes its own kind of sense. The tension in Isaiah 48 between Israel's resistance to God and God's promises to redeem Israel sets up a problem to be solved, and the tension's "resolution will begin only with ch. 49."[8] Brevard Childs thus argues that "the specific role played" by chapter 48 in Second Isaiah is to announce that "now something new is planned," something "signaled by the introduction of a new messenger" whose message begins to unfold in chapter 49.[9] Does Nephi wish to highlight the announcement of the new at a moment of ripe tension and then to move onto the new itself?

Certainly, the work of Isaiah 48's "new messenger" is of particular importance to First Nephi. When one sets that chapter as Nephi quotes it side by side with the King James Version, numerous differences appear. They indicate a clear pattern, a systematic effort in the Book of Mormon version to clarify and exaggerate the messenger's work of *declaration*, which is more muted and ambiguous in the biblical version.[10] Despite such attention to detail in reproducing Isaiah 48, though, Nephi never again—whether in his commentary in 1 Nephi 22 or elsewhere in his record—so much as alludes to that chapter. Its amplified announcement of a new messenger with something to declare stands on its own. The tension between Israel's attitude toward God and God's attitude toward Israel seems to serve for Nephi solely as a self-explanatory context for the sudden and unexpected appearance of the new messenger. And then Nephi goes on to quote—and to explain at length—Isaiah 49, where the new thing announced by the messenger begins to unfold. All this suggests a text-savvy recognition on Nephi's part of the literary continuity between Isaiah 48 and Isaiah 49.

It also indicates thematic continuity with Mormon's project. Here again, God aims to restore Israel's fortunes in a way that involves non-Israelite peoples, or gentiles, in a global project of redemption. The text thus has God straightforwardly explain Israel's role in his plan in Isaiah 49:6 (quoted in 1 Nephi 21:6). "It is a light thing that thou shouldst be my servant to raise up the tribes of Jacob, and to restore the preserved of Israel!" he tells Israel. "I will also give thee for a light to the gentiles, that thou mayest be my salvation unto the ends of the earth!" This promise—so closely aligned with Isaiah 52:7–10, central to Mormon's Isaian project—takes a still more definite shape later, in two verses that become Nephi's first favored passage. As Jerusalem laments the loss of its inhabitants to death and exile, God urges the forsaken city to see that peoples are gathering to repopulate the land. The city's response is confusion: "Who hath begotten me these, seeing I have lost my children? . . . These, where have they been?" (Isaiah 49:21, quoted in 1 Nephi 21:21). The city does not recognize those who gather. God himself provides an explanation: "Behold, I will lift up mine hand to the gentiles and set up my standard to the people, and they shall bring thy sons in their arms, and thy daughters shall be carried upon their shoulders! And kings shall be thy nursing fathers and their queens thy nursing mothers! They shall bow down to thee with their face towards the earth and lick up the dust of thy feet, and thou shalt know that I am the Lord! For they shall not be ashamed that wait for me!" (Isaiah 49:22–23, quoted in 1 Nephi 21:22–23).[11] In these words, thematically continuous with the interests of Mormon's Christ, Nephi finds an image he can liken to his own people's future.

An example of likening comes in Nephi's commentary. He provides two interpretive contexts for Isaiah 49:22–23 (and thus for Isaiah 49 as a whole), two historical experiences of Israelite scattering that then motivate redemption.

They are both contexts Nephi apparently assumes Isaiah himself had in mind in originally issuing the prophecy. First, Nephi says, "It appears that the house of Israel, sooner or later, will be scattered upon all the face of the earth—and also among all nations" (1 Nephi 22:3). This first scattering occurs sooner rather than later, since Nephi goes on to say (from his sixth-century-BCE position) that "there are many"—in fact "the more part of all the tribes"—that "are *already* lost from the knowledge of they which are at Jerusalem" (22:4, emphasis added). Nephi here seems to refer to the traditional scattering of the ten tribes, the former northern Kingdom of Israel conquered by the Assyrian empire in the eighth century BCE (during the lifetime of Isaiah of Jerusalem).[12] Second, however, Nephi says that Isaiah's words apply also to all those "which shall *hereafter* [that is, after Nephi's sixth-century-BCE moment in history] be scattered and be confounded because of the Holy One of Israel, for against him will they harden their hearts" (22:5, emphasis added). This second context for the fulfillment of Isaiah 49:22–23 points to a moment in later history, one focused on different people than the first interpretive context. Where the first group referred to is "led away" and "lost from the knowledge" of the world (22:4), the second group is "scattered" and "hated by all men" (22:5), clearly recognized for who they are rather than lost to the world.

These details indicate that Nephi understands the second group to be specifically Jews. He never identifies them as such in 1 Nephi 22 and never once uses any form of the word *Jew*. And yet, in light of other passages, the unfortunate word *hated* suggests that Nephi has Jews in mind. Four other times in Nephi's record is a people described as "hated," and three of them have specific reference to Jews (1 Nephi 19:14; 2 Nephi 6:11; 29:5). It thus seems best to understand 1 Nephi 22's prediction about a second scattered group that will "harden their hearts" against "the Holy One of Israel" as a reference to the general (but obviously not universal) refusal, by first-century Jews, to identify Jesus of Nazareth as God's Messiah.[13] In providing Isaiah 49:22–23 with a second interpretive context, Nephi asks his readers to imagine a scattering of Jews early in the common era. For Nephi, then, the prophecies in Isaiah 48–49 deliberately concern both (1) indiscernible Israelites descended from those scattered during and in the wake of Assyria's destruction of the northern Kingdom of Israel eight centuries before Christ, and (2) discernible (because historically hated) Israelite persons descended from those who remained in and around Jerusalem as late as the first centuries after Christ.

Crucially, just a few chapters later (in 2 Nephi 6), Nephi's younger brother Jacob quotes the same Isaiah passage and explains it to Nephi's uncomprehending people. And, initially, Jacob follows his older brother interpretively. In fact, Jacob speaks on Isaiah 49—on Isaiah 49:22–23 in particular—only because Nephi asks him to do so (2 Nephi 6:4). Mirroring Nephi's notion that Isaiah 49 would be fulfilled twice in formally similar but materially distinct contexts, Jacob explains that he understands Isaiah to concern "things which are and which are to come" (2 Nephi 6:4). Since the text presents Jacob as speaking during the literal exile of Jerusalem's inhabitants in Babylon during the sixth century BCE (something the text explicitly notes; 2 Nephi 1:4),[14] it would seem that the text takes Isaiah's references to "things which are" as references to events current in Isaiah's own time. As for "things . . . which are to come," Jacob anticipates the second and ultimate fulfillment of Isaiah 49 as occurring through the eschatological redemption of literal Jews, those who retain Jewish identity long after the first-century destruction of Jerusalem. To clinch his interpretation, in fact, Jacob offers a novel gloss on a clause from Isaiah 49:23: "they shall not be ashamed that wait for me." Jacob takes "they . . . that wait for me" to refer (somewhat esoterically) to Jews, those who would come to be viewed from a (traditional) Christian perspective as "still wait[ing] for the coming of the Messiah" after his having come in Jesus of Nazareth (2 Nephi 6:13). Like Nephi, Jacob sees Isaiah 49 as having two fulfillments, one centered on his own time and another centered on a post-Christian eschaton—but both concerned with the literal redemption of literal Israelites.

Returning to Nephi, one finds him, after providing two distinct contexts for the fulfillment of Isaiah 49:22–23, commenting directly on the passage, weaving his own language into Isaiah's. Nephi's comments are difficult, however, because they appear incomplete—an unfinished thought or interrupted sentence. "Nevertheless," he says, "after that they have been nursed by the gentiles and the Lord hath lifted up his hand upon the gentiles and set them up for a standard, and their children shall be carried in their arms, and their daughters shall be carried upon their shoulders . . ." (22:6). This thought never resolves itself, perhaps because the need to clarify the prophecy's application distracts Nephi.[15] That is, that Nephi in his haste leaves the thought unfinished suggests eagerness to move from Old World Israelite history to likening, finding hope in applying the fulfillment of prophecy to his own people in the future.

Nephi's haste to liken provocatively contrasts with his brother's later preference to tarry with Old World (and specifically Jewish) history. This difference in the two commentaries reflects larger discrepancies between Nephi and Jacob. Jacob, after the family's departure from Jerusalem, apparently finds himself lingering on Jerusalem's fate, while Nephi, raised in Jerusalem and happy to leave it, claims to have no interest in reading Isaiah after "the manner of the Jews" (2 Nephi 25:2). Where Nephi begins likening only one verse after (re)quoting Isaiah 49:22, Jacob takes whole chapters to work through (what he takes to be) the prophecy's literal meaning before he turns to likening. Jacob, that is, quotes Isaiah 49:22–23 in 2 Nephi 6:6–7 and, although he dwells on the passage's meaning at length, he comes to likening only in 2 Nephi 10:10, on the second day of a two-day sermon.[16] Of course, it should be said that Nephi announces his interest in likening from the moment he begins to quote Isaiah. In his introductory note to Isaiah 48, he instructs his hearers to "liken it unto yourselves" (1 Nephi 19:24; see also 1 Nephi 21:1). It is thus no surprise when, unlike Jacob, Nephi shifts abruptly from speaking about Old World Israelites to speaking about "all our brethren which are of the house of Israel" and then particularly about "us," his own people's future "in the days to come" (1 Nephi 22:6).

It comes as no surprise that Nephi and Jacob also have distinct pet formulas within Isaiah 49:22–23, different points of emphasis that inflect their respective interests. And each selects a different favored passage from Nephi's triad of Isaian texts to bring to bear, interpretively, on the meaning of Isaiah 49:22–23. Nephi connects the passage to Isaiah 29:14 as he begins his (explicit) work of likening. Isaiah 49, he explains, "meaneth that the time cometh that, after all the house of Israel have been scattered and confounded, that the Lord God will raise up a mighty nation among the gentiles—yea, even upon the face of this land—and . . . the Lord God will proceed to do a marvelous work among the gentiles, which shall be of great worth unto our seed. Wherefore, it is likened unto the being nursed by the gentiles and being carried in their arms and upon their shoulders" (1 Nephi 22:7–8).

Here one discerns what phrases from Isaiah 49:22–23 most interest Nephi ("they shall bring thy sons in their arms, and thy daughters shall be carried upon their shoulders," for instance, or "I will lift up mine hand to the Gentiles"). One also sees that Nephi wishes to liken by linking the passage to Isaiah 29:14, which reads in part, "I will proceed to do a marvellous work among this people."[17] It becomes clear as Nephi's record proceeds that Nephi takes the "marvellous work" in question to be the coming forth of the Book of Mormon itself, and here it is *this* to which Isaiah 49:22 "is likened." Through the circulation of the Book of Mormon—especially among latter-day descendants of Nephi and his brothers—New World gentiles will be "nursing fathers" and "nursing mothers" to the remnant of Israel.

Where Nephi seems most interested in verse 22 of Isaiah 49, Jacob seems particularly interested in verse 23. He interprets "they that fight against Zion," for example, taking the phrase to refer to kings: "And he that fighteth against Zion shall perish," he explains, "for he that raiseth up a king against [God] shall perish" (10:13–14).[18] Jacob thus contrasts kings and queens who become nursing fathers and mothers (Isaiah 49:22) with kings and queens who fight against Zion and so have to "lick up the dust of [Israel's] feet" (Isaiah 49:23). It is interesting that, within the context of Isaiah 49 itself, licking dust from Israel's feet in verse 23 is something paternalistic gentile kings and queens from verse 22 do—a symbol of their humble and rueful servitude. For Jacob, the nursing kings and queens are repentant gentiles, contrasting with verse 23's talk of retributive subjection for unrepentant gentiles. Jacob goes on in his explanation thus: "And behold, according to the words of the prophet, the Messiah will set himself again the second time to recover [Old World Israelites]—wherefore, he will manifest himself unto them in power and great glory, unto the destruction of their enemies, when that day cometh when they shall believe in him. And none will he destroy that believeth him. And they that believe not in him shall be destroyed, both by fire and by tempest, and by earthquakes and by bloodsheds, and by pestilence and by famine" (2 Nephi 6:14–15).

These are strong words, a harsh interpretation of Isaiah 49:23 potentially at odds with Nephi's gentler appropriation. But Jacob's interpretation not only confirms the violence of his understanding of Isaiah 49:23, it shows him borrowing from Isaiah 11 (rather than Isaiah 29) in working out his interpretation. Isaiah 11:11, which commentators often tie to Isaiah 49:22,[19] predicts that "the Lord shall set his hand again the second time to recover the remnant of his people." Drawing on that language, Jacob affirms the relevance of the two favored Isaiah texts to each other.

The contrasts between Nephi's and Jacob's interpretations of Isaiah 49:22–23 indicate a semi-instability of interpretation for this text in Nephi's record. It is of interest, then, that Nephi returns once more to Isaiah 49:22–23 late in his record, and that he there reshapes his approach to the text, parting from his earlier interpretation (although more subtly than his brother). Thus, in 2 Nephi 29:2, Nephi quotes God as saying, "My words shall hiss forth unto the ends of the earth for a standard unto my people which are of the house of Israel" (29:2). Here Nephi confirms his interest in Isaiah's talk of a standard being set up, but what is specifically set up for a standard has changed. Earlier, it is "the gentiles" that are set up "for a standard" (1 Nephi 22:6), but in 2 Nephi 29:2, the standard is God's "words" that hiss forth—the Book of Mormon itself. Whether this is supposed to indicate interpretive looseness or interpretive development on Nephi's part, the record provides distinct understandings of a single Isaian phrase.[20]

Amid discontinuity, however, stands continuity, and the stable interpretation of Isaiah 49:22–23 in Nephi's record can be discerned and summarized. The passage has, for Nephi and Jacob alike, a literal meaning first, an intended meaning in its native (that is, biblical) context. This first meaning is twofold: Isaiah 49 predicts that Israelites scattered from their divinely granted lands in the Old World centuries before Christ were to be restored to their lands through the kindness of servile gentiles *and* that Israelites scattered again in the first century of the common era will be restored to them again at the eschaton. But beyond this (double) first meaning, literal in nature, Isaiah 49 has also for Nephi and Jacob a likened meaning, an implied meaning because Israel has many branches to which the prophet's words can be applied. Nephi and Jacob feel free to liken the prophecy to their distant descendants, who will be restored to an understanding of their Israelite identity through gentiles who will discover and publish the Book of Mormon. They will come to "know that the Lord is their Savior and their Redeemer, the Mighty One of Israel" (1 Nephi 22:12).

The complexity of Nephi's and Jacob's hermeneutic involves both continuity and discontinuity throughout Nephi's record. But such complexity in turn raises questions about the nature of the continuity between the Isaian project of Nephi's small plates and the Isaian project of Mormon's long history and abridgment. What larger continuities and discontinuities structure the whole Book of Mormon? This question has to be answered before our ideal listener/reader can bring the history of Isaian interpretation to bear in earnest on Nephi's work.

Continuity and Discontinuity with Mormon's Project

In several places in the Book of Mormon, one finds clear continuity between Nephi's Isaian project and Mormon's sustained interest in Isaiah 52:7–10. An early allusion to Isaiah 52:7–10 appears in a long and detailed vision that Nephi has (an expansion of a prophetic dream his father, Lehi, had), recounted in 1 Nephi 13. The allusion in fact occurs when Nephi witnesses in vision the latter-day coming forth of the Book of Mormon itself. An angelic guide explains that God's "gospel" will appear in the book (1 Nephi 13:36) and goes on to pronounce a blessing on those who "shall seek to bring forth [God's] Zion at that day" (13:37). The angel then extends this blessing, first with traditional Christian language but then with Isaian language: "And if they endure unto the end, they shall be lifted up at the last day and shall be saved in the everlasting kingdom of the Lamb. Yea, whoso shall publish peace, that shall publish tidings of great joy—how beautiful upon the mountains shall they be!" (13:37). In the focus on precisely these words in the Abinadi narrative and Christ's sermons, one sees again the continuity with Mormon's project. Because Mormon's Christ applies Isaiah 52:7 to those who assist in redeeming "the land of Jerusalem" in the last days (3 Nephi 20:29) and Nephi applies it to those who "seek to bring forth [God's] Zion at that day" (1 Nephi 13:37), the continuity between the climax of Mormon's Isaian project and the point of departure for Nephi's Isaian project is perfectly clear.[21]

There is still further and broader early confirmation of continuity between Mormon's and Nephi's projects (in a passage mentioned earlier). It comes shortly after Nephi's vision, when he finds that his brothers refuse to seek having a vision themselves and he decides to explain Lehi's dream for them. Without citing any particular passage, he "did rehearse unto them the words of Isaiah which spake concerning the restoration of the Jews or of the house of Israel" (1 Nephi 15:20). The general alignment here of "the words of Isaiah" with the restoration of Jews too suggests thematic continuity with the hermeneutic of Third Nephi's Christ. The latter never uses the word *restoration* in Third Nephi (preferring instead *gathering*),[22] but Mormon frames Christ's sermons with the noun "restoration" and the verb "to restore,"[23] and Nephi speaks of "gathering" in just the same way that he speaks of "restoration."[24] Continuity is clear.

Continuity proves easy to establish, then, but what are the substantial points of difference between the interpretive approaches exemplified in Third Nephi and First Nephi? Right from the outset of Nephi's project, as already noted, the range of Isaian texts is broader. Nephi clearly touches on passages central to Christ's sermons in Third Nephi, but they appear only at the blurry edges of the Isaian picture that Nephi paints in bright colors. In First Nephi, it is Isaiah 49, especially Isaiah 49:22–23, that receives sustained attention; Isaiah 52 just confirms the general orientation of Nephi's hermeneutic. In other words, the Isaiah passages most central to Third Nephi's Christ do no more in Nephi's record than establish *general* continuity. The actual focus of Nephi's project is different. While the prophetic history of Israel draws his attention, he apparently sees Isaiah's writings as much more illustrative of this history than Mormon's Christ does. Is it therefore possible to see Nephi as obediently (and anachronistically) fulfilling the command of Mormon's Christ "to search ... the words of Isaiah" and to do so "diligently" (3 Nephi 21:1)? For our ideal listener, sitting in the room with Joseph Smith and listening for everything Isaian, would Nephi not exemplify what it means for someone to take Christ's commandment seriously?

Also distinguishing Nephi's project from the climax of Mormon's, however, is its systematicity. Where Christ's sermons in Third Nephi work through various biblical texts in a somewhat haphazard fashion,[25] Nephi offers a full-blooded program of interpretation. He identifies key sources by telling the story of retrieving the brass plates containing Isaiah's writings (1 Nephi 1–5). He describes and summarizes prophetic sources on his own people's future (1 Nephi 6–14), which he then connects to the task of likening Isaiah's writings (1 Nephi 15, 22). And, of course, he brings all this to fruition by quoting directly from Isaiah for two full chapters (1 Nephi 20–21). As will become clear later, moreover, this is only the tip of the iceberg of Nephi's systematicity. The architecture of Nephi's project smacks more of the doctoral dissertation than of the pastor's sermon. Nephi's systematicity, contrasting with the apparently unsteady presentation in Third Nephi, thus marks a crucial point of difference. For our ideal listener sitting in the room in 1829, Third Nephi would have blazed a meandering trail through the Isaian woods, but Nephi's record would have suggested deep familiarity with the whole terrain—clear points of entry and identifiable destinations connected by plainly visible roads. The basic starting and ending points are perhaps the same for Nephi and Mormon's Christ, but Nephi's record is a near-encyclopedic guide to the journey.

A perhaps less obvious but particularly crucial point of discontinuity concerns method. It is clear that Nephi favors what he calls "likening." The word, however, appears in Third Nephi only in two verses drawn from Matthew's Sermon on the Mount (3 Nephi 14:24, 26) and is found nowhere else in Mormon's project.[26] The term is Nephi's, especially in its technical usage. Key to Nephi's method is his reception of a specific vision of his people's future history, the vision with which he compares prophecies from Isaiah. Nowhere does Mormon suggest that Christ has, Nephi-like, had such a vision. At the same time, however, Mormon's Christ is the Johannine Jesus, the all-knowing God of heaven come to earth. He thus arguably just knows what Nephi has to be given to see. And, in fact, Mormon reports that Christ provides his hearers with a detailed exposition of exactly the same covenantal history covered in Nephi's vision (3 Nephi 26:1–4). This would suggest a deeper continuity between Nephi and Christ, except that Christ crucially discusses the meaning of Isaiah's prophecies *before* he provides his exposition of "all things," while Nephi takes up Isaiah's prophecies only *after* his account of his own vision of "all things." Isaiah paves the way to the exposition of all things in Third Nephi; he prepares Christ's hearers for the bigger picture only he can provide in full. In First and Second Nephi, though, Isaiah comes only after the bigger picture is sketched; his prophecies are what the reader must be prepared for. Put in a nutshell, Mormon's Christ uses Isaiah as a means to an apocalyptic end, while Nephi uses apocalyptic vision as a means to an Isaian end.

The result of all this is a distinction between the ways Christ and Nephi apply Isaiah to sacred history. Mormon's Christ understands at least parts of Isaiah as having their immediate or original application specifically to Jewish history. Thus, when Christ quotes Isaiah 52 late in 3 Nephi 20, his focus is on Jews rather than some (other) branch of Israel. He introduces his quotation with the following words: "I will remember the covenant which I have made with my people, and I have covenanted with them that . . . I would give unto them again the land of their fathers for their inheritance, which is the land of Jerusalem, which is the promised land unto them forever" (3 Nephi 20:29; see also 20:46).[27] Other Isaiah passages Christ applies—in a non-Nephi-like and non-Jacob-like fashion—to uniquely New World events as their direct and original referents. The key example here is the "sign" to mark "the time" when the eschatological redemption of Old World Israel "shall be about to take place" (3 Nephi 21:1). According to the Christ of Third Nephi, the sign concerns New World Israel, specifically their reception of the Book of Mormon through the gentiles after the loss of part of the Book of Mormon manuscript.[28] Christ applies this Isaiah passage directly to New World events and never suggests that it has its primary fulfillment in events of Jewish or Old World history. For Mormon's Christ, then, different Isaiah passages have different peoples as their referents, some pointing to Old World Jewish history and others to New World Israelite remnant history. For Nephi and Jacob, however, *all* of Isaiah points originally and intentionally just to Old World Jewish history, but then also—and only secondarily, through likening—to New World history.

For our ideal listener sitting in the room with Joseph Smith and his scribes in 1829, Nephi's project would therefore have simultaneously appeared to have two distinct relationships to the Isaian climax of Mormon's project. First, Nephi's project would have felt like an attempt to systematize the hermeneutic unveiled by the resurrected Christ, fulfilling the commandment to search Isaiah's words diligently. Where Third Nephi covers just two chapters from

Isaiah and advances toward its goal haphazardly, Nephi's project is a thoroughly systematic attempt at establishing a hermeneutic that allows for eschatological interpretation with an eye to the coming forth of the Book of Mormon. Second, Nephi's project was limited by the visions its all-too-human creator could scrabble out of the brass plates or receive himself through God's grace. Where the sermons of Third Nephi offer—however fragmentarily—a total vision of providential world history as glimpsed by God enfleshed, Nephi's project offers perspectivally limited (but prophetic) views of just parts of the world's providential history, running in parallel and occasionally intersecting. Putting all this together, it seems that the limit of Mormon's project lies in its refusal to provide a *systematic* exposition of Isaiah's meaning (which Nephi's gives), but the limit of Nephi's project lies in its inability to access the divine perspective *directly* (which Mormon's Christ has, being God).

The continuity between the hermeneutic program of Mormon's Christ and that of Nephi is thus rather complicated, which means that situating Nephi's project within the context of its publication in 1830 is somewhat complicated as well. It is already clear from chapter 5 herein that Christ's hermeneutic in the Book of Mormon looks most like the styles of interpretation found on the margins of nineteenth-century American Christianity, at a distance from establishment and mainstream styles of Isaian interpretation. But how do the complex developments of an Isaian hermeneutic within Nephi's project—at least as regards key texts from Second Isaiah—complicate the relationship the Book of Mormon sustains with interpretations offered in the antebellum American context? What would our ideal listener/reader have to say about the contribution—if any—made by Nephi's treatment?

Nursing Kings and Nursing Queens in America

Isaiah 49 is in no way unfamiliar in the Christian tradition. Quite apart from the interests of scholarly interpreters, Christians have long heard sermons on this chapter in liturgical celebrations of Epiphany.[29] It speaks successively of "a light to the gentiles" (49:6), of "kings" who "shall see and arise" (49:7), of "a woman" and "her sucking child" (Isaiah 49:15), of a God who engraves his people "upon the palms of [his] hands" (49:16), and of "kings" who "bow down" and "know" their God as "the Lord" (49:23). It takes little Christian imagination to hear in such talk an outline of the magi's visit to the Christ child, celebrated historically in a variety of Christian liturgies as the festival of Epiphany.[30] The relevance of Isaiah to Epiphany would in fact be confirmed for Christian readers by the close literary connection (noted by historical-critical scholars) between Isaiah 49 and Isaiah 60.[31] The latter text—also often used in lectionaries for Epiphany[32]—speaks explicitly of "gold and incense" being brought to "shew forth the praises of the Lord" when "kings" come to "the brightness" of God's light (60:3, 6). For many Christians through much of history, then, the first chapter of Isaiah that Nephi privileges has held specific significance, as a series of predictions of the visit of "wise men from the east" to the infant Christ (Matthew 2:1).

Set liturgies, however, were largely foreign to Joseph Smith and most of the Book of Mormon's first adherents—which our ideal listener/reader would know. Puritans famously rejected such forms of worship (and the *Book of Common Prayer* in particular),[33] as did Methodists and Baptists—although these latter traditions provided worship-focused familiarity with language from Isaiah 49 through the circulation of hymns. But hymns provided the American Christian public with a different approach to Isaiah 49. One well-known hymn in antebellum America adapted the language of Isaiah 49:20 by declaring, "'Give us room, that we may dwell,' / Zion's children cry aloud; / See their numbers, how they swell; / How they gather like a cloud!" It concluded by weaving language from Isaiah 49 and Isaiah 60 into one image, albeit without any reference to the story of the Magi: "Zion, now arise and shine; / Lo, thy light from heaven is come; / These that crowd from far are thine; / Give thy sons and daughters room."[34] These lines draw from Isaiah 49:20 straightforwardly, suggesting an interpretation of Isaiah 49 that focused on the successes of Christian preaching. This exactly is the sort of interpretation offered in most commentaries from the seventeenth and eighteenth centuries.[35]

A good example of the major English commentators is the Non-Conformist Matthew Henry, who says of Isaiah 49:18–23 that what is "here promised" was "to be in part accomplished in the reviving of the Jewish church, after its [sixth-century BCE] return out of captivity, but more fully in the planting of the Christian church, by the preaching of the gospel of Christ."[36] Unlike many other early modern English interpreters, Henry explicitly rejects the idea that Jews would be excluded from being numbered among gentile Christians in the work of preaching and gathering.[37] Despite this nod to literalist interpretation (eventually relegated to the margins of the interpretive tradition), Henry mostly persists in applying the meaning of the text principally to "the Church," seeing in Isaiah 49:23 an indication that "some of the princes of the nations shall become patrons and protectors to the church."[38] Other interpreters had even less room for literalist gestures. The Non-Conformist Matthew Poole, for example, concedes to Jews only an ancient application of the verse, never a latter-day or eschatological one.[39] And in the nineteenth century, the

Methodist interpreter Adam Clarke, whose notes on Isaiah 49:22–23 incline more to historicizing than to theologizing, sees the only possible latter-day application of the passage to be to the Christian church rather than to Jews. The whole second half of Isaiah 49 describes, he says, "the tender mercies of God to His people, with the prosperity of the church in general, and the final overthrow of all its enemies."[40] Methodist reports at the popular rather than the learned level confirm the common nature of this application of Isaiah 49.[41]

More akin to Henry and his eschatological concessions than to other English divines is the American Jonathan Edwards, who includes Isaiah 49:22–23 among passages fulfilled twice over—first "in the times of the apostles and of Constantine," but then again in the time "which is to succeed the fall of Antichrist."[42] In Edwards, though, talk of double fulfillment concerns two *Christian* fulfillments, leaving Jews out of the eschatological picture altogether. For explicit interest in eschatological applications of the text to Jews, one must turn to the millenarians. Thus, closer to the Book of Mormon's appearance, John Evans, in a late-eighteenth-century review of various Christian denominations, reports growing popularity among Christians on the margins for seeing the eschatological fulfillment of Isaiah 49:22–23 as applying to Jews. When Evans concludes his volume with a sketch of millenarianism, despite his evident desire to be neutral, he wishes his readers to know he is "not unmindful of the prophetic language of Isaiah, chap. xlix. 22, 23"—a passage he evidently takes as a potentially literal description of eschatological Jewish redemption.[43] A glance at one of Evans's examples of millenarianism confirms that such believers were ready to apply the fulfillment of Isaiah 49:22–23 to events in projected Jewish history: the maverick Universalist Elhanan Winchester explicitly contended against the learned opinions of the commentators in an eighteenth-century lecture series. Winchester directly argues that the second half of Isaiah 49 remained to be fulfilled despite "the common opinion that the Christian church" received the covenant once had by Jews.[44]

A more systematic argument than Winchester's against figurative interpretation of Isaiah 49:22–23 illustrates the interpretation from the margins during the early modern period. The literalist Joseph Eyre, in an eighteenth-century work titled *Observations upon the Prophecies Relating to the Restoration of the Jews*, quotes Isaiah 49:14–26 and then explains that

> Whoever reads the words of this Prophecy with the least attention, must (I think) be convinced, that they can relate to nothing else but the future Restoration of Israel. For they are not applicable either to the return from Babylon, or to the Christian church. Not the former, because they were never so straitened

for room, as is here foretold in ver. 19, 20. Nor did kings and queens ever bow down to them, and lick up the dust of their feet, according to ver. 23, but, on the contrary, rather tyrannized over them. Nor can they be applied to the Christian church; because this allegorical Zion has, as yet, had not of its waste and desolate places rendered too narrow by reason of the inhabitants; nor can she be said to be a captive, removing to and fro, or to be left alone."[45]

Insisting on a literal restoration of Israel, Eyre saw himself on the margins of the interpretive tradition. He in fact found that he had to append "an answer to the objections of a late author" to his book to respond to a mainstream book "in which the restoration of the Jews . . . is absolutely denied."[46]

Thus, as with the interpretations of Mormon's Christ in Third Nephi, it is again only on the margins of the Christian tradition—among millenarians positioned outside the mainstream—that one finds approaches to the prophet's meaning analogous to Nephi's. What Nephi assumes about the basic (that is, prelikening) meaning of Isaiah 49—its original and intentional meaning, with an eye to double fulfillment—would have struck almost any nineteenth-century reader (and certainly our deeply informed ideal reader) as aligned with the marginal millenarian tradition of interpretation. Even on the margins of the interpretive tradition, however, Nephi's interpretive method is peculiar. The peculiarity resides in Nephi's notion of likening and its connection to a prophetic vision of the eschatological history of New World Israel. To bring out the particularities of his uniqueness, then, it might be useful to consider something closer in time and place to the Book of Mormon's publication. A few years before the publication of the Book of Mormon, an important variant on occasional marginal millenarian expectations about Isaiah 49:22–23 appeared in New England. The Congregationalist Ethan Smith (unrelated to Joseph Smith) in *View of the Hebrews*—a text often mined by critics as a potential source for the Book of Mormon[47]—several times takes up Isaiah 49 to articulate a vision of eschatological Jewish redemption. (Our ideal listener/reader would naturally wonder about the relevance of *View of the Hebrews* to the Book of Mormon.) Like mainstream commentators (and Nephi's brother Jacob), Ethan Smith cites Isaiah 11:11–12 and Isaiah 49:22–23 together. Unlike mainstream commentators (and Nephi's brother Jacob), however, Smith takes neither the literal nor the figurative meanings of the two passages to be clear. For him, they do not straightforwardly predict a restoration of historically identifiable Jews, whether anciently (in the sixth century before Christ) or eschatologically (in a projected future for Jews). Neither do they figuratively predict the successes of the Christian church, attended to by powerful rulers.

Among the options, Smith is closer to the marginalized anticipation of Jewish restoration, but he complicates that position in key ways.[48]

Working to show that his approach to texts like Isaiah 11 and 49 is reasonable despite its distance from the mainstream, Ethan Smith first defends the very idea of literal—rather than figurative—interpretation of Old Testament prophecy. He finds "great evidence" that the prophets had strictly literal meanings in mind in "the preservation of the Jews, as a distinct people, among the many nations whither they have been dispersed, now for nearly eighteen hundred years."[49] Smith takes this as "a most signal event of providence"[50] and says that Jews "have never, as yet, possessed *all* the land promised to them; nor have they possessed any part of it *so long* as promised. Hence their restoration to that land is essential to the complete fulfilment of those ancient promises."[51] Then, having prepared his readers for literal interpretation, Smith turns to providing exegeses of prophetic passages, but now with a focus peculiar to his project—distinct from his many predecessors whether mainstream or marginal. Smith's *View of the Hebrews* aims not simply at defending the literal fulfillment of Old Testament prophecy among Jews, but rather at arguing that the prophets anticipated a restoration of the *whole* of ancient Israel—Jews *and* the so-called "lost ten tribes." And the burden of Smith's book is to show that the native peoples of the Americas are those lost tribes from ancient Israel's northern kingdom, and so to promote a program of enabling their return to Palestine, the land of their original inheritance.[52] Thus, when *View of the Hebrews* turns from theoretically justifying to practically illustrating Smith's literal hermeneutic, it considers passages that predict restoration for scattered Israelite northerners as much as for scattered Israelite southerners. Smith thus takes as a first and crucial prooftext a passage that would become dear to Latter-day Saints: Ezekiel 37:15–28, concerning the sticks of Judah and Ephraim that, although separated for a time, will be reunited in God's hand.[53] When Ezekiel prophesied, the northern nation of Ephraim was already lost to history, and so Ethan Smith takes Ezekiel 37's insistence on a reunification of Judah and Ephraim to indicate to every believer in the Bible that the lost ten tribes must be literally recovered and restored to their Palestinian lands.

To confirm the meaning of Ezekiel 37, Smith turns to Isaiah 11, emphasizing the same two verses that often draw Nephi's attention (and are the subject of chapter 8): "And it shall come to pass in that day, that the Lord shall set his hand again the second time to recover the remnant of his people, which shall be left, from Assyria, and from Egypt, and from Pathros, and from Cush, and from Elam, and from Shinar, and from Hamath, and from the islands of the sea.

And he shall set up an ensign for the nations, and shall assemble the outcasts of Israel, and gather together the dispersed of Judah from the four corners of the earth" (Isaiah 11:11–12). After quoting the text, Smith comments, "Here just before the Millennium, the Jews and ten tribes are collected from their long dispersion, by the hand of Omnipotence, set *a second time* for their recovery. A body of the Jews, and some of several other tribes, were recovered from ancient Babylon. God is going, in the last days, to make a *second*, and more *effectual* recovery from mystical Babylon, and from the four quarters of the earth."[54] Further interpreting, Smith emphasizes the use of the words *outcasts* and *dispersed* in the text, "which distinction will afford some light in our inquiries."[55] Because the word *outcasts* appears in connection with Israel, while *dispersed* appears in connection with Judah, he explains that "The Jews are '*dispersed*'; scattered over the nations as Jews, as they have long been known to be; but Israel are '*outcast*'; cast out from the nations; from society; from the social world; from the knowledge of men, as being Hebrews." Such a distinction, Smith avers, "is repeatedly found in the prophets."[56] This he demonstrates by turning, at last, to Isaiah 49:18–22.

Smith's first comment on Isaiah 49 shows that he sees its fulfillment occurring when the lost tribes of Israel reunite with Jews in their originally promised lands in Palestine:

> Accordingly, when Israel are recovered, and united with the Jews at last, the Jews express their astonishment; and inquire *where they had been*? They had utterly lost them, as is the fact. See Isai. xlix. 18–22. The Jews here, while *"removing to and fro"* through the nations in their dispersed state, had been *"left alone,"* i.e. of the ten tribes. The latter being now restored to the bosom of the mother church, the Jews inquire, *"Who hath brought up these? Behold, I was left alone; these, where had they been?"* Here we learn that the ten tribes had, during the long dispersion of the Jews, been utterly out of their sight and knowledge, as their brethren. This implies the long *outcast state of the ten tribes.*[57]

Smith here simultaneously prooftexts and provides interpretive argument. He takes phrases and lines from Isaiah 49 as self-evidently referring to the reactions of Jews, once reestablished in their own lands, to the eschatological arrival in their midst of some other children of Zion (Isaiah 49:21).[58] Smith confirms this interpretation and argument a few pages later: "There is no avoiding this conclusion. If God will restore [the ten tribes] at last as his Israel, and as having been '*outcast*' from the nations of the civilized world for 2500 years, . . . they must during that period have been unknown to the Jews as Israelites; and consequently unknown to the world as such; or the Jews would not at last (on their being united to them) inquire, 'These, where had they been?' Isai. xlix. 21."[59]

In all this interpretive work on Isaiah 49, Ethan Smith only cites—never quotes—the specific verses that interest Nephi most.[60] This fact raises questions about how the references to gentiles in Nephi's favored verses might fit into Smith's interpretation in *View of the Hebrews*. To leave out the actual words of Isaiah 49:22–23 is to leave out the passage's direct talk of gentiles. And, in fact, Smith's quotations of Isaiah 11 also omit that text's references to the gentiles. In both Isaiah 11 and Isaiah 49, at key junctures that deeply interest Nephi, one finds a "summoning" of the gentiles. The passages are related: "[Isaiah] 49.22 declares that the promise of 11.10–12 . . . is now to be fulfilled," a modern interpreter points out.[61] Smith seems to recognize this connection between the two passages, several times linking Isaiah 11:11–12 with Isaiah 49:18–23, but he just as consistently omits both passages' references to the gentiles. And, in fact, Smith seldom refers to gentiles in *View of the Hebrews*; the word appears just nineteen times in a publication that runs to nearly three hundred pages.[62] All but one of Smith's references to gentiles come in discussions of Romans 11:11–26 or in recommendations of *View of the Hebrews* printed at the beginning of the book.[63] The only time the word appears otherwise is in a quotation of Isaiah 60:3: "The gentiles shall come to thy light, and kings to the brightness of thy rising."[64] Smith appears reticent to admit Isaiah's talk of gentiles, despite his interest in Romans 11.

The reason for Smith's reticence can be reconstructed. He sees it as the responsibility of the gentiles *in general* to restore "dispersed" but identifiable Jews to their lands, but it is a rather *specific* subset of the gentiles who bear the unique burden of restoring the "outcast" or lost ten tribes to Palestine. In Isaiah 18 (a chapter never quoted or even alluded to in the Book of Mormon), Smith finds a "singularly enigmatical" prophecy whose "true intent" can only become clear "near the time of [its] fulfillment." Smith interprets the prophecy as "an address to some Christian people of the last days, just at the time of the final restoration of God's ancient people; an address to such a people beheld in vision away over the mouths of the Nile, or in some region of the west; a call and solemn divine charge to them to awake and aid that final restoration."[65] Despite having argued in an earlier publication that this prophecy concerned Great Britain (because of its references to naval power),[66] in *View of the Hebrews*, Smith argues that it is "far more probable that the Christian people of the United States of America are the subjects of the address"—or at least are "especially included in it" since they are geographically positioned near the lost Israelite tribes to be redeemed.[67] Taking this approach to Isaiah 18, Smith must be delicate in handling references to gentiles in passages he interprets as predicting the restoration of the outcast tribes of Israel to their promised lands. Doing so allows him to reserve the unique task of fulfilling these prophecies to specifically American gentile Christians.

It is worth considering carefully how Ethan Smith's interpretations of Isaiah 49 (and Isaiah 11) compare with those in Nephi's record, particularly since many have argued that *View of the Hebrews* lay behind the Book of Mormon.[68] The continuity between the style of Smith's approach to the Bible and the style of the marginalized tradition of literal interpretation is clear.[69] That Smith sees biblical prophecy, Isaiah in particular, to have its grandest and most important fulfillment in the literal (but eschatological) redemption of historical Jews places him among the minority of learned interpreters.[70] And there on the margins of the interpretive tradition, Nephi can be said to join Smith, also insisting that the original and intentional meaning of Isaiah's prophecies was to predict eschatological (as well as, to a lesser extent, ancient historical) restoration of Jews. There on those same margins, however, Smith and Nephi would have to pursue a controversy or take up a debate. Smith would happily concede that certain prophecies in Isaiah concern the eschatological redemption of Jews, but he would also argue that other prophecies in Isaiah literally and intentionally point to the eschatological redemption of the lost ten tribes of Israel, specifically understood to be located in modern America. This might make Smith reminiscent of Mormon's Christ (albeit with a focus on a different set of Isaiah texts), but Nephi never makes the last of Smith's moves. Nephi certainly understands Isaiah 49:22–23 to predict the gathering of the lost ten tribes. Setting up his interpretation of the passage in 1 Nephi 22, Nephi says that it applies not only to those "which are at Jerusalem," the people of Judah or Jews, but also to "the more part of all the tribes," the lost tribes who are "scattered to and fro upon the isles of the sea" (1 Nephi 22:4). But the differences between Nephi's and Smith's applications of this passage to the redemption of the lost tribes are crucial.

A first key difference is the fact that Nephi sees Jews and the lost tribes of Israel as twin intentional targets of Isaiah's prediction of a people "nursed by the gentiles" and "carried in their arms" (1 Nephi 22:6). For Smith, such Isaian talk refers *solely* to the redemption of the lost tribes, who are to be brought to an already restored Jewish nation. Nephi's interpretation thus lacks Smith's differentiation of distinct Israelite roles in the fulfillment of Isaiah 49:22–23, with Jews baffled as they receive the lost tribes and the lost tribes coming to know who they are as they arrive among Jews. A second difference is the fact that the Book of Mormon is explicit that the lost ten tribes are not among the peoples whose history it recounts (despite a long history of readers of the Book of Mormon thinking it so).[71] The Book of Mormon occasionally refers to the lost ten tribes, but it explicitly distinguishes them from the latter-day descendants of Nephi and his brothers (2 Nephi 29:12–13; 3 Nephi 16:1–3). Thus, where Smith seeks to identify the location of the lost tribes and then sifts Isaiah's prophecies for references to their redemption, Nephi forges a way of applying Isaiah's prophecies to an unintended group of Israelites, irreducible either to the historically identifiable Jewish people or to the lost tribes of so much legend and myth. A third and final key difference is the fact that Nephi so consistently inserts his own people within the scope of Isaiah's prophecies—Isaiah 49:22–23 included—only through what he calls likening. Through this interpretive move, Nephi extends to a New World remnant of Israel a prophecy he regards as originally predicting the redemption only of Old World peoples (Jews and other Israelites). Smith sees Isaiah as literally and intentionally anticipating through his prophetic gifts the existence of the latter-day nation of the United States of America, assigning them a specific task in the redemption of the lost ten tribes. Nephi sees Isaiah only as applicable to a New World Israelite people and their American gentile caretakers through a hermeneutic diversion. Even among marginal or heterodox interpreters in antebellum American Christianity, then, Nephi's approach to the first of his three favored passages looks peculiar.

In the end, the example of Ethan Smith serves to bring out the real peculiarity of Nephi's Isaian project, and perhaps of the entire Book of Mormon's Isaian project. Smith's interpretation of Isaiah 11 and 49 is reminiscent in certain ways of the interpretation of Isaiah 52 and 54 by Mormon's Christ. He, like the Christ of Third Nephi, takes certain of Isaiah's prophecies to be about Old World Israel and others among Isaiah's prophecies to be about New World Israel (although Smith identifies the latter with the lost ten tribes, which Mormon's Christ does not). This, though, distances Smith from Nephi, who limits the scope of Isaiah's prophecies to just Old World Israel while he likens those prophecies to New World Israel (again, a small remnant rather than the lost ten tribes as a whole) through a secondary and derivative reappropriation, conscious and deliberate. The conjunction of Nephi's and Mormon's projects suggests that it requires a resurrected and glorified God to see the whole scope of world history and so to see how to read Isaiah as outlining that history without a project of likening. Every human being is necessarily limited in what she can see of history. Next to the Book of Mormon, Ethan Smith's study would (ironically) look hubristic to our ideal listener/reader, as if the human preacher had somehow the ability to see world history with the eyes of God and so to understand the global scope of Isaiah's prophecies without needing to lean—like Nephi—on the crutch of likening.

The approach to Isaiah 49 on display in Nephi's record thus accomplishes two things at once. On the one hand, it leaves behind the liturgical association of Isaiah 49 with the feast of Epiphany featured in the oldest Christian interpretive tradition, and it sidelines figural interpretations focused on the successes of Christian preaching, which came to occupy the mainstream of early modern English-speaking Isaiah interpretation. Our ideal listener/reader would certainly assign Nephi's approach its natural place at the time of the Book of Mormon's publication on the populist margins of the interpretive tradition, where millenarian approaches tended to thrive. Even among the marginalized, however, as our listener/reader would point out, Nephi's approach is strange. And so, on the other hand, in its methodological discontinuity with the interpretive style of Mormon's Christ, Nephi's record, as it were, concedes to other marginalized interpreters that Isaiah predicts the literal redemption of Jews in an otherwise deeply Christian eschaton, but he concedes this only to turn his attention to his unique project of likening. This peculiarity about Nephi's interpretive style is, though, not self-arrogating, an act of audacity or hermeneutic daring. Rather, as comparison with Ethan Smith's *View of the Hebrews* confirms and clarifies, Nephi and Jacob seem actually to represent a kind of humility, a recognition of the limited perspective of any human interpreter of history and of Isaian prophecy. Nephi's record suggests that the best human interpretations of Isaiah will begin from solid exegesis, slowly develop clear patterns of God's working in certain limited stretches of history, and finally ask whether and how those same patterns might informatively be found elsewhere—but always with an eye to the recovery of scattered Israel.

As the First Book of Nephi concludes, then, the larger but still preliminary stakes of Nephi's Isaian project begin to make themselves clear. What within Mormon's project is a gradually developed program of literalist and eschatological interpretation of Isaiah is in Nephi's writings literalist and eschatological right from the outset, but with a deeply human dimension. Nephi's Isaian hermeneutic is more at home in its human skin, and more comfortable with its position on the margins of the Christian tradition. Certainly, no battles between establishment priests and prophets from the wilderness are necessary for Nephi to set forth his interpretive style. Also, though, Nephi's and Jacob's hermeneutical method does not aspire to be the kind that could only be offered to the world by God himself come down in exalted flesh. Nephi is a founding figure, king and priest over his people, writing his interpretive principles into a record meant to serve for "the instruction of [his] people" (1 Nephi 19:3). He pursues his task calmly and methodically, and always with a sense of his own humanity. Perhaps it is precisely for this reason that he can add to his hermeneutic a dimension missing from the hermeneutic models in Mormon's project. Where Noah's priests and Abinadi debate the literal meaning of Isaiah, and where Mormon's Christ simply sets forth (what he claims to be) the prophet's literal meaning, Nephi explores literal *and* figurative meanings simultaneously, recognizing the former through an earnest reading of the prophet and producing the other through the prophetic and intellectual work of likening. That there seems to be a deliberate and systematic architecture at work in Nephi's presentation of this hermeneutical theory, however, requires further exposition. Exactly how does Nephi organize his larger (two-book) record, and how does that organization shape his new interpretive method?

7

The Structure of Nephi's Record

Continuous with but departing from Mormon's record, Nephi's writings contain the Book of Mormon's most sophisticated interaction with Isaiah. Its sophistication consists not only in the new hermeneutic operation (likening) that Nephi introduces, but also in the way Nephi introduces the new operation and establishes its aims. Close reading reveals that this culminating approach to Isaiah rises to a level of systematicity unimagined elsewhere in the Book of Mormon. Isaiah is the beating heart of Nephi's record. With Nephi, the Isaian project is positive rather than reactive, constitutive rather than explanatory. The character of the project might not be obvious in the First Book of Nephi, but it is evident to any reader of the Second. Where First Nephi concludes on an Isaian note, Second Nephi never lets the Isaian symphony end. Yet it remains a question for most readers *just how* Isaiah is essential to Nephi, *just what* is essential about Isaiah for Nephi's purposes. To answer these questions, the total picture of Nephi's approach, stretched across *both* of his books, must become clear. At this point, even our ideal listener/reader would naturally feel prompted by the Isaian obsession over the text to set reception history aside and examine Nephi's project for Isaiah's place in it. It is necessary to investigate the structure and scope of Nephi's entire record.[1]

Readers too easily miss the fact that the text explicitly presents Nephi as having had decades to reflect on his life and prophetic experiences before writing his two books (2 Nephi 5:28–34). Although the story opens with Nephi as a young man, he writes it as an old one. Readers are thus not intended to expect in Nephi's writings the haphazard reflections of a journal written in near-real time (which is how lay Latter-day Saints often read it); rather, they are meant to encounter something developed and carefully wrought, the result of extended reflection. Further, that Nephi occasionally interrupts his record with asides that explain its organization confirms that the thing has a definite shape that should belie its underlying motivations and overarching intentions. What do we find if we examine the structure of Nephi's record? The thing is organized, from beginning to end, around the task of interpreting Isaiah.

Here, then, to grasp clearly what Isaiah is doing in Nephi's record, we must do more than analyze the historical and theological context in which each major interaction with Isaiah appears. We have seen the importance of such contexts in analyzing Abinadi and Mormon's Christ. Nephi, however, explicitly expresses the hope that his readers can understand Isaiah *regardless* of historical and cultural contexts (2 Nephi 25:4). The text thus does not intend for them to believe that Nephi's approach to Isaiah is right because of its historical or cultural proximity to Isaiah's original production. Instead, Nephi openly acknowledges that he reads Isaiah through the lens of prophecy of his own (25:7) in his hope to make Isaiah plain (25:4). There is a context for Nephi's reading of Isaiah, but it is *extra*historical; the relevant theological motivations derive from structural rather than historical dimensions of Nephi's record.

Nephi develops his method of likening precisely to signal the fact that Isaiah aligns with his prophetic visions. Repeatedly in his record, Nephi and his brother Jacob speak of likening Isaiah's words to their people's distant future, anticipated prophetically (1 Nephi 19:23, 24; 22:8 2 Nephi 6:5; 11:2, 8). Although readers often understand Nephi's references to likening as simple recommendations to apply scripture to their own devoted lives,[2] the term indicates—as already glimpsed in chapter 6—the hermeneutic relationship Nephi creates between various Isaiah passages and parts of his own visions.[3] Thus, the task of the present chapter is to examine thoroughly Nephi's program of likening, guided by the systematic organization of his writings. How does Nephi arrange things to place Isaian texts in "likenable" relation to his own visions? And how might this clarify Nephi's project before one crosses the threshold between First Nephi and Second Nephi, between the gentle beginnings and the serious climax of the record's treatment of Isaiah?

Structure as Message

When devoted readers seek the meaning of Nephi's record, the literature suggests, they look for one of two things. First, many seek practical understanding, watching for illustrations of the universal human struggle for faith. The relevant narratives appear in 1 Nephi 1–5, 7, 10, 15–18, 22, and 2 Nephi 1, 5. With an eye to this sort of reading, Susan Elizabeth Howe nicely sums up this common view among readers:

> There is an epic dimension to the story of Lehi and his family, a joyful story in that they undertake a perilous journey into the unknown—first into the wilderness and then across a vast uncharted ocean—and arrive at "a land of promise," a land "choice above all other lands." But it is a tragic story in that it chronicles the disintegration of a family into warring peoples who fight against each other for over a thousand years.[4]

Readers see their own struggles in Nephi's efforts to be faithful, their own temptations in the doubts of Nephi's family, and their own blessings in the divine graces recounted by Nephi. In many ways, the text invites this reading. As Grant Hardy rightly says, the book "is very didactic. . . . Even casual readers come away with a fairly accurate impression of the point of the book; it is hard to miss its insistence that readers change their lives and accept its values and assertions as an authoritative revelation from God."[5]

A second approach predominates alongside the first. Many readers, following a mid-twentieth-century Latter-day Saint model of interpreting scripture, look for "doctrine," meaning (in the words of its key defender, apostle Bruce R. McConkie) "the tenets, teachings, and true theories found in the scriptures; it includes the principles, precepts, and revealed philosophies of pure religion."[6] Traditional commentaries emphasize the doctrinal aspect of the text,[7] focusing especially on 1 Nephi 8, 11–14, 19, and 2 Nephi 2–3, 9, 28–32, as do well-circulated collections of essays.[8] Monte Nyman and Charles Tate illustrate this approach: "The book of 1 Nephi firmly establishes the major doctrine of the Book of Mormon—that Jesus Christ is the Savior of the world. . . . Other doctrines such as faith in Christ, the value of his word, the power of the Holy Ghost, and the relevance of his prophets are among many substantiated in that first book."[9] For most Latter-day Saints early in the twenty-first century, what matters in reading Nephi is an understanding of his doctrine.

These two approaches—reading for application and doctrinal insight—prevail among lay readers and believing scholars. Consequently, the literature on Nephi's record seldom asks about textual organization, obscuring the way basic structures might outline literary aims that are in tension with received pragmatic and doctrinal readings. There are, of course, exceptions to the pattern of overlooking structure and literary intention. Noel Reynolds and Brant Gardner have each argued separately that Nephi's record is a "political tract" (Reynolds) or "story of ethnogenesis" (Gardner)[10] and attempted structural analyses of

Nephi's two books (Reynolds in more detail).[11] Following John Welch's work on chiasmus in the Book of Mormon, Reynolds argues that complex chiastic patterns organize each of Nephi's two books.[12] Less comprehensive sketches of structures for First and Second Nephi have appeared as well. Sidney Sperry provides a "scheme of analysis" for each of Nephi's two books but without much argument.[13] Appropriate to his work on connections between the story in First Nephi and the archaeology of the Arabian peninsula, Kent Brown outlines First Nephi as a series of events in distinct geographical settings.[14] More recently, Christopher Thomas has outlined a threefold structure of First Nephi, signaled by the repeated concluding refrain, "and thus it is, amen."[15] From my perspective, however, the most interesting structural analysis of Nephi's record to date is that of Frederick Axelgard, who examines explicit editorial indications within the text about how Nephi himself carves up the text.[16] Although Axelgard's proposal requires development,[17] he is among the very few writers who have noted that Nephi directly explains the basic organization of his record. Too many who have examined structure in Nephi's record neglect these editorial comments, preferring their own aesthetic feel for what Thomas helpfully calls "the overall movement" of Nephi's record.[18]

The fact is that Nephi's record is interspersed with numerous editorial interruptions that focus directly on matters of organization. On this score, Nephi's writings differ from Mormon's. Editorial comments are scattered throughout Mormon's record, but they primarily mark shifts between literary sources or introduce sequences of narrative.[19] Nephi, by contrast, interrupts with editorial comments that explain the larger organization of entire books. Further, Nephi does his most important structural work by using *pairs* of editorial interruptions, with the two elements of a pair located at different points in his record so that one anticipates the other. That is, for each pair, Nephi interrupts his narrative at a relatively early point to explain an aspect of the text's larger structure, but also wording the interruption so as to explicitly anticipate some later moment in his record; then, at the anticipated later point, he interrupts again to mark the fulfillment of the earlier editorial anticipation, confirming the structure. Because these pairs of linked editorial interruptions involve passages at some textual distance from each other, their significance is easily missed by lay and even scholarly readers. To develop a sense for the structure of Nephi's record, these pairs require close attention.

One first pair of editorial comments that helps to clarify the structure of Nephi's record occurs in First Nephi. Its first element appears within a few paragraphs of the beginning of the book (in 1 Nephi 1:16–17). In the middle of the first story Nephi tells, he suddenly breaks off the narrative to explain his literary intentions: "And now I, Nephi, do not make a full account of the things which my father hath written . . . , but I shall make an account of my proceedings in my days. Behold, I make an abridgment of the record of my father upon plates which I have made with mine own hands; wherefore, after that I have abridged the record of my father, then will I make an account of mine own life." Nephi here indicates that his record—or at least some part of it—divides evenly into two halves: a first containing a shortened version of his father's record, and a second addressing the details of his own life. With words like "after" and "then," moreover, Nephi develops a sense of anticipation, and so the careful reader feels obligated to search for the anticipated moment later in the text when one half gives way to the other. One might initially guess that the two halves indicated here are in fact the two books of Nephi, with First Nephi abridging the record of Nephi's father and Second Nephi addressing the details of Nephi's life. A close reading of Nephi's record, however, makes clear that this first editorial comment means to describe the basic organization just of First Nephi. In other words, Nephi indicates that there are, in fact, two halves just to his first book.[20]

The division becomes clear when the anticipated moment of transition from the abridgment of Nephi's father's record arrives. It comes in 1 Nephi 10:1 when Nephi editorially announces, "And now I, Nephi, proceed to give an account upon these plates of my proceedings—and my reign and ministry."[21] Not only does this language directly resume the language of 1:16–17, it draws also on the often-overlooked subtitle of First Nephi: "The Book of Nephi, *His Reign and Ministry*."[22] Together, then, 1 Nephi 1:16–17 and 1 Nephi 10:1 form the first pair of editorial comments, marking out the basic structure of First Nephi. 1 Nephi 1–9 clearly forms what Nephi calls the abridgment of his father's record, while 1 Nephi 10–22 forms the basic account of Nephi's own life, his "reign," and his "ministry."[23]

Another pair of editorial interruptions sketches the outline of Second Nephi (although the first element of this pair appears in First Nephi). It is this feature of the text that Axelgard examines. The first passage of this pair is 1 Nephi 19:1–5, where, as Axelgard puts it, one gets a "rare glimpse into [Nephi's] organizational thoughts."[24] At this point in Nephi's narrative, he and his family have just arrived in the New World after years of travel, and God commands Nephi to create a record of his people. Nephi breaks off the story at just this point to explain that the record just referred to is *not* the small-plates record we are reading. "I did make plates of ore," he explains, but "I knew not at the time which I made them that I should be commanded of the Lord to make *these* plates," the small plates (1 Nephi 19:1–2, emphasis added). Here, as at other various points in his record (1 Nephi 6:1–6; 9:2–6), Nephi distinguishes the small-plates record from other records kept on plates.

Nephi goes on to explain that when he later received a command to make the small plates, that command was accompanied by divine instructions about what should go into them: "the ministry and the prophecies, the more plain and precious parts of them" (19:3). Since this record would not actually be produced until a later point in his story, however, Nephi makes a kind of promise to his reader: "An account of my making these plates [the small plates] shall be given hereafter" (19:5). Here, again, an editorial interruption from Nephi, appearing relatively early in the record, points anticipatorily to a later moment in the record ("hereafter"). And, to be sure, Nephi later tells the story of when, eventually, he was commanded to create a second record, the small plates containing the two books of Nephi familiar from the Book of Mormon. This anticipated passage occurs at the end of Nephi's life's story, in 2 Nephi 5. After Nephi becomes the founder of a people named for him, a people living "after the manner of happiness," he reports that "thirty years had passed away" since the family had left Jerusalem, and that he had dutifully "kept the records" on the large plates for years (2 Nephi 5:27–29). But then, he tells us, "the Lord God said" that he should "make other plates," the small plates at last, and Nephi was "obedient to the commandments of the Lord" (5:30–32).

Here, then, is a second pair: 1 Nephi 19:1–5 and 2 Nephi 5:28–34.[25] This pair also has structural implications. As Axelgard points out, not only does 1 Nephi 19:1–5 explain that the story of the small plates' physical production is to come later in Nephi's record, it *also* "marks that account as a threshold [Nephi] will cross before he conveys 'more sacred things.'"[26] When Nephi's editorial aside in 1 Nephi 19:1–5 is taken together with the narrative report of 2 Nephi 5:28–34, a key organizational detail in Nephi's record comes to light. Nephi understands his small-plates record to serve principally as the receptacle of a particular set of plain and precious prophecies, and he wants his readers to know that they are found at a specific place within his record: beginning immediately after 2 Nephi 5:28–34—that is, beginning with 2 Nephi 6. It seems clear, moreover, that this stretch of "more sacred things" comes to an end with 2 Nephi 30, which concludes when Nephi says that he "must make an end" of his sayings (2 Nephi 30:18; see also 31:1). Nephi thus indicates in his editorial aside in 1 Nephi 19 that a specific set of twenty-five chapters, 2 Nephi 6–30, makes up the plain and precious prophecies, "the more sacred things," he has been commanded to record.[27]

This second pair of editorial comments helps to make clear in a general way that Nephi expects readers to grant a certain privilege to Second Nephi, making it the focal point of Nephi's record. Further, because Nephi designates a core within Second Nephi as containing "the more sacred things," the general structure of Second Nephi becomes apparent. It opens with a few chapters (2 Nephi 1–5) that presumably serve as a narrative introduction, providing context for the key prophecies in 2 Nephi 6–30. And then it closes with a few chapters (2 Nephi 31–33) that presumably serve as an exhortative epilogue, allowing Nephi to follow his presentation of the key prophecies of 2 Nephi 6–30 with a conclusion.[28]

Further structure in Second Nephi can be discerned in light of another editorial comment in 2 Nephi 11, this one standing on its own rather than as part of a pair. The first handful of chapters in Nephi's "more sacred things" consists of a two-day sermon delivered on some unstated occasion by Nephi's priestly younger brother Jacob. The sermon appears in 2 Nephi 6–10. After the sermon, Nephi provides a few words of editorial explanation. He first states that he has edited Jacob's words to meet his own editorial interests (2 Nephi 11:1) and then outlines the basic principle of organization for 2 Nephi 6–30: "And now I, Nephi, write more of the words of Isaiah . . . , for he verily saw my redeemer, even as I have seen him, and my brother Jacob also hath seen him, as I have seen him. Wherefore, I will send their words forth unto my children to prove unto them that my words are true. Wherefore, 'by the words of three,' God hath said, 'I will establish my word'" (11:2–3). Nephi makes perfectly clear here that his "more sacred things," 2 Nephi 6–30, divide into three sequences. First comes Jacob's two-day sermon in 2 Nephi 6–10 (a first witness). There follows a lengthy quotation from the Book of Isaiah in 2 Nephi 12–24 (a second witness). Finally, the section concludes with Nephi's own prophecies in 2 Nephi 25–30 (a third witness).[29]

It is possible to refine still further the structure of Second Nephi, as well as the structure of First Nephi. Refinement, however, requires moving beyond the most straightforward editorial comments Nephi provides. Before turning to such refinements, then, it is perhaps worth drawing up a kind of balance sheet. From Nephi's explicit editorial comments alone, it is possible to provide a general preliminary outline of the contents of Nephi's record. Nephi of course and most obviously divides his record into two distinguishable books, First

Nephi and Second Nephi. But his interruptive editorial comments, functioning most often in structurally significant pairs, divide these two books up into clear and distinct sections:

The First Book of Nephi
 Part 1—The Abridgment of the Record of Nephi's Father (chs. 1–9)
 Part 2—The Record of Nephi's Own Reign and Ministry (chs. 10–22)
The Second Book of Nephi
 Part 1—Introduction (chs. 1–5)
 Part 2—The Plain and Precious Prophecies (chs. 6–30)[30]
  Subpart A—The Witness of Nephi's Brother Jacob (chs. 6–10)
  Subpart B—The Witness of the Prophet Isaiah (chs. 11–24)
  Subpart C—The Witness of Nephi Himself (chs. 25–30)
 Part 3—Epilogue (chs. 31–33)

Refining the Structure of Nephi's Record

The general structure of Nephi's record is already helpful. It makes clear that First Nephi introduces readers to Nephi and his prophetic style—moving from his beginnings within the context of his father's prophetic ministry to his more mature days as a prophet himself.[31] And it makes clear that Second Nephi then launches a deeper investigation into Nephi's ministry and prophecies, using other relevant witnesses to clarify and to confirm what Nephi has to say in his own prophetic voice. The feel and flow of Nephi's record are thus clear just in light of Nephi's explicit editorial comments. Closer investigation, however, reveals a level of structural detail at once startling and highly instructive.

To refine the apparent structures organizing Nephi's record further, it is necessary to consider the original chapter breaks in the text. Readily available editions of the Book of Mormon published by the Church of Jesus Christ of Latter-day Saints today—as well as numerous derivative editions—utilize chapter breaks and versification introduced into the text only in the 1870s by the Latter-day Saint apostle Orson Pratt.[32] This late-nineteenth-century rechaptering was intended both to give the book a more biblical or scriptural feel and to make study and reference easier for readers.[33] It also in some ways obscured the flow and organization of the text as originally dictated by Smith to his scribes, especially in places where original chapter breaks now find themselves in the middle of current chapters.[34] The chapters Smith originally dictated play a deliberate role in organizing the narrative and contents of the book. The first two original chapters of First Nephi, for instance, both utilize the classic literary device biblical scholars call an *inclusio*, a framing device where "a repeated phrase or whole line . . . stands at the beginning and end of a poetic [or more generally textual] unit." The function of every *inclusio* "is obvious and straightforward"; it "delimits a poetic [or textual] unit, providing a strong sense of beginning and closure."[35] Thus, the original first chapter of First Nephi (today made up of 1 Nephi 1–5) opens and closes with clearly parallel narrative pericopes, in each of which Nephi's father, Lehi, has a book brought down to him from above that, when he reads it, fills him with the divine spirit and spurs him to prophesy (1 Nephi 1:9, 11–12, 18; 5:1, 10, 17). Similarly, the original second chapter of Second Nephi (today made up of 1 Nephi 6–9) opens and closes with clearly parallel editorial interruptions that distinguish Nephi's small plates from other textual sources (1 Nephi 6:1–6; 9:2–6).[36] These structural details make perfectly clear that the original chapter breaks, as dictated by Smith to his scribes in 1829, are intentional structural features of the text. They must not be overlooked in a further refinement of the structure of Nephi's record.

Whereas most readers of the Book of Mormon today are familiar with First Nephi as divided into twenty-two chapters, what Smith originally dictated came in only seven chapters. The seven original chapters map onto current chapters and verses in Latter-day Saint editions of the Book of Mormon as follows. (I use Roman numerals for original chapters, while I continue to use Arabic numerals for current chapters and verses.)

Chapter I—1 Nephi 1–5
Chapter II—1 Nephi 6–9
Chapter III—1 Nephi 10–14
Chapter IV—1 Nephi 15
Chapter V—1 Nephi 16:1–19:21
Chapter VI—1 Nephi 19:22–21:26
Chapter VII—1 Nephi 22

Two things are immediately apparent from these details. First, in some cases—especially where original chapters were reasonably short—Orson Pratt followed original chapter breaks. Thus the original chapters IV and VII are equivalent to today's chapters 15 and 22. Elsewhere, Pratt's concern was apparently to create shorter chapters for easier reading and reference. Second, Pratt apparently felt free to obscure some original chapter breaks by locating them in the middle of one of his own new chapters. Thus, the break between the original chapters V and VI does not match a chapter break in today's text, but instead appears within chapter 19. In this case, it is not difficult to guess at Pratt's reasons for such heavy-handed manipulation.[37] In creating the shorter current chapters 20 and 21, each of which reproduces a chapter of Isaiah (Isaiah 48 and 49 respectively), Pratt apparently wished for them to follow the exact versification of familiar editions of the Bible, so that readers might compare the texts verse by verse to see textual variants in the Book of Mormon.[38]

Now, how do the original chapters of First Nephi refine the structure of the book? To answer this question, it is necessary to assign the original seven chapters to their respective places within the two halves of First Nephi already identified (thanks to Nephi's paired editorial comments in 1 Nephi 1:16–17 and 1 Nephi 10:1). A basic outline of the whole First Book of Nephi thus takes shape (with basic descriptions of each chapter's content):

First Nephi, Part 1—The Abridgment of the Record of Nephi's Father
Ch. I (chs. 1–5)—Nephi's family leaves Jerusalem, but not without a collection of sacred Jewish writings recorded on brass plates.
Ch. II (chs. 6–9)—Intrigue in the family spurs Lehi to receive a crucial prophetic dream that inaugurates a new prophetic tradition.
First Nephi, Part 2—The Record of Nephi's Own Reign and Ministry
Ch. III (chs. 10–14)—Nephi seeks and receives his own experience of Lehi's dream, expanded into a massive apocalyptic vision.
Ch. IV (ch. 15)—Finding that his brothers do not understand the dream, Nephi explains its meaning to them.
Ch. V (16:1–19:21)—The family journeys across the desert to the ocean, builds a ship, and then crosses the ocean to the New World.
Ch. VI (19:22–21:26)—Nephi reads to the family, now settled in the New World, from the prophecies of Isaiah.
Ch. VII (ch. 22)—Finding that his brothers do not understand Isaiah, Nephi explains the meaning of the text to them.

Revisiting the fact that Nephi explicitly divides First Nephi into two halves, one now sees that each half has its own implicit shape. The original chaptering reveals, for example, that the abridgment of Lehi's record consists of only two blocks of text, two overarching stories (however complex each of those stories might be). In turn, although five original chapters make up the second half of First Nephi, a relatively obvious pattern organizes them. Chapter III provides a detailed vision that Nephi then has to explain to his confused brothers in chapter IV, just as chapter VI provides a lengthy quotation of Isaiah that Nephi then has to explain to those same brothers in chapter VII. There is an order and a flow to the seven original chapters of First Nephi.

The basic relationships among the original chapters of First Nephi become clear with a little bit of analysis. Chapter I contains various materials, yet there is an unmistakably central narrative serving as a focal point. The primary subject of chapter I is the retrieval from Jerusalem of the brass plates, a Jewish scriptural record that features the writings of Isaiah. Everything before the story of the record's retrieval—Lehi's call as a prophet and the family's removal from Jerusalem—sets up that central story, which then occupies center stage for the remainder of the original first chapter. For its part, chapter II tells only two stories: that of a second return journey to Jerusalem (this time to retrieve another family to accompany Nephi's), which concludes with a protracted confrontation between Nephi and his brothers; and that of Lehi's long and complex dream about a tree. The relationship between these two stories is easy to see. The violent confrontation between Nephi and his brothers is the obvious spur of and interpretive lens for the subsequent telling of the dream, which focuses intensely on the soteriological status of Nephi's rebellious brothers. The dream is then the obvious emphasis of chapter II. Finally, taken together, Nephi's first two original chapters recount the circumstances under which his family came to possess two sources of divine revelation: an Old World collection of scriptures, featuring especially the writings of Isaiah (chapter I) and the beginnings of a New World prophetic tradition, starting from Lehi's rich and justly famous dream (chapter II).

These same two sources of divine revelation form the heart of the second half of First Nephi as well. Chapter III opens that second half by recounting in protracted detail Nephi's own experience of the same dream his father had. In effect, what chapter II introduces already at some length chapter III drastically expands—and clarifies as well thanks to helpful commentary by an angelic guide. Chapter IV then gives Nephi an opportunity to explain Lehi's dream to his brothers. In turn and in fact in parallel, chapter VI does its own work of expanding the other source from the first half of First Nephi, providing the first extended quotation from the writings of Isaiah featured on the brass plates. Chapter VII then gives Nephi an opportunity to explain that text to his brothers. The second half of First Nephi thus provides expansions of and explicit commentaries on precisely the two revelatory sources introduced in the first half.[39]

The larger structure of First Nephi thus becomes readily apparent. Nephi's abridgment of Lehi's record, despite its complexity, reduces to two basic stories, each introducing a key revelatory source that will undergird Nephi's own prophetic activity. It is therefore possible to reproduce the structure of First

Nephi anew, but now with more instructive titles for the two halves of the book, and with new titles and refocused summaries for each original chapter:

First Nephi, Part 1—The Provenance of Two Revelatory Sources
Ch. I, "The Writings of Isaiah"—Nephi's family leaves Jerusalem, but Nephi and his brothers then return to retrieve the brass plates, containing the writings of Isaiah.
Ch. II, "The Dream of the Tree"—Partly in response to the rebellion of Nephi's brothers, Lehi has a dream that inaugurates a new and living prophetic tradition for the migrating family.

First Nephi, Part 2—Investigating the Two Revelatory Sources
Ch. III, "The Dream Expanded"—Nephi seeks and then experiences his father's dream, but in dramatically expanded form and with explanatory comments from an angelic attendant.
Ch. IV, "The Dream Explained"—Because his brothers do not understand the dream's meaning, Nephi interprets it for them.
Ch. V, "The Journey"—The family crosses the Arabian desert, builds a seaworthy ship, and then sails to the New World.
Ch. VI, "Isaiah Quoted"—Nephi reads aloud and copies into his record two substantial chapters from the Book of Isaiah, with a few introductory comments to guide interpretation.
Ch. VII, "Isaiah Explained"—Because his brothers do not understand Isaiah's prophecies, Nephi explains their meaning.

One further detail about the structure of First Nephi deserves at least preliminary notice at this point. Not only does the second half of the book develop and explain the two revelatory sources introduced in the first half, it also suggests that what makes for full comprehension of each revelatory source is, in fact, the *other* revelatory source. When Nephi explains his father's dream to his brothers in chapter IV, he states that he "did rehearse unto them the words of Isaiah" to clarify the dream's meaning (1 Nephi 15:20). Similarly, if less explicitly, chapter VII makes clear that Nephi's chief resource for clarifying the meaning of Isaiah for his brothers is Lehi's dream as he himself experienced it (1 Nephi 22:2–28). First Nephi therefore places these two sources into relationship, with each bearing explanatory power for the other. This, it will turn out, has major implications for understanding the nature of Second Nephi, and especially for understanding the relationship between Nephi's two books.

In Second Nephi, original chaptering is less crucial for sorting out structure, but it is helpful for clarifying thematic development.

Second Nephi, Part 1—An Introduction to the More Sacred Things
   Ch. I (chs. 1–2)—Lehi addresses his final words to his first sons born in Jerusalem (Nephi's brothers Laman and Lemuel), and to his first son born in the desert (Nephi's brother Jacob).
   Ch. II (ch. 3)—Lehi delivers to his youngest son (Nephi's youngest brother, Joseph) a series of prophecies focused on the redemption of the Lamanites in the last days.
   Ch. III (ch. 4)—Lehi speaks to his grandchildren who will become Lamanites and then dies; Nephi records a psalmlike prayer that illuminates his conflict with his brothers.[40]
   Ch. IV (ch. 5)—The Nephites and the Lamanites, after Lehi's death, finally divide into warring nations as a racializing curse falls on the Lamanites.

Even these cursory summaries of the first four original chapters of Second Nephi make clear the basic structural purpose of what immediately precedes Nephi's "more sacred things." Each chapter focuses intensely on the question of the Lamanites' fate—through direct address to the Lamanites' founders (chapter I), through prophetic articulation of their future (chapter II), through further prophecy and a focused psalm on the conflict (chapter III), and through the actual narrative account of the divide between the Nephites and the Lamanites (chapter IV). This fixation prepares the reader for Nephi's plain and precious prophecies, which outline God's plan to restore the Lamanites out of covenantal fidelity. What is now 2 Nephi 1–5 indeed serves as a straightforward introduction to Second Nephi's prophetic core.

The witness then offered by Nephi's brother Jacob has a clear shape of its own:

Second Nephi, Part 2 (The More Sacred Things), Subpart A—Jacob's Witness
   Ch. V (chs. 6–8)—Under Nephi's direction, Jacob reads from and comments on a few chapters from Isaiah, applying them at first solely to Jewish (and not to Lamanite) history.[41]
   Ch. VI (ch. 9)—Jacob diverts from his Isaian and covenantal theme to speak about resurrection and to offer practical exhortations to his audience.
   Ch. VII (ch. 10)—On a second day of sermonizing, Jacob returns to Isaiah and the covenant theme, reviewing Jewish history before turning to future Lamanite history.

Nephi divides Jacob's lengthy (but nonetheless truncated) sermon into three sequences, sandwiching his more specifically Christian and soteriological reflections between two more strictly Isaian sequences about the covenant. Jacob's comments on Isaiah, focused especially on the same passage that features at the end of First Nephi (Isaiah 49:22–23), effectively resume Nephi's earlier commentary and foreshadow Nephi's later prophetic words.

Still more to the point, however, is the witness offered in the infamously long quotation of Isaiah that follows Jacob's sermon. Here, if anywhere in Second Nephi, original chapter breaks help to clarify the meaning and flow of the text, because they group the much shorter chapters familiar from the King James Version of the Bible into larger blocks that together tell a clear three-part story. A first (original) chapter articulates the problem, a second outlines the solution, and a third celebrates success by recounting the elimination of God's opponents:

> *Second Nephi, Part 2 (the More Sacred Things), Subpart B—Isaiah's Witness*
> Ch. VIII (chs. 11–15)—The text develops a stark contrast between Israel's divinely appointed destiny (leading other nations to peace and truth) and Israel's present situation (imitating those nations).
> Ch. IX (chs. 16–22)—God bridges present and future by sending a prophet with the task of hardening the people, reducing them to a remnant that will return and fulfill the covenantal task.
> Ch. X (chs. 23–24)—With the covenant fulfilled, Babylon (Israel's most representative enemy) falls spectacularly, freeing the covenant people from bondage.

Nephi's original chapter breaks organize the long Isaiah quotation into three sequences that emphasize a pair of repeating images: the remnant (of Israel) and the (messianic) branch. The remnant theme is, of course, classic in Isaiah, in which a sacred band of Israelite survivors live to receive the promises God intends for the covenant people. In Nephi's chapter VIII, they appear only in Isaiah's vision of the distant future, where those who "are escaped of Israel" are "called holy" (2 Nephi 14:2–3). Nephi's chapter IX then tells how God sends Isaiah to harden the people until such a remnant can return; and this they do while a "consumption decreed" against the land nonetheless "overflow[s] with righteousness" (16:13; 20:22). Finally, in Nephi's chapter X, Babylon is left without a remnant, so that it will not "rise nor possess the land, nor fill the face of the world with cities" again (24:21). The branch, for its part, is a classically messianic image, referring to "the legitimate Davidic scion who is associated with Yahweh's postexilic restoration of Israel and Judah."[42] The branch appears in Nephi's chapter VIII as "beautiful and glorious," offering "the fruit of the earth . . . to them that are escaped of Israel" (that is, to the remnant, precisely) at the predicted day of fulfillment (14:2). Chapter IX then describes how "a branch" grows out of the roots of "Jesse," the father of biblical King David—this only after God winnows Israel to a remnant ready for such a guiding ruler (21:1). Finally, in chapter X, not only is Babylon left without any remnant, the city's fallen king is "cast out of [his] grave like an abominable branch," a kind of antimessiah, an inversion of the promised king (24:19). The original chapter breaks thus clarify Nephi's basic interests in Isaiah, where he apparently finds a three-part story organized around a delivered remnant and a delivering branch.

Original chapter breaks show that Nephi divides his own, climactic prophecies into two clear sequences:

Second Nephi, Part 2 (the More Sacred Things), Subpart C—Nephi's Witness
Ch. XI (chs. 25–27)—Nephi outlines a prophetic sketch of history from ancient Israel through the advent of Christ to the last days, when the Book of Mormon itself comes forth amid real opposition.
Ch. XII (chs. 28–30)—Nephi pauses on the problem of gentile resistance to the Book of Mormon, criticizing opponents before resuming his prophecy and detailing the end of history.

Nephi's own climactic prophecy unfolds straightforwardly, beginning with a few words about the need for prophecy to interpret Isaiah (2 Nephi 25:1–8) and then proceeding through sacred history all the way to the final fulfillment of Israel's covenant.[43] Nephi interrupts this sequence only twice, in both instances to describe the corruption of latter-day gentiles, opponents of the Book of Mormon (26:20–33; 28–29). Here, finally, is the straightforwardly plain and precious prophecy Nephi promises so much earlier in his record—its interpretation prepared for by the witnesses of Jacob and Isaiah.

Last of all, and only after the close of "the more sacred things," comes a conclusion:

Second Nephi, Part 3—a Conclusion to the More Sacred Things
Ch. XIII (ch. 31)—Nephi offers a few words about what he calls "the doctrine of Christ," centering on baptism and the reception of the Holy Ghost.
Ch. XIV (ch. 32)—Prophetically recognizing that his readers do not understand what life under the influence of the Holy Ghost looks like, Nephi (somewhat despairingly) attempts further explanation.
Ch. XV (ch. 33)—In a few words of exhortation and testimony, Nephi offers a clear farewell, praying for the welfare of his readers and especially of his people.

The chapter breaks at the end of Second Nephi are the same in the original dictated text as in more recent Latter-day Saint editions. Each chapter is short and to the point, the succession among them clear. Before this conclusion, Nephi has worked through a series of prophecies, detailing the historical process through which latter-day Lamanites will come to know "the very points of [Christ's] doctrine, that they may know how to come unto him and be saved" (1 Nephi 15:14). These final chapters therefore logically place the capstone on Nephi's plain and precious prophecies by laying out in detail those "very points" of Christ's doctrine (chapter XIII),[44] addressing apparent confusion about the doctrine (chapter XIV), and offering a decisive and forceful farewell (chapter XV).

At this point, the full structure of each of Nephi's two books is clear, as is the basic flow of ideas that runs through each book. How, finally, do the two books work together?[45] We have seen that First Nephi focuses principally on the relationship between two prophetic sources—the written records brought from Jerusalem, in which Isaiah features prominently, and the oral tradition inaugurated by Lehi, which explores the spiritual state of Nephi's rebellious brothers. In turn, it seems clear that Second Nephi offers a prophetic sketch of all of sacred history, but especially as it comes to focus on the latter-day redemption of the Lamanites—prepared for by the prophecies of Isaiah, partially clarified by Nephi's brother Jacob. In short, then, First Nephi explains the provenance and then provides a first exposition of the two prophetic sources that address the basic question asked and then answered in Second Nephi. The brass-plates text of Isaiah, bent toward Lehi's prophetic concern for his sons and their posterity, proves to be Nephi's key source for clarifying the latter-day redemption of the Lamanites. Second Nephi is, in fact, saturated with Isaiah—not only because of the thirteen-chapters-long quotation from Isaiah at the heart of the book, but also because both Jacob and Nephi quote from and comment on Isaiah in their own contributions. Isaiah, interpreted from the standpoint of Lehi's dream, is the unmistakable focus from the beginning to the end of Second Nephi, while First Nephi establishes what it means to approach the Israelite prophet in what Nephi regards as the right way.

This last point, however, requires further elaboration. And because addressing it provides an opportunity, at last, for serious investigation of what Isaiah is doing in Nephi's record, it is worth taking up the point at some length. What do Nephi's two books, in their respective internal arrangements and their shared conjunction, indicate about the role of Isaiah?

Some Implications about Isaiah

The preceding analyses of textual structure have only touched on the fact that passages from the Book of Isaiah appear in Nephi's record. They do little to clarify what these structures collectively suggest about Nephi's intentions. As my previous chapters have shown, Isaiah plays an occasional but structurally crucial role in Mormon's hundreds-of-pages-long record of Nephite history. Only a few chapters of Isaiah make any appearance there, and the point seems to be primarily to illustrate how just *one* passage of Isaiah was interpreted in radically different ways by different persons and groups and at different moments in Nephite history. By contrast, Isaiah quotations appear with startling frequency in Nephi's record, and it is far less obvious to even an ideal listener or reader why exactly that is so. The fact is that the overwhelming ubiquity of Isaiah's writings in Nephi's record makes it difficult for readers to discern purpose—leading Claudia Bushman, ever a judicious reader, to quip that Nephi's long quotations of Isaiah are "no doubt the 'chloroform in print' spoken of by Mark Twain."[46] Grant Hardy, who has provided the most astute study to date of the Book of Mormon's authorial, editorial, and narratological voices, therefore finds it necessary to explain to his readers that Nephi is more than Nephi's (auto)biography. Although, as Hardy notes, "when Latter-day Saints think of Nephi, they generally have in mind the young man featured so prominently in the opening chapters" of First Nephi, closer reading shows that "Nephi appears oddly disconnected from the present."[47] His record quickly becomes obsessed with the details of Isaian prophecy and seems largely detached from the matters of everyday faith. Nephi's record is not—certainly not *primarily*—about the concrete life of faith before God. It has something larger than individuals in view.

Considering these facets of Nephi's text carefully, Hardy incisively concludes that "This means that trying to understand Nephi from his writings is something like interpreting the *Confessions*. Augustine's spiritual autobiography also begins with chapters of narrative (books 1–9), and those include the stories that most readers remember. Yet we cannot come to know the man as a whole without figuring out why he finishes his memoir with meditations on the nature of memory and time and a commentary on the opening chapter of Genesis (books 10–13). Similarly, we have to ask what Nephi was trying to accomplish with his own non-narrative chapters."[48]

The structure of Nephi's record as reassembled in the preceding sections of this chapter already goes far toward clarifying what Nephi's "spiritual autobiography" has to do with the way he concludes his memoir. Nephi's abridgement of Lehi's record, even as it simultaneously illustrates a life of faith, primarily serves to explain the paired provenances of Nephi's two prophetic sources: the brass plates, which feature Isaiah most prominently, and Lehi's dream, which Nephi expands into a panoramic vision of the world's sacred history. Further, subsequent details of the story do little more than move the colony from Jerusalem to the New World and then divide the family into rival factions. These events provide only the minimal necessary narrative details for the reader to understand the stakes of Nephi's prophecies. One must know who the Lamanites are and where they are generally located, since Nephi's and Jacob's prophecies predict their future in the New World. No more is needed, however, and the narrative covered in First and Second Nephi covers just these basics. In Nephi's record, then, there is ultimately Isaian prophecy and narrative props that foreground Isaian prophecy.[49]

Can we, then, become clearer about what the respective structures of Nephi's two books indicate about his intentions with Isaiah? Can we help our ideal listener/reader see what is important about all this structural work for anyone trying to understand Nephi's Isaian project? It is already clear how the two halves of First Nephi relate to each other. The abridgment of Lehi's record (the first half of First Nephi) provides the provenance for two prophetic sources that interest Nephi, while Nephi's own proceedings (the second half) clarify and interpret each source. By the end of First Nephi, the reader has in hand a set of interdefining prophetic resources, the book of Isaiah and Lehi's dream. These two revelatory assets come into full clarity only when each serves as the hermeneutic lens for the other—a relationship we can perceive by investigating the basic content of each.

Lehi's dream famously focuses on a life-giving tree, which delivers him from "a dark and dreary waste" (1 Nephi 8:4). Upon tasting the fruit of the tree, Lehi seeks to share it with his family. Although Nephi, his mother Sariah, and his brother Sam eat from the tree, Nephi's rebellious oldest two brothers refuse to partake. The dream then expands in scope, revealing "numberless concourses of people" who seek in various ways to come to the same tree (8:21). Most of the people in the dream either fail to reach the tree or do not remain there long. The dream deploys powerful and even primordial imagery, casting a long shadow.[50] At least one astute literary reader of the Book of Mormon argues compellingly that the basic imagery of the dream saturates the Nephite imagination, reappearing throughout the Book of Mormon.[51] Despite the dream's general appeal, however, its actual recounting within the context of 1 Nephi

8 makes clear that its focus is more or less exclusively on Nephi's immediate family.[52] As Grant Hardy rightly points out, the dream immediately follows (and is positioned within the same original chapter as) the story of the first serious rebellion on the part of Lehi's two oldest sons, and the dream account opens and closes with expressions of Lehi's grief and anxiety. Lehi "does not offer allegorical interpretations or universalizing commentary; instead, he goes straight to exhortation, pleading, and preaching."[53] This is a dream about Nephi's family and their fate, about Lehi's sons "and also many of their seed" (8:3). The implication is that the "numberless concourses of people" in the dream represent "the world" or "the human family"[54] less than they do a more specific group: the Lamanites, the descendants of those who, a moment earlier in the same dream, refuse to eat from the tree (8:17–18). The dream explains the distance of a specific people from God, and then it outlines in images the means for their eventual return to God—despite certain obstacles.[55]

It is, of course, exactly this story that Nephi's expanded version of Lehi's dream explains in the second half of First Nephi. His vision details the historical events through which Lamanites come to "dwindle in unbelief" after the destruction of Nephi's own descendants (1 Nephi 12:22). It then outlines the complex process through which they are eventually "convinc[ed] . . . that the records of the prophets and of the twelve apostles of the Lamb are true" (13:39). The process involves several key moments: the arrival and then political ascendency of (European) gentiles among Lamanites early in the modern period (13:10–19), gentile religious confusion after establishing independence in the New World (13:1–9, 20–29), and the overcoming of all such religious confusion through the Book of Mormon (13:30–41).[56] The details here are essential. First, the story concerns a remnant of the house of Israel, what remains of the Israelite colony in the New World after a devastatingly tragic history. Second, redemption for this remnant in exile, "cut off from the presence of the Lord" (2:21), begins only when it finds itself in a position of political submission to a conquering gentile people—a gentile people apparently guided and supported by God himself, although they are unmistakably presented as religiously confused or even apostate. Third, what triggers the redemption of the remnant is the unexpected appearance of a once-sealed book of prophecy, a book addressed to the remnant that nonetheless gathers repentant gentiles into a project of establishing a land of real promise and peace. Why are these details so crucial? Because, for anyone deeply familiar with biblical prophecy, they seem in so many ways to summarize the Book of Isaiah—especially certain portions of Isaiah: those quoted at various places in Nephi's record.

Isaiah is a complexly organized assemblage of diverse prophetic texts produced in response to various historical and political crises. Scholars working on Isaiah today, though, generally agree that it has a definite and apparently intentional literary shape.[57] Further, that literary shape assumes a kind of story about Israel's role in history. As Edgar Conrad and Hugh Williamson have shown, the Book of Isaiah (especially Isaiah 2–55) organizes itself around a story about Israel being winnowed down by foreign imperial powers to a mere remnant that God eventually sends into exile among religiously confused and politically oppressive gentiles. There in exile, however, Israel's remnant finds itself confronted by a once-sealed book of prophecy (that is, Isaiah's own prophecies) that calls them to trust in the God who will redeem them from exile. Israel's consequent redemption, moreover, unfolds in such a spectacular fashion that many of its benighted gentile oppressors become the remnant's generous benefactors and coreligionists, assisting them to return to their promised land in peace, and even joining with them at their temple to worship the true God.[58]

These historical events of course took place during the eighth, seventh, and sixth centuries before Christ. It was the ascendant Assyrian Empire that eliminated one of the two Israelite nations during the eighth century and winnowed the other down to a remnant. The first half of the Book of Isaiah depicts these events as the consequence of Israelite waywardness, and it predicts exile for the Judean remnant as well. Exile came early in the sixth century, now under the oppressive hand of the Neo-Babylonian Empire. In the context of Jewish exile, however, it seems that the writings of Isaiah of Jerusalem took on new significance, and Isaiah's "vision of all," which had "become . . . as the words of a book that is sealed" (Isaiah 29:11), was reopened.[59] The exiled remnant was now fired by "good tidings" from heaven, and they hoped that God would make "bare his holy arm in the eyes of all the nations" (52:7, 10). Such might inspire their gentile oppressors in Babylon not only to carry them home on their shoulders and in their arms (49:22), but also to join them at "the mountain of the Lord's house" and "beat their swords into plowshares, and their spears into pruninghooks" (2:2, 4). The exiles' desires were fulfilled late in the sixth century, even if not quite as spectacularly as the prophecies in Isaiah anticipated.[60]

What Lehi reports seeing impressionistically and Nephi in stark clarity is a history that runs in perfect parallel to the one assumed in Isaiah (or at least in Isaiah 2–55). In the place of the kingdoms of Judah and Israel in the eighth century before Christ, he focuses on the Nephites and the Lamanites in the

New World during the fourth century after Christ. His "remnant of Israel" is therefore the remaining Lamanites after the wars that conclude the history recounted in the Book of Mormon. And in the place of exile for a Judean remnant in Babylon, Nephi sees the Lamanite remnant of Israel in a kind of exile in the context of conquest in early modern America. The oppressors here are gentiles of European descent, and the exiles are Native Americans. In the place of a fresh reading of the metaphorically sealed vision of Isaiah, Nephi places his hope in the translation and circulation of the literally sealed record of his people, the Book of Mormon itself. And in the place of a Jewish return from Babylonian exile to peace and prosperity in the anciently promised land of Canaan, Nephi anticipates the establishment of peace and the promise of prosperity for the latter-day Lamanites to whom the promised land of the American continent rightly belongs. The latent story assumed in the assembled prophecies of Isaiah parallels the explicit story laid out in Nephi's vision point by point, except that every detail has been shifted from the Old World main root of Israel to the New World branch of Israel. And for this shift it seems that Nephi has a name, a kind of *terminus technicus* he uses throughout his record: *likening*. His vision is *like* or *likened to* Isaiah's prophecies. The two prophetic resources run in parallel.

Nephi most famously speaks of likening in a passage that—in the original chaptering of First Nephi—serves as an introduction to his first substantial quotation of Isaiah (preliminarily discussed in chapter 6). Hoping to spur his unsteady older brothers to faith, he says that he "did read unto them that which was written by the prophet Isaiah—for I did liken all scriptures unto us, that it might be for our profit and learning" (1 Nephi 19:23). Stripped from its context by the more recent chapter divisions, this passage is often read as a general recommendation to read scripture with an eye to concrete and practical application, "applying scripture to our everyday lives," as Latter-day Saints often say.[61] In their literary and especially structural context, however, Nephi's words serve as a bridge between the two prophetic sources that interest him, between his own visionary expansion of his father's dream and biblical Isaiah. He thus reports that he introduced his reading of Isaiah's own words with an injunction: "Hear ye the words of the prophet, ye which are a remnant of the house of Israel, a branch which have been broken off! Hear ye the words of the prophet which was written unto all the house of Israel, and liken it unto yourselves that ye may have hope as well as your brethren from whom ye have been broken off!" (19:24). Here Nephi's meaning becomes substantially clearer. He enjoins his brothers to see themselves and their descendants as a branch of Israel, an Israelite remnant like that described by Isaiah. And then he enjoins them to see in Isaiah's prophecies an outline of God's intentions with "all the house of Israel" so that they might trust that God will do much the same in their own local (but still Israelite) history and circumstances. In this way alone might they "have hope" like their "brethren" to whom Isaiah's words were originally and intentionally addressed.

Other uses of the verb "to liken" in Nephi's record confirm this technical meaning. After quoting from Isaiah 48–49, Nephi explains the text by speaking of how his family's future history "is likened unto" specific passages from Isaiah 49 (1 Nephi 22:8). At the outset of the "more sacred things," he quotes his brother Jacob as explaining that what "Isaiah spake concerning all the house of Israel . . . may be likened unto" the New World remnant of Israel, specifically "because that [they] are of the house of Israel" (2 Nephi 6:5).[62] And then, a few chapters later, when Nephi transitions from quoting his brother's sermon to quoting thirteen chapters of Isaiah at once, he states his general intention to "liken [Isaiah's] words unto my people" and "send them forth unto all my children" (11:2). His last sentence before undertaking the lengthy quotation is this: "Now these are the words [of Isaiah], and ye may liken them unto you and unto all men" (11:8). The record of Nephi speaks of likening in a perfectly consistent way, always understanding it to signal the task of finding parallels between Isaian prophecy and Nephi's and his father's own prophetic visions.[63]

The whole of First Nephi organizes itself around this highly specific hermeneutical program. As an attentive reader comes to the end of First Nephi, she has been trained in the art of likening. Nephi has introduced her to two key prophetic resources and taught her about their relevance to each other. More specifically, Nephi has introduced her to Isaiah and how it is meant both to clarify and be clarified by the visionary tradition unique to the Book of Mormon's earliest prophets. As First Nephi gives way to Second Nephi, the one book sends its readers to the other prepared to engage earnestly with the tight weave of Nephite and Isaian prophecy that forms the hard core of Nephi's "more sacred things." First Nephi serves as a handbook for Second Nephi, which is the real substance of Nephi's project. And, of course, as the analyses in this chapter have made clear, Second Nephi is from start to finish about nothing *but* Isaiah.

Nephi's own prophecies, the climactic final chapters of his "more sacred things" (in 2 Nephi 25–30, the original chapters XI–XII), are especially important in this regard. They form the ultimate *telos* of Nephi's preparatory material. He prefaces his own prophecies with the words of two corroborating witnesses, of course—the two-day sermon of his brother Jacob and the chapters-long block taken from Isaiah. These only help to confirm the hermeneutic project outlined in full in First Nephi. Jacob quotes from and comments on Isaiah, explicitly likening the latter's prophecies to the same future history of the Lamanites in the last days. And then the long quotation of Isaiah 2–14 provides more Isaian grist for Nephi's prophetic mill (phrases and theological opinions from those chapters appear throughout Nephi's own prophecy in 2 Nephi 25–30).[64] But the whole of Nephi's project comes to its real culmination and genuine climax only when he provides what he calls "mine own prophecy, . . . in the which I know that no man can err" (2 Nephi 25:7). Everything before that point in Second Nephi is arguably a prolongation of the preparatory work of First Nephi. But when Nephi speaks up in his own prophetic voice, something genuinely new occurs, because he *no longer talks about likening*. He no longer differentiates his two prophetic sources, because he instead weaves them seamlessly into one prophetic whole. For the first time, in fact, Nephi *does not even mention Isaiah* when he uses his words; he simply uses them as if they were his own.[65] It is as if the many mechanical steps of likening outlined in First Nephi and even in earlier parts of Second Nephi are finally behind the reader—certainly behind Nephi. Now Nephi asks the reader (borrowing an image from the philosopher Ludwig Wittgenstein) to "throw away the ladder after he has climbed up it."[66]

In this way, the whole structure of Nephi's record yearns toward its end. First Nephi's startlingly tight organization establishes the basic nature of Nephi's hermeneutic. Isaiah serves as a prophetic window onto God's dealings with Israel, and what one sees through that window is an outline of the covenantal history of the nations growing out of Nephi's own family. Isaiah thus serves both to clarify and to be clarified by the dreams and visions that set Nephite and Lamanite history in motion. Nephi apparently sees Isaiah as useful, a kind of means to a non-Isaian end: the clarification of his own prophecies. But he also sees Isaiah's writings as intrinsically valuable, although he understands their import as intelligible only to those who either develop a familiarity with "the manner of prophesying among the Jews" (2 Nephi 25:1) or happen to be "filled with the spirit of prophecy" themselves (25:4). Ignoring what might be learned from historical and textual study along the first of these two lines of interpretation, Nephi indicates that his own prophetic tradition helps to make Isaiah's real value clear, even if only through the lens of likening. And at some point, when Nephi has done enough preparatory work, it becomes possible to forget the technical details and just read Isaiah prophetically, weaving his images and phrases directly into new prophetic work. Nephi explains in technical detail what it means to read scripture prophetically, but then he finally simply *models* what it looks like when "a prophet reads scripture"—as Benjamin Sommer nicely puts it in a parallel context.[67]

All this helps to clarify the basic nature of Nephi's approach to Isaiah. It is possible, once again, to hand all this structural work over to that imagined ideal listener, sitting through the dictation of the Book of Mormon in 1829, who then brings deep familiarity with the history of Isaiah's interpretation to the task of understanding the book's Isaian project. Naturally, the richness of Nephi's particular interactions with Isaiah—by far the most complex and the most sustained in the Book of Mormon—comes out in full only when considering the details, and especially those at the heart of Nephi's project in his "more sacred things." It is necessary next, therefore, to turn directly to the long quotation of Isaiah at the very center of Second Nephi, to look once again through the eyes of our ideal listener/reader. In light of the larger structural frame of Nephi's record and its associated hermeneutic program, what can we say about Nephi's most sustained interaction with Isaiah? And how might those living at the time of its initial presentation in English have ideally read or heard it?

8

He Shall Set His Hand Again the Second Time

When we begin swimming through First Nephi, the likening of Isaiah 49:22–23 perhaps looks like a ladder bolted to the wall across the pool. All our movement is toward it, and we will use it to climb out and look back over the pool. The same passage appears in Second Nephi, but there it looks more like a diving board, securely bolted to the deck. In other words, Isaiah 49:22–23 appears early this time, as a familiar point of departure from which—as we liken—we leap into an immersive experience with Isaiah. In what makes up the hard core of Second Nephi—those twenty-five chapters of "more sacred things" (1 Nephi 19:5)—Isaiah 49:22–23 is the first of many Isaiah texts encountered. As discussed in chapter 6, Jacob there quotes the passage when addressing his people at Nephi's request. The passage thus serves as a distant limit and final goal for First Nephi, but a fresh beginning for Second Nephi. In fact, right after Jacob quotes from Isaiah 49 and offers commentary, he proceeds to quote whole chapters of Isaiah that never appear in First Nephi.[1] And Jacob's expansion of the Isaian scope in Nephi's project is only the beginning. Some fourteen further chapters of Isaiah appear before long.

Despite going further than First Nephi, Jacob's sermon in 2 Nephi 6–10 continues First Nephi's emphasis on Second Isaiah, prophecies of restoration from Isaiah 40–55. Nephi, though, seems impatient with perpetuating his first book's focus. After a few chapters, he truncates his account of Jacob's sermon and hurries on to other things. "Jacob spake many more things to my people at that time," he explains; "nevertheless, only these things have I caused to be written, for the things which I have written sufficeth me" (2 Nephi 11:1). What interests Nephi is "more of the words of Isaiah," more words to liken to Nephi's people (11:2). Jacob serves as a second witness for Nephi, but Nephi has much more to say; at the core of Second Nephi he apparently wishes to abandon the predominantly positive tone of Second Isaiah for the predominantly negative tone of First Isaiah. This forceful transition thus introduces the most recognizable (because by far the longest) Isaiah quotation in the whole Book of Mormon. Full chapters of Isaiah appear elsewhere, but when Latter-day Saints speak of "the Isaiah chapters," they always have reference to what immediately follows Jacob's preaching. In modern chaptering, some thirteen chapters from First Isaiah (Isaiah 2–14) appear in one solid block in 2 Nephi 12–24.

At this point in Nephi's record, as devoted readers often confess, it becomes easy to miss the forest for the trees. Without guidance, readers wonder what they are meant to seek or to find in a fifteen-page quotation.[2] As we saw in chapter 7, larger structures and original chapter divisions provide some orientation. Rather than a meandering thirteen-chapter quotation from Isaiah (what readers find in recent editions), for example, earlier editions organize the long quotation into three blocks of text with a clear sense of progression. The original chapter VIII (2 Nephi 11–15) contrasts the wicked state of God's covenant people during Isaiah's day with their promised condition when God's work in the world is done. The original chapter IX (2 Nephi 16–22) then tracks the path from Isaiah's present to that glorious future, reached through Israel's reduction to a sacred remnant and the intervention of a promised messiah. Finally, the original chapter X (2 Nephi 23–24) explains how Israel's enemies collapse under their own oppressive weight as God redeems his people. The central stretch of Second Nephi thus consists of Isaiah's words without much commentary, but nonetheless organized into an overarching story.

Original chapter divisions help readers watching for larger structures, but are there more obvious clues for readers? There are. Only one passage from the long block of Isaiah appears before the full quotation of the text. Nephi thus grants a certain privilege to this passage, and attentive readers naturally feel its familiarity when, after having heard it alluded to, they encounter it in canonical context. The passage is Isaiah 11:11–12, about God reaching out a second time to reclaim Israel's remnant. Although Nephi and Jacob have quoted and commented on several chapters from Second Isaiah and a few shorter passages from First Isaiah before 2 Nephi 11, none of them appears in the long quotation starting in 2 Nephi 12. The only familiar note the reader encounters in "the Isaiah chapters" is the passage from Isaiah 11. Nephi's placement of Jacob's citation of Isaiah 11:11 early in Second Nephi (along with his own subtle preparations at the end of First Nephi) makes this passage—and all of Isaiah 11 with it—a focal point for the long quotation of Isaiah at the heart of Nephi's "more sacred things."

In this chapter, then, the task is to clarify Nephi's interpretation of Isaiah 11:11–12, the second of his three favored passages, along with all of Isaiah 11 within the long quotation in Second Nephi. How does the fact that Isaiah 11:11–12 appears in a protracted quotation give shape to its meaning for Nephi? How does it sit within the triad of Isaian texts Nephi favors? And how, to nod again toward the question most important to our ideal listener/reader, does Nephi's handling of this passage from Isaiah compare with known interpretations around the time when the Book of Mormon was published?

Quotation in Long Form

Although Nephi quotes full chapters of Isaiah at several points in his record (as do both Abinadi and Christ in Mormon's project), the quotation of Isaiah 2–14 in Second Nephi is unique within the Book of Mormon. The writings of Isaiah come at the reader so relentlessly there that skeptics begin to ask where reasonable quotation ends and immoral plagiarism begins. Even believers find themselves puzzled by the unswerving commitment embodied in Nephi's long excerpt, a puzzlement that is fully on display when Claudia Bushman speaks of "the wasteland of 2 Nephi with its endless transcriptions of Isaiah."[3] It really takes someone like our ideal listener/reader to exhibit the patience necessary to investigate the stakes of such inclusion.

To understand Nephi's motivation in including so much of Isaiah, it would be helpful to extend our analysis of the original chapter divisions. Recall that when Joseph Smith originally dictated Isaiah's long and corroborating witness, immediately following Jacob's sermon and immediately preceding Nephi's own culminating prophecy, it consisted of three distinct sequences. The original chapter VIII of Second Nephi corresponds to the quotation of Isaiah 2–5 (now in 2 Nephi 12–15), along with a few verses of introduction (now in 2 Nephi 11). The original chapter IX corresponds in turn to the quotation of Isaiah 6–12 (now in 2 Nephi 16–22). And the original chapter X corresponds, finally, to the quotation of Isaiah 13–14 (now in 2 Nephi 23–24). As pointed out before, these divisions allow the long quotation of Isaiah to tell a clear, three-part story. The first of the three chapters (chapter VIII) articulates a specific problem, a tension between the disastrous present for God's rebellious people and their prophetically predicted destiny, glorious but historically distant in the future. The second (chapter IX) then outlines God's complex way of solving this problem, intervening in history in unexpected and theologically paradoxical ways to move his people from their lost and fallen state to their full and glorious redemption. Finally, the third and last chapter (chapter X) contains a somewhat raucous celebration of God's involvement in his people's history, littered with taunts against those who have fallen because they chose to fight against the divine purpose.

A subtle but consistent literary feature marks both the individual coherence of each of the three divisions and the real continuity that holds them together as telling one total story. As noted before also, this literary feature is the repetition, within each of the original three chapters making up the long quotation of Isaiah, of a pair of related images. The first is the remnant of Israel, a classically Isaian theme, referring to a sacred band of survivors who are preserved to receive all the blessings promised to God's covenant people. In the original chapter VIII of Second Nephi, the remnant remains still to come in the distant future, those who are "escaped of Israel" and "written among the living in Jerusalem" and who are therefore "called holy" (2 Nephi 14:2–3). Chapter IX then tells how God sends a prophet (Isaiah) to harden his people, leading them into disaster so that just a remnant will survive to return to their lands; in that the remnant results from disaster, though, "the consumption decreed shall overflow with righteousness" (20:22). Finally, in chapter X, Israel's most dangerous enemy, the empire of Babylon that eventually and cruelly drives them into exile, not only collapses under the weight of its own power structures; it is also predicted to be left *without* a remnant, precisely so that it cannot again "fill the face of the world with cities" (24:21).[4] The repeating theme of the remnant marks the continuity of the nonetheless decidedly three-part story: (1) the remnant is a promised thing in the distant future, (2) God's intervention in history allows for the remnant's creation, and (3) the enemies of God's people are, in their punishment, left without any promised remnant at all.

The second image that confirms the literary coherence of the tripartite extract from the Book of Isaiah is the image of the branch, classically a messianic image in the prophetic texts of the Hebrew Bible.[5] This image too appears in a significant way once in each of the three divisions of the long Isaiah quotation in Second Nephi. It appears in the original chapter VIII as something "beautiful and glorious" that will (like the life-giving tree of Nephi's own vision) offer to the sacred remnant "the fruit of the earth" in the distant and promised future (2 Nephi 14:2). The original chapter IX then famously describes in its reproduction of Isaiah 11 how "a branch" grows out of the roots of "Jesse," the father of the biblical King David, in order to rescue and then to rule over the preserved remnant of Israel (2 Nephi 21:1). Finally, in the original chapter X of Second Nephi, not only does the royal household of the dangerous Babylonian empire find itself left without any remnant, the empire's fallen king is taunted as having been "cast out of [his] grave like an abominable branch," thus treated as a kind of antimessiah (or even, from the perspective of the Christian Nephites, an anti-Christ)—certainly an inversion of the promised ruler for Israel (24:19).[6] Just as each of the three sequences of the long quotation of Isaiah contributes its unique part to the larger three-part story of the remnant, each also contributes its unique part to the larger three-part story of the branch (the promise of a branch to feed the remnant, the arrival of the branch among the remnant in its redemption, and the parody of the true branch represented by the leader of Israel's enemies).

The coherence of 2 Nephi 11–24 is thus clear and would have been clearer to our ideal listener/reader than it is to many readers today. At the heart of Nephi's "more sacred things," the long quotation of Isaiah is anything but haphazard, and anything but filler material. It is not, as Fawn Brodie suggested with a wry smile, a telling example of how, whenever Joseph Smith's "literary reservoir . . . ran dry," he "simply arranged for his Nephite prophets to quote from the Bible."[7] The long quotation is, rather, a systematically conceived extraction from the Book of Isaiah with a discernible three-part story to tell about an Israelite remnant and its relationship to the branch-Messiah that would redeem it in the end. Of course, the several parts of this three-part story require further elaboration, especially so that the moment the text prepares its readers to receive at the climax of the long quotation can find its specific place there.

The first of the three original chapters making up "the Isaiah chapters," the original chapter VIII (now 2 Nephi 11–15), consists of a few paragraphs of editorial introduction and then the full quotation of Isaiah 2–5.[8] That Nephi groups these four chapters from Isaiah together as a single block determines their meaning in a way that runs, at least somewhat, against the grain of the canonical version in the Bible. Most Isaiah scholars today distinguish within Isaiah 2–5 at least two larger blocks of text—Isaiah 2–4 on the one hand, and Isaiah 5 on the other—arguing further that each was assembled from numerous originally distinct oracles.[9] Isaiah 2–4 is shaped as a single unit by the fact that it opens and closes with parallel predictions on the fate of Judah and Jerusalem "in that day" (Isaiah 4:2) or "in the last days" (2:2).[10] Isaiah 5 seems straightforwardly to be a separate unit, a gathering of woe oracles appended to a parabolic song about Israel's inequities.

The version of Isaiah 2–5 found in Second Nephi, however, introduces subtle but interpretively crucial variants into the prophetic text, one of which seems meant to cover over the apparent seam between what Isaiah scholars discern as the two larger units within these chapters. In the King James Version of the Bible, Isaiah 5 opens with an abrupt instance of the word *now*: "Now will I sing to my well-beloved a song of my beloved touching his vineyard" (Isaiah 5:1). In Nephi's version of Isaiah 2–5, however, the word *now* is replaced with "and then": "And then will I sing to my well-beloved a song of my beloved touching his vineyard" (2 Nephi 15:1). This version of the text helps to smooth the abrupt transition between Isaiah 2–4 and Isaiah 5, rendering what in the Bible looks like two units into one overarching unit. At first, this might seem to introduce incoherence into the biblical text, breaking the solid symmetry of the carefully bookended unit of Isaiah 2–4 by appending to it the unwieldy discourse from Isaiah 5.[11] If one ignores for a moment the formal analyses of scholars working with the biblical text rather than Nephi's, another possibility comes into view. The version of Isaiah 2–5 in Second Nephi can be read as built on a pattern of alternating (short) celebrations of the future (Isaiah 2:2–4 and 4:2–6) and (long) laments about the present (Isaiah 2:5–4:1 and Isaiah 5:1–30). Rather than an unwieldy appendix of sorts, Isaiah 5 becomes a reiteration of woes pronounced in an earlier and structurally parallel part of the larger unit, extending them from Judah to all of Israel.

In Second Nephi, then, the biblical units of Isaiah 2–4 and Isaiah 5 are fused into one prophetic discourse that halts between the miserable present condition of the wayward covenant people during Isaiah's own time and the glorious future predicted for that same people when God works to draw a remnant from them. Another variant in the original chapter VIII of Second Nephi confirms the emphasis on deliberate contrast in its version of Isaiah 2–5. This variant is found in Nephi's version of Isaiah 2:5. As predictions for Jerusalem's ultimate exaltation come to an end in Isaiah, the reader of the biblical text finds this address by the prophet, in the second person, to the house of Jacob: "O house of Jacob, come ye, and let us walk in the light of the LORD" (Isaiah 2:5). There then awkwardly follows a sudden second-person address by the prophet to, it seems, God: "Therefore thou hast forsaken thy people the house of Jacob"

(2:6). The transition from glorious prediction to thundering denunciation is awkward and unclear.[12]

In Nephi's version of the text, by contrast, the transition is smooth and the meaning unambiguous, thanks to a rather long stretch of additional text introduced by the word *yea*. The verse reads as follows in Second Nephi: "O house of Jacob, come ye, and let us walk in the light of the Lord—yea, come! for ye have all gone astray, every one to his wicked ways!" (2 Nephi 12:5). Thanks to the fourteen additional words that appear here, the beginning of the following verse also has a more apparent context and therefore a determinate meaning: "Therefore, O Lord, thou hast forsaken thy people, the house of Jacob" (12:6). Isaiah 2:6 in Nephi's version still shifts somewhat awkwardly from addressing Jerusalem's inhabitants to addressing God, but the connecting "therefore" gains a clear sense and the abruptness of transition fades. The contrast between the brilliant future of redemption for Israel and the dismal present of inequity within Israel becomes, in all this, a good deal sharper.

The altered verse in Second Nephi does more than smooth out a transition and sharpen a contrast, however. The additional words of Nephi's version—"yea, come! for ye have all gone astray, every one to his wicked ways!"—makes a very early verse in the Book of Isaiah anticipate a much later one, a verse that would have come immediately to the mind of an ideal listener/reader like the one we have imagined throughout this study. Isaiah 53:6, sitting at the heart of the song of the suffering servant quoted in full by Abinadi in Mormon's record, reads rather similarly to the words that conclude Nephi's Isaiah 2:5: "All we like sheep have gone astray; we have turned every one to his own way; and the LORD hath laid on him the iniquity of us all."[13] Although the later verse exchanges the second-person "ye" for the first-person "we," adds a simile about wayward sheep, replaces the more explicit "wicked" with "own," and reduces the plural "ways" to the singular "way," the relationship between Nephi's version of Isaiah 2:5 and the Bible's (and Abinadi's) version of Isaiah 53:6 is obvious. The reader of the Book of Mormon is meant to understand that the Nephites' copies of Isaiah traced a slow historical transformation, from a time when the prophet has to confront Israel harshly with an accusation of going astray (Isaiah 2) to a time when Israel, ready for redemption, is willing to confess directly that it has gone astray (Isaiah 53). The contrasts between unfortunate present and redemptive future in Isaiah 2–5 thus serve in the Nephite version of Isaiah to invite readers to receive the prophet's accusation humbly and penitently, preparing to make a confession.

If Second Nephi's original chapter VIII identifies a problem in Israel—the asymmetry between actually existing Israel and the future Israel of promise—its original chapter IX (now 2 Nephi 16–22) outlines God's complex solution to the problem.[14] Chapter IX consists of Isaiah 6–12, a block of text that Isaiah scholars have sometimes called Isaiah's *Denkschrift* (or "memoir"), thanks to a once-popular idea that an autobiographical sketch that went all the way back to Isaiah of Jerusalem lay behind these chapters. Although recent years have seen increasing doubt about any original unity for Isaiah 6–12, even today few question that the chapters were given a unified shape by editors.[15] Thus, in general, scholars recognize some kind of continuity across these several chapters in their final form, acknowledging that they function as a total unit. Nephi acknowledges the same, allowing these seven chapters of the Isaiah text to function as one continuous story from disaster to promised redemption. The unit is long and remarkably complex. Even interpreters who tend to emphasize ultimate unity in the text point to shifting historical contexts and changing thematic emphases as Isaiah 6–12 unfolds. For example, Isaiah 6 opens "in the year that king Uzziah died" (Isaiah 6:1), while the next chapter occurs "in the days of Ahaz the son of Jotham, the son of Uzziah" (Isaiah 7:1)—the two chapters are therefore separated by the whole reign of Ahaz (lasting some sixteen years according to 2 Kings 16:2).

Several sequences with Second Nephi's original chapter IX are nonetheless discernible, and something like a continuous story can be found running through them. The opening sequence, in Isaiah 6, recounts "Isaiah's inaugural vision through which God called him to his prophetic office and commissioned him with his particular message."[16] The closing sequences in Isaiah 11 and 12 form a fitting conclusion, since there the branch-messiah appears to the remnant of Israel at last, and a brief psalm of praise appears in Isaiah 12.[17] There is, then, a clear point of departure, as well as a clear point of termination, for the story told in Isaiah 6–12. The pathway from the one to the other, however, is somewhat obscure and rests on the prophetic commission that comes to Isaiah at the outset of these chapters.

Isaiah's is no simple or straightforward task. As Walter Brueggemann explains his prophetic commission in Isaiah 6, "The intention of the decree of Yahweh is that Judah and Jerusalem should be narcoticized so that they will not be healed. God wills an unhealed people!"[18] The actual words of commission in the text include these: "Make the heart of this people fat, and make their ears heavy, and shut their eyes; lest they see with their eyes, and hear with their ears, and understand with their heart, and convert, and be healed"

(Isaiah 6:10). The passage is theologically difficult—and has long been recognized as theologically difficult[19]—both because human agency is here overridden by the sovereign intentions of Israel's God and because the good God of Israel here explicitly wills that his people be hardened and so be prevented from redemption for a time. Hyun Chul Paul Kim notes that "the prophet's task to harden this people may be taken as a part of divine judgment already pronounced in the preceding chapters [that is, in Isaiah 2–5]. As an essential component of divine punishment, the moral and theological shipwreck [of Israel] is unavoidable, and this hardening is in fact a 'strategy of prolongation' in the divine verdict."[20]

However one makes sense of the theological difficulty of the text,[21] it is clear that the prophet knows in advance of his mission that he will fail. As one commentator summarizes, "He receives no promise of success. His task will be to preach to deaf ears: Israel will become even more hardened."[22] What follows then, as Isaiah 6–12 begins to unfold, is first two successive stories that illustrate perfectly what Isaiah learns during his commission: that Israel will fail to believe his words. Parallel oracles are offered in Isaiah 7 and 8 about babies being born and given illustrative names, neither of which will grow into early childhood before certain threats facing Jerusalem during the days of King Ahaz fade. Jerusalem's elite, however, refuse to listen to Isaiah's warnings, and so he begins to predict disaster: Assyria will come and subjugate God's covenant people, resulting ultimately in devastation and exile. In the meanwhile, as a particularly important subsequent sequence of the text reports, "the message against which Jerusalem hardened its heart is to be written down for a generation to come. At that time—such is Isaiah's meaning—all that had fallen on completely deaf ears in his own day and generation will be fulfilled."[23] Isaiah puts his trust, as the text says, in the paradoxical God "that hideth his face from the house of Jacob" (Isaiah 8:17) as he "bind[s] up the testimony" and "seal[s] the law" he has spoken (8:16).[24] Once the book is sealed so that it can await the construction of Israel's promised remnant and the arrival of the promised branch, the covenant people's Assyrian (and then Babylonian) enemies invade and wreak havoc in the holy land. It is at this end of these disastrous events that a remnant emerges, prepared to return to Israel's God.

Such is the pathway, then, from the first to the final sequence of Isaiah 6–12. From the beginning, Isaiah knows that his people will hear no divine word he can utter. He faithfully delivers his message nonetheless, meanwhile just as faithfully writing his words down for a later remnant of Israel that might be prepared to hear them. When Israel has demonstrated its rebellion against God long enough, massive imperial forces overrun the holy land, leaving just the promised sacred remnant behind, but the remnant is joined—at long last—by the promised branch-Messiah, and so there is reason for celebration as peace comes to Israel and its neighbors. Key words running through these (and other) chapters of First Isaiah all relate to the idea of a divine *plan* for history: *work, counsel, operation, act*, and so on.[25] What stands at the climax and culmination of the historical plan is the emergence of an Israelite remnant, joined by the messianic branch, ready to be restored to its lands and to receive peace and rest. This moment of culmination and climax occurs in Isaiah 11, surrounding the second of Nephi's three favored excerpts from the Book of Isaiah. It marks the end of the trail leading from the miserable condition of the covenant people during Isaiah's time to their exalted condition at the promised last day.

The third and final portion of the long quotation of Isaiah in Second Nephi, the book's original chapter X (now 2 Nephi 23–24), is the simplest, maybe a bit of respite for even an ideal listener/reader. After chapter IX historically solves the problem posed in chapter VIII, chapter X, reproducing Isaiah 13–14, seems just to place a kind of capstone on the whole project of Nephi's long quotation of Isaiah. It predicts the collapse of the Babylonian empire and sets forth the covenantal motivations for this collapse: "the LORD will have mercy on Jacob, and will yet choose Israel, and set them in their own land" (14:1). And, famously, it includes a long taunt against the fallen "king of Babylon" (14:4), a bit of mockery of the antimessiah or "abominable branch" (14:19), in a text that the Christian tradition has often appropriated as a description of the devil's fall from glory in heaven.[26] Within the three-part schema of Second Nephi's long quotation of Isaiah, this prophecy against Babylon neatly brings closure to the story of Israel's promised redemption. The enemies of God's people all fall as the remnant returns and sees the fulfillment of the divine promises. In the context of Second Nephi—presented as having been written by someone who left Jerusalem when it was under Babylonian control and who later prophetically learned of the city's actual fall to Babylon—this ties up any loose ends of Isaiah 2–12.

In all, a careful analysis of the long quotation of Isaiah at the heart of Second Nephi reveals thoughtful purpose and real awareness of the biblical text. It recognizes the natural seams in the Book of Isaiah and reflects creatively on how successive portions might be presented as telling a story with a clear and theologically significant arc. When we read it as a prolonged series of individual biblical chapters, the quotation naturally feels like a haphazard affair, unsure of its purpose or direction. But when we approach it in light of original chapter divisions, subtle variants in Nephi's version of the text, and parallels with Nephi's vision from 1 Nephi 11–14, the whole presentation reveals itself to have a shape and a sense. And it is clear, even from a preliminary analysis, that Isaiah 11 serves as the climax and culmination of the long quotation. It is also there that we find the lone instance of a single passage from Isaiah 2–14 being quoted in advance of the long excerpt.

Israel's Second Redemption

In the several places where the language of Isaiah 11:11–12 appears in the small plates—both before and after the long quotation of Isaiah in 2 Nephi 11–24—one phrase consistently draws attention. The key words are "set his hand again the second time." Thus, when Nephi's brother Jacob alludes to the passage in 2 Nephi 6:14, introducing it explicitly into Nephi's record for the first time, it is this line he quotes. Jacob much later confirms his particular interest in this one line when, in a short book that appears under his own name after Nephi's record, he quotes it again. There, in the course of commenting on a complex allegory (which equates Israel with an olive tree in the fashion of Romans 11:16–25), Jacob turns again to Isaiah 11 to explain the meaning of a prophetic text. "The things which this prophet Zenos spake concerning the house of Israel, in the which he likened them unto a tame olive tree, must surely come to pass," Jacob says. "And in the day that he shall set his hand again the second time to recover his people is the day—yea, even the last time—that the servants of the Lord shall go forth in his power to nourish and prune his vineyard" (Jacob 6:1–2). As when Jacob's words appear within Nephi's record, what interests him in Isaiah 11 is just the idea that God will recover his people *twice*, an implied first time but then "again the second time."[27] The force of the passage apparently lies in its ability, as prooftext, to indicate the repetitive nature of God's work of gathering and so to show that Isaiah's prophecies might in general be fulfilled more than once.[28]

That Jacob is supposed to have seen Isaiah's prophecies as having two *literal* fulfillments (quite apart from any fulfillments of either a figurative or a likening nature) is clear from the text. When Jacob begins his long discourse in 2 Nephi 6–10, starting from the assigned passage of Isaiah 49:22–23, he explains that what he wishes to say about Isaiah will be different from his previous (and unrecorded) sermons to Nephi's people. While on previous occasions he has dealt with the historical past (2 Nephi 6:3), with this sermon Jacob intends to speak "concerning things which are and which are to come"—about the present and the future—apparently simultaneously (6:4). When Jacob speaks on Isaiah, he offers prophecies that have a first literal fulfillment in his own present (coinciding with the exile of Jerusalem's inhabitants in Babylon)[29] and then a second literal fulfillment in a distant eschatological future ("the second time" of gathering). This whole hermeneutic approach seems to be one Jacob builds on Isaiah's own significant use of the phrase "the second time" in Isaiah 11.

On this score, Nephi and Jacob align hermeneutically. After the long quotation of Isaiah 2–14, Nephi himself twice alludes to Isaiah 11:11, and in both cases he too seems interested primarily in the phrase "the second time." Thus, in 2 Nephi 25:16–17, Nephi looks to a time, after Jews "have been scattered . . . for the space of many generations," when "the Lord will set his hand again the second time to restore his people from their lost and fallen state." The allusion to Isaiah 11:11 is clear here. And, similarly, in 2 Nephi 29:1 Nephi quotes God describing the Book of Mormon's emergence in the last days as happening so that "I may set my hand again the second time to recover my people which are of the house of Israel." This passage thus serves more as prooftext than as text in Nephi's record, as the means of securing a hermeneutic of double (literal) fulfillment.

Yet, as has been shown in this chapter, Isaiah 11:11–12 sits comfortably at the climax of the long quotation of Isaiah 2–14 in 2 Nephi 11–24. If the passage is a prooftext for Nephi's project, it is a prooftext consciously drawn from and carefully set back into a rich and developed context. The long quotation of the whole of Isaiah 2–14 is in fact sandwiched precisely between Jacob's prooftexting allusion to Isaiah 11:11 in 2 Nephi 6 and Nephi's own prooftexting allusions to the same passage in 2 Nephi 25 and 29—as if Nephi were inviting his readers to see that his and his brother's uses of Isaiah 11 are in no way at odds with the plain meaning of the Isaian text. What looks like prooftexting might thus, in the end, actually be further thoughtful reflection on the overall shape of a significant portion of Isaiah, excerpted and reflectively given a clear shape in Second Nephi. In view of both Jacob's and Nephi's penchant for quoting the one line from Isaiah 11 about God setting his hand "the second time" to recover Israel, how might we sharpen our analysis of the long quotation of Isaiah? The allusions to Isaiah 11:11 in Nephi's and Jacob's prophecies find in that text a clear indication of a repeating pattern in God's dealings with historical (Old World) Israel. Is this something to be found responsibly in Isaiah 2–14 as it is quoted in 2 Nephi 11–24?

Because the Hebrew text of Isaiah 11:11 presents potential difficulties, little consensus among Isaiah scholars about the text's meaning exists today.

Scholars leaning toward the liberal end of the spectrum tend to argue that the word translated as "second" (Hebrew *šinīt*) is corrupted and so that the phrase could be read as "once again 'raise high' his hand" or simply "again raise his hand."[30] For such interpreters, there simply is no reference to a "second time" in the passage. Scholars working at the conservative end of the spectrum tend to be slower to suggest emendations and so usually accept the traditional Hebrew rendering, regardless of grammatical difficulties.[31] These latter scholars almost universally take the implied "first" setting of God's hand to recover his people to have occurred in Israel's exodus from Egypt.[32] As in the ever-present "second exodus" motif of Second Isaiah,[33] such scholars see the prophet predicting here in Isaiah 11 also a second exodus in the anticipated recovery of Israelites after being conquered by Assyria.

Nephi and Jacob follow neither of the major tendencies among modern biblical critics in interpreting or using Isaiah 11:11; they raise no questions at all about whether the word *second* deserves emendation. Further, their various quotations of and allusions to the passage make clear that they understand the implied first gathering or recovery of the covenant people to have happened not in the famous exodus from Egypt, but rather in the centuries immediately after Isaiah's prophetic activity in Jerusalem. Does that mean that they have a naïve interpretation of Isaiah 6–12, Second Nephi's original chapter IX? Or is it possible to discover a reasonable reading of Isaiah 6–12 that sees in it two distinct and identifiable moments of divine recovery for the Israelite remnant—a second one referred to straightforwardly as a second one in Isaiah 11, but a first one earlier in the text, somewhat more subtly referred to? For an answer, it is instructive to turn from twentieth- and twenty-first-century biblical criticism to the English-language biblical commentaries of the early modern period, where we occasionally find interpretations of Isaiah 11's "second time" that seem akin to Second Nephi's.

Early modern commentators who would have been familiar to our ideal listener/reader, taken together with Nephi and Jacob, form a peculiar spectrum of overlapping interpretive possibilities for the meaning of Isaiah 11:11. At one extreme stands the Non-Conformist Matthew Henry, for whom Israel's first recovery is from Egypt and its second is from Assyrian domination—these as literal events that would find their figural double in the Messiah's arrival at the dawn of the Christian age.[34] At the other extreme stand Nephi and Jacob, for whom the literal meaning of Isaiah 11 is that Israel's first recovery is from Babylon and second is from its scattered condition at history's end. Between these extremes are positioned the English Non-Conformist Matthew Poole and the Anglican William Lowth. Poole argues, Nephi- and Jacob-like, that Israel's first recovery is its ancient return from Babylon but, he also argues, much more Henry-like, that Israel's second recovery occurs with the arrival of the Messiah and the rise of the Christian age.[35] Lowth, by contrast, agrees with Henry that Israel's first recovery is in its exodus from Egypt, while he concurs with Nephi and Jacob that Israel's second recovery will be found in its eschatological redemption at the end of history.[36] The interpretation of Isaiah 11:11 that Second Nephi sets forth (or at least assumes) is a far cry from that of the towering figure of Matthew Henry, but it incorporates interpretive moves offered by others: a bit from Poole and a bit from Lowth. All this makes perfectly clear that there is a kind of coherence—a kind of mainstream respectability—to the assumed interpretation of Isaiah 11:11–12 in Nephi's record. It is decidedly at odds with current critical biblical scholarship in various ways, but it has a recognizable place in the largely precritical interpretive tradition available to the earliest readers of the Book of Mormon.

Confirming that Isaiah 11 is the whole focus and center of the long quotation of Isaiah is the fact that Nephi quotes from that particular chapter again at the close of his own prophetic contribution to his "more sacred things." The setting for this further quotation—this time not of verses 11–12, however—is important. Having prophesied at length of the coming forth of the Book of Mormon and of the problematic reactions to that book that can be anticipated, Nephi concludes his prophecy with "somewhat more concerning the Jews and the gentiles," turning his attention at last to the "many" who "shall believe the words which are written" (2 Nephi 30:3). Believing gentiles will take the Book of Mormon, he predicts, to his own people's latter-day descendants, "and then shall the remnant of our seed know concerning us," from their origins in Jerusalem to their eventual knowledge of the gospel of Jesus Christ (30:4). Once gentiles have united in faith with the latter-day descendants of the Book of Mormon's peoples, Nephi predicts, "the Jews which are scattered also shall begin to believe in Christ, and they shall begin to gather in upon the face of the land" (30:7). This event, finally, marks the commencement of God's work to restore his people (30:8).

As soon as Nephi reaches this threshold in his prophecy, he begins to quote from Isaiah 11 again, now from an earlier part of the chapter and at substantial length (albeit with an editorial insertion of his own, italicized below):

> And with righteousness shall the Lord God judge the poor and reprove with equity for the meek of the earth. And he shall smite the earth with the rod of his mouth, and with the breath of his lips shall he slay the wicked. *For the time*

speedily cometh that the Lord God shall cause a great division among the people, and the wicked will he destroy, and he will spare his people—yea, even if it so be that he must destroy the wicked by fire. And righteousness shall be the girdle of his loins and faithfulness the girdle of his reins. And then shall the wolf dwell with the lamb, and the leopard shall lie down with the kid, and the calf and the young lion and the fatling together, and a little child shall lead them. And the cow and the bear shall feed. Their young ones shall lie down together, and the lion shall eat straw like the ox. And the sucking child shall play on the hole of the asp, and the weaned child shall put his hand on the cockatrice's den. They shall not hurt nor destroy in all my holy mountain, for the earth shall be full of the knowledge of the Lord as the waters cover the sea. (2 Nephi 30:9–15)[37]

Here Nephi quotes in full Isaiah 11:4–9, already encountered by the reader in the full quotation of Isaiah 11 in 2 Nephi 21. Never providing even a word of explanation or commentary for this requotation of Isaiah 11:4–9, Nephi seems to assume that its meaning is straightforward or obvious. The reader is supposed to recognize that Isaiah 11 describes the end of history, the dawning of global peace. A self-interpreting passage of Isaiah is allowed to stand in for the climax of Nephi's "own" prophesying.

Thus Nephi makes his understanding of Isaiah 11 perfectly plain. It is the climactic prophetic description of how God brings his work in the world to a close. There will be peace, in the end (even if, Nephi inserts into the prophecy, that has to be accomplished through the destruction of the wicked by fire!). Isaiah 11 he takes to be a straightforward description of the eschaton, the time when God intervenes at last in the world to see justice established. This is the load-bearing wall of his Isaian construction in Second Nephi. Because Isaiah 11 wears its meaning on its sleeve, for Nephi—especially the description of eschatological peace—he can assume that Isaiah's words can be likened rather easily "unto all men" (2 Nephi 11:8). Many of the details scattered throughout the rest of his long quotation of Isaiah might need clarification and exposition, but Isaiah 11 can be presented as simply describing what every believer in the Bible is supposed to recognize as the truth. History will culminate with a millennial era of peace, established by God's own work at "the restoration of his people upon the earth" (2 Nephi 30:8).

The Peaceable Kingdom

There is something surprising in Nephi's final quotation from Isaiah 11 at the conclusion of his own prophetic contribution—the aforementioned insertion about God destroying the wicked by fire (2 Nephi 30:10). That such talk should interrupt what might be the Christian Bible's best-known description of messianic peace brings one up short. It was, after all, this same extract from Isaiah 11 that inspired Edward Hicks, the nineteenth-century American Quaker artist, to produce "perhaps a hundred lustrous, thickly coated" paintings—now quite famous—of the "Peaceable Kingdom," the messianic kingdom where lion and lamb dwell together.[38]

Hicks's beautiful paintings are justifiably more famous today than other nineteenth-century illustrations of Isaiah 11, which were largely didactic in purpose. They grew, moreover, out of a rather more complex social situation. Hicks painted "at least sixty-two versions of the allegorical *Peaceable Kingdom* . . . between about 1820 and 1849," using them as a way of expressing his adherence to one side of a major schism in the Pennsylvania Society of Friends during those decades.[39] Hicks found in Isaiah 11:6–9 a scriptural passage that both mirrored the theology for which he argued and anticipated the sort of peace he wished to see return to his religious community. "His paints and brush, as well as his sermons [at the time], were eloquent statements against the world's disappointments," as Hicks's biographer says.[40] (Hicks even set the passage from Isaiah to verse in his own words.)[41] Reception historian John Sawyer argues that Hicks's paintings were responsible for the growing popularity of this particular passage of Isaiah, although only belatedly—beyond the historical scope, for instance, of our ideal listener/reader.[42] Hicks's work "remained virtually unknown to historians, critics, and other artists until the 1920s," and was not widely exhibited until the early 1930s.[43] Since that time, however, *The Peaceable Kingdom* has inspired musicians, poets, and theologians—and the iconography of at least one branch of the Latter-Day Saints movement begun by Joseph Smith.[44] A century after their production, Hicks's illustrations of Isaiah 11 were enough removed from their conflictual context that they could be received as inspiring visions of what peace might look like in the world. Although they are now valued for their "bucolic nature" and expression of God's peace,[45] in the 1820s and 1830s, when Hicks originally and repeatedly painted the scene, Isaiah 11:6–9 was arguably more a site for interpretive conflict than a simple prophetic appeal for peace. The immediate context is useful for understanding Nephi's interpolation about the fiery fate of the wicked.

It is important to note, moreover, that the quotation from Isaiah 11 that Nephi interrupts with a prediction of violent destruction is not limited to verses 6–9; it begins with verse 4, which contains its own violent language. Only two verses before the parade of peaceful animals begins, Isaiah 11 says of the Spirit-endowed branch that "he shall smite the earth with the rod of his mouth, and with the breath of his lips shall he slay the wicked." Modern commentators discussing Isaiah 11, fired by the celebrated ethical vision of Israel's prophets, emphasize that the wicked are contextually the oppressors of the poor. Thus Walter Brueggemann comments, "The public responsibility of the king for justice and righteousness exercised in fidelity requires that the royal government should have at its disposal leverage for sanctions, penalties, and punishments for those who violate the vision. The positive power to create social good requires the capacity for curbing 'the wicked.' Thus the king has the capacity to 'smite' and to 'slay' the wicked, who are here seen to be those who prey upon, exploit, and abuse the meek, vulnerable, and poor."[46] Nephi seems similarly concerned, alluding to Isaiah 3:15 as he insists that the wicked gentiles are those who "preach up unto themselves their own wisdom and their own learning, that they may get gain and grind upon the face of the poor" (2 Nephi 26:20). He concludes his long quotation of Isaiah with these words quite specifically, in fact: "What shall then answer the messengers of the nations? That the Lord hath founded Zion! And the poor of his people shall trust in it!" (24:32, quoting Isaiah 14:32). Perhaps most important, in a text directly related to Nephi's interruptive insertion into Isaiah 11:4–9, Nephi says that those who "need fear and tremble and quake" are those who seek "to get gain," "to get power over the flesh," and "to become popular in the eyes of the world" (1 Nephi 22:23). For Nephi as much as for modern interpreters of Isaiah 11:4, the text seems to be about violence toward and judgment for the oppressors of the poor.

The mainstream Protestant interpreters writing a century before the publication of the Book of Mormon, but still popular and available when our ideal listener/reader would have been around, emphasize these same points about Isaiah 11. They do not, in other words, tend toward what would become a largely contextless celebration of "the peaceable kingdom" after Hicks's art became fashionable. Thus, Matthew Henry says of God, in connection with Isaiah 11:4, that "he shall in righteousness plead for the people that are poor and oppressed; he will be their Protector"—adding further that "it is the duty of princes to defend and deliver the poor" and that Christ "is the poor man's King."[47] Such interpreters, however, work in some way to soften the impact of the violent language used to describe the punishment that will come to the oppressors of the poor. Henry, for example, interprets "with the breath of his lips" as meaning "by the operation of his Spirit, according to his word," and he explains that the words "slay the wicked" must find their fulfillment "in the other world" where "everlasting tribulation will be recompensed to those that trouble [God's] poor people."[48] Even less learned interpreters, such as a lay Methodist writing within years of the Book of Mormon's publication, argued that the passage's references to animals "is, without doubt, figurative; and the meaning of [it] is, that men of savage characters, of beast-like passions, shall be so subdued by the mild and peaceful spirit of the gospel as to do no mischief.[49]

At first glance, Nephi appears to contrast with the mainstream interpreters in the English-speaking tradition of commentary, leaving little room for any softening of Isaiah's meaning. For Nephi, the wicked *in history* are to be destroyed, and that—if necessary—*by fire*.[50] And, in fact, one might naturally be inclined to root Nephi's connection between the violent "breath of [God's] lips" and the destruction of the wicked "by fire" in other (uncited) passages of Isaiah that millenarians tended to emphasize in the nineteenth century, as our always-present ideal listener/reader would remind us. One millenarian tract published two decades after the Book of Mormon connects Isaiah 11:4 with Isaiah 30:27–33, in which God's "lips are full of indignation, and his tongue as a devouring fire"; God's enemies are reduced to "fire and much wood," while "the breath of the LORD, like a stream of brimstone, doth kindle it."[51] Despite such networkings of texts available to early readers of the Book of Mormon, there is reason to think that Nephi as much as the mainstream commentators wishes to soften the impact of the violent language of Isaiah—despite his own editorial interruption and its own apparently violent language.

In his apocalyptic vision in the first of his two books, Nephi describes the same events to which he applies Isaiah 11 in 2 Nephi 30, but there he does so in terms that suggest he has in mind the natural consequences of human enmity rather than a divinely imposed act of punishment. He speaks of "the wrath of God" being "poured out" on the wicked, but what this actually looks like as Nephi watches events unfold is that "there were wars and rumors of wars among all the nations and kindreds of the earth" (1 Nephi 14:15). Much in the spirit of his heir, Mormon, Nephi seems to indicate that "it is by the wicked that the wicked are punished," because they incite others to bloodshed (Mormon 4:5). In this sense, it is possible that Nephi is—against superficial appearances—prepared to offer an interpretation of Isaiah 11:4 like that of the mystic Emanuel Swedenborg, for whom the meaning of the verse "is, not that Jehovah should smite with the rod of his mouth, and slay the wicked with the breath of his lips, but that the wicked do thus to themselves."[52] That Nephi couples Isaiah 11:4–5 with Isaiah 11:6–9 may not, then, necessarily imply that he embraces a less peaceful vision of the millennial dawn than does Edward Hicks, who preached and painted at the very time that Nephi's words became public. Or if he feels compelled by his prophetic gift to believe that violence must necessarily come, he expresses discomfort with such a vision of things.

What Nephi emphasizes in his final appropriation of Isaiah 11 is that peace lies only in the (distant) future, after God accomplishes his strange work with the remnant of Israel. After every historical difficulty, Nephi avers, the faithful can expect God to intervene to bring goodness and rest to the world—and especially to the downtrodden of Israel. "They shall not hurt nor destroy in all my holy mountain," the last verse Nephi quotes from Isaiah runs, "for the earth shall be full of the knowledge of the Lord as the waters cover the sea" (2 Nephi 30:15). This final eschatological revelation is what apparently brings peace to the world,[53] which is what Nephi emphasizes. And so, readers of Nephi's record in the nineteenth century, if they were acquainted with available Isaiah scholarship, would likely have seen him as standing in respectable interpretive company as he highlights Isaiah 11 within his thirteen-chapters-long quotation. Although scholarship contemporary with our ideal listener/reader consistently disagreed about whether to apply aspects of Isaiah 11 to pre-Christian, Christian, or eschatological events, all seem to have agreed—with Nephi—that the chapter deserves particular and peculiar attention.

What really distinguishes Nephi from the dominant and even marginal interpreters of our ideal listener/reader's contemporaries, then, lies as always in his unique hermeneutical methods. However much Nephi fits into the larger English-language interpretative tradition on the literal meaning of Isaiah 11, it is his penchant for likening that sets him apart. Nephi likens Isaiah 11 much more gently than he does Isaiah 49, however, and he does so explicitly only in 2 Nephi 30 at the close of his record when he weaves the language of Isaiah 11 into his own prophetic anticipations of the last-days fate of his people. Even when Nephi and his brother Jacob take Isaiah 11's distinction between a first and a "second time" to motivate multiple literal applications of Isaiah's prophecies, they fit well into the mainstream English-speaking interpretive tradition. When, however, Nephi's method of likening pushes him toward a third application of Isaiah's prophecies—to every branch of Israel, and especially to his own as seen in a vision—he moves beyond the margin into a space of his own. Thus, although Nephi's understanding of the *literal* meanings of Isaiah 11 always fits on the map of available mainline antebellum interpretations (albeit with a tendency toward the millennialist margins of the interpretive tradition), the fact that he *likens* the text moves him onto unfamiliar terrain.

All this helps to explain why the long quotation of Isaiah at the heart of Second Nephi largely stands on its own, without guiding interpretive glosses. For the latter-day audience of Nephi's record, then, the first dozen or so chapters of the Book of Isaiah are supposed to be largely self-interpreting, plain enough in their general meaning at the literal level. Nephi, in fact, asserts this straightforwardly after concluding the long quotation of Isaiah. He concedes that, for his own people, "the words of Isaiah are not plain" (2 Nephi 25:4), but he insists that they will be wholly plain for those who live "in the last days" (25:8). That is, Nephi assumes that Isaiah's readers in the time and place of the Book of Mormon's coming forth would have little difficulty in understanding the basic (literal) message of the prophet—about Jews' redemption from Babylon anciently and from a general scattering at the end of time. What he adds that no nineteenth-century reader would guess on her own comes only *after* the long quotation, as Nephi shifts from quoting to, once again, likening.

As he shifts from quoting to likening, however, Nephi makes a surprising move. Not only does he announce that what he has quoted at such length will be perfectly plain to (millenarian) latter-day readers, he delimits the intended audience of the likening he goes on to set out. He, as he puts it, "confine[s]" his words to his "own people" (2 Nephi 25:8)—especially to the several generations of his people that would follow his own death.[54] Nephi's own culminating prophecy in 2 Nephi 25–30, following Jacob's sermon and the long quotation of Isaiah 2–14, is supposed to be directed *not* to latter-day readers, but primarily if not exclusively to ancient ones. As Nephi approaches his final and fullest likening work with the prophecies of Isaiah—work to be examined in full in chapter 9 herein—he asks the Book of Mormon's latter-day audience to take a back seat while he speaks to his own ancient people. After all that has become clear here about the nature of Nephi's unique hermeneutical method, we suddenly find him explaining to us that he means his labors in likening to land on just a certain sort of reader—a sort that had been dead for almost two thousand years by the time the Book of Mormon was published.

Nephi's comments immediately following his long quotation of Isaiah thus confirm but then dramatically develop his notion of likening. And what is the result for our charitable and informed ideal listener sitting in the room with Joseph Smith and his scribes in the summer of 1829—especially if such a person could sit later with the printed text to study it further? It becomes suddenly apparent that readers in the nineteenth century and beyond are intended, as they read Nephi's record, not only to see Nephi as adding metaphorical interpretations (likening) to standard literal interpretations of Isaiah's prophecies. They are also to see themselves as somewhat awkwardly listening in on Nephi's attempts to instruct ancient peoples about how they, *specifically those ancient people*, might come to understand Isaiah. Latter-day readers are supposed to understand Isaiah's general meaning enough not to require the kinds of explanations Nephi provides. They might, however, benefit from listening in as Nephi works to explain Isaiah's relevance to the ancients. Nephi's own people have to see why it matters that God would restore the people they left behind from exile in Babylon, but then especially why it matters that God would restore those same people again from a much broader and more complex form of exile at the end of history. To see why such things matter, they would have to be shown—through the resources of Nephi's "own prophecy" (2 Nephi 25:7)—that their own future descendants would be a part of that complex story of exile and redemption, part of the mystery of covenantal history.

I have repeatedly emphasized that our ideal listener, sitting in the room with Joseph Smith and his scribes in 1829 and listening hard for anything touching on Isaiah, would have heard something of a clear climax for the Book of Mormon in Nephi's record. Second Nephi introduces a new level of complexity to the millennialist approach that is entirely lacking in Mormon's project and not even really glimpsed in Nephi's own first book. What is new at *this* point, though, is that Nephi eventually asks his latter-day readers—those living through the eschaton that the Book of Mormon projects—to undertake something other than just the standard millennialist interpretation if they are really to understand the prophet's meaning. They need to know something of an *ancient* conversation if they are really to see their place in the unfolding events of the last days. Why this is so can become clear only in a close investigation of how Nephi addresses himself to the third—the last—of his three favored Isaiah passages, Isaiah 29:11–14. This is what absorbs him, finally, when he sets long quotations of Isaiah behind to turn to a far more intricate engagement with the Isaian text, this in the course of presenting what he calls his "own prophecy" (2 Nephi 25:7).

Key to Nephi's project, then, is the idea that something is essentially missing from the reconstructed picture of salvation history that rightly oriented millennialists in the latter days associated with Isaiah's prophecies. According to Nephi, such millennialists really do understand the basic meaning and thrust of Isaiah's predictions about the final gathering of Israel, prior to the dawn of millennial peace. What they lack is, at the very least, a sense for *when* such events can be expected to occur. This is a worry for Mormon's Christ as well, who pauses in his articulation of eschatological history to explain "a sign" that would mark the beginning of the eschaton (3 Nephi 21:1). Nephi too works to provide latter-day readers with a clear and forceful understanding of when to expect apocalyptic events. But where the Christ of Third Nephi simply states what the sign is—the coming forth of the Book of Mormon itself—Nephi instead takes up a startlingly complex hermeneutic project that allows him to find likened traces of that sign right in Isaiah's prophecies. He effectively creates a layered Isaian text, one that tells not only the straightforward story of the eschaton but also, when read in a kind of figurative way, the less straightforward story of the events that immediately precede the eschaton. If Isaiah is taken to be likenable to other visionary traditions—visionary traditions not at all known to the larger Christian world—then it becomes possible to discern details about the eschaton that Christians are unaware of. They stumble in their millennialist hopes because they fail to know of the ancient American remnant of Israel. But, coming to know that remnant and its unique visionary experiences (and their connection to Isaiah), gentile Christians might well come to see what it really means to advance the work of the millennium.

For Nephi, what latter-day readers of the Book of Mormon really need is to become aware of the remnant of Israel. Redemption for the world and for humanity can occur only if that remnant—the Book of Mormon's own peoples, surviving into modernity—can receive gentile Christians who understand their place in a complex eschatological history. Christians in late modernity need to listen in as the visionary Nephi works to instruct his own ancient people about what God would do with every unrecognizable remnant of Israel, scattered around the world. Gentile Christians, in other words, need to watch as the Book of Isaiah is once more and most definitively alienated from itself in a likening hermeneutic that displaces the text's meaning. Then, only as the meaning of Isaiah returns to itself from such an alienation, might the whole plan of God's intervention in latter-day history become clear. This, it seems, is what Nephi aims to do in a kind of grand finale. He is strangely simultaneously aware that he writes principally for his own descendants during the centuries immediately after his own lifetime *and* that latter-day gentiles will read his words and reflect on what they mean for the final fulfillment of Isaiah's prophecies.

It is only with this whole picture in mind that we can be fully prepared to consider the last of Nephi's three favored passages: Isaiah 29:11–14. It is the last Isaian text that Nephi takes up in earnest and at length. And what he puts together in his final treatment of Isaiah is more complex and more probing than anything he does prior to it. This project, finally, deserves the closest attention.

9

As One That Hath a Familiar Spirit

The last crucial use of Isaiah in the Book of Mormon (as Joseph Smith dictated the text to his scribes, and to our imagined ideal listener) comes a few pages after the long quotation of Isaiah 2–14.[1] It has drawn more scholarly attention than other uses of Isaiah in the Book of Mormon, if for no other reason than its sheer inventiveness. This is no slavish reproduction of Isaiah but a creative adaptation of it to a new context, the sort of thing that would have especially intrigued our ideal listener/reader. In 2 Nephi 25–27, the original chapter XI, a virtuosic exploration of Isaiah 29 appears, virtuosic especially in its comparison between prophecy and a sealed book. Here, Nephi's readers encounter likening in its most mature form. The two sources of Nephi's practice of likening are so developed by this point in his record that he mentions neither while he uses both. That is, for the first time in all his more extensive interactions with Isaiah, Nephi never uses the prophet's name while exploring his text. Further, although Nephi occasionally interrupts his predictions in these chapters with "I prophesy," he never explains to his readers that these prophecies and predictions derive from the vision in 1 Nephi 11–14. Nephi's and Isaiah's voices come at the reader in such tight harmony that they register—or are meant to register—as one sound.

It cannot be accidental that this final fusion of Nephi's and Isaiah's prophetic voices occurs when Nephi's burden is to clarify his unique contribution to Isaiah's prophecy. Chapter 8 has shown how Nephi assumes the Book of Mormon's *latter-day* readers will understand the eschatological import of

Isaiah, as well as its ancient fulfillments. But what Nephi uniquely brings to the hermeneutic table is his project of likening, an interpretive alienation of Isaiah's literal meaning through application to a New World branch or remnant of Israel; and this, he makes clear, has as its primary audience Nephi's own *ancient* people, with latter-day (gentile) readers mostly listening in on the ancient conversation. And yet that latter-day eavesdropping is something Nephi both anticipates and intends, since the likened prophecies of Isaiah—refracted through the prism of Nephi's vision—introduces latter-day readers to the event meant to launch the fulfillment of the unlikened prophecies of Isaiah. That is, Nephi wishes his latter-day readers to listen as he admonishes his own people thousands of years earlier to remain faithful and produce a book that might eventually resurface and inaugurate the eschaton anticipated by the prophets. Nephi makes this subject—that of his sermons to his own people, uttered with a sideways glance at the modern reader—the focus of his climactic reading of Isaiah.

What remains to be pursued in concluding this study, then, is an investigation of how Nephi brings off his final engagement with Isaiah. It is necessary, at last, to consider the Book of Mormon's most theologically potent interaction with Isaiah. What does Nephi do with Isaiah 29 when the training wheels of his hermeneutic are off and he can ride freely? How does this moment—a wholly unique contribution to the history of Isaiah's interpretation—compare with the larger interpretive tradition? And what should one think about while sitting in striking silence after the fading echoes of the Book of Mormon's Isaian finale, when the crescendo of the whole project has come to an end? For one last examination of what the Book of Mormon does with Isaiah, we have to lean once again on our charitable and informed ideal listener-turned-reader, with us from the beginning of this study.

What Nephi Does and Does Not Do with Isaiah 29

The bulk of the Isaian material in the Book of Mormon strikes most readers as either straightforward quotation or simple allusion. Long excerpts and short borrowings look uninventive if left unprobed. Especially where excerpts and borrowings receive Christological or apocalyptic interpretations, readers tend to guess that the Book of Mormon understands Isaiah as any millenarian Christian from the antebellum American frontier would—predictable and therefore largely uninteresting. There is, however, one crucial exception to this pattern. Just once in the Book of Mormon, the treatment of Isaiah becomes so obviously unique that readers cannot ignore it: when Nephi experiments with Isaiah 29. Because this treatment clamors for attention, scholars of various stripes have given it special consideration.[2] And because existing analyses of what Nephi does with Isaiah 29 are often problematic, we must briefly consider how Nephi's handling of this text has been seen.

Isaiah 29 contains twenty-four verses—742 words in the King James translation. The text in which Isaiah 29 appears in 2 Nephi 25–27, however, runs to about forty verses, some 1,739 words.[3] Nephi's "version" of Isaiah 29 is thus more than twice as long as the Bible's, despite the fact that Nephi entirely omits the first two verses of Isaiah 29 in his appropriation. The disparity is real, and it is this disparity that draws attention—reinforced by the paratextual apparatus in modern editions that invite readers to "compare Isaiah 29" when they come to 2 Nephi 27 (or to "compare 2 Nephi 27" when they come to Isaiah 29 in the Bible).[4] The inevitable impression on any reader is either that Nephi greatly expanded Isaiah 29 or that the editors of the biblical text dramatically condensed what Nephi found on the brass plates. Readers have drawn both conclusions. Is Nephi supposed to provide the true and original text of Isaiah 29, which was corrupted or at least truncated by scribes? Or are we meant to see Nephi at his inventive best here, prophetically manipulating the Bible's accurate text of Isaiah 29 into something appropriate to his own interests? The question is essential. To answer it one way is to decide that biblical Isaiah himself directly predicted the coming forth of the Book of Mormon in the last days. To answer it the other way is to decide that Isaiah made no such prediction; Nephi simply uses Isaiah's words to explain the Book of Mormon's appearance. Latter-day Saints have traditionally decided in favor of the first option, arguing that Christians have overlooked the Bible's own direct prophecy that the Book of Mormon would trigger a "marvellous work and a wonder" (Isaiah 29:14).

The first Latter-day Saint scholar with training in biblical languages to work directly on this issue was Sidney B. Sperry. Sperry trained at the University of Chicago, receiving his doctorate there in 1931 before taking up a position in the Division of Religion at Brigham Young University.[5] As early as 1939, Sperry addressed in print what he called the Isaiah problem in the Book of Mormon—the potential difficulties surrounding the presence of Second Isaiah in a volume purportedly produced by Israelites who left Jerusalem before the Jewish exile in Babylon.[6] This came hard on the heels of Sperry's directing Grant Vest's 1938 dissertation, "The Problem of Isaiah in the Book of Mormon."[7] Not until 1952, however, did Sperry address the use of Isaiah 29 in Second Nephi. Despite his serious training and his sustained interest in Isaiah in the Book of Mormon, Sperry's treatment is brief. He identifies allusions to Isaiah 29:3–7 in 2 Nephi 26 and early in 2 Nephi 27. He then states his view that, "commencing with the fourth clause of 2 Nephi 27:3, Nephi quotes verbatim Isaiah 29, beginning with verse 8."[8] Sperry's use of the word *verbatim* naturally puzzles anyone comparing 2 Nephi 27 with Isaiah 29, but he explains: "When I say 'verbatim' I mean the true and ancient text of Isaiah 29 as found upon the Brass Plates."[9] According to Sperry, then, Nephi preserves rather than expands the original and uncorrupted text of Isaiah 29 (or at least of Isaiah 29:8–24).

Sperry's understanding reflected that of certain well-received leaders within the Latter-day Saint tradition at the time.[10] His treatment, however, suggests more nuance than popular references by ecclesiastical leaders writing in pastoral contexts. In fact, what apparently motivated Sperry's approach most was a volume of ambiguous scriptural status—the so-called "inspired version" of the Bible produced by Joseph Smith.[11] Just months after publishing the Book of Mormon, Smith began an ambitious revision of the Bible, working on the project for three years.[12] Although he made some efforts to publish the revision, no full printing would appear until the 1860s, and then only as a result of the efforts of the second-largest denomination from within Smith's religious tradition, the Reorganized Church of Jesus Christ of Latter Day Saints (now Community of Christ). Because Smith's immediate family members mostly joined the Reorganized Church after its formation, it rather than the larger Church of Jesus Christ of Latter-day Saints had possession of the relevant manuscripts. Growing friendliness between the two branches of the Restoration movement would eventually result in sharing the manuscripts, but Sperry wrote before any such later developments. He therefore worked delicately and somewhat skeptically with resources published by a rival tradition.[13] Even after the full manuscripts of Smith's revision became available, however, the "Inspired Version" did not formally become scripture within Sperry's Latter-day Saint tradition. It remains today quasi-scripture, its authoritative status uncertain.

Joseph Smith's revision of the Bible is unsure of itself in several ways. In addition to its murky authoritative status within the Latter-day Saint tradition, Smith's own efforts with the project were of two dramatically different sorts, although scholars have often downplayed the differences. When Smith began revising the Bible in June 1830, his method was to dictate a dramatically altered biblical text in full for his scribes to take down in longhand. In this early stage of the project, his revisions were striking and provocative, inserting long sections of text and drastically altering the extant narratives. For nearly two years, he labored in this way on half of Genesis, the whole of Matthew, Mark, and Luke, and the first few chapters of John. Then, however, after Smith and a scribe experienced, during their labors on the Bible, an epoch-making vision,[14] the project changed. As if the long-form project had served its purpose, Smith now worked with his scribes simply to mark up a copy of the Bible, writing out relatively minor revisions where advisable.[15] As a result, the project became hurried and conservative rather than ponderous and experimental. Where Smith and his scribes had taken nearly two years to work through three and half of the Bible's sixty-six books in the first version of the project, they raced through the remainder of the Bible in just a year and a half.[16]

Because the Old Testament came last in Joseph Smith's revisions, and because the prophetic writings come last in the Old Testament, revisions to Isaiah occurred late in the project and are rather minimal. Moreover, they often (but not always) reproduce variants from the Book of Mormon's quotations of Isaiah. Typically, they involve a word here or a phrase there, but when Smith and his scribes came to Isaiah 29:8–24, he had his scribe copy out the text of 2 Nephi 27:3–35 in full (perhaps as Smith read the text aloud).[17] Sperry, as we can now see, took the change in procedure to mean that Smith understood Isaiah 29:8–24 (but not Isaiah 29:3–7) to appear in its original and uncorrupted form in Second Nephi. Is it clear, however? It falls very much within the range of orthodox Latter-day Saint belief to hold that parts of Smith's Bible revision aimed not at restoring original text but at providing "inspired commentary" or harmonizing "doctrinal concepts that were revealed to the Prophet Joseph Smith independently of his translation of the Bible."[18] Why not conclude that Smith's handling of Isaiah 29 was intended to be an instance of harmonizing or clarifying? And why not think that the decision to copy from the Book of Mormon only beginning with Isaiah 29:8 was the result of a midrevision change of mind?[19] Smith or his scribe simply may have remembered, partway through revising Isaiah 29, that there was some treatment of the text in the Book of Mormon, and they therefore copied a long text over from 2 Nephi 27 without reflecting on the implications.

Despite these ambiguities, however, many Latter-day Saint scholars have followed Sperry's approach, such as today's most established Latter-day Saint biblical scholar, Donald Parry. Parry studied Near Eastern languages at the University of Utah before becoming a professor of the Hebrew Bible at Brigham Young University in 1992. His contributions to the ancient textual history of

Isaiah are many and important.[20] He has also, however, written about Isaiah for average Latter-day Saints. In his most substantial such work (with two coauthors), he discusses Isaiah 29 as if it were originally (basically) equivalent to 2 Nephi 27 in the Book of Mormon.[21] "Evidently," he and his coauthors write, "Nephi's citations of Isaiah were from the brass plates." Parry apparently arrives at this conclusion from the fact that the Book of Mormon text appears also in "the Joseph Smith Translation."[22]

During the half-century between Sperry and Parry, presumably encouraged by these experts' opinions, other Latter-day Saint authors (many with far less training in biblical studies) made far stronger statements about Isaiah 29 and Second Nephi. Victor Ludlow, for instance, in what has long been regarded among Latter-day Saints as the best work on Isaiah for lay readers, expanded on Sperry's view by providing a detailed and systematic argument for the idea that 2 Nephi 27 contains large swaths of Isaian text that were lost at some point after Nephi's family departed from Jerusalem.[23] Monte Nyman was more specific (but less systematic) in claiming that 2 Nephi 27 includes "at least eighteen complete verses which undoubtedly are some of the 'plain and precious things' that were taken away from the record of the Jews by the 'great and abominable church' (see 1 Nephi 13:23–29)."[24] Clay Gorton went so far as to outline "the apostate condition of Israel" and its direct effects on "the wording of Isaiah" in considering differences between the Book of Mormon's Isaiah texts and those in the King James Version.[25]

Even during the twentieth century, however, the view that Nephi had a lost and fuller version of Isaiah was not universal. Scholars working in the Reorganized Church were untouched by the conclusions of scholars like Sperry and Parry who worked within the Latter-day Saint tradition. Thus, Charles Hartshorn simply observed that the words of 2 Nephi 26–27 "follow Isaiah 29 quite closely,"[26] and Richard Howard stated that Joseph Smith "revised these King James Isaiah 29 passages" in creating the Book of Mormon.[27] Writing from entirely outside the Restoration tradition and skeptically, Wesley Walters argued that 2 Nephi 26–27 is "designed to bend the Isaiah passage to fit the situation that had transpired before the production of the Book of Mormon."[28] Even scholars working within the boundaries of the Latter-day Saint tradition sometimes concluded that Nephi (or Joseph Smith writing in Nephi's name) does not simply reproduce the supposed original of Isaiah 29 but rather adopts it to Nephi's own purposes. Thus, at the orthodox extreme, Joseph McConkie and Robert Millet followed apostle Bruce R. McConkie in asserting that Nephi "has given us an interpreting paraphrase" of Isaiah 29.[29] At the unorthodox extreme, David Wright, attributing the Book of Mormon to Joseph Smith as sole author, took 2 Nephi 26–27 to be "interpretation . . . interwoven with the citation of the text."[30] Somewhere between these extremes lay Avraham Gileadi, who, in a "new translation" of Isaiah published by Church-owned Deseret Book, entirely ignored 2 Nephi 26–27 in providing a rendering of Isaiah 29.[31] And even before Sperry, early commentators like George Reynolds and Janne Sjodahl wrote that Nephi "applies the prophecy of Isaiah 29 to the coming forth of the Book of Mormon" rather than provides access to a lost original.[32] The dominant position taken by Sperry and Parry has in no way been decisive for the tradition.[33]

Even Parry may be more nuanced than his most popular writings suggest. Both in his commentary and in a collation of Isaiah texts in translation, he refers readers to a study by Robert Cloward.[34] Cloward's position not only differs from but diametrically opposes Parry's (apparent) position. Cloward, that is, takes Nephi to be an inventive appropriator of the biblical Isaiah 29 rather than a passive reproducer of a lost original. That Parry cites Cloward for his readers' consideration is suggestive, and even more suggestive is the fact that Parry edited the volume in which Cloward's essay appears. All this indicates that Parry takes a less nuanced approach in his popular writings simply because he believes average Latter-day Saints are unprepared for the complexity of how Nephi handles Isaiah. He nonetheless places subtle suggestions for further reading in footnotes, pointing serious readers to sources that address complexity.

Cloward's essay, at any rate, largely put an end to the careless readings that often appeared and sometimes dominated twentieth-century discussions of Isaiah 29 in the Book of Mormon. Published in 1998, the essay outlines what has since become the standard scholarly Latter-day Saint understanding of Nephi's treatment of Isaiah 29: that the biblical version of Isaiah 29 is neither corrupted nor derivative.[35] He identifies four contexts for the prophecy's literal fulfillment as Nephi sees it: (1) Assyria's campaign against Judah in the eighth century before Christ, (2) Babylon's campaign in the sixth century before Christ, (3) Rome's devastation of Jerusalem in the first century, and (4) the latter-day eschaton.[36] Then, however, Cloward comes to his principal task: to ask what happens with the *text* of Isaiah 29 in the Book of Mormon. Here he makes a clear case that 2 Nephi 26–27 prophetically experiments with—rather than scribally reproduces—Isaiah 29. He insists that the Book of Mormon's handling of Isaiah 29 begins from what "Nephi and Jacob call 'likening,'" introducing a fifth angle of fulfillment for the biblical text.[37] Only this nonliteral or likening fulfillment of Isaiah 29 concerns the coming forth of the Book of Mormon, and this Nephi adds to the general patterns of millenarian interpretations of Isaiah in antebellum America.

Cloward rightly focuses on a subtle and—before him—often overlooked difference between the Bible's and Nephi's "versions" of Isaiah 29:11. In the King James Version, it reads thus: "And the vision of all is become unto you as the words of a book that is sealed, which men deliver to one that is learned, saying, Read this, I pray thee: and he saith, I cannot; for it is sealed." Latter-day Saints have long taken this verse to describe exactly an event that occurred in 1828, shortly after Joseph Smith received the gold plates from which he would translate the Book of Mormon. Hoping to secure assistance, Smith sent Martin Harris to New York City with a copy of characters drawn from the plates to see what a learned expert might say.[38] Cloward, however, points out that Isaiah 29:11 presents a simile about Isaiah's own visionary experience, not a literal prediction about the coming forth of the Book of Mormon: "Isaiah lamented in Isaiah 29:11 that the vision of Jerusalem's people had become *as* the words of a sealed book. No specific book is mentioned. Isaiah's concern was the lost vision of his people, not books. His expression is symbolic—a simile, one of many similes and metaphors in Isaiah 29." Cloward therefore concludes that "it was Nephi who made Isaiah's symbolic book into a literal book," that is, the Book of Mormon itself coming forth in the last days.[39]

Cloward's basic approach is the dominant one among scholars today, despite lingering interest in twentieth-century approaches at the popular level. Grant and Heather Hardy use a musical metaphor to describe Nephi's method in 2 Nephi 25–27: "Much as Mozart brings together three separate musical genres in a complicated interweaving of voices [in 'Ah! vous je-dirai Maman'], Nephi here reworks phrases from multiple sources into a kind of bravura prophetic performance."[40] Brant Gardner compares Nephi's use of Isaiah 29 to the inventive treatment of biblical texts found in the Dead Sea Scrolls (quoting in part from Robert Eisenman, a Dead Sea Scrolls scholar): "What Nephi is doing corresponds to the later practice called *pesher*.... 'Often this takes the form of citing a biblical passage or quotation out of context or even sometimes slightly altered.... The text then proceeds to give an idiosyncratic interpretation having to do with the history or ideology of the group, with particular reference to contemporary events.' This description matches closely what Nephi is doing with Isaiah."[41] Whatever the right term or image is for Nephi's handling of Isaiah 29, today's scholarly consensus is that he is not to be understood as reproducing some uncorrupted original but "likening" his source material. In 2 Nephi 25–27, Nephi brings his method to its fullest expression, incorporating Isaiah's words into his own visions or incorporating his own visions into Isaiah's words. The details deserve close attention.

Nephi's Novel Hermeneutic at Its Height

It is easy to sum up where Nephi differs most from both mainstream and marginal interpretations of Isaiah known to our ideal listener/reader when the Book of Mormon appeared. As the preceding chapters make clear, what Nephi understands to be the literal meaning of Isaiah's prophecies falls within the range of recognizable interpretive options in about 1830. He straightforwardly predicts of his nineteenth-century readers that they would "understand" Isaiah's prophecies without trouble (2 Nephi 25:8). Where Nephi ventures out on his own hermeneutically, though, is in likening. He deliberately divorces Isaiah's words from their literal meaning, extracts from them larger patterns of God's interactions with his covenant people, and then reapplies them to his own New World branch of Israel. When he does so, his interpretations take a shape unfamiliar to the Book of Mormon's earliest readers. His pursuit reaches an extreme when Nephi takes up Isaiah 29, because there he likens in the most explicit fashion, and he likens Isaiah's prophecies to events no one would have anticipated without the Book of Mormon (since they involve the Book of Mormon itself).[42]

Isaiah 29 strings together various prophecies into what reads as one fluid story. Brevard Childs argues that the chapter "divides into three larger units," each showing "signs of literary tension and editorial expansion," although "there is a clear movement rendering the unit into a literarily coherent whole."[43] Childs's summary is worth quoting in full:

> Verses 1–8 depict the strangeness of God's work, which first lays siege to Jerusalem and humiliates its inhabitants with great distress. Suddenly without motivation there is a reversal and the divine judgment falls on the hordes who are attacking the city. Verses 9–12 pick up the theme of the blindness and stupor of the inhabitants who are unable to comprehend what is happening. Verses 15–24 return to the theme of the failure of the leaders of Judah to comprehend God's purpose as they engage in their own secretive plans for political survival. This portrayal of utter ignorance then forms the background for a radical transition in vv. 17ff. as God intervenes to transform both the darkness of the corrupted world and the folly of its inhabitants, the house of Jacob.[44]

It is this address to Jerusalem, with clear roots in the eighth-century-BCE Assyrian threat, that Nephi dismantles and redeploys. In Isaiah's strong language against both Jerusalem and its enemies, Nephi finds imagery to describe the destruction facing his own divided people. In Isaiah 29's description of the blindness of Jerusalem's elite, Nephi sees the oppressive gentiles of the last days. In one image of blindness and stupor—an unreadable sealed book—he finds a cipher for the Book of Mormon's reception, witnessed in his own prophetic experiences. Finally, in the long sequence that concludes Isaiah 29, he finds a reversal he can liken directly to God's triumph at the end of history. In broad terms, then, Nephi's likening of Isaiah 29 is straightforward. What interests is not the big picture, but the details.

A preliminary example comes from Nephi's appropriation of Isaiah 29:3–4.[45] Nephi offers a prediction that, if stripped of all its Isaian content, could not be simpler: "After that my seed [the Nephites] and the seed of my brethren [the Lamanites] shall have dwindled in unbelief and shall have been smitten by the gentiles . . . , yet the words of the righteous shall be written, and the prayers of the faithful shall be heard, and all they which have dwindled in unbelief shall not be forgotten!" With these words, Nephi bluntly predicts the final Nephite-Lamanite wars, during which a lone prophet, Moroni, steals away with the gold plates; Moroni finishes and seals the record before burying it so that it might come forth as the Book of Mormon. Into this simple prophecy, however, Nephi inserts the language of Isaiah 29:3–4, enriching it through likening:

> After that my seed and the seed of my brethren shall have dwindled in unbelief and shall have been smitten by the gentiles—yea, after that the Lord God shall have camped against them round about, and shall have laid siege against them with a mount, and raised forts against them, and after that they shall have been brought down low in the dust, even that they are not—yet the words of the righteous shall be written, and the prayers of the faithful shall be heard, and all they which have dwindled in unbelief shall not be forgotten!

Using the word *yea* as a bridge, Nephi here appends Isaiah's language to his own prophecy without attribution. He draws first on Isaiah 29:3: "And I will camp against thee round about, and will lay siege against thee with a mount, and I will raise forts against thee." These words Nephi alters only slightly to insert it into its new context. He then adds words drawn from Isaiah 29:4: "And thou shalt be brought down, and shalt speak out of the ground, and thy speech shall be low out of the dust." Here Nephi has a stronger hand with Isaiah's text, condensing a longer line into just "brought down low in the dust."

Nephi's modifications to the Isaian text here are minor. What impresses is how he weaves the biblical text directly into his prophecy, dividing his own prediction neatly into two sequences that bookend Isaiah's words. He thus forcefully indicates a likeness between his vision and Isaiah's words. Of course, as already noted, the original words of Isaiah 29:3–4 are for Jerusalem, predicting disaster when Assyria arrives. But, for the first time, Nephi never acknowledges original or literal meanings. He likens the text immediately to his own prophecy, failing even to mention that the borrowed words come from Isaiah (or even that they *are* borrowed).[46] Unless Nephi's reader knows Isaiah 29 well, in fact, she would likely assume that Nephi's words are all his own as he paints a picture of disaster. Nephi's predictions for his people's future have become one with Isaiah's predictions for his own people's future, the seams invisible except to those familiar with the sources.

This early example does not reach the level of virtuosity. Nephi grows most interesting only when he weaves into Isaiah's words specifically his foreknowledge of the coming forth of the Book of Mormon. This happens in connection with two passages from Isaiah 29. The first comes immediately after the passage just reviewed, adapting Isaiah 29:4:

ISAIAH 29:4	NEPHI'S ADAPTATION IN 2 NEPHI 26:16
And thou shalt be brought down, and shalt speak out of the ground, and thy	They which shall be destroyed shall speak unto them out of the ground, and their
speech shall be low out of the dust, and thy voice shall be, as of one that hath a familiar spirit,	speech shall be low out of the dust, and their voice shall be as one that hath a familiar spirit—
	for the Lord God will give unto him power that he
	may whisper concerning them, even as it were
out of the ground, and thy speech shall whisper out of the dust.	out of the ground— and their speech shall whisper out of the dust.

The destruction of Nephi's people in the New World looks very much like the destruction of Isaiah's people in Jerusalem here, except that Nephi seems to see in Isaiah's simile about "a familiar spirit" much more than an image to figure destruction. He sees in it an apt and basically literal description of the production of the Book of Mormon in the early nineteenth century.

Here, though, one must step carefully. King James Isaiah 29:4, with its talk of "a familiar spirit," makes reference to necromantic practices. The phrase "familiar spirit," as the *Oxford English Dictionary* explains, came into English from the "post-classical Latin *spiritus familiaris*" and means "a spirit, often taking the form of an animal, which obeys and assists a witch or other person."[47] Because early modern English terms for necromantic practices are part of a specialist lexicon today, however, Latter-day Saints have often taken the phrase "a familiar spirit" in 2 Nephi 26:16 to mean that the Book of Mormon would come forth with a clearly recognizable or immediately resonant message. To cite a simple example, Cleon Skousen, a popular Latter-day Saint writer in the twentieth century, paraphrases Isaiah 29:4 thus: the Nephites' "writings would come forth and speak to modern man like a 'voice from the dust.' These writings would have a familiar spirit and arouse a compelling attraction to the children of Israel in the latter days."[48] This interpretation goes back much further, however—in fact to the 1840s—when apostle Orson Pratt wrote into a polemical tract an explanation of Isaiah 29:4 and its talk of "a familiar spirit." The Book of Mormon, he wrote, was not to speak with "the voice of a distant, vague, uncertain spirit, but 'as a familiar spirit,' one that could be familiarly understood, and that too, by the most ordinary capacity."[49] Unlike less biblically literate Latter-day Saints after him, Pratt was fully aware that "familiar spirit" usually has a negative connotation in biblical texts. He nonetheless attempted to work out a broader meaning of *familiar* that might encompass familiar interaction with evil spirits and familiar interaction with good spirits—obviously including the Book of Mormon's connection among the latter sort of interaction.[50]

Other well-informed Latter-day Saint interpreters have more recently acknowledged that the Hebrew text of Isaiah 29:4 has reference to ghosts or spirits while denying that it refers to necromancy. John Tvedtnes, for instance, argues that "the King James Version of the Bible takes great liberty in construing statements about 'them that have familiar spirits' as referring to spirit mediums, even when that is not always included in the Hebrew.... In the case of Isaiah 29:4 the Hebrew is best read as 'thy voice shall be as a ghost out of the ground'; it has nothing to do with spirit mediums."[51] Critical commentators writing on Isaiah generally agree with Tvedtnes, at least broadly. Thus, although Philip Johnston points out that the Hebrew word in question "can mean both medium and ghost," two things that were "indistinct to the Israelites," nonetheless "the context clarifies the reference" in Isaiah 29:4. It seems to refer just to the spirit of the deceased and not necessarily to any particular necromantic practice used to gain access to that spirit.[52] To hypothesize that the more obviously necromantic resonance of the King James Version is unimportant to the use of Isaiah in the Book of Mormon, however, requires further argument. Because (benign) necromantic practices surrounded Joseph Smith's quest for and subsequent translation of the gold plates, the issue certainly deserves closer attention.[53]

A single Hebrew word, 'ōb, underlies the whole phrase "one that hath a familiar spirit" in King James Isaiah 29:4. This longer phrase in English seems to refer to two distinct figures: the familiar spirit, of course, but also the "one that hath" that familiar spirit. The whole phrase appears in 2 Nephi 26:16, rather than some discerning simplification of it. One might argue that this fact is immaterial, except that the whole phrase seems to be important to Nephi. The importance is clear from the fact that he later refers back not only to the familiar spirit, but also—it appears—to the one who has the familiar spirit.[54] "The Lord God will give unto *him* power," Nephi explains, "that *he* may whisper concerning them [that is, concerning the deceased Nephite and Lamanite peoples], even as it were out of the ground—and their speech shall whisper out of the dust" (2 Nephi 26:16). If, as so many commentators claim, the familiar spirit is itself that of "the departed of [Nephi's] own people who, through the Book of Mormon, speak to those of the last days from the grave,"[55] then it has to be asked who *he* is in Nephi's text who has power given *him* to give voice to the deceased. For Nephi, there is not only a ghostly voice but also a medium through which the ghostly voice speaks.[56] The medium is gendered masculine and left ambiguous in the text. The picture hints more at necromancy than of a simple ghost or spirit.

Who voices the long-past Nephites and Lamanites, according to Nephi? Commentators occasionally ask about the "mysterious character" who has a masculine pronoun.[57] Joseph McConkie and Robert Millet thus suggest that it is "Mormon, the great prophet-editor of the Book of Mormon."[58] This is a real possibility. The Book of Mormon places its eponymous author at the end of Nephite history, from which vantage point he looks back and constructs a text to present that history to others, "even as it were out of the ground" (2 Nephi 26:16). Another and more likely possibility, though, is the one noted by Monte Nyman, that "the pronoun 'him' . . . may be a reference to Joseph Smith."[59] On this interpretation, although the many voices of the deceased Nephites and Lamanites come ultimately under the editorial control of Mormon, Joseph Smith serves as the medium through whom their voices are heard. It is he, as necromantic medium, who has "power" given to him "that he may whisper concerning them" (26:16). In a scene that is often portrayed as something like a séance,[60] Joseph Smith literally whispered the text of the Book of Mormon to his scribes as he gazed at a seer stone, his face buried in his hat to keep the natural light from darkening the spiritual light in the stone. Our imagined ideal listener would have watched this very process unfold while listening to the unfolding text for traces of its interaction with Isaiah. The possibility that Isaiah is being put directly in conversation with that translational event here would have been, for such a listener, interpretively provocative to say the least.

As Samuel Brown crucially points out, however, "Smith was careful to distinguish his religious behaviors from what he saw as base imitations.... For the Latter-day Saints, spirits crying from the dust were prophets, lost ancestors, rather than ghoulish specters."[61] That necromancy appears in King James Isaiah 29, and that Nephi adopts it to provide an image for Joseph Smith's dictation of the Book of Mormon, suggests *benign* necromancy, a gentle sort of communication with the dead. Joseph Smith appears right within the text of the Book of Mormon as a sympathetic medium, one graced with "the gift and power of the Lamb" (1 Nephi 13:35).

This picture grows more detailed, as well as more theologically interesting, when Nephi takes up the second passage he associates with the Book of Mormon's coming forth. This second passage is Isaiah 29:11–14, which comes a page or two later in Nephi's appropriation of the prophet. Here Nephi develops a few Isaian words into a rich and complex parable—intertwined with identifiable nineteenth-century historical events—to justify the peculiar circumstances surrounding Smith's translation of the gold plates. Especially important is Nephi's likening development of Isaiah 29:11, already quoted earlier: "And the vision of all is become unto you as the words of a book that is sealed, which men deliver to one that is learned saying, Read this, I pray thee: and he saith, I cannot; for it is sealed." Nephi reads this passage so closely that it surprises even the believing reader, although he simultaneously reworks the text dramatically. Apparently noting that the verse does not speak simply of "a book that is sealed," but instead of "the words of a book that is sealed," Nephi in his long and complex appropriation carefully distinguishes the book from its words (2 Nephi 27:7–8), a contrast that is only subtly implied in Isaiah. With "the *book*," Nephi seems straightforwardly to refer to the gold plates, the physical artifact from which Joseph Smith would translate the text of the Book of Mormon. With "the *words* of the book," however, he seems to have reference instead to the Book of Mormon, the published and circulatable intellectual content of the book. Nephi finds much theological significance, it seems, in the gulf that separates the singular material artifact from the mechanically reproducible text made available through the work of printing and publication.[62] This gulf has much to do, once again, with (benign) necromancy. As he explains the general unavailability of the book but the universal availability of the *words* of the book, Nephi testifies that "the Lord God hath said that the words of the faithful should speak as if it were from the dead" (27:13).[63]

With the difference between the book and its words firmly established, Nephi provides a prophetic prediction, still drawing on and developing the possibilities within Isaiah 29:11:

> But behold, it shall come to pass that the Lord God shall say unto him to whom he shall deliver the book, "Take these words, which are not sealed, and deliver them to another, that he may shew them unto the learned, saying, 'Read this, I pray thee!' And the learned shall say, 'Bring hither the book, and I will read them.' (And now because of the glory of the world and to get gain will they say this, and not for the glory of God.) And the man shall say, 'I cannot bring the book, for it is sealed.' Then shall the learned say, 'I cannot read it!'" (2 Nephi 27:15–18)

These verses tell what seems a relatively straightforward story, even as they deepen and develop Nephi's likening of Isaiah 29:11. The book—the gold plates themselves—end up in the possession of some man, obviously Joseph Smith. He finds himself divinely commanded to get the unsealed words of the book (but not the book itself) into the hands of "the learned" to read. Smith does not have the task of approaching the learned directly, but of sending the words to the learned through "another," some other man involved with the translation effort. For apparently problematic reasons, the response of the learned is that a specific condition must be fulfilled before the words of the book can be learnedly read, namely access to the book itself. When it turns out that the book (the gold plates) is unavailable for general circulation, the response of the learned is decisive. The book and its words will go unread.

From the very beginning of Latter-day Saint history, believers and critics alike have taken Nephi's appropriation of Isaiah 29:11 here as describing a specific historical event. In 1828, Joseph Smith sent Martin Harris—his first real supporter who nonetheless battled bouts of skepticism about Smith's claims—to seek out scholars who might help to orient the project of the translation from its outset. Harris took with him a sheet of characters copied from the gold plates, perhaps hoping to get help to produce a basic alphabet that might be used in the work of translation. He visited first with Luther

Bradish, a statesman in Albany, New York, who had formerly lived in Harris's hometown of Palmyra, New York. Harris's hope with Bradish was likely just to see whether he "could help him find scholars to translate the characters."[64] Thanks to leads he picked up along the way to New York City (whether from Bradish himself or during a stopover in Philadelphia at Bradish's direction), he sought out Samuel Mitchill, someone familiar with certain Native American languages and cultures. Mitchill could make little of the characters but apparently sent Harris to visit with a young teacher of classics at Columbia College, Charles Anthon, along with a note of introduction.[65] Anthon would become recognized for his studies in classics, but he had already gained a reputation for his interest in Native American artifacts. Harris made the visit, about which there are conflicting accounts. Harris later declared that Anthon was prepared to authenticate the characters until he learned that Smith was claiming that he received the plates from an angel, while Anthon later claimed that he tried from early in the visit to convince Harris that he was being duped.[66] According to Harris's account (relayed to the public by Smith), when Anthon asked Harris to "bring the plates to him" because "he would translate them" and Harris responded that "part of the plates were sealed," Anthon allusively "replied 'I cannot read a sealed book.'"[67] Whatever actually took place in Anthon's office, as Richard Bushman points out, "Martin Harris came back more convinced than before. He went right to translating and later funded publication of the Book of Mormon."[68]

Generations of Latter-day Saints have taken "the Anthon incident" as faith-inspiring in much the way Harris himself did, and from Harris to the present, the event has been seen by believers as a remarkable fulfillment of Isaian (or quasi-Isaian) prophecy.[69] It may be, however, that a reader who has no reason to force the text through the interpretive bottleneck of one possible historical meaning might be *better* positioned to receive the text in all its richness. That is, awareness of the Anthon incident might hinder rather than deepen a reader's ability to see what Nephi does with the text.[70] (We might well insist that our ideal listener, sitting in the room with those directly familiar with the Anthon incident, had heard nothing of that peculiar episode.) For example, it is potentially important that every reference to "the learned" in 2 Nephi 27 is clearly *plural* rather *singular*. That is, the text does not refer to "the learned one," Charles Anthon, the one person who reportedly told Martin Harris that he could not read a sealed book. It refers, rather, to "the learned" in the plural, consistently using the pronoun "they." If the Anthon incident is the or even *a* referent of the text, then the Anthon incident itself is broadened or generalized in its signification. Nephi's reworking of Isaiah 29 is not about one latter-day scholar's frustrated exclamation that he cannot read a sealed book. It is rather about a global latter-day culture of skepticism. Anthon and *all* the learned respond to the words of the book—that is, to the Book of Mormon itself—by insisting on first having a look at the book itself, at the material artifact of the gold plates. The learned response is to demand proof, to require material evidence before dealing with the words. And, according to Nephi, it is "because of the glory of the world and to get gain" that "they say this" (2 Nephi 27:16).

Nephi thus uses Isaiah 29 to develop not just a prophecy of, but also and especially a theology about, the Book of Mormon. In the Isaian text he finds the resources for thinking through a mystery, namely the idea that God would—in the context of a globally dominant gentile culture that obsessively presses the case for secularism—ask the world to believe in a new set of scriptural *words* without any actual access to the material *book* from which they are drawn. In the image of (benign) necromancy, he finds the rich idea that "the words of the faithful should speak as if it were from the dead" (2 Nephi 27:13)—that is, as a disembodied voice, a ghostly collection of words without any material corpse that just anyone could dig up. The whole point of the Book of Mormon's coming forth under such peculiar circumstances, it seems, is to force anew in a skeptical era the question of faith or of miracles. The question is whether the coming forth of the Book of Mormon might enact afresh the founding paradoxes of Christianity, showing that God is "the same yesterday, today, and forever" (27:23). Thus, to early Christianity's empty tomb there corresponds the empty box where Joseph Smith claimed to find the gold plates, empty because an angel took the plates away from the world after the translation was complete. To early Christianity's twelve apostles or witnesses to Jesus's resurrection there correspond the twelve men who testified to having seen the gold plates in person (Joseph Smith, the so-called three witnesses referred to directly in 2 Nephi 27:12, and the so-called eight witnesses also mentioned obliquely in 2 Nephi 27:13). In fact, even early Christianity's Mary Magdalene, the singular woman who witnessed Jesus's resurrected body outside his tomb, has a correspondence in the witness of Mary Whitmer, the only woman who claimed to have had the gold plates revealed to her by an angel one day during the translation.[71]

In his culminating use of the Book of Isaiah, then, Nephi finally puts that book to thoroughly novel use. It is only with this last and most inventive deployment of Isaiah, the weaving of Isaiah 29's words and phrases directly into a prophecy wholly unique to the Book of Mormon, that the real audacity of the project begins to show itself. Nephi here brings to a real climax the Isaian project of the Book of Mormon as Joseph Smith dictated it to his scribes. The Book of Isaiah is no longer solely something that has to be interpreted *correctly*, a testimony of the truth that might become clear to those who rightly understand the nature of prophecy. It is also something that can be dealt with *inventively*, a resource for theological reflection that might help to make a real intervention in the intellectual world. It is too easy for people to "draw near unto [God] with their mouth" or "with their lips . . . honor" him (2 Nephi 27:25). What Nephi calls for is "a marvelous work and a wonder," the kind of reading that might trump "the wisdom of their wise and learned," that might amount to a real "turning of things upside down" (27:26–27). This, Nephi claims, is supposed to happen with the Book of Mormon, and Isaiah 29 provides the resources for thinking through that idea theologically.

A Book That Remains Sealed

Because Nephi, right within the Book of Mormon, likens Isaiah 29 to the book's coming forth, there is little need to demonstrate any further the uniqueness of his likening interpretation within the larger interpretive tradition.[72] At the same time, as our ideal listener/reader, familiar with the larger history of Isaiah's reception would immediately point out, there is a sense in which the place for Nephi's unique appropriation of Isaiah 29 is prepared precisely by the larger tradition from which it unmistakably departs. That is, despite the particular prediction bound up with Nephi's use of the text—the prediction, of course, of the Book of Mormon's own coming forth—Nephi's handling of Isaiah 29 has a kind of precedent in certain apocalyptic and decidedly nonmainstream interpretations. Such interpretations appeared in the English-speaking world of the centuries leading up to the Book of Mormon's publication, but they also appeared much earlier in history. Really, from the very beginning of Isaiah 29's circulation in the ancient world, a line of interpretation began to appear in which the Book of Mormon would find its place centuries and centuries later. The basic interpretive history of Isaiah 29 thus proves instructive one last time, now in the work of sorting out the real significance of the Book of Mormon's most peculiar and recognizable experimentation with the Book of Isaiah.

The basic motivations underlying the interpretive history of Isaiah 29:11–12, of its talk of a sealed book and those unable to read it, are relatively obvious. Whether read in isolation or in the context of the verses immediately surrounding it, the passage suggests the simple theme of incomprehension due to faithlessness. As one interpreter sums it up (and as Nephi himself might have written), it "speaks of the closed eyes and dull perception of the prophets and of anyone who seeks to understand [Isaiah's] vision."[73] At issue, according to Isaiah's own text, is a kind of double failure: "This vision of God's future is completely beyond access by reason of a Catch-22. Those who would understand either can read but cannot open the seal, or can open the seal but cannot read. Either way, an understanding of what is happening is beyond the horizon."[74] In short, the passage accuses a motley people of being wholly incapable of reading or understanding prophecy, Isaiah's prophecy in particular. The accused are not a monolithic group, it is important to note, since the text distinguishes between the literate and the illiterate; it is, rather, a people stratified into classes. It is, nonetheless, a people unable to understand the crucial words of the prophet.

Commentators consistently point out that these two verses are in prose, while the text surrounding it is poetry. It is a "brief narrative illustration"[75] or an "editorial comment"[76] that serves to sharpen the critique of the verses before and after the passage. For many interpreters, the change from poetry to prose is a clue to the earliest reception of Isaiah's prophecies. That is, many scholars conclude that Isaiah 29:11–12 is the work of a redactor decades or even centuries after Isaiah's time, reflecting on the prophet's reception (in something like the way we have done here).[77] In its reflective spirit, early or late, the comment in Isaiah 29:11–12 unquestionably has "further layers of meaning" than a mere gloss might.[78] Joseph Blenkinsopp thus imagines a scribe copying out some version of the Book of Isaiah and then adding to the text a marginal note about his growing despair over whether anyone can make sense of the spiritually crucial writings he is copying—something like Nephi's own lament that he was "left to mourn because of the unbelief and the wickedness and the ignorance and the stiffneckedness" of his readers (2 Nephi 32:7). The literate and the learned might naturally feel that Isaiah's prophecies—so critical of the elite and so focused on coming doom—are arrogant and arcane and ultimately not for them. The illiterate and downtrodden, meanwhile, to whom Isaiah's prophecies are deeply relevant, simply cannot read and so cannot know the prophecies meant for their comfort. In a period when the fieriest prophecies are to be found only in books, who could make real sense of them? As Blenkinsopp goes on to discuss at length, however, what might have been a relatively innocuous (or at most a semiapocalyptic) note in the margins of a copy of Isaiah's prophecies—if it was not in fact a saying from Isaiah of Jerusalem himself—eventually drew the apocalyptic attention of religious separatists as early as the last centuries before the common era. The same interpretive tradition would stretch into the modern world.

The fact is that various groups from very early in Isaiah's reception history took Isaiah 29:11–12 and its image of a sealed book to be particularly meaningful. The passage became the focus of sectarian interpretations of Isaiah during the first several centuries of its circulation.[79] For such interpreters, Isaiah's sealed book came "to be read as a corpus of eschatological teaching intelligible only in the context of the apocalyptic worldview" eventually canonized in the Bible's books of Daniel and Revelation, the only two other biblical books interested in sealed books.[80] Linking Isaiah 29:11–12 with Isaiah 8:16–18, apocalyptic interpreters saw Isaiah as having received—and then sealed up—esoteric visions and revelations that might give a full understanding of history's end. Thus, a whole apocalyptic literature produced during the several centuries surrounding the time of Jesus of Nazareth eventually came to understand Isaiah's "sealed testimony" as "a transcription of the heavenly tablets, . . . an esoteric record revelatory of future events."[81] This interpretive tradition about the sealed book resided on the religious margins of formative Judaism, clearly in contrast with the mainstream interpretations—first those of the so-called Deuteronomists and eventually those of the rabbinical tradition.[82] Sectarians saw themselves as privileged to know the hidden or sealed meaning of the prophet, while those in the religious mainstream were among the blind prophets and veiled seers Isaiah denounces.

It is significant that early Christianity was among the traditions that found significance in Isaiah 29:11–12—in those centuries before it became something more powerful than a marginalized and fledgling sect within (still-formative) Judaism. The early Christian fathers in that context occasionally referred to Isaiah's sealed book to explain how the whole collection of the Old Testament's prophets was closed to rival Jewish interpreters in the Rabbinic mainstream.[83] By the fourth and early fifth centuries, such applications of Isaiah 29 to Jews had become not only standard but also, because of the changing political fortunes for Christianity, a discourse of power against (rather than a discourse of resistance from) the margins.[84] What began as a sectarian reading among some marginal separatist Jewish groups thus became, in the hands of imperial Christians, a defense of the powerful Christian mainstream against the displaced Jews and their hermeneutic practices. Nonetheless, as so often happens with such reversals, the same passage those in power use to justify themselves against the marginalized becomes a tool in the hands of separatists who eventually break from the central power. Thus one finds in the interpretations of the early leaders of the Reformation a redeployment of Isaiah 29:11–12 against the main body of Christians. In his lectures on the Book of Isaiah, for instance, Martin Luther simultaneously reaffirms the anti-Semitic interpretation—by then a long-standing tradition—but immediately repurposes the text to criticize his own contemporary theological enemies in Rome or under Rome's sway. He writes, "It is as if [Isaiah] were saying: 'I will demonstrate by an example that you are blind, that by your ungodliness you are closing the Scripture for yourselves,' as we observe with regard to the Jews, who do not see the very clearest prophecies of all the prophets. So today we see that the papists do not recognize the plainest testimonies of Scripture."[85]

Of course, the Protestant tradition eventually became an institution in its own right, with Anglicans of course assuming power in English and Calvinists becoming the Christian foundation for mainstream American biblical interpretation in the northern United States. It is unsurprising, then, that during the centuries following the Reformation, a passage like Isaiah 29:11–12 drew relatively little attention from establishment Protestant commentators.[86] By the end of the eighteenth century and the beginning of the nineteenth, therefore, when the Book of Mormon was set to appear in print, it was principally on Protestantism's margins that the passage could draw fresh attention in newly emergent movements separating themselves from the mainstream. Thus, even before the passage found its way into the Book of Mormon, it featured prominently in the preface to the first published book of Joanna Southcott's prophecies, *The Strange Effects of Faith*.[87] Southcott, a self-proclaimed prophetess with a following that lasted more than a century, often addressed sealed and unsealed revelations, as much with an eye to the Books of Daniel and Revelation as to the Book of Isaiah. She nonetheless used the passage that Nephi in the Book of Mormon would favor to explain her place in history in the preface to her own prophetic writings. "The Word of God is as a book that is sealed," the preface reads, "so that neither the learned nor the unlearned, can read, (that is to say, understand it,) for it was sealed up in the bosom of the Father, till he thought proper to break the seals, and reveal it to a woman, as it is written in the Revelation."[88]

It is clear that Southcott's use of Isaiah 29 in this way offended mainstream sensibilities, but it is interesting to note that it apparently offended for reasons of both gender and theology. That is, it was apparently not only because Southcott claimed that the unsealing of the prophecies was the work of a woman, but that she claimed that there were prophecies to be unsealed at all, that offended her contemporaries. Thus, in R. Hann's *Letter to the Right Reverend the Lord Bishop of London*, a petition "for the removal of so great a nuisance," the first objectionable doctrine attributed to Southcott is simply "that the Bible is a Sealed Book." Hann explains, "Whoever believes this doctrine, my Lord, is an infidel; for infidelity is a belief that the scriptures do not contain the revealed will of God, which they cannot do if the Bible is a sealed book, for to be sealed and revealed is a manifest contradiction."[89] On the margins once again leading up to the publication of the Book of Mormon, the literal interpretation of Isaiah consistently played the role of marking apocalyptic possibilities, and Isaiah 29:11–12 confirms this in particularly striking ways.

When Joseph Smith dictated the Book of Mormon to his scribes, concluding with Nephi's climactic and remarkable use of Isaiah 29, he gave the world yet another plea from the margins for esoterically reading Isaiah 29:11–12. Nephi's use of the passage, though, sparkles with sheer inventiveness—applying the sealed book to the Book of Mormon, and especially dividing and arranging the text of Isaiah 29 into a whole theologically forceful series of fragments. Nephi's handling of Isaiah 29 not only calls for vigilance regarding the apocalypse but also studies what it might mean to restore to Christianity its original radical nature. Nephi places his version of Isaiah 29 amidst long tirades against pervasive gentile skepticism in the modern age and so gives the Book of Mormon's coming forth a rather specific meaning. More than just a long-lost scripture, evidence that God has orchestrated a more complex salvation history than the Bible suggests, it also directly performs the theological scandal of faith. It presents a collection of words that *cannot* be approached in a "learned" way. Nephi finds in Isaiah 29 resources to explain what it might mean to read scripture outside or beyond dawning secularism. What might an *unlearned* reading of scripture—the Book of Mormon, but perhaps especially the Bible, and the Book of Isaiah in particular—look like? If, as Sean Leahy argues, Nephi "holds the unlearned man as the one at whom the text is directed," how might a *deliberately* and *self-consciously* unlearned approach to scripture unfold?[90]

Intentionally and provocatively speaking from the margins, the Book of Mormon's last and most impassioned treatment of Isaiah calls on the unlearned to lay claim to the sacred books the learned can no longer read. It confidently dismisses mainstream approaches to the prophets, wondering whether faith can flourish at the center of power. It roots its defiance in a passage of Isaiah that has spurred similar denunciations of interpretive institutional power, from the beginning of Isaiah's reception to the present. Going further, though, it ties that passage directly to the very book of new scripture within which it builds its barricades against the world. The Book of Mormon, in this climactic handling of Isaiah, becomes simultaneously subject and object, preacher and preached about, the thing that asks to be read earnestly and the thing that defies standard approaches to reading. For Nephi, bringing the Book of Mormon's Isaian explorations to their peak, Isaiah is and ought to be the occasion for deep reflection on whether anyone in history has been reading scripture rightly.

In light of this, there is something wonderfully ironic about the history of how people have written about Isaiah in the Book of Mormon, the subject of this long study. From the moment that fully trained scholars began to discuss Isaiah in the Book of Mormon, they questioned whether the presence of Isaian material might prove or disprove the volume's claim to be an ancient document. Already in Sidney Sperry's 1926 master's thesis at the University of Chicago, this was the principal question.[91] It remains, today, the chief subject of debate in scholarly literature on Isaiah in the Book of Mormon—whether authors defend the Book of Mormon's antiquity[92] or attempt to show it to be a decidedly modern production.[93] From within the Book of Mormon's own pages, however, Nephi himself argues against the validity of all such debate. He calls—directly and with Mormon standing at his side—for an entirely different approach to the problem of Isaiah within its pages. To debate only the antiquity of the book, especially if such antiquity becomes a prerequisite for taking the book seriously, is to imitate precisely the refusal of Isaiah's learned ones, those who "cannot read" what is before them. To insist that the verified or falsified antiquity of the book wholly or even largely determines its spiritual value undermines Nephi's conviction that God "work[s] not among the children of men save it be according to their faith" (2 Nephi 27:23).

Naturally, some have argued passionately for a middle ground on questions of the Book of Mormon's historicity. Some have argued, for instance, that "members of the Church of Jesus Christ of Latter-day Saints should confess in faith that the Book of Mormon is the word of God but also abandon claims that it is a historical record of the ancient peoples of the Americas."[94] And some have proposed "a rhetorical approach" to the book as a way of occupying the middle ground, an approach that "focuses on the internal literary features of the text and how these forms address its original nineteenth-century audience, while setting aside the issue of authorship."[95] These are interesting and valuable contributions to the conversation. Middle-ground positions have generally, however, been minority ones, and many still and understandably insist that the ultimate truth of the Book of Mormon depends on the relevant historical facts.[96] Nephi never denies that historical issues matter, nor does any other voice within the Book of Mormon. One might say, though, that Nephi's final treatment of Isaiah makes clear that he sees questions of historicity as wholly decisive only *in the last instance*.[97] For Nephi, this means that such questions come only after a genuinely *faithful* reading of the book, one that does not decide on its meaning or its value or its truth without having first demonstrated a kind of fidelity to its call.[98]

As regards Isaiah's place in the Book of Mormon, the implication is that questions of whether, say, Second Isaiah should or should not be present in a (barely) pre-exilic text that exists only in a nineteenth-century translation are really only to be asked on the other side of a great deal of close, theological interpretation. *First*, it has to be asked how the book uses Isaiah, or what aims or purposes the book achieves through Isaiah. *First*, it has to be asked where Isaiah shows up in the book, according to what patterns and through what hermeneutic lenses, and how consistently. *First*, it has to be asked how the text of the Book of Mormon presents the meanings of Isaiah within the context of its appearance on the nineteenth-century American frontier. And, of course, *first*, it has to be asked whether the Book of Mormon even allows for a historicizing analysis of Isaiah's place in the book. That Nephi uses Isaiah and even reflects on what it means to use Isaiah in his writings is suggestive enough. That he also talks with his readers about whether and how *they* might relate rightly to Isaiah is much more suggestive.

We might return just one last time to that ideal listener that has accompanied us all along the way—that listener who sat in the room with Joseph Smith and his scribes in the summer of 1829, noting carefully everything in Smith's dictation of the Book of Mormon that touches on Isaiah. This listener was, remember, well versed in the history of how various Jewish and Christian groups have interpreted or appropriated Isaiah and was sympathetic to (but not uncritical about) Smith and his scribes and their investment in their project. We imagine, too, that this listener had an opportunity to sit down with a printed copy of the Book of Mormon later, to go back over particularly thick parts of the text, looking for nuance and riddling out subtleties. As this listener hears Nephi's climactic treatment of Isaiah 29 in the last part of Second Nephi, would her sympathy not be stressed to the breaking point? This listener is an ideal, and yet even such a person would have to raise an eyebrow at the audacity of the Book of Mormon's culminating Isaian gestures. Nephi describes the very scene the listener has witnessed firsthand as a kind of séance, a channeling of the dead, deliberately staged so as to separate material artifacts from ghostly words and thereby testing latter-day faith. Even sympathetic readers are warned at this late point in the book to become more serious, to put off questions of truth until the last instance while giving themselves to the book in abandon. Nephi makes perfectly clear that he means to upset norms. Using Isaiah's own words, he imagines the Book of Mormon's opponents accusing it of "turning . . . things upside down" (2 Nephi 27:27). Nephi, again with Isaiah's words, has only a confident retort to such talk: "The wisdom of their wise and learned shall perish, and the understanding of their prudent shall be hid" (27:26).

The Book of Mormon's handling of Isaiah deserves much more attention than it has received—and apparently a different sort of attention than it has received. The foregoing pages have really aimed only to spell out the basic framework of the volume's uses of Isaiah. The details warrant close scrutiny, but always of the kind that is willing to put off until the right time—*the last instance*—all questions of historicity. To do otherwise is to refuse the Book of Mormon its own considered opinion about what it means to read the book with an eye to its uses of Isaiah.

The Book of Mormon's Book of Isaiah is a rich and malleable source, one with certain determinate meanings and applications but also with literary and theological possibilities that go well beyond the obvious meaning of the text. The Book of Mormon deserves a closer reading, if only because it is itself an experimental theorization of reading as such. That it stages its intervention on hermeneutical questions through sustained interaction with one of the most richly interpreted books in the Judeo-Christian tradition makes it a worthy contender for the status of great literature and world scripture. The book is supposed to utter its Isaian message "low out of the dust" (2 Nephi 26:15). The sad truth is that it has had to do so largely because of the dust that has settled on the Isaian portions of the book. Believers mostly confess bafflement at the volume's interactions with Isaiah, skimming or skipping or dutifully reading but only in confusion. Nonbelievers still generally ignore the book, and even when they give it attention, the Isaiah portions seem at best an odd digression, a distraction from the romance of the volume's narratives. There is reason, though, to blow the dust away and allow the book to speak, and to speak in its native Isaian tongue. It might, in fact, "speak a word in season," as Isaiah says he was gifted to do (2 Nephi 7:4).

Notes

Introduction

1. See throughout Miller, *Speculative Grace*.
2. See, classically, W. Smith, *What Is Scripture?*; and, more recently, Wimbush, *Theorizing Scriptures*.
3. O'Dea, *The Mormons*, 26.
4. J. Smith, "Joseph Smith—History," in *The Pearl of Great Price*, published by the Church of Jesus Christ of Latter-day Saints (hereafter, JS—H). Quotations of Smith's 1838 history are drawn from this most-circulated presentation of the text. For some context, see R. Bushman, *Joseph Smith, Rough Stone Rolling*, 322–55.
5. JS—H 1:18.
6. Contemporary accounts of Smith's earliest vision appear in Jessee, "The Earliest Documented Accounts of Joseph Smith's First Vision." For discussion, see Harper, *First Vision*.
7. JS—H 1:19.
8. JS—H 1:19. In the words Smith attributes to God, one finds not only the words of Isaiah 29:13, somewhat creatively truncated, but also the language of New Testament quotations of the same passage (in Matthew 15:9 and Mark 7:7) and a snippet from 2 Timothy 3:5.
9. The most detailed of these accounts is Oliver Cowdery's, outlined in letters published in 1835, which can be read in Vogel, *Early Mormon Documents*, 2: 426–44.
10. JS—H 1:36.
11. JS—H 1:40.
12. This period between the acquisition of the gold plates and the dictation of the Book of Mormon has recently been the subject of close study; for example, MacKay and Dirkmaat, *From Darkness unto Light*, 1–117.

13. On the use and place of the Bible in the Latter-day Saint tradition, see Barlow, *Mormons and the Bible*.

14. For a general introduction to this field of research, see Sawyer, *Fifth Gospel*. In Sawyer's more recent *Isaiah through the Centuries*, only a few passing references to the Latter-day Saint tradition appear, on pages 172, 174, 197, and 205.

15. Grant Hardy's *Understanding the Book of Mormon* so far represents the most impressive attempt at sorting out the basic shape of the Book of Mormon. He gives serious but introductory attention to the volume's engagement with Isaiah on pages 58–86, and 199–209.

16. I have offered preliminary studies of this larger-scale debate in both Spencer, *Anatomy of Book of Mormon Theology*, 1: 45–62, and *An Other Testament*. What I present here corrects, reworks, and drastically expands my previous conclusions.

17. See, of course, Williamson, *The Book Called Isaiah*.

18. Variants in Book of Mormon Isaiah texts have provoked a small but important literature on what connections these variants might have with the earliest texts of Isaiah. The two most important studies, one arguing for the antiquity of the Book of Mormon and the other against it, are Tvedtnes, "The Isaiah Variants in the Book of Mormon"; and D. Wright, "Isaiah in the Book of Mormon."

19. Hugh Nibley nicely captured the strange status of the Book of Mormon when he described it as "the only ancient text in a modern language" (*An Approach to the Book of Mormon*, 6).

20. Von Rad, *Old Testament Theology*, 2: 147.

Chapter 1. Preliminaries

1. See, from rather different perspectives, Van Dyke and Galbraith, "The Jerusalem Center for Near Eastern Studies," and Sharkansky, *Governing Jerusalem*, 167–68.

2. Steinberg, *The Lost Book of Mormon*, 44, emphasis in original.

3. On "a land of promise" in America, see 1 Nephi 2:20. For the "new Jerusalem," see 3 Nephi 20:22; 21:23–24. Throughout this book, I use the critical text of the Book of Mormon reconstructed by Royal Skousen, although I supply my own punctuation. See R. Skousen, *The Book of Mormon*. For references, I follow the versification used in editions from the Church of Jesus Christ of Latter-day Saints, since these are more standard than the alternative versification used in editions published by Community of Christ, the second-largest branch of Mormonism.

4. O'Dea, *The Mormons*, 26.

5. Steinberg, *The Lost Book of Mormon*, 44.

6. Twain, *The Innocents Abroad / Roughing It*, 617.

7. Brodie, *No Man Knows My History*, 58.

8. See especially Frederick, *The Bible, Mormon Scripture, and the Rhetoric of Allusivity*.

9. The obstacles to producing such a list are formidable. On this point, see Barlow, *Mormons and the Bible*, 27–29.

10. I privilege talk of the "Old Testament" here over talk of the "Hebrew Bible," since Latter-day Saints refer to the first biblical testament as the "Old Testament" and use the canonical Old Testament of the Christian tradition.

11. Hilton, "Old Testament Psalms in the Book of Mormon."

12. There are, though, extended interactions with one psalm in particular (Psalm 95); see Hilton's discussion, but also D. Wright, "'In Plain Terms That We May Understand.'"

13. Frederick, "Evaluating the Interaction between the New Testament and the Book of Mormon"; and Frederick, "The Book of Mormon and Its Redaction of the King James New Testament."

14. Hardy, *Understanding the Book of Mormon*, 5–6; Barlow, *Mormons and the Bible*, 28.

15. Most famously, Jesus provides an exposition of John 10:16, the passage about Jesus's "other sheep." There are, however, other Johannine aspects of the narrative of Jesus's visit that deserve notice and are discussed in chapter 4.

16. The quotation of the Ten Commandments appears in Mosiah 12:33–37; 13:11–26. Next to Isaiah, the Book of Revelation arguably draws the most biblical attention in the Book of Mormon. Two visions are explicitly connected to Revelation's vision (1 Nephi 11–14 and Ether 3–5), and the volume contains other references to it (see, for instance, Mormon 8:33). For a preliminary comparison of John's revelation with one of the two visions mentioned, see Hopkin, "Seeing Eye to Eye." Finally, the relationship between Paul's description of spiritual gifts and that of Moroni 10:8–19 is enough to have made Sidney Sperry call the latter's inclusion one of the Book of Mormon's "problems" (*Answers to Book of Mormon Questions*, 113–21).

17. Frederick, *The Bible, Mormon Scripture, and the Rhetoric of Allusivity*, 1–55.

18. For some analysis of Malachi texts in the Book of Mormon, see Townsend, "'Behold, Other Scriptures I Would That Ye Should Write.'"

19. Micah and Isaiah were contemporaries, and the books bearing their names contain numerous thematic parallels—and at least one common prophecy (compare Isaiah 2:2–4 and Micah 4:1–3).

20. Stendahl, "The Sermon on the Mount and Third Nephi."

21. See the discussion of borrowed biblical authority in Frederick, *The Bible, Mormon Scripture, and the Rhetoric of Allusivity*, 1–19.

22. See Spencer, "Moderate Millenarianism."

23. All biblical texts discussed in the preceding paragraphs deserve close investigation, and ideally the fruits of such analysis might be productively compared with those of the present study.

24. Consensus never fully emerged during this earlier period on whether one or two authors originally stood behind Second and Third Isaiah, but the majority opinion certainly tended toward distinguishing Third from Second Isaiah. For some helpful discussion, see Blenkinsopp, *Isaiah 56–66*, 27–29.

25. This shift in approach to the Book of Isaiah was largely precipitated by Brevard Childs and his plea for a "canonical" reading of the Hebrew Bible. See Childs, *Introduction to the Old Testament as Scripture*, 311–38. For an important transitional work that lays out a systematic critique of the earlier view, see Seitz, *Zion's Final Destiny*, 1–35.

26. For a helpful outline of this development, see Williamson, "Recent Issues in the Study of Isaiah." For a fantastic overview of current views of Isaiah, see Stromberg, *An Introduction to the Study of Isaiah*.

27. As in earlier scholarship, there remains a lack of consensus about dividing Third Isaiah from Second Isaiah. For a recent argument against distinguishing the two, see Sommer, *A Prophet Reads Scripture*, 187–95.

28. There is, of course, much excellent work to be done in investigating borrowings from and allusions to Isaiah that do not seem to have an obvious connection to the book's larger program with Isaiah. Although taking these up in detail lies beyond the scope of this study, nothing in my argument should be taken to imply that these are of less literary value.

29. Isaiah 48–49 appear in 1 Nephi 20–21; Isaiah 50–51 appear in 2 Nephi 7–8; most of Isaiah 52 appears in Mosiah 15 and 3 Nephi 20–21; Isaiah 53 appears in Mosiah 14; and Isaiah 54 appears in 3 Nephi 22.

30. A few passages potentially draw on the language of Third Isaiah, generally through the mediating influence of the New Testament's borrowing of Third Isaiah's language. There is no *programmatic* interest in Third Isaiah in the Book of Mormon. For a good introduction to possible interactions with Third Isaiah in the Book of Mormon, see Townsend, "Robe of Righteousness."

31. For comments on the relationship between these two texts, see Blenkinsopp, *Isaiah 56–66*, 207–18.

32. See, for instance, the use of Isaiah 40:3 in markedly similar situations in all four New Testament Gospels and in 1 Nephi 10:8.

33. Blenkinsopp, *Isaiah 40–55*, 60.

34. The historical setting in question is the Syro-Ephraimite War, the setting of both Isaiah 7–8 and Isaiah 28–33. For context, see Cogan, "Into Exile."

35. After William Brownlee's *The Meaning of the Qumrân Scrolls for the Bible*, some have insisted on dividing Isaiah into two halves: Isaiah 1–33 and Isaiah 34–66. This makes real sense of certain textual data, especially the close stylistic relationship between Isaiah 34–35 and Isaiah 40–55. For discussion, see G. Brooke, "On Isaiah at Qumran," 77–81. If this reconceptualization is on the mark, First Isaiah would consist of just four subsections: the first three noted here, along with a fourth and final sequence, Isaiah 28–33, all made up of prophecies originating in the Syro-Ephraimite crisis.

36. Many interpreters find close linguistic connections between Isaiah 1 and Isaiah 65–66, and it may be that the Book of Mormon's lack of interest in Third Isaiah is therefore connected to its lack of interest in Isaiah 1. This is something deserving closer attention. For a summary treatment of the relationship between Isaiah 1 and Isaiah 65–66, see G. Smith, *Isaiah 1–39*, 96–97.

37. See, for instance, Wagner, "Isaiah in Romans and Galatians"; and Wilk, "Isaiah in 1 and 2 Corinthians."

38. Ethan Smith's 1823 *View of the Hebrews* is often cited as a possible source for the Book of Mormon, since it draws on Isaiah and argues that Native Americans are of Israelite descent. Yet Smith's references to and quotations of Isaiah reveal a

far more evenly distributed interest in Isaian prophecy. See Riley, "A Comparison of Passages from Isaiah and Other Old Testament Prophets in Ethan Smith's *View of the Hebrews* and the Book of Mormon."

39. Expositions of Isaiah in the Book of Mormon almost universally focus on the inclusion of Isaiah at these three points. For a representative example, see V. Ludlow, *Unlocking Isaiah*.

40. For the sake of simplicity, I refrain from repeatedly referring to the writings the Book of Mormon attributes to Nephi as "the writings attributed to Nephi" and speak instead of "Nephi's writings." I do not mean to decide questions of authorship in doing so, since Nephi is as much a literary construction as a potentially historical person. I use the same approach in speaking of other Book of Mormon figures.

41. See Grant Hardy's succinct analysis: "It seems obvious that the climax of the Book of Mormon is Christ's three-day visit to the Nephites. Jesus is the central figure of the book's theology, and his earthly ministry and redemptive sacrifice had been prophesied, discussed, and anticipated among the Nephites since the time of Lehi" (Hardy, *Understanding the Book of Mormon*, 180).

42. For a fuller exposition of the role of Isaiah in the larger trajectory of the Book of Mormon, read in the familiar way, see Spencer, *Anatomy of Book of Mormon Theology*, 1: 45–62, and Spencer, *An Other Testament*. In the next section, however, I offer an alternative to this conventional approach.

43. There is a well-worn joke among Latter-day Saints about a Mormon soldier whose copy of the Book of Mormon, tucked into his breast pocket, saves his life when a bullet strikes it rather than him. Upon opening the damaged book, he finds the bullet stopped somewhere in Nephi's record and remarks that not even a bullet can "get through the Isaiah chapters" (Bytheway, *Isaiah for Airheads*, 1).

44. It has thus become common to speak of an "Isaiah barrier" in the Book of Mormon, and many lay readers confess that they skip "the Isaiah chapters" when reading the book devotionally. Consequently, Latter-day Saint publishing companies have created a cottage industry producing resources—some less, some more scholarly in nature—for lay readers to understand Isaiah in the Book of Mormon. For an example that explicitly names "the Isaiah barrier," see Chase, *Making Isaiah Plain*, v.

45. This is evident already from the title page of the Book of Mormon, where the volume is addressed to "the remnant of the house of Israel" and its purpose is identified as one of "shew[ing] unto the remnant of the house of Israel how great things the Lord hath done for their fathers, and that they may know the covenants of the Lord, that they are not cast off forever."

46. I provide a slightly different—and fuller—exposition of this interpretation in Spencer, *An Other Testament*.

47. Abinadi's preaching occurs somewhat earlier than a century before the birth of Christ. For a good discussion, see Sperry, *Book of Mormon Chronology*, 8–11.

48. I myself took the final form of the text essentially for granted in my earliest research on Isaiah's place in the Book of Mormon; see Spencer, *An Other Testament*.

49. The best account of the production of the Book of Mormon is MacKay and Dirkmaat, *From Darkness unto Light*. For a wider range of approaches to the issue of

translation for Smith, see MacKay, Ashurst-McGee, and Hauglid, *Producing Ancient Scripture*.

50. Royal Skousen's critical textual work on the Book of Mormon identifies where changes have been made (sometimes intentionally, often unintentionally) to the text as (most likely) originally dictated by Smith. Although there are many minor changes, there are few significant changes to the substance of the text. For the full analysis, see R. Skousen, *Analysis of Textual Variants of the Book of Mormon*.

51. For helpful historical investigation and fruitful speculation, see Bradley, *The Lost 116 Pages*.

52. This is well established today. For a solid review of the relevant events with historical sources, see R. Bushman, *Joseph Smith, Rough Stone Rolling*, 61–69; as well as MacKay and Dirkmaat, *From Darkness unto Light*, 79–117. For a thorough—if decidedly naturalizing—treatment of textual evidence for the order of dictation, see Metcalfe, "The Priority of Mosiah."

53. Curiously few studies of the Book of Mormon follow dictation order rather than final form. All available commentaries follow final form, and almost all substantive monographs follow final form. One major exception, although it has been reviewed poorly for its heavy-handed style of interpretation, is Vogel, *Joseph Smith*.

54. This can be felt in most published treatments of Isaiah in the Book of Mormon (always directed to a lay believing audience). See, for instance, V. Ludlow, *Unlocking Isaiah*.

55. However interesting this reconfiguration of the Isaian trajectory within the Book of Mormon might be, some will express discomfort at how it might appear to decide in favor of the book's critics (that is, in favor of nineteenth-century rather than ancient origins). It seems to me, however, that reasons of faith as much as of scholarship recommend taking seriously the order of the Book of Mormon's dictation alongside the volume's final form. Certainly, believers (like myself) might ask why God should not have had Joseph Smith turn immediately to the replacement record of Nephi after the loss of the first-dictated manuscript, rather than to Mormon's history. Might there be, from a believing perspective, a providential reason that Smith and his scribes were given to hear the text out of sequential order?

56. For an outline of apologetic work on the Book of Mormon, see Givens, *By the Hand of Mormon*, 89–154. For a sampling of such work, see Parry, Peterson, and Welch, *Echoes and Evidences of the Book of Mormon*.

57. A history of criticism of the Book of Mormon can be read in Givens, *By the Hand of Mormon*, 155–84. For a survey, see Wunderli, *An Imperfect Book*.

58. See, for instance, the justifiable handwringing in Hardy, *Understanding the Book of Mormon*, xi–xix.

59. See, already in the first half of the twentieth century, Sperry, "The 'Isaiah Problem' in the Book of Mormon"; and, earlier but less sophisticatedly, B. Roberts, *New Witnesses for God*, 2: 25–27. For the most significant contributions to the question from the last several decades, see, respectively, Parry and Welch, *Isaiah in the Book of Mormon*; and D. Wright, "Isaiah in the Book of Mormon."

60. I take it that a point equivalent to Nephi's is made when Dallin H. Oaks, a leader in the Church of Jesus Christ of Latter-day Saints, insists on the Book of

Mormon's historicity as "fundamental" but insists that "it rests first upon faith in the Lord Jesus Christ" (Oaks, "The Historicity of the Book of Mormon," 238).

61. Pfisterer Darr, *Isaiah's Vision and the Family of God*, 30 (for the full theoretical justification of this move, see 13–45).

62. Pfisterer Darr, *Isaiah's Vision and the Family of God*, 29, 31.

63. Pfisterer Darr, *Isaiah's Vision and the Family of God*, 35–36.

64. I imagine here a reader with a decent theological education, up to date on learned debates in the 1820s but also broadly familiar with popular and even marginal approaches to Isaiah.

65. This is perfectly evident from early learned responses to the Book of Mormon, beginning already with the famed Disciples preacher Alexander Campbell's in 1832 (for example, Campbell, *Delusions*).

66. This is evident in turn from the interests early believing readers of the Book of Mormon displayed in their readings, which were, despite their eschatological bent, given to the populist hermeneutics characteristic outside of learned discourse in antebellum American Christianity. See, for instance, Underwood, *Millenarian World of Early Mormonism*.

Chapter 2. Controversy in a Nephite Colony

1. That is, Abinadi strikes the reader as closely following the tradition of the Former Prophets: figures summoned by God to critique Israel's wayward kings, but figures whose stories are told for them in third-person narratives contained in the historical books. If the Book of Mormon contains a prophet figure who most directly embodies the tradition of the Latter Prophets, the prophets represented by books written in their own names, it would be Lehi, whose story is presented at the opening of the Book of Mormon in final form. On connections between Lehi and the tradition of the Latter Prophets, see Ostler, "The Throne-Theophany and Prophetic Commission in 1 Nephi."

2. It may be significant that at one point in his precaptivity preaching, Abinadi comes among the people "in disguise," only to cast away this disguise and reveal his true identity moments later (Mosiah 12:1).

3. The narrative presents Abinadi as aware of the peculiarity of fusing the Hebrew prophetic tradition and Christian scriptural interpretation, evidenced in his "speaking of things to come as though they had already come" (Mosiah 16:6).

4. In this regard, one might read Abinadi's trial as an inversion of the late medieval trials in which Jews attempted unsuccessfully to defend their reading of Isaiah 53 against Christian accusers. See, for example, Maccoby, *Judaism on Trial*.

5. John Welch summarizes the priests' intentions: they planned "to expose a contradiction in Abinadi's teachings and thus convince him—and the people—of the error of his ways" (Welch, *Legal Cases in the Book of Mormon*, 169).

6. Others have discerned elements of what follows in my analysis. See McConkie and Millet, *Doctrinal Commentary*, 2: 208; Nibley, *Teachings of the Book of Mormon*, 2: 71; Pike, "How Beautiful upon the Mountains," 264; Gardner, *Second Witness*, 3: 270–71; Welch, *Legal Cases in the Book of Mormon*, 176–77; and my own previous work in Spencer, *An Other Testament*, 142–45. The most thorough analysis of the priests'

interpretation—largely identical to my own here—can be found in Belnap, "For the Lord Redeemeth None Such."

7. Christensen, *Nahum*, 259.

8. Goldingay and Payne, *Critical and Exegetical Commentary on Isaiah 40–55*, 2: 262. See also Tull Willey, *Remember the Former Things*, 117–20.

9. See the discussion in Sorenson, *Mormon's Map*, 32–34.

10. Goldingay notes that "it is the three nouns [in this verse] describing the news that indicate its goodness. All three could have been used to refer to military successes." Goldingay, *Message of Isaiah 40–55*, 452.

11. Goldingay, *Message of Isaiah 40–55*, 453. See also Koole, *Isaiah III*, 2: 229; G. Smith, *Isaiah 40–66*, 423–24.

12. See echoes of the remainder of Second Isaiah listed in Goldingay, *Message of Isaiah 40–55*, 452.

13. Goldingay, *Message of Isaiah 40–55*, 456.

14. Brueggemann, *Isaiah 40–66*, 138–39.

15. G. Smith, *Isaiah 40–66*, 424.

16. Blenkinsopp, *Isaiah 40–55*, 342. Blenkinsopp provides a series of passages in the Hebrew prophets where the image of a watchman is used to figure a prophet, one of which appears earlier in Isaiah (21:8–9).

17. Brueggemann, *Isaiah 40–66*, 139. See similar comments in Goldingay, *The Message of Isaiah 40–55*, 456.

18. This seems to imply that the Lamanite occupation has indeed been a military one, parallel to Babylon's conquest of Judah in the sixth century.

19. G. Smith, *Isaiah 40–66*, 426.

20. Brueggemann, *Isaiah 40–66*, 139.

21. This bloodthirsty boasting in military might is the last narrative event described before Abinadi's first appearance in the Nephite colony. The suggestion is that God's intervention among Noah's people is in direct response to their development of a taste for violence.

22. Some interpreters suggest that the emphasis on the Law of Moses in Abinadi's confrontation with the priests indicates that the latter are prepared to prosecute Abinadi with reference to Deuteronomy's prescriptions for dealing with false prophets (Deuteronomy 18). See especially Welch, *Legal Cases in the Book of Mormon*, 176–77. Significantly, Abinadi himself somewhat indirectly alludes to a key passage from that part of Deuteronomy (Mosiah 13:33; compare Deuteronomy 18:15–19). See also the discussion in Spencer, *An Other Testament*, 149–55.

23. This literary connection may partially explain Abinadi's lack of interest in what most interpreters today regard as the three-verse opening of the poem mostly made up of Isaiah 53. Most today regard Isaiah 52:13–15 as the first stanza of a poem that stretches to the end of Isaiah 53. Abinadi, however, quotes only Isaiah 53. This seems to be in major part due to his interest in opening his quotation of further Isaian prophecy with the double rhetorical question from Isaiah 53:1 that directly calls into question the priests' problematic appropriation of Isaiah 52:10.

24. Recent scholarship has begun to question the viability of separating out the song of the suffering servant (along with other supposedly identifiable songs about

the servant in Isaiah 40–55) from the weave of its larger literary context. See especially Mettinger, *Farewell to the Servant Songs*.

25. Blenkinsopp, *Isaiah 40–55*, 349.

26. On minor variants in the Book of Mormon's reproduction of Isaiah 53, see Hopkin, "Isaiah 52–53 and Mosiah 13–14: A Textual Comparison."

27. It would not be difficult to construct a Zeniffite approach to Isaiah 53 along methodologically similar lines to their implicit approach to Isaiah 52:7–10.

28. The claim that "God himself should come down among the children of men" is repeated almost verbatim in Mosiah 15:1. The statement that God would "take upon him the form of man" is echoed in Mosiah 15:2, where Abinadi claims that God as Son "dwelleth in flesh." The insistence that God would "go forth in mighty power" finds its correlate in Mosiah 15:6, where Abinadi predicts that the Son will work "many mighty miracles among the children of men." God's "bring[ing] to pass the resurrection of the dead" is the subject of extended discussion throughout Mosiah 15. Finally, the idea that God would "be oppressed and afflicted" finds an echo in Abinadi's description of the Son suffering "temptation" and being "mocked and scourged and cast out and disowned by his people" in Mosiah 15:5.

29. Abinadi quotes another part of the same verse in his commentary in Mosiah 15:6, describing the Messiah's being "led—yea, even as Isaiah said: as a sheep before the shearer is dumb, so he opened not his mouth."

30. Justin Martyr, *Dialogue with Trypho*, 13.1. The question of whether the first generation of Christians saw the story of Jesus in Isaiah 53 is more complicated. See, for instance, Hooker, "Did the Use of Isaiah 53 to Interpret His Mission Begin with Jesus?" Concurrent with and sometimes earlier than the earliest Christians, some non-Christian Jews saw in the poem an outline of the Messiah's fate, albeit distancing the anticipated Messiah from the poem's talk of suffering. For the Isaiah Targum, for instance, see Ådna, "The Servant of Isaiah 53 as Triumphant and Interceding Messiah"; Chilton, *The Glory of Israel*, 86–96; and, for the text, Chilton, *The Isaiah Targum*. For the still earlier Great Isaiah Scroll from the Qumran community, see Hengel and Bailey, "The Effective History of Isaiah 53 in the Pre-Christian Period"; and for the text, see Ulrich and Flint, *Qumran Cave 1*. Another common Jewish interpretation of Isaiah 53 understands the suffering servant to be Israel, forced historically to suffer in persecution. For a classic statement of this interpretation, see Maccoby, *Judaism on Trial*, 112. For a whole collection of Jewish interpretations of the poem, see Neubauer, *The Fifty-Third Chapter of Isaiah according to the Jewish Interpreters*.

31. Abinadi never attempts to justify hermeneutically the reference to Jesus's miracles. In his commentary on Isaiah 53, he simply *asserts* that Jesus will do miracles before his death: "And after all this, and after working many mighty miracles among the children of men, he shall be led—yea, even as Isaiah said: 'as a sheep before the shearer is dumb, so he opened not his mouth'—yea, even so he shall be led, crucified, and slain" (Mosiah 15:6–7).

32. For helpful reviews of the standard variations of critical interpretation of this question, see Koole, *Isaiah III*, 2: 305–8, and Goldingay and Payne, *Critical and Exegetical Commentary on Isaiah 40–55*, 2: 312–13.

33. See, for instance, the suggestion by Joseph Blenkinsopp that, with an eye to cognates in Akkadian and Arabic, the word be translated as "fate": "And who gives a thought to his fate?" Blenkinsopp, *Isaiah 40–55*, 345, 348.

34. Brant Gardner, interpreting Abinadi's discourse, clearly recognizes this possible connection, although I believe he misunderstands what Abinadi takes to be the referent of "generation." See his discussion in Gardner, *Second Witness*, 3: 303.

35. In an influential work of apologetics, Sidney Sperry labeled the passage one of the Book of Mormon's "problems" (Sperry, *Answers to Book of Mormon Questions*, 31–38).

36. Moench Charles, "Book of Mormon Christology," 81.

37. Givens, *Wrestling the Angel*, 72.

38. For an attempt to trace the development of Smith's view of God, see Harrell, *"This Is My Doctrine,"* 105–24.

39. In a parallel discourse, the Book of Mormon's King Benjamin uses the same imagery of a son's submission to his father to describe achievable sainthood; on this, see Mosiah 3:19.

40. The focus is here emphatically on those living *before* the Messiah's coming. This remains throughout Abinadi's exposition of Isaiah. See, for instance, his definition of the "first resurrection": "a resurrection of those that have been, and which are, and which shall be—even until the resurrection of Christ" (Mosiah 15:21).

41. There are difficulties of interpretation here. Although there is no church described as existing in the narrative before Alma organizes his, in 3 Nephi 5:12, Mormon (the editor of the Nephite history) refers to Alma's church as "the first church which was established among [the people] after their transgression." One possible interpretation of this passage is that there was some church before Alma's that Alma meant in some way to restore.

42. The title "the apostles of the Lamb" is introduced in Nephi's record (1 Nephi 11:34–36; 12:9; 13:24, 26, 39–41; 14:20, 24, 25, 27). It then appears a few times late in the Book of Mormon, after the beginning of the apostolic age (Mormon 9:18; Ether 12:41; Moroni 2:2). The continuity between the prophetic and the apostolic is an idea expressed elsewhere in the Book of Mormon. See especially Moroni 7:20–32.

43. Two classic "burdens" in Isaiah 21 use the image of the prophet as a watchman. One quotes the Lord's words of instruction to Isaiah as follows: "Go, set a watchman, let him declare what he seeth" (Isaiah 21:6). Significantly, what this watchman sees is, as in Isaiah 52:7–10, that "Babylon is fallen, is fallen; and all the graven images of her gods he hath broken unto the ground" (Isaiah 21:9). The other burden has God calling to Isaiah: "Watchman, what of the night? Watchman, what of the night?" (Isaiah 21:11). For commentary, see Blenkinsopp, *Isaiah 1–39*, 323–30.

44. This classic Isaian text connects this scene of international peace to a gathering on the Lord's mountain (Isaiah 2:2–4, quoted by Nephi in 2 Nephi 12:2–4).

45. Abinadi speaks of God's relationship to "his people" ten times (Mosiah 13:28, 33; 15:1, 5, 11, 18–19, 30; 16:4).

46. The shift from the prophets to the apostles occurs, it seems, because the pre-Christian prophets who declare the Messiah's generation have limited geographical

Chapter 3. Tradition and Innovation

1. See the treatments of Paul's use of Isaiah 52:7 in Wagner, *Heralds of the Good News*, 170–78, and Seifrid, "Romans," 660–67.

2. See, generally, the essays in Moyise and Menken, *Isaiah in the New Testament*.

3. This is, in fact, the title of John Sawyer's classic study of the history of Isaiah interpretation.

4. Childs, *The Struggle to Understand Isaiah as Christian Scripture*.

5. Jerome, *Commentary on Isaiah*, 67.

6. For important medieval uses of Isaiah (and other Old Testament scripture) to "prove" the Christian gospel, see Maccoby, *Judaism on Trial*.

7. See the occasionally academic presentation, for instance, of Bock and Glaser, *Gospel According to Isaiah 53*.

8. A good example of standard transatlantic approaches in the first half of the nineteenth century can be found in the commentaries by Joseph Addison Alexander, published in the 1840s. Although American commentaries were by Joseph Smith's time increasingly aware of hermeneutical problems with simple Christological interpretations, they still dedicated much space to defending those interpretations. Alexander's commentaries are a key example. See Alexander, *The Earlier Prophecies of Isaiah*, and Alexander, *The Later Prophecies of Isaiah*.

9. For an introduction to the fathers' interpretation of Isaiah generally, see Childs, *The Struggle to Understand Isaiah as Christian Scripture*, 32–147. For a more summary treatment, see Sawyer, *The Fifth Gospel*, 42–64.

10. Sawyer, *The Fifth Gospel*, 52.

11. Sermon 195, in Mark Elliott, *Isaiah 40–66*, 167. See also Augustine's Sermon 171, in Wilken, *Isaiah Interpreted*, 429.

12. Justin Martyr, *First and Second Apologies*, 58 (paragraph 51), Justin Martyr, *Dialogue with Trypho*, 65 (43.3). See also the discussion in Markschies, "Jesus Christ as a Man before God," 245, 68. For helpful commentary on Justin's uses of Isaiah 53, see Bailey, "'Our Suffering and Crucified Messiah' (Dial. 111.1)."

13. Jerome, *Commentary on Isaiah*, 671 (14.24).

14. On the dating of *On the Incarnation*, see Anatolios, *Athanasius*, 11–12. For an excerpt, see Elliott, *Isaiah 40–66*, 167.

15. Hanson, *The Search for the Christian Doctrine of God*, 141.

16. Thus an Arian council at Sirmium decided in 357 that "no mention ought to be made of [claims about the shared substance of the Father and the Son], nor any exposition of them in the church, . . . because no one can explain the birth of the Son, of whom it is written 'Who shall explain [declare] his generation?' (Is. Liii.8)" Bettenson and Maunder, *Documents of the Christian Church*, 45.

17. Hanson, *The Search for the Christian Doctrine of God*, 403–4, 518, Elliott, *Isaiah 40–66*, 167–68.

18. Hanson, *The Search for the Christian Doctrine of God*, 429.

19. For a brief summary of the various ways this single passage was used throughout the controversy, see Hanson, *The Search for the Christian Doctrine of God*, 833.

20. See, for example, Wilken, *Isaiah Interpreted*, 419.

21. For a helpful introduction to Reformation-era interpretation of Isaiah, critical about popular reception of the changes the Reformation introduced, see Childs, *The Struggle to Understand Isaiah as Christian Scripture*, 181–229.

22. Luther, *Lectures on Isaiah Chapters 40–66*, 227.

23. Calvin, *Commentary on the Book of the Prophet Isaiah*, 4: 120–21. Note that late medieval Catholic interpreters themselves began to move in similar directions. For example, see Lapide, *Commentaria in Scripturam Sacram*, 11: 634.

24. As at least one major Catholic commentator from the early seventeenth century notes, Nicholas of Lyra, writing in the fourteenth century, moved in a similar direction (Lapide, *Commentaria in Scripturam Sacram*, 11: 634).

25. Grotius, *Annotationes in Vetus Testamentum*, 2: 105, and Vitringa, *Commentarius in Librum Prophetiarum Jesaiae*, 2: 787.

26. Poole, *Annotations upon the Holy Bible*, 2: 448–49. See the nearly identical discussion in Henry, *Exposition of the Old and New Testament*, 4: 246.

27. On the relationship between the Latter-day Saint tradition and Methodism, see Jones, "'We Latter-day Saints Are Methodists.'"

28. Wesley, *Wesley's Notes on the Bible*, 335. See a direct dismissal of the medieval reading in Patrick et al., *Critical Commentary and Paraphrase*, 3: 565.

29. For some introduction to Lowth, see Childs, *The Struggle to Understand Isaiah as Christian Scripture*, 250–54.

30. Lowth, *Isaiah*, 2: 325, 327.

31. Clarke, *The Holy Bible*, 3: 848. On the potential influence of Clarke's commentary on Joseph Smith, see Wayment and Wilson-Lemmon, "A Recovered Resource."

32. Scott, *The Holy Bible*, s.v. Isaiah LIII:8.

33. Woodward, *A System of Christian Theology*, 77.

34. Hunter, *Sacred Biography*, 7: 22.

35. "On the Sonship of Jesus Christ," 133–34.

36. A., "Answers to Queries," 533.

37. N., "Observations on Isa. liii.8."

38. J. Edwards, *History of Redemption on a Plan Entirely Original*, vi.

39. J. Edwards, *History of Redemption on a Plan Entirely Original*, 249–50. See, though, J. Edwards, *Works of President Edwards*, 5: 65.

40. Dabney, *Annotations on the New Testament*, 21. Significantly, even Catholic commentaries in the early modern period distanced themselves from the medieval interpretation. See Lapide, *Commentaria in Scripturam Sacram*, 11: 634–35, Knabenbauer, *Commentarius in Isaiam Prophetam*, 2: 331–34.

41. See the summary in Stout, *The New England Soul*, 302: "In a very real sense, the Old Testament had always served as New England's 'ancient constitution,' and each generation had read and interpreted it from their own unique vantage point." For further applications, see Hatch and Noll, *The Bible in America*. On the foundations of this hermeneutic, however, see Byrd, *Sacred Scripture, Sacred War*, and Noll, *In the Beginning Was the Word*.

42. Shalev, *American Zion*, 99–101.

43. The Book of Mormon seems out of step historically with much of the pseudo-biblical literature traced by Shalev, coming afterward (and therefore able to critique it) (Park, "The Book of Mormon").

44. Interpretations of Isaiah 52:8–10 along Abinadi-like lines can be found in the early Christian fathers (see Wilken, *Isaiah Interpreted*, 405–6, Eusebius of Caesarea, *Commentary on Isaiah*, 259–60, and Jerome, *Commentary on Isaiah*, 660–61 [14.18–19]) and their modern heirs (see, for example, Lapide, *Commentaria in Scripturam Sacram*, 11: 618–19, Knabenbauer, *Commentarius in Isaiam Prophetam*, 2: 303–4). They can be found as well in the early Reformers (Luther, *Lectures on Isaiah Chapters 40–66*, 211, and Calvin, *Commentary on the Book of the Prophet Isaiah*, 4: 102) and their later heirs (Scott, *The Holy Bible*, s.v. Isaiah LII:9–10, Patrick et al., *A Critical Commentary and Paraphrase*, 3: 563, Poole, *Annotations upon the Holy Bible*, 2: 446, Henry, *Exposition of the Old and New Testament*, 4: 240, and Clarke, *The Holy Bible*, 3: 844). Right into the nineteenth century, the larger Christian tradition interpreted Isaiah 52:7–10 as about Christian preaching.

45. See, for example, Jerome, *Commentary on Isaiah*, 673 (14.25), and Eusebius of Caesarea, *Commentary on Isaiah*, 265 (338). It should be noted that the application of Isaiah 53:7–10 to the early Christian work of missionizing can be found already in the New Testament, in Romans 10:14–15.

46. Luther, *Lectures on Isaiah Chapters 40–66*, 229.

47. Calvin, *Commentary on the Book of the Prophet Isaiah*, 4: 125.

48. See, for instance, Vitringa, *Commentarius in Librum Prophetiarum Jesaiae*, 2: 792, Poole, *Annotations upon the Holy Bible*, 2: 448–49. See also the nearly identical discussion in Henry, *Exposition of the Old and New Testament*, 4: 449, Patrick et al., *Critical Commentary and Paraphrase*, 3: 565, Wesley, *Wesley's Notes on the Bible*, 335, and Scott, *The Holy Bible*, s.v. "Isaiah LIII:10."

49. Clarke, *The Holy Bible*, 3: 850.

50. This same pattern can be found also in Catholic commentaries published throughout the modern period (Lapide, *Commentaria in Scripturam Sacram*, 11: 637, and Knabenbauer, *Commentarius in Isaiam Prophetam*, 2: 341).

51. Henry, *Exposition of the Old and New Testament*, 4: 247.

52. Stendahl, *Paul among Jews and Gentiles*.

53. Abinadi's approach to Isaiah 53:10 is presented within the Book of Mormon itself as controversial and difficult. Two generations after Abinadi, the Nephite church's high priest Alma (the son of Alma, the church's founder) has to correct misinterpretations of Abinadi's teachings (Alma 40:16–20).

54. I borrow the term "church of anticipation" from Hugh Nibley, who uses it to describe Alma's church organized in the wake of Abinadi's defense (Nibley, *An Approach to the Book of Mormon*, 183–93).

55. Commentators more or less universally regard—as do Noah's priests—Isaiah 52:7–10 as a cohesive unit. See, for example, Blenkinsopp, *Isaiah 1–39*, 338–39.

56. On Abinadi's discussion of typology, see Spencer, *An Other Testament*, 159–64.

57. Pascal, *The Provincial Letters*, 290.

58. Pascal, *The Provincial Letters*, 300.

59. Badiou, *Being and Event*, 216–17, translation modified.

60. N. T. Wright, *The New Testament and the People of God*, 40.

61. Givens, *By the Hand of Mormon*, 50.

62. For Benjamin's similar statement, see Mosiah 3:13.

63. The answer in the text is that souls before Christ's advent are "as precious unto God" as those afterward (Alma 39:17), with the consequence that it is "as necessary that the plan of redemption should be made known" in both eras (39:18).

64. On this theme, see Givens, *By the Hand of Mormon*, 45–51, Spencer, *Anatomy of Book of Mormon Theology*, 2: 279–87, and, most recently, J. Thomas, *A Pentecostal Reads the Book of Mormon*, 199–204.

65. This was, according to Samuel Brown's argument, a consistent theological concern for Joseph Smith. See his discussion in S. M. Brown, *In Heaven as It Is on Earth*, 219–22.

66. Campbell, *Delusions*, 12.

67. I have articulated this point elsewhere (Spencer, *An Other Testament*, 157–58).

68. For some commentary on the use of Isaiah 53:4 in Matthew 8:17, see Blomberg, "Matthew," 30–33.

69. Brief outlines of each of the Book of Mormon's several books can be found in Largey, *Book of Mormon Reference Companion*.

70. The Book of Mosiah "clearly juxtaposes an unrighteous ruler (Noah) and the dire consequences such a man could bring on his people, with rulers who tried to follow the Lord" (Thomasson, "Mosiah," 25). For further discussion and development, see Sturgess, "The Book of Mosiah," 118–23. For important context for the Book of Mormon's political rhetoric about monarchy, see R. Bushman, "The Book of Mormon and the American Revolution."

71. Grant Hardy has shown that a major literary feature of the Book of Mormon—especially those portions presented as written by Mormon (as is the case in the Book of Mosiah)—is the use of parallel narratives to highlight points of contrast (Hardy, *Understanding the Book of Mormon*, 152–79).

72. The divine messages sent to each dynasty's second king—to Benjamin in Zarahemla and to Noah in Nephi—are clearly parallel (Spencer, *An Other Testament*, 120–25).

73. Grant Hardy analyzes the text's unique presentation of Zeniff as a sensitive personality (Hardy, *Understanding the Book of Mormon*, 123–32).

74. Zeniff's reign is presented as aligned with God's purposes in many ways also, but Zeniff's reign comes in a first-person account and Mosiah's reads in the third person. Thus, while Mosiah's account is, as it were, *objectively* presented as divinely guided, the reader is left with the impression that Zeniff only wishes his reign had been divinely guided.

75. There are clear literary links between the two narrative reports of removal (although Nephi moves his people *to* and Mosiah *from* the land of Nephi).

76. Hardy, *Understanding the Book of Mormon*, 121–51.

77. On the relationship between these two texts, see Goff, "Historical Narrative, Literary Narrative," 85–86. Gardner, *Second Witness*, 3: 227, contests the connection but unconvincingly in my view. Apparently attempting again to make himself

Nephi's heir, Zeniff also writes into his record an impassioned defense of Nephi in relation to his rebellious brothers, the ancestors of the Lamanite people. In this way, Zeniff presents himself and his people as fighting the same war—and for the same causes—that Nephi was fighting centuries earlier in the same land. For helpful analyses of this defense, see R. Bushman, "The Lamanite View of Book of Mormon History," and Hardy, *Understanding the Book of Mormon*, 129–30.

78. The text emphasizes that the sword of Laban, symbol of Nephi's power and legitimacy, is in the possession of the dynasty founded by Mosiah. It is Benjamin, Mosiah's son, not Zeniff and his heirs, who wields the sword.

79. I have offered an interpretation of this major shift in the context of final form in Spencer, *An Other Testament*, and more briefly in Spencer, *Anatomy of Book of Mormon Theology*, 1: 45–62.

80. Spencer, *An Other Testament*, 120–25.

Chapter 4. A New Direction at the Meridian of Time

1. Skinner, *Third Nephi*, 1, and Sawyer, *The Fifth Gospel*, 1–3.

2. Current chapter divisions in Latter-day Saint editions of the Book of Mormon were introduced only in the 1870s.

3. Hardy, *Understanding the Book of Mormon*, 180.

4. Hardy, *Understanding the Book of Mormon*, 180.

5. Hardy, *Understanding the Book of Mormon*, 180–81.

6. Hardy, *Understanding the Book of Mormon*, 183.

7. Hardy, *Understanding the Book of Mormon*, 183.

8. See the discourse of the war captain Moroni in Alma 46:23–27, which uses the biblical idea of the Israelite remnant to curse Nephites who refuse to fight for freedom.

9. On the uniqueness of this early Christian claim in the context of ancient Judaism, see Harvey, *The True Israel*.

10. The exact repetition of "Jesus Christ, the Son of God" from 3 Nephi 5:13 in 3 Nephi 9:15—in Mormon's editorial interruption and in Christ's interruption of destruction—suggests a deliberate parallel, running alongside parallel references to the covenant theme.

11. Even with careful literary warnings of a shift, many readers remain confused at Third Nephi's heavy focus on Israel's covenantal history. In a devotional work on Third Nephi, for instance, Andrew Skinner (in *Third Nephi*) entirely ignores everything said about Israel and the covenant.

12. 3 Nephi 26:13 claims that "the Lord truly did teach the people for the space of three days," but Mormon's account either says nothing of the events of the third day of Christ's visit, or what is reported of the second day is supposed to have stretched over two days.

13. For a representative summary of the sermon, see V. Ludlow, "The Father's Covenant People Sermon."

14. The fusion of law and covenant can be found directly in the writings of the New Testament, of course, or at least can be rather easily read into texts from the New Testament—especially the Letter to the Hebrews.

15. For the critical textual details here, see R. Skousen, *Analysis of Textual Variants of the Book of Mormon*, 3539–41.

16. A few words from the first sequence of Christ's covenant sermonizing anticipate the second-sequence quotation of Micah 5:8–9 (3 Nephi 16:14–15), weaving quasi-Mican language into language borrowed directly from the Sermon on the Mount quoted earlier in Third Nephi (compare 3 Nephi 16:15 with 3 Nephi 12:13). It is significant that Mormon as narrator and editor later comes back to the same Mican language as he concludes his record (Mormon 5:24).

17. The quotations of Genesis 22 and Deuteronomy 18 are unmistakably filtered through the New Testament's quotation of the same passages in Acts 3:22–25.

18. Stendahl, "The Sermon on the Mount and Third Nephi." Critics have taken the relationship between Third Nephi and the New Testament as a chief evidence against the Book of Mormon's historicity; see, most classically, Larson, "The Historicity of the Matthean Sermon on the Mount in 3 Nephi," and Larson, "The Sermon on the Mount." The classic apologetic response is Welch, *The Sermon at the Temple and the Sermon on the Mount*. Stendahl's approach largely ignores debates about historicity.

19. Stendahl notes also that the Book of Mormon version include John-like terms and phrases like "my commandments" and "come unto me and be saved" (Stendahl, "The Sermon on the Mount and Third Nephi," 143–44).

20. Stendahl, "The Sermon on the Mount and Third Nephi," 149.

21. Stendahl, "The Sermon on the Mount and Third Nephi," 150.

22. Stendahl, "The Sermon on the Mount and Third Nephi," 150–51.

23. Stendahl, "The Sermon on the Mount and Third Nephi," 150.

24. Frederick, *The Bible, Mormon Scripture, and the Rhetoric of Allusivity*, 2–8.

25. The Matthew text, an adaptation of the apparently earlier Markan report (with which the Third Nephi text is less resonant), itself contains allusions, specifically to Psalms 2:7 and Isaiah 42:1. See the brief discussion in Blomberg, "Matthew," 14.

26. Raymond Brown points out the possibility that Jesus's prayer in John 12 may be a Johannine adaptation of a few words from the Lord's Prayer in the Sermon on the Mount ("Hallowed be thy name"; Matthew 6:9) (R. Brown, *Gospel According to John*, 476). Rudolf Bultmann similarly suggests that the scene in John 12 marks an adaptation of the Transfiguration scene of the synoptics (Bultmann, *Gospel of John*, 428).

27. After identifying himself as "Jesus Christ, of which the prophets testified that should come into the world," he says, "I am the light and the life of the world, and I have drank out of that bitter cup with the Father hath given me and have glorified the Father in taking upon me the sins of the world—in the which I have suffered the will of the Father in all things from the beginning" (3 Nephi 11:10–11). This stitches together, in order, John 8:12, John 1:4, John 18:11, John 1:29, and John 5:30.

28. One interesting example comes when Mormon's Christ presents his doctrine in thoroughly Johannine terms. See especially 3 Nephi 11:33–34, 37–38, which weaves language from John (John 1:18; 3:35; 5:26, 32, 36, 37; 6:37, 39; 7:16–17; 8:18; 10:29–30; 12:49; 13:3; 14:7, 9, 11, 26, 31; 15:26; 17:11, 24; 18:11) into a doctrine that is otherwise directly from Mark 16:16 or Acts 2:38; 17:30.

29. In lieu of concentric circles, the Luke story of Jesus's Gethsemane suffering places the disciples as a group simply at some distance from Jesus (he is "withdrawn from them about a stone's cast"; Luke 22:41). When an angel appears during the scene, it attends only Jesus, "strengthening him" (22:43); it never interacts with the disciples, nor does it demarcate any boundary as the angels do in 3 Nephi 17.

30. The similarity has been noted by Douglas Davies, but he also adds this warning: "Because the context is different from the biblical Gethsemane, due caution is demanded not only because the focus of the angelic ministration is that of little children but also because the descending fiery angels might just as well be regarded in loose parallel with the Day of Pentecost" (Davies, *Joseph Smith, Jesus, and Satanic Opposition*, 136–37).

31. This replacement—and perhaps subtle equation—of Christ's disciples and little children may well play on the synoptic Gospels' investigations of the relationship between disciples and children. In Mark 9:42, "little ones" is a name Jesus gives to his disciples, and Matthew later connects this same saying to Jesus's encouragement to his disciples to "become as little children" (Matthew 18:3). This same injunction appears in 3 Nephi 11:37–38.

32. With the disciples in the place of the children, the second day's scene is reminiscent of the throne room vision of Revelation 4–5, where twenty-four elders surround the throne where Christ appears and is slain, while larger multitudes surround the twenty-four elders. It almost appears as if the more strictly transcendent second day's experiences approach those depicted as occurring in heaven in the Bible.

33. This Davies notes, saying that the likeness of 3 Nephi 19's event "to the biblical Gethsemane is too striking to be accidental" (Davies, *Joseph Smith, Jesus, and Satanic Opposition*, 137). Despite this obviousness, Latter-day Saint commentators tend not to note the connections in their discussions. See, for instance, Gardner, *Second Witness*, 5: 513–21, Skinner, *Third Nephi*, 104–8.

34. Davies, *Joseph Smith, Jesus, and Satanic Opposition*, 137 (spelling and punctuation Americanized).

35. See Stendahl, "The Sermon on the Mount and Third Nephi," 149; Gardner, *Second Witness*, 5: 518; and Skinner, *Third Nephi*, 106–7.

36. One major difference between the two accounts might be noted, namely, that the New Testament emphasizes Christ's body as "given" for his people, while the Book of Mormon emphasizes Christ's body as "shown" to his people. This is a consistent theme—linked to what appears to be a consistent theology—in the Book of Mormon, more deserving of attention than it has yet received. See, for instance, 2 Nephi 9:5; 10:19; Ether 3:17; Moroni 9:25.

37. Gardner notes the obvious parallel (Gardner, *Second Witness*, 5: 522–23). Hardy notes it as well but notes also the contrast between the two events, one instance of several where Third Nephi "amplifies the miraculous aspects of the gospels" while "stay[ing] close to the parameters of biblical supernaturalism." Thus, "in Palestine, Jesus miraculously multiplied five loaves to feed five thousand people; in the Americas he fed even greater numbers by producing bread out of nothing" (Hardy, *Understanding the Book of Mormon*, 181).

38. Once again, see Stendahl, "The Sermon on the Mount and Third Nephi," 149. And, once again, these connections are noted often enough by Latter-day Saint commentators (Gardner, *Second Witness*, 5: 523).

39. Dana Pike notes the delay in the second day's sermon, providing a brief outline of the material leading up to and contextualizing Christ's second-day treatment of Isaiah 52 (Pike, "'How Beautiful upon the Mountains,'" 269–70).

40. I put "our" in brackets because it does not appear in Christ's quotation of Isaiah 52:8–10 in 3 Nephi 16:18–20, as noted before, although it appears in the King James Version of Isaiah 52:8–10 and its full quotation by Noah's priests in Mosiah 12:21–24.

41. Some even attempt to discern patterns of corrupting editorial work in Isaiah by comparing the Book of Mormon's Isaiah texts with those in the manuscript tradition. See, for instance, Gorton, *Legacy of the Brass Plates*.

42. On this kind of move, see Handley, "Reading and the Menardian Paradox in 3 Nephi," and, more generally, Webb, "Slumbering Voices," and Handley, "On the Moral Risks of Reading Scripture."

43. R. Brown, *Gospel according to John*, 406.

44. For some further discussion of these points, see Spencer, *An Other Testament*, 106–8.

45. There is a general consensus that different portions of Isaiah 52 play different roles. For a good overview, see Westermann, *Isaiah 40–66*, 238–60. Christ's several divisions within Isaiah 52 in the Book of Mormon, however, do not correlate with consensus scholarship.

46. The role Isaiah 52:6 plays here in confirming Israel's response to Isaiah 52:1–3 may explain the excision of Isaiah 52:4–5 in 3 Nephi 20. It may also explain the use of the Johannine "verily, verily" formula, which clearly serves in its Third Nephi context to confirm the immediately preceding verses.

47. See even conservative commentators: G. Smith, *Isaiah 40–66*, 430–34, and Oswalt, *The Book of Isaiah*, 2: 376.

48. See the helpful structural analyses in Galland, "A Short Structural Reading of Isaiah 52:13–53:12," and Goldingay, *The Message of Isaiah 40–55*, 469–73.

49. Actually, one other passage from Isaiah 52 makes another appearance, since Isaiah 52:12 is quoted as the final line of 3 Nephi 21. This particular quotation, however, serves just to introduce the full quotation of Isaiah 54 in 3 Nephi 22; it receives no other clarification or development.

50. For the full argument, see Strathearn and Moody, "Christ's Interpretation of Isaiah 52's 'My Servant' in 3 Nephi."

51. See, again, MacKay and Dirkmaat, *From Darkness unto Light*, 79–104.

52. If by no other means, our ideal listener/reader would learn of the lost manuscript when picking up a first edition of the Book of Mormon in 1830, since Smith included in that edition a brief preface about the loss.

53. The canonical source for this text is D&C 10:43. See the discussion in Strathearn and Moody, "Christ's Interpretation of Isaiah 52's 'My Servant' in 3 Nephi," 186–87. Because Smith's revelation likely preceded the dictation of the relevant portion of the

Book of Mormon, it seems best to understand that the translation alludes directly to the revelation, making the meaning of the use of Isaiah 52 all the clearer.

54. Only a few differences, none crucial, distinguish King James Isaiah 54 from Isaiah 54 in Third Nephi.

55. This is so much the case that the contribution to Parry and Welch, *Isaiah in the Book of Mormon*, that focuses on Isaiah 54 in Third Nephi never bothers to say anything about the placement or interpretation of the chapter in the Book of Mormon. Instead, it addresses just the meaning of Isaiah 54 as such (Hallen, "The Lord's Covenant of Kindness").

Chapter 5. A Radical Hermeneutic in Outline

1. For the idea of realized eschatology (especially in the Gospel of John), see Bultmann, *Theology of the New Testament*, 2: 78; and Dodd, *Interpretation of the Fourth Gospel*, 7. In some sense, Third Nephi promotes the idea of a realized eschatology within its messianic expectation, but it separates out from this a second eschatology, yet unrealized, to be accomplished in the very distant future.

2. Histories of Isaiah interpretation tend to focus on the mainstream. By contrast, histories of interpretation of the Book of Revelation tend to focus on the marginal and millenarian, providing a helpful contrast in interpretive communities (Chilton, *Visions of the Apocalypse*; Kirsch, *History of the End of the World*; Beal, *Book of Revelation*).

3. Hatch, *Democratization of American Christianity*, 162, 170–71 (emphasis added).

4. For a similar view of much of early Latter-day Saint belief, see Hill, *Quest for Refuge*. For some problematization of Hill's thesis, see Harper, "Infallible Proofs, Both Human and Divine."

5. Moorhead, "Apocalypticism in Mainstream Protestantism," 72.

6. Moorhead, "Between Progress and Apocalypse," 525.

7. Stein, "Apocalypticism outside the Mainstream," 108.

8. Stein, "Signs of the Times," 61.

9. Naturally, a long and complex history of millenarianism and apocalypticism has followed in the wake of the Book of Mormon's publication among Latter-day Saints. For an important summary history, see Blythe, *Terrible Revolution*.

10. Cross, *Burned-Over District*, 287.

11. Underwood, *Millenarian World of Early Mormonism*, 76–82.

12. Justin Martyr, *Dialogue with Trypho*, 22 (13.1–2).

13. M. Elliott, *Isaiah 40–66*, 152 (*Proof of the Gospel* 6.24). See the fuller exposition in Eusebius of Caesarea, *Commentary on Isaiah*, 257–58.

14. Jerome, *Commentary on Isaiah*, 660 (14.18).

15. Patrick et al., *Critical Commentary*, 3: 563. (William Lowth was the father of the famed Isaiah scholar Robert Lowth.) See, similarly, Henry, *Exposition of the Old and New Testament*, 4: 239.

16. Clarke, *The Holy Bible*, 3: 843–44.

17. Asbury, *Journal of Rev. Francis Asbury*, 470.

18. Jerome, *Commentary on Isaiah*, 653 (14.15).

19. Jerome, *Commentary on Isaiah*, 663 (14.20).
20. Henry, *Exposition of the Old and New Testament*, 4: 238–41.
21. See the April 17, 1818, letter by Messrs. Lawson, Carey, Yates, and Penny, in the *Baptist Magazine for 1819*, 43.
22. Scott, *The Holy Bible*, s.v. Isaiah LII:1; 11, 12.
23. Scott, *The Holy Bible*, s.v. Isaiah LII:1.
24. Scott, *The Holy Bible*, s.v. Isaiah LII:7, 8.
25. Scott, *The Holy Bible*, s.v. Isaiah LII:11, 12.
26. For some commentary, see Silva, "Galatians."
27. Holmes, *Apostolic Fathers*, 68–69 (2 Clement 2).
28. J. Elliott, *Apocryphal New Testament*, 577 ("Epistle of the Apostles" 33).
29. Justin Martyr, *First and Second Apologies*, 60 (First Apology 53).
30. Wilken, *Isaiah Interpreted*, 436 (*Against Heresies* 1.10.3). For other extremely early Christian citations, as well as for a few sources on early Jewish uses of the same passage, see Betz, *Galatians*, 248–49.
31. M. Elliott, *Isaiah 40–66*, 174; Eusebius, *Commentary on Isaiah*, 266; Jerome, *Commentary on Isaiah*, 679–81 (15.2–3); and, for a host of examples, Wilken, *Isaiah Interpreted*, 434–37.
32. Jerome, *Commentary on Isaiah*, 681 (15.2).
33. Henry, *Exposition of the Old and New Testament*, 4: 248.
34. Henry, *Exposition of the Old and New Testament*, 4: 248. See also and especially Poole, *Annotations upon the Holy Bible*, 2: 450.
35. See, for example, Coggeshall, "Progress and Final Triumph of the Gospel," 68.
36. Patrick et al., *Critical Commentary and Paraphrase*, 3: 565.
37. Clarke, *The Holy Bible*, 3: 850.
38. See the February 13, 1810, letter by Joseph Fox in the *Baptist Magazine for 1810*, 271.
39. Patrick et al., *Critical Commentary and Paraphrase*, 3: 493.
40. Clarke, *The Holy Bible*, 3: 724; Scott, *The Holy Bible*, s.v. Isaiah XI.11–16; and Lowth, *Isaiah*, 2: 115.
41. See, for instance, E. Smith, *View of the Hebrews*, 37, where Robert Lowth (son of the aforementioned William Lowth) and Thomas Scott serve as principal sources for interpreting Isaiah 11.
42. E. Smith, *View of the Hebrews*.
43. McDonald, *Isaiah's Message to the American Nation*. Eran Shalev finds the motivation for McDonald's interpretation in the revitalization of patriotism after the War of 1812 (Shalev, *American Zion*, 119).
44. Horsley, *Critical Disquisitions*, 86–115. Horsley worked tirelessly to counter the heretical views of Joseph Priestley, while Faber helped to lay the foundation for nineteenth-century dispensationalism.
45. Scott, *The Holy Bible*, s.v. Isaiah XVIII, V. 7.
46. Hatch, *Democratization of American Christianity*, 59.
47. It is, of course, true that the Disciples movement produced a "compellingly fresh reinterpretation of Scripture," but it must be said that the majority of what it

introduced as novel was largely confined to the New Testament, and especially to the Book of Acts (Noll, *America's God*, 184). For a good study of biblical interpretation in the Disciples tradition, see Boring, *Disciples and the Bible*. As for Baptists and Methodists as parts of a protest movement within the mainstream, see Heyrman, *Southern Cross*.

48. Mark Noll comments: "American denominations such as the Disciples of Barton Stone and 'Christians' of Alexander Campbell, or even the Baptists and Methodists, took pains to distinguish themselves from the older denominations that had dominated the colonial period. But . . . once they had achieved a certain measure of success, they moved easily into the mainstream. Their Protestantism was more an extension of the dominant evangelical trends than a contrast to them" (Noll, *History of Christianity in the United States and Canada*, 192). For a helpful account of the Disciples' shift toward the mainstream, see Hughes and Allen, *Illusions of Innocence*, 170–87.

49. See the discussion in Hatch, *Democratization of American Christianity*, 93–101.

50. In the Methodist Richard Watson's *Biblical and Theological Dictionary* too one finds under the entry on millenarianism a detailed argument that scriptural passages traditionally used by millenarians are all to be read spiritually, as being about human beings in their ultimately resurrected state (Watson, *Biblical and Theological Dictionary*, 649–53).

51. Noll, *History of Christianity in the United States and Canada*, 191–92.

52. Underwood, *Millenarian World of Early Mormonism*, 112.

53. For an overview of Miller's life, see Dick, *William Miller and the Advent Crisis*. For the standard biography of Joseph Smith, see, of course, R. Bushman, *Joseph Smith, Rough Stone Rolling*.

54. For a comparison of the marginalizations of Millerites and Latter-day Saints together, see Doan, *Miller Heresy, Millennialism, and American Culture*, 217–20.

55. Noll, *History of Christianity in the United States and Canada*, 195. See also Doan, *Miller Heresy, Millennialism, and American Culture*, 21–22.

56. D. Howe, *What Hath God Wrought*, 286; see, more generally, pages 243–327. For important qualifications of how this thoroughly American vision was related to the status of religion in the early Republic, see Porterfield, *Conceived in Doubt*.

57. The idea that Millerism was pessimistic in some ways approaches caricature, but certainly Miller himself and the movement had some doubts about progress. For some discussion, see Land, "Historians and the Millerites."

58. Doan, *Miller Heresy, Millennialism, and American Culture*, 31.

59. For a recent, detailed study of the panic of 1837, see Lepler, *Many Panics of 1837*.

60. Miller, *Evidence from Scripture and History*, 4.

61. Miller, *Evidence from Scripture and History*, 5.

62. It seems significant, for example, that Reverend William R. Weeks, in his serialized "Mistakes of Millerism" published in 1843 in the *New York Evangelist*, never once addresses Miller's uses of Isaiah, despite enumerating well over a hundred "mistakes" in Miller's uses of the biblical text.

63. See especially Miller, *Evidence from Scripture and History*, 6.

64. Miller, *Evidence from Scripture and History*, 284.

65. This sometimes leads to interpretive peculiarities. For example, although Miller sees Isaiah 40:3 as a simple prediction of the Baptist's preaching, he sees Isaiah 40:5 as predicting the general revelation of God's glory at the last day (Miller, *Evidence from Scripture and History*, 17).

66. Miller, *Evidence from Scripture and History*, 19, 20–21, 173.

67. Givens, *Wrestling the Angel*, 34–41; see also Givens, "'We Have Only the Old Thing.'"

68. Isaiah 35:1–2 is quoted in an 1831 revelation to Joseph Smith—given, significantly, in the context of an early mission among the Shakers—that promises that the Book of Mormon's "Lamanites shall blossom as the rose." See also, though, Sawyer, *Isaiah through the Centuries*, 205. It is interesting that some Methodists used the passage in similar contexts, albeit without the Book of Mormon's account of Native origins (Case, "Grand River Mission," 111).

69. Miller, *Evidence from Scripture and History*, 274.

70. Miller, *Evidence from Scripture and History*, 270–71.

71. Miller, *Evidence from Scripture and History*, 28.

72. Miller, *Evidence from Scripture and History*, 41.

73. Miller, *Evidence from Scripture and History*, 228. Other Isaian texts help to confirm Miller's interpretations of the marital relationship between God and the church, the meaning of the imagery in Jesus's famous parable of the ten virgins, or the idea that prophets throughout the Bible have similar visionary experiences (Miller, *Evidence from Scripture and History*, 164–67, 206, 235–36; see also p. 98).

74. Miller, *Evidence from Scripture and History*, 82.

75. For a helpful, contextualizing discussion of Miller's methods, see Doan, *Miller Heresy, Millennialism, and American Culture*, 31–53.

76. Miller explicitly sets himself "against Judaizing teachers," presumably meaning scholars with an increasingly historicist sensibility in the early nineteenth century (Miller, *Evidence from Scripture and History*, 59–61). As Epperson points out in contrasting the Book of Mormon with Miller's views, "Jewish people dropped out altogether from Miller's picture" in a clearly supersessionist gesture (Epperson, *Mormons and Jews*, 20).

77. Holland, *Sacred Borders*, 127–69. Actually, Holland makes a triad of, precisely, Shakers, Latter-day Saints, and Millerites—although his deepest interest is in the developments within the Millerite movement after the Great Disappointment of 1844, when Ellen G. White emerged as a prophetic voice. Stephen Stein also notes a handful of parallels between the Book of Mormon and Philemon Stewart's *Sacred and Divine Roll* (Stein, *Shaker Experience in America*, 182).

78. Foster, *Religion and Sexuality*, and Taysom, *Shakers, Mormons, and Religious Worlds*. There were crucial direct interactions between the two groups, documented in part within a canonical revelation to Joseph Smith. The original text of the revelation, along with helpful context, is in MacKay, Dirkmaat, Underwood, et al., *Joseph Smith Papers, Documents*, 1: 297–303.

79. An 1879 *Bible of Bibles* analyzed a variety of alternatives to orthodox Christian scripture and suggestively grouped together the Qur'an, the Book of Mormon, and the Shakers' *Sacred and Divine Roll* (Graves, *Bible of Bibles*, 57–60).

80. A note "to printers" about "amendments and corrections" points out that Isaiah 53:1–3 is supposed to appear in the list of passages cited about the first coming of Christ, although it does not actually appear there (Stewart, *Holy, Sacred and Divine Roll and Book*, 224).

81. Stewart, *Holy, Sacred and Divine Roll and Book*, 129. The passages quoted in a long list are Isaiah 4:2; 9:6; 11:1–6, 9–10, 12; 27:2–3, 5–6; 26:20–21; 32:1, 17–18; 35:1–2, 5, 8–10; 42:9; 52:1, 7–9; 55:1–9; 57:14–15, 19–21; 60:1–4, 15, 18, 21–22; 66:5, 13, 15–16, 22. Note that a few of these appear in the Book of Mormon, sometimes with similar and sometimes with different interpretations.

82. They are Isaiah 1:25; 2:19; 13:13; 24:13–15; 29:17; 52:2. Note here again that some of these passages are quoted in passing in the Book of Mormon.

83. Stewart, *Holy, Sacred and Divine Roll and Book*, 187. Preceding portions of the volume derive from an experience had on May 4, 1842, while those in the last portion of the volume were given months later, near the end of 1842 (Stewart, *Holy, Sacred and Divine Roll and Book*, ix, 200).

84. Archers are twice mentioned in the Book of Isaiah (Isaiah 21:17; 22:3), but it is not clear whether these references are supposed to be relevant to Isaiah's archers in *Sacred and Divine Roll*.

85. Stewart, *Holy, Sacred and Divine Roll and Book*, 187.

86. Stewart, *Holy, Sacred and Divine Roll and Book*, 191.

87. The words of the first archer, for instance, do not draw in any obvious way on Isaiah before the fourth and fifth paragraphs. At that point, though, obvious borrowings from Isaiah 28:17 ("Have not I promised that my judgments should be to the line, and my righteousness to the plummet?") and Isaiah 35:3 ("Have I not strengthened the feeble and tottering knee . . . ?") appear. Stewart, *Holy, Sacred and Divine Roll and Book*, 188.

88. The strangeness of the volume was apparent from the outset, and the unfortunate reception of the book after its rapid publication—in Stephen Stein's view— "certainly contributed to the rapidly declining fortunes of the volume and to the society's decision to withdraw it from public circulation before the end of the decade [of the 1840s]" (Stein, *Shaker Experience in America*, 183).

89. Stewart, *Holy, Sacred and Divine Roll and Book*, 199.

90. Stewart, *Holy, Sacred and Divine Roll and Book*, 200.

91. Stewart, *Holy, Sacred and Divine Roll and Book*, 248.

92. Stewart, *Holy, Sacred and Divine Roll and Book*, 249.

93. Seth Perry speaks appropriately of "performed biblicism" in such contexts, as when "Methodist itinerant Fanny Newell imagined the prophet Isaiah coming to prayer meeting with her" (Perry, *Bible Culture and Authority*, 69).

94. Harper, "Infallible Proofs, Both Human and Divine," 107. Harper cites Jan Shipps, Thomas O'Dea, and Klaus Hansen on this point, all of whom underscore

the rationality of the Book of Mormon. Their evaluation extends, without question, to the Book of Mormon's intricate engagement with Isaiah. For discussions of the rationality in question, see Shipps, *Mormonism*, 33; O'Dea, *The Mormons*, 31; and Hansen, *Mormonism and the American Experience*, 41.

95. O'Dea, *The Mormons*, 35.

96. Note that Abinadi makes comments on the events at Sinai, for instance, but sees them as singularly oriented toward Christ in a typological way (Mosiah 13:27–33).

97. Among the more important theological differences would be that Abinadi's Christological interpretation of Isaiah tends toward what theologians call a "replacement theology," that is, an understanding of Christianity as having superseded Judaism. Christ's interpretation of Isaiah, however, would clearly amount to a contrasting "remnant theology" that insists on the persistence of the literal covenant given to historical Israel. (It should be noted that Abinadi's replacement theology may not be exactly supersessionist. He claims, in essence, that Christianity was present before Judaism, or that Judaism as historically understood was a misguided development within a Christianity that began long before the arrival of Christ. Note that Abinadi's schema of the Jewish-Christian relationship has no place in Donaldson's recent typology of supersessionisms [Donaldson, "Supersessionism and Early Christian Self-Definition].")

98. Further, of course, Abinadi's foundational philosophy of history, which roots itself in turn in his Christology, provides him with a basic interpretive approach to Isaiah. For him, everything in the pre-Christian era looks forward to the Christ event, sometimes more clearly or knowingly and sometimes less.

99. On this point, see Dunn, *Partings of the Ways*, 156–60, 220–29.

100. I took this approach, somewhat too strongly or without enough evidence, in a previous study: Spencer, *An Other Testament*; see also Spencer, *Anatomy of Book of Mormon Theology*, 1: 45–62.

101. I have provided a similarly brief analysis of Moroni's use of Isaiah 52 and Isaiah 54 in Spencer, *Anatomy of Book of Mormon Theology*, 2: 194–96.

102. Significantly, the covenantal theme introduced into Mormon's project alongside the revitalization of Isaiah never lapses again in any way. It remains a focus of Mormon's editorial project through the last part of Third Nephi (3 Nephi 28:24–32; 29–30); it shows up in a number of editorial asides in Mormon's concluding autobiographical sketch (Mormon 3:17–22; 5:8–24; 7); it appears obsessively in Moroni's reflections after his father's death (Mormon 8–9); it frames Moroni's telling of the story of a non-Nephite and non-Lamanite people, the Jaredites (Ether 2:9–12; 4:4–19; 12:22–41; 13:4–12); and it appears in Moroni's conclusion, as already noted (Moroni 10:30–31). For more on the covenantal framing of Ether, see Spencer, *Anatomy of Book of Mormon Theology*, 1: 280–84.

Chapter 6. Nursing Fathers and Nursing Mothers

1. One major interpreter has recently insisted that the common opinion that Isaiah 29:11–12 is a later addition rests on "highly subjective" evidence and is based on "the assumption that prose passages must be late expansions on the prophet's

original, purely poetic oracles." This, though, "remains simply that, an unproven assumption" (J. Roberts, *First Isaiah*, 368). For a statement of the usual position, see Blenkinsopp, *Isaiah 1–39*, 404.

2. Here again Roberts criticizes the consensus opinion that Isaiah 11 is a late text (J. Roberts, *First Isaiah*, 189). For a statement of the usual position and how it has developed, see Blenkinsopp, *Isaiah 1–39*, 263–64.

3. I have elsewhere offered a preliminary assessment of a key passage (2 Nephi 29:1–3) where all three Isaiah passages appear together (Spencer, *Vision of All*, 279–85).

4. Nephi alludes first here to Genesis 22:18, quoted in the preceding verse with the wording found in Acts 3:25. The passage from Acts appears in Christ's sermonizing in Third Nephi, underscoring continuity yet again (3 Nephi 20:23–26; Acts 3:22–26).

5. See S. K. Brown, "What Is Isaiah Doing in First Nephi?" 9: "At first blush, the question about Isaiah seems to be out of place or, at the very least, out of focus."

6. Blenkinsopp, *Isaiah 40–55*, 59–60.

7. Goldingay, *The Message of Isaiah 40–55*, 339.

8. Goldingay, *The Message of Isaiah 40–55*, 340.

9. Childs, *Isaiah*, 377.

10. Four instances of the verb "to declare" are added to the text in the Book of Mormon rendering of Isaiah 48, and many other differences in the text concern already extant references to declaration. For some discussion, see Spencer, *Vision of All*, 98–102.

11. For good commentary on the Isaiah text itself, see Goldingay and Payne, *Critical and Exegetical Commentary on Isaiah 40–55*, 2: 194–95; and Goldingay, *The Message of Isaiah 40–55*, 390–92.

12. For useful histories of the idea of the lost ten tribes—including some comments on the Book of Mormon—see Benite, *The Ten Lost Tribes*; and especially Fenton, *Old Canaan in a New World*. It is of note that Nephi explicitly indicates that Isaiah 48–49 was written at some point after the scattering.

13. Two of the passages linking Jews to a history of being hated connect that history directly to the fact that "they which are at Jerusalem" will have "crucified the God of Israel" (1 Nephi 19:13; see 2 Nephi 6:8–9).

14. This is a point that Terryl Givens has expanded on at length (Givens, *2nd Nephi*).

15. Commentaries on 1 Nephi 22:6 ignore the grammatical difficulty here. A possibility I ignore here is that the thought *is* finished, but in a sentence using non-standard English grammar. On this point, see R. Skousen, *History of the Text of the Book of Mormon*, 2: 362–76 (although Skousen does not include this example in his treatment).

16. I have commented on these points in Spencer, *Vision of All*, 132–35; and Spencer, *Anatomy of Book of Mormon Theology*, 2: 19–44.

17. The word *work* is one of several terms that form a technical lexicon in Isaiah, referring to what God accomplishes in and through history (Wildberger, *Isaiah 1–12*, 202–4). It is striking and important that, from the very beginning, Nephi fixes on the importance of this central term from Isaiah.

18. Nephi, however, entirely ignores the references to kings and queens, focusing on the fact that it is from among the gentiles that those who nurse Israel come. Jacob seems more invested in the political stakes of Isaiah's reference to royalty, drawing out political consequences for latter-day America in his likening in 2 Nephi 10.

19. See, for instance, Goldingay, *The Message of Isaiah 40–55*, 391; and Williamson, *The Book Called Isaiah*, 63–67. In connection with the Book of Mormon, see Bowen, "'The Messiah Will Set Himself Again.'"

20. It is worth noting that in both texts, Nephi seems to understand Isaiah's reference to "the people" ("set up my standard to the people") to refer to Israel, while it seems straightforwardly to refer to gentiles in its original context in Isaiah. See, for instance, the straightforward assumption of a standard commentary that this is the meaning of the term: G. Smith, *Isaiah 40–66*, 369–71.

21. It is interesting that the angel attributes beauty directly to those publishing peace, rather than to their feet—as in the original Isaiah text. We have seen that Nephi expresses less interest than Jacob in Isaiah's prediction that gentile kings and queens will "lick up the dust" of Israel's feet. Further, though, Nephi's quotation of Isaiah 49 in 1 Nephi 21 contains an addition (to the biblical version) that also focuses on feet: "the feet of them which are in the east shall be established" (1 Nephi 21:13). This line appears immediately before a command issued to the "mountains" to "break forth into singing" (21:13).

22. Christ uses the verb "to gather" eighteen times in Third Nephi, and Mormon uses it twice in anticipation of Christ's uses of it (3 Nephi 5:24, 26; 10:4–6; 16:5; 20:13, 18, 29, 33; 21:1, 24, 28; 22:7).

23. See 3 Nephi 5:25; 29:1.

24. The verb "to gather" appears twelve times in Nephi's record, sometimes in quotations of Isaiah (e.g., 1 Nephi 21:5, 8; 2 Nephi 21:12), sometimes in quotations of other Hebrew prophets (e.g., 1 Nephi 19:16), but most often in his own name (e.g., 1 Nephi 10:14; 22:12, 25; 2 Nephi 6:11; 9:2; 10:8; 29:14; 30:7). The verb *to restore* and the noun *restoration* appear thirteen relevant times in Nephi's record (1 Nephi 15:19–20; 21:6; 2 Nephi 3:13, 24; 9:2; 10:2, 7; 25:11, 17; 30:5, 8).

25. There is little question that the Third Nephi sermons feel roughhewn. Is the reader to understand that Christ works his way toward his point by taking several approaches in a row, reviewing the same general theme in different ways and through different texts? Or is the reader to assume that Mormon's editorial hand plays a role in obscuring Christ's sermons, since Mormon explains that he largely eliminates many of Christ's teachings (3 Nephi 26:6–12)?

26. Apart from the two borrowings from Matthew 7, the only instances of the verb "to liken" appear in Nephi's record and in the small Book of Jacob, written by Nephi's brother (1 Nephi 19:23–24; 22:8; 2 Nephi 6:5; 11:2, 8; Jacob 5:3; 6:1).

27. Jews are specifically in view here because New World Israel is to be established "in this land," the Americas, which "shall be a *New* Jerusalem" (3 Nephi 20:22, emphasis added).

28. See the discussion in chapter 4 herein and, again, in Strathearn and Moody, "Christ's Interpretation of Isaiah 52's 'My Servant' in 3 Nephi."

Notes to Chapter 6

29. Isaiah 49 has a privileged place also in Jewish lectionaries (Sawyer, *Isaiah through the Centuries*, 289).

30. Saint Augustine already drew such a connection in an Epiphany sermon in the early medieval period (Wilken, *Isaiah*, 373–74).

31. See, for example, Blenkinsopp, *Isaiah 56–66*, 215–16.

32. Sawyer, *Isaiah through the Centuries*, 362. The Book of Common Prayer establishes Isaiah 60 as the focus of the lesson for Matins on Epiphany and Isaiah 49 as the focus of the lesson for Evensong on Epiphany.

33. For some context, see Jacobs, *Book of Common Prayer*, 61–112.

34. This is Hymn 805 in Caldwell, *Service of Song for Baptist Churches*, 540–41. That the hymn was familiar earlier is clear from its printing in an 1824 collection of "missionary hymns" (Kelly, *Missionary Hymns*, 16–17).

35. This interpretation is also reflected in well-known musical pieces by George Frederick Handel and Henry Purcell, both originally written for coronation ceremonies (Sawyer, *Isaiah through the Centuries*, 292).

36. Henry, *Exposition of the Old and New Testaments*, 4: 226.

37. Henry, *Exposition of the Old and New Testaments*, 4: 227.

38. Henry, *Exposition of the Old and New Testaments*, 4: 227.

39. Poole, *Annotations upon the Holy Bible*, 2: 439–40.

40. Clarke, *The Holy Bible*, 3: 833.

41. See the June 3, 1817, letter by Rev. Ebenezer Henderson in *Methodist Magazine for the Year of Our Lord 1818*, 28, and Coggeshall, "Progress and Final Triumph of the Gospel," 67.

42. J. Edwards, *History of the Work of Redemption*, 395.

43. Evans, *Sketch of the Denominations of the Christian World*, 291.

44. Winchester, *Course of Lectures*, 1: 157 (Isaiah 49 quoted on 141–42).

45. Eyre, *Observations upon the Prophecies*, 21.

46. Eyre, *Observations upon the Prophecies*, 129.

47. See especially Persuitte, *Joseph Smith and the Origins of the* Book of Mormon.

48. Fenton, *Old Canaan in a New World*, 55–84, has done much more than previous commentators to contextualize the work of Ethan Smith.

49. E. Smith, *View of the Hebrews*, 31.

50. E. Smith, *View of the Hebrews*, 31.

51. E. Smith, *View of the Hebrews*, 31.

52. For some general context, see Benite, *Ten Lost Tribes*, 169–98; but see also, by way of clarification and qualification, Fenton, "Nephites and Israelites."

53. E. Smith, *View of the Hebrews*, 34.

54. E. Smith, *View of the Hebrews*, 36. Smith cites (by name, but not as specific sources) Thomas Scott and Bishop (Robert) Lowth.

55. E. Smith, *View of the Hebrews*, 47.

56. E. Smith, *View of the Hebrews*, 48.

57. E. Smith, *View of the Hebrews*, 48, italics in original.

58. Smith takes Zion, referred to in the text, to refer to Jews gathered anew in Palestine. Modern critical interpreters of the text take Zion instead to be "personified

Jerusalem," the city itself, who asks about her lost children and about the identity of the newcomers (Blenkinsopp, *Isaiah 40–55*, 311). Conservative interpreters are more reticent to reduce Zion to the city rather than to the city *and* its people. See, for example, Oswalt, *The Book of Isaiah*, 2: 304–7.

59. E. Smith, *View of the Hebrews*, 50, italics in original.

60. E. Smith, *View of the Hebrews*, 42, 48.

61. Goldingay, *The Message of Isaiah 40–55*, 391.

62. By contrast, the Book of Mormon refers to gentiles 146 times in its nearly six hundred pages—a frequency almost four times as great as Smith's *View of the Hebrews*.

63. E. Smith, *View of the Hebrews*, xxxii, xxxiv, 41, 42, 187, 192, 193, 198, 201, 208.

64. E. Smith, *View of the Hebrews*, 38.

65. E. Smith, *View of the Hebrews*, 176.

66. E. Smith, *Dissertation on the Prophecies*, 224–25.

67. E. Smith, *View of the Hebrews*, 176. Smith says he was unaware when he published his 1823 first edition of *View of the Hebrews* of McDonald, *Isaiah's Message to the American Nation*, discovering the latter only as he prepared his second edition (Smith, *View of the Hebrews*, 193–94).

68. For a brief outline of the history of such arguments, see Smith, *View of the Hebrews*, ix–xix.

69. See especially Smith's earlier *Dissertation on the Prophecies*.

70. Making Smith still more marginal, of course, was his view that ancient America had been peopled by Israelites. On this point, see Benite, *Lost Ten Tribes*, 184: "By the beginning of the nineteenth century, the idea that Indians were Israelites had exhausted itself in the face of the overwhelming evidence to the contrary. Only a renewed theological thrust [such as that in the Book of Mormon] could keep it alive. In 1832, the polymath and natural scientist Constantine Samuel Rafinesque (1783–1840) attacked in his *Atlantic Journal* the 'singular but absurd opinion that American tribes are descended from the Hebrews or the ten lost tribes.'"

71. See, for example, Brodie, *No Man Knows My History*, 46: "Ethan Smith's theory of the origin of the Indian mounds was exactly the same as that which formed the heart of the Book of Mormon story." By contrast, see Fenton, *Old Canaan in a New World*, 115: The Book of Mormon "refutes the lost tribes version of the Hebraic Indian [theory] and thereby calls into question the theory's place within millenarian eschatology."

Chapter 7. The Structure of Nephi's Record

1. I have undertaken this structural work—in several stages—in previous publications. A first outline of Nephi's project appears in Spencer, *An Other Testament*, 33–68. I offer a critique of this early approximation in the second edition (pp. xiii–xvi). A better analysis appears in Spencer, *Vision of All*, 37–58, and again in Spencer, *1st Nephi*, 10–24.

2. The approach is visible in popular Latter-day Saint usage of Nephi's language, but also in scholarly commentaries. See, for instance, Reynolds and Sjodahl, *Commentary on the Book of Mormon*, 1: 206, and Gardner, *Second Witness*, 1: 373.

Notes to Chapter 7

3. I have laid out this argument in different ways before: in terms of differentiating likening from typological interpretation in Spencer, *An Other Testament*, 69–104; and more specifically in terms of Nephi's interpretive project in Spencer, *Vision of All*, 74–79, 127–29, 147–50.

4. Howe, "Long Consequential Journey," xvii.

5. Hardy, *Understanding the Book of Mormon*, 9.

6. McConkie, *Mormon Doctrine*, 204.

7. See McConkie and Millet, *Doctrinal Commentary*, vol. 1, and Nyman, *I Nephi Wrote This Record*, vol. 1.

8. Nyman and Tate, *First Nephi*; and Nyman, *Second Nephi*.

9. Nyman and Tate, *First Nephi*, ix. See also McConkie and Millet, *Doctrinal Commentary*, 1: xv.

10. Reynolds, "Political Dimension," quote on p. 1; Gardner, *Second Witness*, 1: 43, 47.

11. Gardner, *Second Witness*, 2: 15. Also, more recently, Gardner, *Labor Diligently to Write*, 133–258, Reynolds, "Nephi's Outline," and Reynolds, "Chiastic Structuring."

12. For a summary introduction to Welch's work on chiasmus, see Welch, "Chiasmus in the Book of Mormon"; for debate about Welch's approach, see Wunderli, "Critique of Alma 36 as an Extended Chiasm," and Edwards and Edwards, "Does Chiasmus Appear in the Book of Mormon by Chance?"

13. Sperry, *Book of Mormon Compendium*, 94–95, 144–45.

14. S. K. Brown, "Nephi, First Book of," 590. For a summary statement of Brown's work on Nephi and Arabia, see S. K. Brown, "New Light from Arabia."

15. J. Thomas, *Pentecostal Reads the Book of Mormon*, 31. It is worth noting that Thomas's attention to the "and thus it is, amen" refrain is preceded by Reynolds's chiastic reading of First Nephi, although, as Thomas points out, Reynolds's structuring overlooks or ignores a key instance of the formula (J. Thomas, *Pentecostal Reads the Book of Mormon*, 31–32; Reynolds, "Nephi's Outline," 58).

16. Axelgard, "1 and 2 Nephi."

17. Reynolds has criticized Axelgard's reading and my own attempts to build on Axelgard. Reynolds's critiques—which hit their mark only as regards my earlier work—show the need to accept Axelgard's key insights without drawing hasty conclusions (Reynolds, "On Doubting Nephi's Break between 1 and 2 Nephi").

18. J. Thomas, *Pentecostal Reads the Book of Mormon*, 39. Also recently, William Davis points out ways that book headings in Nephi's writings can work to organize the narrative in a premeditated fashion (W. Davis, *Visions in a Seer Stone*, 122–59).

19. For examples, see not only Mormon's occasional headings (like the ones that appear before Mosiah 9 or Alma 5), but more especially editorial formulas like "now we will return" from one story to another (used in Alma 3:13, 22:1, and 47:1) and "we shall say no more concerning" a specific story (used in Alma 43:2).

20. Evidence from the original manuscript makes clear that Joseph Smith and his scribes did not anticipate any division between the two distinct books of Nephi. When they came to the end of First Nephi, Smith's scribe initially wrote "chapter" in the manuscript, indicating that both he and Smith understood the break after 1

Nephi 22 to be just another chapter break within the single (or at least continued) Book of Nephi. But the first words dictated from the assumed new chapter were "The Book of Nephi, an account of." See the discussion in R. Skousen, *Analysis of Textual Variants of the Book of Mormon*, 1: 490–92.

21. Early commentators noted this point; see Ricks, *Book of Mormon Commentary*, 1: 35, 110; Sperry, *Book of Mormon Compendium*, 93–94. More recent commentators have noted it as well; for example, Reynolds, "Nephi's Outline," 56, and Gardner, *Second Witness*, 1: 187.

22. Sperry, *Our Book of Mormon*, 44–45.

23. It seems peculiar to describe the second half of First Nephi as focused in any way on Nephi's "reign," since he does not assume any kind of strict royal position until Second Nephi (2 Nephi 5:18). Noel Reynolds offers a possible explanation in "Nephite Kingship Reconsidered," proposing that 1 Nephi 17 amounts to a political-theological reflection on the nature of kingship.

24. Axelgard, "1 and 2 Nephi," 55.

25. Commentators tend to recognize the connection between these two passages (see, for instance, Ricks, *Book of Mormon Commentary*, 229; McConkie and Millet, *Doctrinal Commentary*, 1: 145), but only Axelgard seems to have recognized that the connection has specifically *structural* implications.

26. Axelgard, "1 and 2 Nephi," 55. Just as in 1 Nephi 1:16–17, Nephi here uses the words "after" and "then" together to outline the structure of his two books.

27. Even if most commentators have missed the structural significance of the connection between 1 Nephi 19:1–5 and 2 Nephi 5:28–34, most do recognize the clear seismic shift in genre that occurs when 2 Nephi 5 gives way to 2 Nephi 6.

28. These are details Axelgard overlooks. In essence, he simply divides the whole of Nephi's record into two parts, "one historical" and "one spiritual," with the dividing line between 2 Nephi 5 and 2 Nephi 6 (Axelgard, "1 and 2 Nephi," 55). Reynolds seems right to me to worry how such an interpretation effectively disregards "Nephi's division of his writing into two books" (Reynolds, "On Doubting Nephi's Break between 1 and 2 Nephi," 91).

29. The division of 2 Nephi 6–30 into three sequences, each representing the words or prophecies of one of three witnesses, has become traditional—presumably because it is so clear in the text.

30. Here, again, the key passage marking out the general structure of this privileged sequence of Nephi's record is 2 Nephi 11:1–3.

31. J. C. Thomas, *Pentecostal Reads the Book of Mormon*, 31.

32. For a very brief account of the production of the 1879 Latter-day Saint edition, see Turley and Slaughter, *How We Got the Book of Mormon*, 81–91.

33. Gutjahr, *The "Book of Mormon,"* 91–97; as well as Gutjahr, "Orson Pratt's Enduring Influence on the *Book of Mormon*." See also Amy Easton-Flake, "Knowing the Book Better."

34. Other branches of the religious movement begun by Joseph Smith continue to utilize the original chapter breaks.

35. Longman and Enns, *Dictionary of the Old Testament*, 323.

36. All these *inclusio* sequences in the first two original chapters of First Nephi focus on books and records and writings: (1) the pericope that opens the first chapter tells of a book in heaven, which Nephi's father has a chance to read; (2) the pericope that closes the first chapter tells of a book brought from Jerusalem, which Nephi's family takes with them into the wilderness; (3) the editorial comment that opens the second chapter describes the writings of Nephi's father, distinct from Nephi's own writings; and (4) the editorial comment that closes the second chapter describes Nephi's large plates, distinct from the small plates with which Nephi's readers are familiar. Because Nephi turns directly to the account of his own life beginning a verse after the last of these four sequences, it seems that he uses structure to bring his readers from the remotest of books (the book in heaven, and then the book from ancient Jerusalem) to the most proximate of books (his father's record, and then his own large plates) to the one the reader has in her hands.

37. In some other cases elsewhere in the Book of Mormon, it is much more difficult to determine Pratt's reasons for obscuring original chapter breaks in the text.

38. Extracting these from the original chapter VI left Pratt with only a paragraph or two over—words of introduction to Isaiah. These paragraphs would have created an exceedingly short third chapter to be extracted from the original chapter VI. Apparently for this reason, Pratt decided to group the first paragraphs of the original chapter VI with his own chapter 19 (now verses 22–24) as if they were the last paragraphs of the original chapter V.

39. First Nephi in this way embodies structurally what would quickly come to be a basic theological commitment for Latter-day Saints: the need for both ancient written prophecies *and* modern oral prophecies. For some context, see Holland, *Sacred Borders*.

40. There is a substantial literature on Nephi's psalm, but the literature universally overlooks the way the text clearly invites the reader to see the psalm as a direct response to and reflection on the conflict between Nephi and his brothers—and therefore the dawning conflict between warring nations. See especially 2 Nephi 4:13–14, 22, 27; 5:1. See also Sperry, *Book of Mormon Compendium*, 151–53; Sondrup, "Psalm of Nephi"; Rust, *Feasting on the Word*, 71–75; Nickerson, "Nephi's Psalm"; and Hardy, *Understanding the Book of Mormon*, 55–57.

41. For some discussion of Jacob's more direct focus on Jewish history (by contrast with Nephi's prophetic style), see Spencer, *Vision of All*, 127–39. The specific Isaiah texts addressed by Jacob are Isaiah 49:22–52:2.

42. Bracke, "Branch," 1: 776. For a recent and helpful intervention that favors finding messianic imagery in Isaiah, see Heskett, *Messianism within the Scriptural Scrolls of Isaiah*. For a more minimalist reading of the whole of the Hebrew Bible, see Fitzmyer, *One Who Is to Come*.

43. Garold Davis argues that 1 Nephi 10 already sketches this basic history, in words Nephi attributes to Lehi and positions as the opening of his own proceedings in First Nephi (G. Davis, "Pattern and Purpose of the Isaiah Commentaries"). A similar approach appears in Hardy, *Understanding the Book of Mormon*, 61–65.

44. Lehi's prophetic discourse in 1 Nephi 10 centers on two topics that Nephi says preoccupied his father (1 Nephi 10:8, 12): the baptism of Christ by a preparatory prophet

and the complex history of Israelite-gentile relations (summarily treated through the image of an olive tree, as in Romans 11). The vast majority of Nephi's record focuses on the latter of these two themes, but two key texts narrow in on the former topic, Christ's baptism. Nephi witnesses the event in his own vision in 1 Nephi 11:26–28, where the event is suggestively described as "the condescension of God." And then Nephi returns to the topic at the very conclusion of his record, using it as a starting point for explaining "the doctrine of Christ" (in 2 Nephi 31:2, 4–12).

45. It is worth underscoring the fact that Nephi divides his record into two books. No other contributor to the Nephite records is said to have divided his record into two books. There is no "First Alma" and "Second Alma," for instance, but just "the Book of Alma." (Although one might suggest that the books of Third Nephi and Fourth Nephi suggest a parallel, these two books were originally dictated as being, each of them, "The Book of Nephi." Each is associated with a distinct person named Nephi. They do not form parts of a single, larger record.)

46. C. Bushman, "Big Lessons from Little Books," xvi.

47. Hardy, *Understanding the Book of Mormon*, 58–59.

48. Hardy, *Understanding the Book of Mormon*, 59.

49. Of course, some have insisted on seeing the quotations of Isaiah as actually focused on the narrative events recorded in First and Second Nephi. On this score, see especially S. K. Brown, "What Is Isaiah Doing in First Nephi?" Hardy plays up this possibility as well in the last part of First Nephi, although he speaks consistently of "a double perspective," recognizing that the first aim of the Isaiah content is always to attend to Nephi's "prophetic interpretation of world history" (Hardy, *Understanding the Book of Mormon*, 61, 70–76).

50. Underscoring the archetypal nature of the imagery, one student of the Book of Mormon has attempted a full interpretation of the dream through the lens of Jungian psychology (Maddox, "Lehi's Vision of the Tree of Life").

51. Jorgensen, "Dark Way to the Tree" and also Belnap, "Even as Our Father Lehi Saw." The influence of the dream escapes the bounds of the text as well. In a late account of the Smith family's story, Joseph Smith's mother told of her husband having a dream that closely follows the details of Lehi's dream (Anderson, *Lucy's Book*, 297–98). The memoir dates the dream to 1811, long before the dictation of the Book of Mormon, which has led many to claim that Joseph Smith simply reproduced his father's dream in the Book of Mormon. The memoir itself dates to 1853, however, long after the publication of the Book of Mormon. It seems most likely that the Book of Mormon shaped the recollection of Smith's mother, in light of other evidence that she was an avid reader of the book and was given to using its language in her everyday communication (Johnson, "Becoming a People of the Books," 34–36).

52. Spencer, *1st Nephi*, 26–43.

53. Hardy, "Prophetic Perspectives, 202.

54. Gardner, *Second Witness*, 1: 176.

55. Halverson, "Lehi's Dream and Nephi's Vision," 54, 58. Halverson suggests that the dream presents in spatial terms what Nephi's subsequent vision translates into historical or temporal terms.

56. For a remarkably tight literary analysis of the vision and the history it outlines, see Easton-Flake, "Lehi's Dream as a Template."

57. For some of the more influential works that have spurred the current consensus on overall literary unity in the Book of Isaiah, see Clements, "Unity of the Book of Isaiah," Vermeylen, "L'unité du livre d'Isaïe," Rendtorff, "The Book of Isaiah," and Rendtorff, *Canon and Theology*, 146–69. Behind all of these arguably lies Childs, *Introduction to the Old Testament as Scripture*, 311–38.

58. For the literary-structural details, as well as the whole historical story assumed here, see Conrad, *Reading Isaiah*, and Williamson, *The Book Called Isaiah*.

59. Conrad suggests that the command to the new prophetic figure in Isaiah 40, translated "Cry!" in most English versions of the Bible, would be better rendered "Read!" (Conrad, *Reading Isaiah*, 137–38).

60. It was the somewhat lackluster fulfillment of these Isaian expectations that, according to most arguments, spurred the production of Third Isaiah. For a good outline of the consensus position, along with appropriate reviews of the literature, see Blenkinsopp, *Isaiah 56–66*, 27–91. I have tried, throughout this paragraph, to avoid language that would decide questions of Isaianic authorship. The consensus on the multiple authorship of Isaiah is clear, but Latter-day Saints trend against that consensus. Here I leave to one side entirely the task of deciding such questions. For good discussions of the issues, see Hardy, *Understanding the Book of Mormon*, 66–70, 291–92.

61. See, for instance, McConkie and Millet, *Doctrinal Commentary*, 1: 149, commenting on this passage: "Gospel principles do not tarnish with time, nor do they apply with greater effect in one day than in another. . . . The art of gospel teaching is to make timeless principles timely. Nephi did this by taking those prophecies that were made to the entire house of Israel and specifically applying them to his own family, who are part of the house of Israel."

62. Somewhat peculiarly, the same commentators who forgivably repeat the common interpretation of "likening" in 1 Nephi 19:23 provide a more apt analysis when they comment on 2 Nephi 6:5: "Many of Isaiah's prophecies find appropriate application among the Book of Mormon peoples. To show that their experiences harmonize perfectly with the prophecies of Isaiah, however, does not mean that these prophecies have been fulfilled. The Book of Mormon peoples are but a remnant of the house of Israel, and the ancient prophecies can only partially be fulfilled in their experiences, since the promises were given to all of Israel" (McConkie and Millet, *Doctrinal Commentary*, 1: 228).

63. None of this is to say that Nephi uses the word *liken* in a way at odds with its common meaning in English, just that he uses it to signal a rather specific task of likening—of finding likeness between a specific text and specific vision.

64. Grant Hardy has attempted to track these, noting the following quotations: Isaiah 11:11 in 2 Nephi 25:17, 2 Nephi 29:1, and 2 Nephi 29:7; Isaiah 5:24–25 in 2 Nephi 26:6; Isaiah 8:14–15 and Isaiah 3:15 in 2 Nephi 26:20; Isaiah 5:18 in 2 Nephi 26:22; Isaiah 5:26 in 2 Nephi 29:2; and Isaiah 11:4–9 in 2 Nephi 30:9, 11–15. See the footnotes in Hardy, *The Book of Mormon*, 117–34.

65. For an argument that a similar shift occurs in the middle of Abinadi's discussion of Isaiah, see Spencer, "Performative Prophecy." For an exposition of what it means for one prophet to take on the voice of another, see Webb, "Slumbering Voices."

66. Wittgenstein, *Tractatus Logico-Philosophicus*, 89 (proposition 6.54).

67. Sommer, *A Prophet Reads Scripture*.

Chapter 8. He Shall Set His Hand Again the Second Time

1. Jacob quotes Isaiah 49:24–52:2 over the course of 2 Nephi 6–8.

2. In the 1830 first edition of the Book of Mormon, the long quotation of Isaiah stretches from page 86 to page 102.

3. C. Bushman, "Big Lessons from Little Books," xiii.

4. There is a further and somewhat peculiar reference to a remnant in the original chapter X, at 2 Nephi 24:19: "But thou art cast out of thy grave like an abominable branch and the remnant of those that are slain." The parallel Isaiah text in the King James Version of the Bible does not have the word "remnant" here but "raiment." Unfortunately, the original manuscript of the Book of Mormon is no longer extant for this passage, although the copied "printer's manuscript" clearly reads "remnant" here. Royal Skousen suggests that Joseph Smith intended the word "raiment" and that this was accidentally replaced with "remnant" either in the course of original transcription of the dictation or in the copying of the printer's manuscript (R. Skousen, *Analysis of Textual Variants of the Book of Mormon*, 830–31).

5. For a classic (but short) study of the image, see Baldwin, "Ṣemaḥ as a Technical Term." This identification of "the Branch" with a messianic figure was made apparent to early modern English readers of the Bible through the capitalization of "branch" in the Book of Jeremiah in the King James Version (Jeremiah 23:5; 33:15).

6. Commentators consistently express confusion over the Hebrew text of this passage and often suggest emendations, often a reconstruction that would translate as "like a stomach-turning miscarriage" (Wildberger, *Isaiah 13–27*, 71). See also Blenkinsopp, *Isaiah 1–39*, 285; J. Roberts, *First Isaiah*, 206; and even the conservative Oswalt, *The Book of Isaiah*, 1: 324, although Oswalt ultimately concludes that "no such correction is required" to make sense of the text.

7. Brodie, *No Man Knows My History*, 58.

8. A few of the points made in these several paragraphs appear in Spencer, *Vision of All*, 155–66.

9. For a standard exegetical analysis of Isaiah 2–5, see Blenkinsopp, *Isaiah 1–39*, 188–222. For a wider-ranging discussion of the recent exegetical history of these chapters, see Childs, *Isaiah*, 23–49.

10. Sweeney, *Isaiah 1–39*, 88.

11. Perhaps with some such concern in mind, Gardner, *Second Witness*, 2: 228–29, concedes that the version in Second Nephi makes "a tighter connection" between the two biblical units but nonetheless argues that, even in the Book of Mormon, the two units remain distinct and independent. Most Latter-day Saint scholars who have commented on this variant in the Book of Mormon Isaiah text have ignored its effects on structure, preferring instead to consider whether "and then" might

be a good translation of the underlying Hebrew word. On this issue, see Vest, "The Problem of Isaiah in the Book of Mormon," 59; Tvedtnes, "Isaiah Variants in the Book of Mormon," 35; and Ellertson, "Isaiah Passages," 102—and even Wright, "Isaiah in the Book of Mormon," 230.

12. See, for instance, Brueggemann, *Isaiah 1–39*, 26, who says of Isaiah 2:5, "This brief verse seems to stand alone as a liturgical summons to trust in Yahweh. I have placed it with verses 6–22, regarding it as a summons for which the remainder of the chapter is a basis, giving a reason for heeding the summons to trust. It is alternatively possible to treat the verse as a climax to the promissory vision of verses 1–4, inviting Judah to embrace the vision of a torah-based peace."

13. Generally, commentators have failed to note the connection, although at least two mention it briefly (but without any attention to larger structural implications): Tvedtnes, "The Isaiah Variants in the Book of Mormon," 22; and Wright, "Isaiah in the Book of Mormon," 191.

14. Various points in the next several paragraphs find some expression in Spencer, *Vision of All*, 179–201.

15. For a helpful overview of the memoir hypothesis and its problems, see Childs, *Isaiah*, 52–54; but see especially Williamson, *Variations on a Theme*, 73–98. A still more recent summary of the scholarship appears in Williamson, "Recent Issues in the Study of Isaiah," 32–33.

16. J. Roberts, *First Isaiah*, 91.

17. Seitz, *Isaiah 1–39*, 111.

18. Brueggemann, *Isaiah 1–39*, 61.

19. See Evans, *To See and Not Perceive*. See the brief but broad comments in Sawyer, *Isaiah through the Centuries*, 50–51.

20. Kim, *Reading Isaiah*, 55–56. Kim borrows the phrase "strategy of prolongation" from Uhlig, *Theme of Hardening*, 141–42.

21. Some Latter-day Saints suggest, peculiarly, that the Book of Mormon version of the text removes its theological difficulties. Nyman, *Great Are the Words of Isaiah*, 50–51; V. Ludlow, *Unlocking Isaiah in the Book of Mormon*, 117–19; Gorton, *Legacy of the Brass Plates*, 202; Gardner, *Second Witness*, 2: 244; and Swint, *Compare Isaiah*, 54. For a fuller treatment, see Spencer, *Anatomy of Book of Mormon Theology*, 2: 143–67.

22. Ridderbos, *Isaiah*, 78.

23. Von Rad, *Old Testament Theology*, 2: 155.

24. This sealed-book motif is the subject of chapter 9 as well. It is to be noted, for the moment, that several interpreters have pointed out ways that the sealed-book motif gives shape to the whole of the Book of Isaiah in final form. See especially Conrad, *Reading Isaiah*; and Williamson, *The Book Called Isaiah*. Motifs from Isaiah's commission to harden, as Williamson in particular demonstrates, riddle the Book of Isaiah as a whole. It is worth noting that the same is true of the larger Book of Mormon, as Jason Combs has recently begun to demonstrate in Combs, "Narrative Fulfillment."

25. John Goldingay warns that "Isaiah does not speak of Yahweh having a plan for the whole of world history, for the whole of Israel's story or for the lives of individuals,

but it does speak of Yahweh having plans about what to do at particular moments or in particular connections, and of an overall intent that goes back centuries" (Goldingay, *Theology of the Book of Isaiah*, 135).

26. For a brilliant study of this text and this tradition, see Bordjadze, *Darkness Visible*.

27. Modern commentators generally agree that "this passage begins . . . with a reference to God doing something *again*," and "this has usually been understood as referring to the following clause *to recover the remnant of his people*, and so has been taken as a reference either to the first Exodus, with God about to move again as he did on that previous occasion . . . or to the first return from exile under Cyrus." Williamson himself argues for another possibility, with "again" (or "the second time") referring back to earlier talk in Isaiah of God stretching out his hand *against* Israel—but now, this second time, he stretches out his hand to redeem (Williamson, *Critical and Exegetical Commentary*, 2: 689–90).

28. For some speculative and interesting remarks on these connections, see Bowen, "The Messiah Will Set Himself Again."

29. See 2 Nephi 1:4, where Jacob's father Lehi announces—within a discourse that will come to be addressed to Jacob himself—having had "a vision, in the which I know that Jerusalem is destroyed."

30. Wildberger, *Isaiah 1–12*, 486; Williamson, *Isaiah 6–12*, 678. See Williamson, *Critical and Exegetical Commentary*, 2: 678–79, for discussion of other suggested emendations from the scholarly tradition.

31. Edward Young points out a similar construction in a collection of Hittite annals to motivate the grammatically peculiar words in the Hebrew text (Young, *The Book of Isaiah*, 1: 395).

32. See, for example, Young, *The Book of Isaiah*, 1: 394–95; Motyer, *The Prophecy of Isaiah*, 125–26; Oswalt, *The Book of Isaiah*, 1: 287; and G. Smith, *Isaiah 1–39*, 275–76.

33. The "second exodus" motif is often noted in the literature. For a simple introduction to it, see Blenkinsop, *Isaiah 40–55*, 111–12.

34. Henry, *Exposition of the Old and New Testament*, 4: 69–70.

35. Poole, *Annotations upon the Holy Bible*, 2: 354–55.

36. Patrick et al., *Critical Commentary and Paraphrase*, 3: 493.

37. The insertion in the middle of the quotation draws on Nephi's own exposition of Isaiah 48–49 in 1 Nephi 22:16–17. This is one of several connections between the exposition in 1 Nephi 22 and the conclusion to Nephi's own prophecy in 2 Nephi 30 (compare, for instance, 1 Nephi 22:26 and 2 Nephi 30:18).

38. Ford, *Edward Hicks*, 41.

39. Tatham, "Edward Hicks, Elias Hicks, and John Comly," 40.

40. Ford, *Edward Hicks*, 40.

41. Ford, *Edward Hicks*, 41.

42. Sawyer, *Isaiah through the Centuries*, 86.

43. Tatham, "Edward Hicks, Elias Hicks, and John Comly," 37.

44. On Hicks's influence, see Sawyer, *Isaiah through the Centuries*, 87.

45. As in Schwain, "The Bible and Art," 412.

46. Brueggemann, *Isaiah 1–39*, 101.

47. Henry, *Exposition of the Old and New Testament*, 4: 68.

48. Henry, *Exposition of the Old and New Testament*, 4: 68. See also Patrick et al., *Critical Commentary and Paraphrase*, 3: 492, and Poole, *Annotations upon the Holy Bible*, 2: 354.

49. Coggeshall, "Progress and Final Triumph of the Gospel," 66–67.

50. Mainstream commentaries from the last decades before the publication of the Book of Mormon are less forthcoming about the meaning of the text. Thomas Scott speaks of God as "the Protector of the poor and needy," but he speaks only vaguely about how God "would destroy the enemies of his kingdom" (Scott, *The Holy Bible*, s.v. Isaiah XI:2–5). Adam Clarke, moreover, says nothing about the difficulties of the text, giving his attention only to clarifying the Hebrew text underlying "with the rod of his mouth" (Clarke, *The Holy Bible*, 3: 723).

51. Bryant, *Millennarian Views*, 78.

52. Swedenborg, *Arcana Coelestia*, 2: 74.

53. This is apparent enough right within the text of Isaiah 11:9 that commentators note it. See, for instance, Brueggemann, *Isaiah 1–39*, 103.

54. That Nephi means his children in ancient times is clear when he goes on to express his worry that they might "harden their hearts against [Christ] when the law [of Moses] had ought to be done away" (2 Nephi 25:27).

Chapter 9. As One That Hath a Familiar Spirit

1. A few brief allusions appear later, one somewhat longer quotation, and one complex potential adaptation.

2. The only reference to the Book of Mormon in John Sawyer's historical commentary on Isaiah's reception comes in his discussion of Isaiah 29 (Sawyer, *Isaiah through the Centuries*, 172, 174).

3. I include in this count 2 Nephi 26:14–18 and 2 Nephi 27:1–35.

4. These phrases appear in italicized chapter headings for 2 Nephi 27 and Isaiah 29 respectively in the current edition of the volume published by the Church of Jesus Christ of Latter-day Saints.

5. For some context on Latter-day Saints in higher education in the early twentieth century, see Simpson, *American Universities*. For helpful context on Sperry's place in Book of Mormon studies, see Bowman, "Biblical Criticism."

6. Sperry, "The 'Isaiah Problem' in the Book of Mormon." Sperry was, for at least a year prior to the publication of his essay, delivering oral versions of the paper.

7. See in addition Sperry's 1926 master's thesis: Sperry, "The Text of Isaiah in the Book of Mormon."

8. Sperry, *The Book of Mormon Testifies*, 127.

9. Sperry, *The Book of Mormon Testifies*, 127. Sperry provides exactly the same account of the matter almost two decades later in Sperry, *Book of Mormon Compendium*, 249.

10. See especially the often-republished Richards, *Marvelous Work and a Wonder*, 48–49, 68–69.

11. Although dated and devotional in tone, the standard work on Smith's project of revising the Bible is Matthews, *"Plainer Translation."*

12. Faulring, Jackson, and Matthews, *Joseph Smith's New Translation of the Bible*, 3–13, 29–40, 57–59; Bushman, *Joseph Smith, Rough Stone Rolling*, 127–43.

13. For Sperry's attempt at sorting out the reliability of the "Inspired Version," see Sperry and Van Wagoner, "Inspired Revision of the Bible."

14. On the vision, see Bushman, *Joseph Smith, Rough Stone Rolling*, 195–214.

15. All the manuscripts of the revision project are available in typescript in Faulring, Jackson, and Matthews, *Joseph Smith's New Translation of the Bible*.

16. For some further discussion of the change in the revision project, see Spencer, "Moderate Millennialism."

17. Faulring, Jackson, and Matthews, *Joseph Smith's New Translation of the Bible*, 804–15. Some differences between the Book of Mormon's text and the text copied into the revision project's manuscripts occur, of course. They—as well as the whole of Smith's treatment of Isaiah in the revision project—deserve closer investigation.

18. Matthews, *"Plainer Translation"*, 253. Sperry himself argued for nuance and caution in drawing conclusions about the nature of the project. See, again, Sperry and Van Wagoner, "Inspired Revision of the Bible."

19. This inference makes some sense, since Smith's revision of other chapters of the Bible shows signs of some delay before he decided what to do with the text. For a good example (with a text that has been influential in the Latter-day Saint tradition), see Smith's revision of 1 Corinthians 7 in Faulring, Jackson, and Matthews, *Joseph Smith's New Translation of the Bible*, 500–505.

20. See, most recently, Parry, *Exploring the Isaiah Scrolls and Their Textual Variants*.

21. Parry, Parry, and Peterson, *Understanding Isaiah*, 259–74.

22. Parry, Parry, and Peterson, *Understanding Isaiah*, 264. See also Parry, *Harmonizing Isaiah*, 120–27, 273.

23. Ludlow, *Isaiah*, 268–77. Note that Ludlow later softened his approach. See Ludlow, *Unlocking Isaiah*, 203–15.

24. Nyman, *"Great Are the Words of Isaiah,"* 101.

25. Gorton, *Legacy of the Brass Plates*, 66.

26. Hartshorn, *Commentary on the Book of Mormon*, 139.

27. Howard, *Restoration Scriptures*, 112.

28. Walters, "The Use of the Old Testament in the Book of Mormon," 75.

29. McConkie and Millet, *Doctrinal Commentary*, 1: 305.

30. Wright, "Joseph Smith's Interpretation of Isaiah," 196.

31. Gileadi, *The Book of Isaiah*, 147–49. It may have been in response to Gileadi's translation that Parry produced his own. See Parry, review of *The Book of Isaiah*, by Avraham Gileadi. Gileadi's relationship to orthodoxy would prove complicated, but his translation long predated the institutional difficulties that would plague him later.

32. Reynolds and Sjodahl, *Commentary on the Book of Mormon*, 1: 385.

33. For a helpful survey of Latter-day Saint writings on Isaiah through the end of the twentieth century, see Thompson and Smith, "Isaiah and the Latter-day Saints."

34. Parry, Parry, and Peterson, *Understanding Isaiah*, 263; and Parry, *Harmonizing Isaiah*, 273.

35. See, for example, Hardy, *Understanding the Book of Mormon*, 76–86; Gardner, *Second Witness*, 2: 360–61, 377–79; and all the essays in Spencer and Webb, *Reading Nephi Reading Isaiah*.

36. Cloward, "Isaiah 29 and the Book of Mormon," 198–200.

37. Cloward, "Isaiah 29 and the Book of Mormon," 191.

38. For a detailed account of these events, with some important revisions to earlier historical reconstructions, see MacKay and Dirkmaat, *From Darkness unto Light*, 39–59.

39. Cloward, "Isaiah 29 and the Book of Mormon," 200–201;

40. Hardy and Hardy, "How Nephi Shapes His Readers' Perceptions of Isaiah," 40.

41. Gardner, *Second Witness*, 2: 377. Even an author like Victor Ludlow, who argued in the early 1980s that Nephi reveals the uncorrupted original text of Isaiah 29, by the early 2000s was arguing that Nephi weaves "inspired comments" into an expansion of Isaiah 29 (Ludlow, *Unlocking Isaiah*, 204).

42. See Wright, "Joseph Smith's Interpretation of Isaiah," 196: "There are no significant parallels (to my knowledge) to [Nephi's] interpretation of Isaiah 29 in the biblical commentaries of [Joseph Smith's] age, in contrast with the situation that exists in his interpretation" of other chapters from Isaiah.

43. Childs, *Isaiah*, 214.

44. Childs, *Isaiah*, 214.

45. For commentary, see Cloward, "Isaiah 29 in the Book of Mormon," 206–7; Hardy and Hardy, "How Nephi Shapes His Readers' Perceptions of Isaiah," 44–45.

46. Wright, "Joseph Smith's Interpretation of Isaiah," 199.

47. *Oxford English Dictionary*, s.v. "familiar."

48. W. Skousen, *Isaiah Speaks to Modern Times*, 401.

49. Pratt, *Reply to a Pamphlet Printed at Glasgow*, 11.

50. Pratt, *Reply to a Pamphlet Printed at Glasgow*, 11. See, more recently but in a similar vein, D. Ludlow, *Companion to Your Study*, 146.

51. Tvedtnes, "'Fulness of the Gospel' and 'Familiar Spirit,'" 74.

52. Johnston, *Shades of Sheol*, 151–52. See also Wildberger, *Isaiah 28–39*, 75.

53. Joseph Smith's involvement in folk magic in the years leading up to his dictation of the Book of Mormon is well documented and often commented on. See especially Ashurst-McGee, "Pathway to Prophethood."

54. A. Brown, "Out of the Dust," 34–35.

55. McConkie and Millet, *Doctrinal Commentary*, 1: 306.

56. This is often overlooked in the literature. See, for instance, Cloward, "Isaiah 29 and the Book of Mormon," 207, where the familiar spirit and "he" or "him" is conflated.

57. Brown, "Out of the Dust," 35.

58. McConkie and Millet, *Doctrinal Commentary*, 1: 306–7. McConkie and Millet base their interpretation on a related interpretation of 2 Nephi 3, drawn from the Latter-day Saint apostle Bruce R. McConkie. See p. 1: 211.

59. Nyman, *I Nephi Wrote This Record*, 649.

60. See throughout Brooke, *Refiner's Fire*.

61. S. M. Brown, *In Heaven as It Is on Earth*, 120, 124. See also Gardner, *Gift and Power*, 41; and Eliason, "Mormon Folk Culture," 464–66.

62. Here and in the following paragraphs, I adapt and develop the argument in Spencer, *Anatomy of Book of Mormon Theology*, 1: 73–89.

63. Nephi reproduces here the general language of Isaiah 8:19 (quoted in 2 Nephi 18:19), which not only refers to "familiar spirits" and "wizards that peep, and that mutter," but also asks "should not a people seek unto their God? for the living to the dead?" It should be noted, too, that Nephi's long quotation of this passage slightly and suggestively alters it: "Should not a people seek unto their God for the living to hear from the dead?"

64. MacKay and Dirkmaat, *From Darkness unto Light*, 41.

65. MacKay and Dirkmaat, *From Darkness unto Light*, 49.

66. Morris, *Documentary History*, 224–49.

67. Morris, *Documentary History*, 241. This account has been canonized in the Latter-day Saint tradition within the Pearl of Great Price; see J. Smith, "Joseph Smith—History," 1: 65.

68. Bushman, *Joseph Smith, Rough Stone Rolling*, 65.

69. Joseph Smith did not dictate the text of 2 Nephi 27 until 1829, after the Anthon incident occurred and while it was still fresh in the minds of those involved in the translation project. For unbelievers, then, the reworking of Isaiah 29 in 2 Nephi 27 looks rather straightforwardly like *vaticinium ex eventu*, a prophecy written only after the predicted event has taken place (but presented as if it were written beforehand). For most believers—especially those who take 2 Nephi 27 to reproduce the lost original text of Isaiah 29—the antiquity of the Book of Mormon's text and certainly of Isaiah's own prophecy make the Anthon incident a genuine fulfillment of ancient prophecy.

70. Handley, "On the Moral Risks of Reading Scripture," 100–101. I draw heavily from Handley's insights in the reading presented here.

71. Morris, *Documentary History*, 355–56.

72. The striking theoretical force of the fact that the Book of Mormon reflects on and predicts its own coming into existence is something often noted. For a particularly interesting approach to this question, though, see Shipps, *Mormonism*, 41–65.

73. Seitz, *Isaiah 1–39*, 214–15.

74. Brueggemann, *Isaiah 1–39*, 234.

75. G. Smith, *Isaiah 1–39*, 499.

76. Blenkinsopp, *Isaiah 1–39*, 405.

77. See, for example, Wildberger, *Isaiah 28–39*, 82.

78. Blenkinsopp, *Opening the Sealed Book*, 11.

79. Blenkinsopp points out that one of the most significant ancient commentaries on the passage is only fragmentary, found among the scraps of the Dead Sea Scrolls. "The loss of the pesher on this passage," he says, "is particularly unfortunate" (Blenkinsopp, *Opening the Sealed Book*, 122).

80. Blenkinsopp, *Opening the Sealed Book*, 18.

81. Blenkinsopp, *Opening the Sealed Book*, 23.

82. See, for example, Blenkinsopp, *Opening the Sealed Book*, 28–55. It is worth noting that Jacob Neusner's two-volume book on the uses of Isaiah in the rabbinic Talmudic and Midrashic sources contains no citations of or allusions to Isaiah 29:11–12 (Neusner, *Isaiah in Talmud and Midrash*).

83. For a range of early Christian voices making this claim, see McKinion, *Isaiah 1–39*, 201–3; and Wilken, *Isaiah Interpreted*, 246–48.

84. Exemplary are uses of Isaiah 29 by Eusebius of Caesarea and Saint Jerome (McKinion, *Isaiah 1–39*, 201–2 [*Proof of the Gospel* 8.2]; Eusebius of Caesarea, *Commentary on Isaiah*, 146–47 [paragraphs 190–91]; and Jerome, *Commentary on Isaiah*, 449 [9.10]).

85. Luther, *Lectures on Isaiah*, 243. See also Calvin, *Isaiah*, 188.

86. For scattered but dispassionate commentaries, see Henry, *Exposition of the Old and New Testament*, 4: 134; Scott, *The Holy Bible*, s.v. Isaiah XXIX:9–12; Poole, *Annotations upon the Holy Bible*, 2: 393; and Patrick et al., *Critical Commentary and Paraphrase*, 3: 524.

87. For a general introduction to Southcott and her work, see Hopkins, *A Woman to Deliver Her People*.

88. Southcott, *Strange Effects of Faith*, 3.

89. Hann, *Letter to the Right Reverend the Lord Bishop of London*, 9.

90. Leahy, "'Learned' and 'Unlearned' Reading," 183.

91. Sperry, "The Text of Isaiah in the Book of Mormon."

92. For example, Jackson, "Isaiah in the Book of Mormon."

93. For example, Wunderli, *An Imperfect Book*, 77–84.

94. Hutchinson, "The Word of God Is Enough," 1.

95. M. Thomas, *Digging in Cumorah*, 2.

96. See, classically, Midgley, "No Middle Ground"; and, more recently and from a very different angle, Williams, "The Ghost and the Machine."

97. On the idea of determination in the last instance, drawn from Marxian thought, see (in somewhat different registers) Althusser, *For Marx*; and Laruelle, *Introduction to Non-Marxism*.

98. The name I have elsewhere given to this aspect of the Book of Mormon is "nonhistorical," to be distinguished from both "historical" and "ahistorical" (Spencer, *An Other Testament*, 26–29).

Works Cited

A. "Answers to Queries." *Evangelical Magazine* 10 (1802): 533–34.
Ådna, Jostein. "The Servant of Isaiah 53 as Triumphant and Interceding Messiah: The Reception of Isaiah 52:13–53:12 in the Targum of Isaiah with Special Attention to the Concept of the Messiah." In Janowski and Stuhlmacher, *The Suffering Servant*, 189–224.
Alexander, Joseph Addison. *The Earlier Prophecies of Isaiah*. New York: Wiley and Putnam, 1846.
Alexander, Joseph Addison. *The Later Prophecies of Isaiah*. New York: Wiley and Putnam, 1847.
Althusser, Louis. *For Marx*. Translated by Ben Brewster. New York: Verso, 2005.
Anatolios, Khaled. *Athanasius*. New York: Routledge, 2004.
Anderson, Lavina Fielding, ed. *Lucy's Book: A Critical Edition of Lucy Mack Smith's Family Memoir*. Salt Lake City: Signature, 2001.
Asbury, Francis. *Journal of Rev. Francis Asbury, Bishop of the Methodist Episcopal Church*. Vol. 2, *From January 1, 1787, to December 31, 1800*. New York: Eaton and Mains, n.d.
Ashurst-McGee, Mark. "A Pathway to Prophethood: Joseph Smith Junior as Rodsman, Village Seer, and Judeo-Christian Prophet." MA thesis, Utah State University, 2000.
Axelgard, Frederick W. "1 and 2 Nephi: An Inspiring Whole." *BYU Studies* 26, no. 4 (Fall 1986): 53–66.
Badiou, Alain. *Being and Event*. Translated by Oliver Feltham. New York: Continuum, 2006.
Bailey, Daniel P. "'Our Suffering and Crucified Messiah' (Dial. 111.2): Justin Martyr's Allusions to Isaiah 53 in His Dialogue with Trypho with Special Reference to

the New Edition of M. Marcovich." In Janowski and Stuhlmacher, *The Suffering Servant*, 324–417.

Baldwin, Joyce G. "Ṣemaḥ as a Technical Term in the Prophets," *Vetus Testamentum* 14, no. 1 (January 1964): 93–97.

The Baptist Magazine for 1810, Vol. 2. London: J. Burditt and W. Button, 1810.

The Baptist Magazine for 1819, Vol. 11. London: J. Barfield, 1819.

Barlow, Philip L. *Mormons and the Bible: The Place of the Latter-day Saints in American Religion*. New York: Oxford University Press, 1991.

Beal, Timothy. *The Book of Revelation: A Biography*. Princeton, NJ: Princeton University Press, 2018.

Beale, G. K., and D. A. Carson, eds. *Commentary on the New Testament Use of the Old Testament*, Grand Rapids, MI: Baker Academic, 2007.

Belnap, Daniel L. "'Even as Our Father Lehi Saw': Lehi's Dream as Nephite Cultural Narrative." In Belnap, Strathearn, and Johnson, *The Things Which My Father Saw*, 214–39.

Belnap, Daniel L. "'For the Lord Redeemeth None Such': The Abinadi Narrative, Redemption, and the Struggle of Nephite Identity." In *Abinadi: He Came Among Them in Disguise*, edited by Shon D. Hopkin, 27–66. Salt Lake City: Deseret; and Provo, UT: BYU Religious Studies Center, 2018.

Belnap, Daniel L., Gaye Strathearn, and Stanley A. Johnson, eds. *The Things Which My Father Saw: Approaches to Lehi's Dream and Nephi's Vision*. Provo, UT: BYU Religious Studies Center, 2011.

Benite, Zvi Ben-Dor. *The Ten Lost Tribes: A World History*. New York: Oxford University Press, 2009.

Bettenson, Henry, and Chris Maunder, eds. *Documents of the Christian Church*. 4th ed. New York: Oxford University Press, 2011.

Betz, Hans Dieter. *Galatians: A Commentary on Paul's Letter to the Churches in Galatia*. Philadelphia: Fortress, 1979.

Blenkinsopp, Joseph. *Isaiah 1–39: A New Translation with Introduction and Commentary*. New Haven, CT: Yale University Press, 2000.

Blenkinsopp, Joseph. *Isaiah 40–55: A New Translation with Introduction and Commentary*. New York: Doubleday, 2000.

Blenkinsopp, Joseph. *Isaiah 56–66: A New Translation with Introduction and Commentary*. New York: Doubleday, 2003.

Blenkinsopp, Joseph. *Opening the Sealed Book: Interpretations of the Book of Isaiah in Late Antiquity*. Grand Rapids, MI: Eerdmans, 2006.

Blomberg, Craig L. "Matthew." In Beale and Carson, *Commentary on the New Testament Use of the Old Testament*, 1–109.

Blythe, Christopher James. *Terrible Revolution: Latter-day Saints and the American Apocalypse*. New York: Oxford University Press, 2020.

Bock, Darrell L., and Mitch Glaser, eds. *The Gospel According to Isaiah 53: Encountering the Suffering Servant in Jewish and Christian Theology*. Grand Rapids, MI: Kregel, 2012.

Bordjadze, Karlo V. *Darkness Visible: A Study of Isaiah 14:3–23 as Christian Scripture*. Eugene, OR: Pickwick, 2017.

Boring, M. Eugene. *Disciples and the Bible: A History of Disciples Biblical Interpretation in North America*. St. Louis, MO: Chalice, 1997.

Bowen, Matthew L. "'The Messiah Will Set Himself Again': Jacob's Use of Isaiah 11:11 in 2 Nephi 6:14 and Jacob 6:2." *Interpreter* 44 (2021): 287–306.

Bowman, Matthew. "Biblical Criticism, the Book of Mormon, and the Meanings of Civilization." *Journal of Book of Mormon Studies* (2021): 62–89.

Bracke, John M. "Branch." In *Anchor Bible Dictionary*, edited by David Noel Freedman, 1: 776–77. New York: Doubleday, 1992.

Bradley, Don. *The Lost 116 Pages: Reconstructing the Book of Mormon's Missing Sources*. Salt Lake City: Greg Kofford, 2019.

Brodie, Fawn M. *No Man Knows My History: The Life of Joseph Smith, the Mormon Prophet*. 2nd ed. New York: Vintage, 1995.

Brooke, George J. "On Isaiah at Qumran." In *"As Those Who Are Taught": The Interpretation of Isaiah from the LXX to the SBL*, edited by Claire Mathews McGinnis and Patricia K. Tull, 69–85. Atlanta: Society of Biblical Literature, 2006.

Brooke, John L. *The Refiner's Fire: The Making of Mormon Cosmology, 1644–1844*. New York: Cambridge University Press, 1994.

Brown, Amanda Colleen. "Out of the Dust: An Examination of Necromancy as a Literary Construct in the Book of Mormon." *Studia Antiqua* 14, no. 2 (Fall 2015): 27–37.

Brown, Raymond E. *The Gospel According to John (I–XII): Introduction, Translation, and Notes*. New Haven, CT: Yale University Press, 2008.

Brown, Samuel Morris. *In Heaven as It Is on Earth: Joseph Smith and the Early Mormon Conquest of Death*. New York: Oxford University Press, 2012.

Brown, S. Kent. "Nephi, First Book of." In *Book of Mormon Reference Companion*, edited by Dennis L. Largey, 589–92. Salt Lake City: Deseret, 2003.

Brown, S. Kent. "New Light from Arabia on Lehi's Trail." In *Echoes and Evidences of the Book of Mormon*, edited by Donald W. Parry, Daniel C. Peterson, and John W. Welch, 55–125. Provo, UT: FARMS, 2002.

Brown, S. Kent. "What Is Isaiah Doing in First Nephi?" or, "How Did Lehi's Family Fare so Far from Home?" In *From Jerusalem to Zarahemla: Literary and Historical Studies of the Book of Mormon*, 9–27. Provo, UT: BYU Religious Studies Center, 1998.

Brownlee, William Hugh. *The Meaning of the Qumrân Scrolls for the Bible, with Special Attention to the Book of Isaiah*. New York: Oxford University Press, 1964.

Brueggemann, Walter. *Isaiah 1–39*. Westminster Bible Companion. Louisville, KY: Westminster John Knox, 1998.

Brueggemann, Walter. *Isaiah 40–66*. Westminster Bible Companion. Louisville, KY: Westminster John Knox, 1998.

Bryant, Alfred. *Millennarian Views with Reasons for Receiving Them, to Which Is Added a Discourse on the Fact and Nature of the Resurrection*. New York: M. W. Dodd, 1852.

Bultmann, Rudolf. *The Gospel of John: A Commentary*. Translated by G. R. Beasley-Murray. Oxford, UK: Basil Blackwell, 1971.

Bultmann, Rudolf. *Theology of the New Testament*. 2 vols. Translated by Kendrick Grobel, 1951–55. New York: Scribner's.

Bushman, Claudia L. "Big Lessons from Little Books." In *The Reader's Book of Mormon*, 7 vols., edited by Robert A. Rees and Eugene England, 2: vii–xxii. Salt Lake City: Signature, 2008.

Bushman, Richard Lyman. "The Book of Mormon and the American Revolution." In *Believing History: Latter-day Saint Essays*, edited by Reid L. Neilson and Jed Woodworth, 47–64. New York: Columbia University Press, 2004.

Bushman, Richard Lyman. *Joseph Smith, Rough Stone Rolling: A Cultural Biography of Mormonism's Founder*. New York: Alfred A. Knopf, 2005.

Bushman, Richard Lyman. "The Lamanite View of Book of Mormon History." In *Believing History: Latter-day Saint Essays*, edited by Reid L. Neilson and Jed Woodworth, 79–92. New York: Columbia University Press, 2004.

Byrd, James P. *Sacred Scripture, Sacred War: The Bible and the American Revolution*. New York: Oxford University Press, 2013.

Bytheway, John. *Isaiah for Airheads*. Salt Lake City: Deseret, 2006.

Caldwell, Samuel Lunt. *The Service of Song for Baptist Churches*. New and enlgd. ed. New York: Sheldon and Company, 1876.

Calvin, John. *Commentary on the Book of the Prophet Isaiah*. 4 vols. Translated by William Pringle. Grand Rapids, MI: Eerdmans, 1948.

Calvin, John. *Isaiah*. Wheaton, IL: Crossway, 2000.

Campbell, Alexander. *Delusions: An Analysis of the Book of Mormon with an Examination of Its Internal and External Evidences, and a Refutation of Its Pretences to Divine Authority*. Boston: Benjamin H. Greene, 1832.

Case, Rev. Wm. "Grand River Mission." Pp. 110–11 in *The Methodist Magazine, Designed as a Compend of Useful Knowledge, and of Religious and Missionary Intelligence, for the Year of Our Lord 1825*. New York: N. Bangs and J. Emory, 1825.

Chase, Randal S. *Making Isaiah Plain: An Old Testament Study Guide for the Book of Isaiah*. Washington, UT: Plain and Precious, 2010.

Childs, Brevard S. *Introduction to the Old Testament as Scripture*. Philadelphia: Fortress, 1979.

Childs, Brevard S. *Isaiah*. Louisville, KY: Westminster John Knox, 2001.

Childs, Brevard S. *The Struggle to Understand Isaiah as Christian Scripture*. Grand Rapids, MI: Eerdmans, 2004.

Chilton, Bruce D. *The Glory of Israel: The Theology and Provenience of the Isaiah Targum*. Sheffield, UK: JSOT, 1982.

Chilton, Bruce D. *The Isaiah Targum: Introduction, Translation, Apparatus and Notes*. Collegeville, MN: Liturgical Press, 1987.

Chilton, Bruce D. *Visions of the Apocalypse: Receptions of John's Revelation in Western Imagination*. Waco, TX: Baylor University Press, 2013.

Christensen, Duane. L. *Nahum: A New Translation with Introduction and Commentary*. New Haven, CT: Yale University Press, 2009.

Clarke, Adam. *The Holy Bible, Containing the Old and New Testaments: The Text Printed from the Most Correct Copies of the Present Authorized Translation, Including the*

Marginal Readings and Parallel Texts, with a Commentary and Critical Notes. 6 vols. New York: J. Emory and B. Waugh, 1829.

Clements, Ronald E. "The Unity of the Book of Isaiah." *Interpretation* 36 (1982): 117–29.

Cloward, Robert A. "Isaiah 29 and the Book of Mormon." In Parry and Welch, *Isaiah in the Book of Mormon*, 191–247.

Cogan, Mordechai. "Into Exile: From the Assyrian Conquest of Israel to the Fall of Babylon." In *The Oxford History of the Biblical World*, edited by Michael D. Coogan, 321–65. New York: Oxford University Press, 1998.

Coggeshall, S. W. "The Progress and Final Triumph of the Gospel." *Methodist Magazine and Quarterly Review* 20 (1838): 65–80. New York: T. Mason and G. Lane.

Combs, Jason R. "The Narrative Fulfillment of Isaiah 6 in 3 Nephi 11." *Journal of Book of Mormon Studies* 29 (2020): 289–98.

Conrad, Edgar W. *Reading Isaiah*. Minneapolis: Fortress, 1991.

Cross, Whitney R. *The Burned-Over District: The Social and Intellectual History of Enthusiastic Religion in Western New York, 1800–1850*. Ithaca, NY: Cornell University Press, 1950.

Dabney, J. P. *Annotations on the New Testament: Compiled from the Best Critical Authorities and Designed for Popular Use*. Cambridge, MA: Hilliard and Brown, 1829.

Davies, Douglas James. *Joseph Smith, Jesus, and Satanic Opposition: Atonement, Evil, and the Mormon Vision*. Burlington, VT: Ashgate, 2010.

Davis, Garold N. "Pattern and Purpose of the Isaiah Commentaries in the Book of Mormon." In *Mormons, Scripture, and the Ancient World: Studies in Honor of John L. Sorenson*, edited by Davis Bitton, 277–303. Provo, UT: FARMS, 1998.

Davis, William L. *Visions in a Seer Stone: Joseph Smith and the Making of the Book of Mormon*. Chapel Hill: University of North Carolina Press, 2020.

Dick, Everett N. *William Miller and the Advent Crisis, 1831–1844*. Berrien Spring, MI: Andrews University Press, 1994.

Doan, Ruth Alden. *The Miller Heresy, Millennialism, and American Culture*. Philadelphia: Temple University Press, 1987.

Dodd, C. H. *The Interpretation of the Fourth Gospel*. New York: Cambridge University Press, 1968.

Donaldson, Terence L. "Supersessionism and Early Christian Self-Definition." *Journal of the Jesus Movement in Its Jewish Setting* 3 (2016): 1–32.

Dunn, James D. G. *The Partings of the Ways between Christianity and Judaism and Their Significance for the Character of Christianity*. Philadelphia: Trinity, 1991.

Easton-Flake, Amy. "Knowing the Book Better: Orson Pratt, George Reynolds, and Janne M. Sjödahl on the Book of Mormon." *Journal of Book of Mormon Studies* 30 (2021): 41–61.

Easton-Flake, Amy. "Lehi's Dream as a Template for Understanding Each Act of Nephi's Vision." In Belnap, Strathearn, and Johnson, *The Things Which My Father Saw*, 179–98.

Edwards, Boyd F., and W. Farrell Edwards. "Does Chiasmus Appear in the Book of Mormon by Chance?" *BYU Studies* 43, no. 2 (2004): 103–30.

Edwards, Jonathan. *History of Redemption, on a Plan Entirely Original: Exhibiting the Gradual Discovery and Accomplishment of the Divine Purposes in the Salvation of Man; Including a Comprehensive View of Church History, and the Fulfilment of Scripture Prophecies . . . , to Which Are Now Added Notes, Historical, Critical, and Theological, with the Life and Experience of the Author.* London: T. Pitcher, 1788.

Edwards, Jonathan. *A History of the Work of Redemption; Comprising an Outline of Church History.* Rev. and abr. ed. New York: American Tract Society, 1816.

Edwards, Jonathan. *The Works of President Edwards.* 10 vols. New York: S. Converse, 1829.

Eliason, Eric A. "Mormon Folk Culture." In *The Oxford Handbook of Mormonism*, edited by Terryl L. Givens and Philip L. Barlow, 454–69. New York: Oxford University Press, 2015.

Ellertson, Carol F. "The Isaiah Passages in the Book of Mormon: A Non-aligned Text." M.A. thesis, Brigham Young University, 2001.

Elliott, J. K., ed. *The Apocryphal New Testament: A Collection of Apocryphal Christian Literature in an English Translation.* New York: Oxford University Press, 1993.

Elliott, Mark W., ed. *Isaiah 40–66: Ancient Christian Commentary on Scripture.* Downers Grove, IL: InterVarsity, 2007.

Epperson, Steven. *Mormons and Jews: Early Mormon Theologies of Israel.* Salt Lake City: Signature, 1992.

Eusebius of Caesarea. *Commentary on Isaiah.* Edited by Joel C. Elowsky. Translated by Jonathan J. Armstrong. Downers Grove, IL: IVP Academic, 2013.

Evans, Craig A. *To See and Not Perceive: Isaiah 6.9–10 in Early Jewish and Christian Interpretation.* Sheffield, UK: JSOT, 1989.

Evans, John. *A Sketch of the Denominations of the Christian World, to Which Is Prefixed an Outline of Atheism, Deism, Theophilanthropism, Mahometanism, Judaism, and Christianity; with a Persuasive to Religious Moderation.* 15th ed. London: Baldwin, Cradock, and Joy, 1827.

Eyre, Joseph. *Observations upon the Prophecies Relating to the Restoration of the Jews, with an Appendix in Answer to the Objections of Some Late Writers.* London: T. Cadell, 1771.

Faulring, Scott H., Kent P. Jackson, and Robert J. Matthews, eds. *Joseph Smith's New Translation of the Bible: Original Manuscripts.* Provo, UT: BYU Religious Studies Center, 2004.

Fenton, Elizabeth. "Nephites and Israelites: The Book of Mormon and the Hebraic Indian Theory." In Fenton and Hickman, *Americanist Approaches*, 277–97.

Fenton, Elizabeth. *Old Canaan in a New World: Native Americans and the Lost Tribes of Israel.* New York: New York University Press, 2020.

Fenton, Elizabeth, and Jared Hickman, eds. *Americanist Approaches to the Book of Mormon.* New York: Oxford University Press, 2019.

Fitzmyer, Joseph A. *The One Who Is to Come.* Grand Rapids, MI: Eerdmans, 2007.

Ford, Alice. *Edward Hicks, Painter of the Peaceable Kingdom.* Philadelphia: University of Pennsylvania Press, 1998.

Foster, Lawrence. *Religion and Sexuality: The Shakers, the Mormons, and the Oneida Community*. Urbana: University of Illinois Press, 1984.

Frederick, Nicholas J. *The Bible, Mormon Scripture, and the Rhetoric of Allusivity*. Madison, NJ: Fairleigh Dickinson University Press, 2016.

Frederick, Nicholas J. "The Book of Mormon and Its Redaction of the King James New Testament: A Further Evaluation of the Interaction between the New Testament and the Book of Mormon." *Journal of Book of Mormon Studies* 27 (2018): 44–87.

Frederick, Nicholas J. "Evaluating the Interaction between the New Testament and the Book of Mormon: A Proposed Methodology." *Journal of Book of Mormon Studies* 24 (2015): 1–30.

Galland, Corina. "A Short Structural Reading of Isaiah 52:13–53:12." In *Structuralism and Biblical Hermeneutics: A Collection of Essays*, edited and translated by Alfred M. Johnson Jr., 197–203. Eugene, OR: Pickwick, 1979.

Gardner, Brant A. *The Gift and Power: Translating the Book of Mormon*. Salt Lake City: Greg Kofford, 2011.

Gardner, Brant A. "Labor Diligently to Write: The Ancient Making of a Modern Scripture." Special issue, *Interpreter* 35 (2020).

Gardner, Brant A. *Second Witness: Analytical and Contextual Commentary on the Book of Mormon*. 6 vols. Salt Lake City: Greg Kofford, 2007.

Gileadi, Avraham. *The Book of Isaiah: A New Translation with Interpretive Keys from the Book of Mormon*. Salt Lake City: Deseret, 1988.

Givens, Terryl L. *By the Hand of Mormon: The American Scripture That Launched a New World Religion*. New York: Oxford University Press, 2002.

Givens, Terryl L. *2nd Nephi: A Brief Theological Introduction*. Provo, UT: Neal A. Maxwell Institute, 2020.

Givens, Terryl L. "'We Have Only the Old Thing': Rethinking Mormon Restoration." In *Standing Apart: Mormon Historical Consciousness and the Concept of Apostasy*, edited by Miranda Wilcox and John D. Young, 335–42. New York: Oxford University Press, 2014.

Givens, Terryl L. *Wrestling the Angel, the Foundations of Mormon Thought: Cosmos, God, Humanity*. New York: Oxford University Press, 2015.

Goff, Alan. "Historical Narrative, Literary Narrative—Expelling Poetics from the Republic of History." *Journal of Book of Mormon Studies* 5, no. 1 (1996): 50–102.

Goldingay, John. *The Message of Isaiah 40–55: A Literary-Theological Commentary*. New York: T and T Clark, 2005.

Goldingay, John. *The Theology of the Book of Isaiah*. Downers Grove, IL: IVP Academic, 2014.

Goldingay, John, and David Payne. *A Critical and Exegetical Commentary on Isaiah 40–55*. 2 vols. New York: T and T Clark, 2006.

Gorton, H. Clay. *The Legacy of the Brass Plates of Laban: A Comparison of Biblical and Book of Mormon Texts*. Bountiful, UT: Horizon, 1994.

Graves, Kersey. *The Bible of Bibles; or, Twenty-Seven "Divine Revelations": Containing a Description of Twenty-Seven Bibles, and an Exposition of Two Thousand Biblical*

Errors in Science, History, Morals, Religion, and General Events; also a Delineation of the Characters of the Principal Personages of the Christian Bible, and an Examination of Their Doctrines. Boston: Colby and Rich, 1879.

Grotius, Hugo. *Annotationes in Vetus Testamentum*. 2 vols. Edited by George John Ludou Vogel. Halle, Ger.: 1775–76.

Gutjahr, Paul C. *The "Book of Mormon": A Biography*. Princeton, NJ: Princeton University Press, 2012.

Gutjahr, Paul C. "Orson Pratt's Enduring Influence on the Book of Mormon." In Fenton and Hickman, *Americanist Approaches*, 83–104.

Hallen, Cynthia L. "The Lord's Covenant of Kindness: Isaiah 54 and 3 Nephi 22." In Parry and Welch, *Isaiah in the Book of Mormon*, 313–49.

Halverson, Jared M. "Lehi's Dream and Nephi's Vision as Apocalyptic Literature." In Belnap, Strathearn, and Johnson, *The Things Which My Father Saw*, 53–69.

Handley, George B. "On the Moral Risks of Reading Scripture." In Spencer and Webb, *Reading Nephi Reading Isaiah*, 89–104.

Handley, George B. "Reading the Menardian Paradox in 3 Nephi." *Journal of Book of Mormon Studies* 26 (2017): 165–84.

Hann, R. *A Letter to the Right Reverend the Lord Bishop of London, concerning the Heresy and Imposture of Joanna the Prophetess*. London: J. Smith, 1810.

Hansen, Klaus. *Mormonism and the American Experience*. Chicago: University of Chicago Press, 1981.

Hanson, R. P. C. *The Search for the Christian Doctrine of God: The Arian Controversy, 318–381*. Grand Rapids, MI: Baker Academic, 2005.

Hardy, Grant. *The Book of Mormon: A Reader's Edition*. Urbana: University of Illinois Press, 2003.

Hardy, Grant. "Prophetic Perspectives: How Lehi and Nephi Applied the Lessons of Lehi's Dream." In Belnap, Strathearn, and Johnson, *The Things Which My Father Saw*, 199–213.

Hardy, Grant. *Understanding the Book of Mormon: A Reader's Guide*. New York: Oxford University Press, 2010.

Hardy, Heather, and Grant Hardy. "How Nephi Shapes His Readers' Perceptions of Isaiah." In Spencer and Webb, *Reading Nephi Reading Isaiah*, 33–58.

Harper, Steven C. *First Vision: Memory and Mormon Origins*. New York: Oxford University Press, 2019.

Harper, Steven C. "Infallible Proofs, Both Human and Divine: The Persuasiveness of Mormonism for Early Converts." *Religion and American Culture* 10 (Winter 2000): 99–118.

Harrell, Charles R. *"This Is My Doctrine": The Development of Mormon Theology*. Salt Lake City: Greg Kofford, 2011.

Hartshorn, Chris B. *A Commentary on the Book of Mormon*. Independence, MO: Herald, 1964.

Harvey, Graham. *The True Israel: Uses of the Names Jew, Hebrew, and Israel in Ancient Jewish and Early Christian Literature*. New York: E. J. Brill, 1996.

Hatch, Nathan O. *The Democratization of American Christianity*. New Haven, CT: Yale University Press, 1989.

Hatch, Nathan O., and Mark A. Noll, eds. *The Bible in America: Essays in Cultural History*. New York: Oxford University Press, 1982.

Hengel, Martin, and Daniel P. Bailey. "The Effective History of Isaiah 53 in the Pre-Christian Period." In Janowski and Stuhlmacher, *The Suffering Servant*, 75–146.

Henry, Matthew. *An Exposition of the Old and New Testament: Wherein Each Chapter Is Summed Up in Its Contents; the Sacred Text Inserted at Large in Distinct Paragraphs; Each Paragraph Reduced to Its Proper Heads; the Sense Given, and Largely Illustrated; with Practical Remarks and Observations*. 6 vols., edited by George Burder and Joseph Hughes. New York: Robert Carter and Brothers, 1853.

Heskett, Randall. *Messianism within the Scriptural Scrolls of Isaiah*. New York: T and T Clark, 2007.

Heyrman, Christine Leigh. *Southern Cross: The Beginnings of the Bible Belt*. Chapel Hill: University of North Carolina Press, 1998.

Hill, Marvin S. *Quest for Refuge: The Mormon Flight from American Pluralism*. Salt Lake City: Signature, 1989.

Hilton, John III. "Old Testament Psalms in the Book of Mormon." In *Ascending the Mountain of the Lord: Temple, Praise, and Worship in the Old Testament*, edited by Jeffrey R. Chadwick, Matthew J. Grey, and David Rolph Seely, 291–311. Salt Lake City: Deseret; Provo, UT: BYU Religious Studies Center, 2013.

Holland, David F. *Sacred Borders: Continuing Revelation and Canonical Restraint in Early America*. New York: Oxford University Press, 2011.

Holmes, Michael W., ed. *The Apostolic Fathers*. 2nd ed. Translated by J. B. Lightfoot and J. R. Harmer. Grand Rapids, MI: Baker, 1989.

Hooker, Morna D. "Did the Use of Isaiah 53 to Interpret His Mission Begin with Jesus?" In *Jesus and the Suffering Servant: Isaiah 53 and Christian Origins*, edited by William H. Bellinger Jr. and William R. Farmer, 88–103. Harrisburg, PA: Trinity, 1998.

Hopkin, Shon D. "Isaiah 52–53 and Mosiah 13–14: A Textual Comparison." In *Abinadi: He Came among Them in Disguise*, edited by Shon D. Hopkin, 139–66. Salt Lake City: Deseret; Provo, UT: BYU Religious Studies Center, 2018.

Hopkin, Shon D. "Seeing Eye to Eye: Nephi's and John's Intertwining Visions of the Tree of Life." In *Apocalypse: Reading Revelation 21–22*, edited by Julie M. Smith, 66–84. Provo, UT: Neal A. Maxwell Institute Press, 2016.

Hopkins, James K. *A Woman to Deliver Her People: Joanna Southcott and English Millenarianism in an Era of Revolution*. Austin: University of Texas Press, 1982.

Horsley, Samuel. *Critical Disquisitions on the Eighteenth Chapter of Isaiah. In a Letter to Edward King, Esq. F.R.S. A.S.* Philadelphia: James Humphreys, 1800.

Howard, Richard P. *Restoration Scriptures: A Study of Their Textual Development*. Independence, MO: Herald, 1969.

Howe, Daniel Walker. *What Hath God Wrought: The Transformation of America, 1815–1848*. New York: Oxford University Press, 2007.

Howe, Susan Elizabeth. "A Long Consequential Journey." In *The Reader's Book of Mormon*. 7 vols., edited by Robert A. Rees and Eugene England, 1: xvii–xxxix. Salt Lake City: Signature, 2008.

Hughes, Richard T., and C. Leonard Allen. *Illusions of Innocence: Protestant Primitivism in America, 1630–1875*. Chicago: University of Chicago Press, 1988.

Hunter, Henry. *Sacred Biography; or, The History of the Patriarchs.* 7 vols. 3rd American ed. Hallowell, ME: Glazier, 1828.

Hutchinson, Anthony A. "The Word of God Is Enough: The Book of Mormon as Nineteenth-Century Scripture." In Metcalfe, *New Approaches to the Book of Mormon*, 1–19.

Jackson, Kent P. "Isaiah in the Book of Mormon." In *A Reason for Faith: Navigating LDS Doctrine and Church History*, edited by Laura Harris Hales, 69–78. Salt Lake City: Deseret; Provo, UT: BYU Religious Studies Center, 2016.

Jacobs, Alan. *The Book of Common Prayer: A Biography.* Princeton, NJ: Princeton University Press, 2019.

Janowski, Bernd, and Peter Stuhlmacher, eds. *The Suffering Servant: Isaiah 53 in Jewish and Christian Sources.* Translated by Daniel P. Bailey. Grand Rapids, MI: Eerdmans, 2004.

Jerome. *Commentary on Isaiah, Including St. Jerome's Translation of Origen's Homilies 1–9 on Isaiah.* Translated by Thomas P. Scheck. New York: Newman, 2015.

Jessee, Dean C. "The Earliest Documented Accounts of Joseph Smith's First Vision." In *Opening the Heavens: Accounts of Divine Manifestations, 1820–1844*, 1–33. Provo and Salt Lake City, UT: Brigham Young University Press and Deseret, 2005.

Johnson, Janiece. "Becoming a People of the Books: Toward an Understanding of Early Mormon Converts and the New Word of the Lord." *Journal of Book of Mormon Studies* 27 (2018): 1–43.

Johnston, Philip S. *Shades of Sheol: Death and Afterlife in the Old Testament.* Downers Grove, IL: IVP Academic, 2002.

Jones, Christopher C. "'We Latter-day Saints Are Methodists': The Influence of Methodism on Early Mormon Religiosity." M.A. thesis, Brigham Young University, 2009.

Jorgensen, Bruce W. "The Dark Way to the Tree: Typological Unity in the Book of Mormon." In *Literature of Belief: Sacred Scripture and Religious Experience*, edited by Neal A. Lambert, 217–31. Provo, UT: BYU Religious Studies Center, 1981.

Justin Martyr. *Dialogue with Trypho.* Translated by Thomas B. Falls. Edited by Michael Slusser. Revised by Thomas P. Halton. Washington, DC: Catholic University of America Press, 2003.

Justin Martyr. *First and Second Apologies.* Translated by Leslie William Barnard. New York: Paulist Press, 1997.

Kelly, Thomas. *Missionary Hymns.* London: J. Power, 1824.

Kim, Hyun Chul Paul. *Reading Isaiah: A Literary and Theological Commentary.* Macon, GA: Smyth and Helwys, 2016.

Kirsch, Jonathan. *A History of the End of the World: How the Most Controversial Book in the Bible Changed the Course of Western Civilization.* San Francisco: HarperCollins, 2006.

Knabenbauer, Joseph. *Commentarius in Isaiam Prophetam.* 2nd ed. 2 vols. Paris: P. Lethielleux, 1923.

Koole, Jan L. *Isaiah III.* 2 vols. Translated by Anthony P. Runia. Leuven, Belg.: Peeters, 1998.

Land, Gary. "The Historians and the Millerites: An Historiographical Essay." *Andrews University Seminary Studies* 32, no. 3 (Autumn 1994): 227–46.

Lapide, Cornelius. *Commentaria in Scripturam Sacram*. New ed. 26 vols. Paris: Ludovicus Vives, 1877.

Largey, Dennis L., ed. *Book of Mormon Reference Companion*. Salt Lake City: Deseret, 2003.

Larson, Stan. "The Historicity of the Matthean Sermon on the Mount in 3 Nephi." In Metcalfe, *New Approaches to the Book of Mormon*, 115–63.

Larson, Stan. "The Sermon on the Mount: What Its Textual Transformation Discloses concerning the Historicity of the Book of Mormon." *Trinity Journal* 7 (Spring 1986): 23–45.

Laruelle, François. *Introduction to Non-Marxism*. Translated by Anthony Paul Smith. Minneapolis: Univocal, 2015.

Leahy, Sean. "'Learned' and 'Unlearned' Reading in the Book of Mormon." *Journal of Book of Mormon Studies* 27 (2018): 175–86.

Lepler, Jessica M. *The Many Panics of 1837*. New York: Cambridge University Press, 2013.

Longman, Tremper III, and Peter Enns, eds. *Dictionary of the Old Testament: Wisdom, Poetry, and Writings*. Downers Grove, IL: IVP Academic, 2008.

Lowth, Robert. *Isaiah: A New Translation; with a Preliminary Dissertation, and Notes, Critical, Philological, and Explanatory*. 2 vols. 2nd ed. Glasgow, UK: University Press, 1822.

Ludlow, Daniel H. *A Companion to Your Study of the Book of Mormon*. Salt Lake City: Deseret, 1976.

Ludlow, Victor L. "The Father's Covenant People Sermon: 3 Nephi 20:10–23:5." In *Third Nephi: An Incomparable Scripture*, edited by Andrew C. Skinner and Gaye Strathearn, 147–74. Salt Lake City: Deseret; Provo, UT: Neal A. Maxwell Institute, 2012.

Ludlow, Victor L. *Isaiah: Prophet, Seer, and Poet*. Salt Lake City: Deseret, 1982.

Ludlow, Victor L. *Unlocking Isaiah in the Book of Mormon*. Salt Lake City: Deseret, 2003.

Luther, Martin. *Lectures on Isaiah, Chapters 1–39*. Edited by Jaroslav Pelikan. Saint Louis, MO: Concordia, 1969.

Luther, Martin. *Lectures on Isaiah, Chapters 40–66*. Edited by Hilton C. Oswald. Saint Louis, MO: Concordia, 1972.

Maccoby, Hyam, ed. and trans. *Judaism on Trial: Jewish-Christian Disputations in the Middle Ages*. Portland, OR: Littman Library of Jewish Civilization, 1993.

MacKay, Michael Hubbard, Mark Ashurst-McGee, and Brian Hauglid, eds. *Producing Ancient Scripture: Joseph Smith's Translation Projects in the Development of Mormon Christianity*. Salt Lake City: University of Utah Press, 2020.

MacKay, Michael Hubbard, and Gerrit J. Dirkmaat. *From Darkness unto Light: Joseph Smith's Translation and Publication of the Book of Mormon*. Provo, UT: Brigham Young University Religious Studies Center; Salt Lake City: Deseret, 2015.

MacKay, Michael Hubbard, Gerrit J. Dirkmaat, Grant Underwood, Robert J. Woodford, and William G. Hartley, eds. *The Joseph Smith Papers, Documents*. Vol. 1, *July 1828–June 1831*. Salt Lake City: Church Historian's Press, 2013.

Maddox, Julie Adams. "Lehi's Vision of the Tree of Life: An Anagogic Interpretation." MA thesis, Brigham Young University, 1986.

Markschies, Christoph. "Jesus Christ as a Man before God: Two Interpretive Models for Isaiah 53 in the Patristic Literature and Their Development." In Janowski and Stuhlmacher, *The Suffering Servant*, 225–323.

Matthews, Robert J. *"A Plainer Translation": Joseph Smith's Translation of the Bible: A History and Commentary*. Provo, UT: Brigham Young University Press, 1985.

McConkie, Bruce R. *Mormon Doctrine*. 2nd ed. Salt Lake City: Bookcraft, 1966.

McConkie, Joseph Fielding, and Robert L. Millet. *Doctrinal Commentary on the Book of Mormon*. 4 vols. Salt Lake City: Bookcraft, 1987–1992.

McDonald, John. *Isaiah's Message to the American Nation: A New Translation of Isaiah, Chapter XVIII, with Notes Critical and Explanatory, a Remarkable Prophecy, Respecting the Restoration of the Jews, Aided by the American Nation; with an Universal Summons to the Battle of Armageddon, and a Description of That Solemn Scene*. Albany, NY: E. and E. Hosford, 1814.

McKinion, Steven A. *Isaiah 1–39: Ancient Christian Commentary on Scripture*. Downers Grove, IL: InterVarsity, 2004.

Metcalfe, Brent Lee. *New Approaches to the Book of Mormon: Explorations in Critical Methodology*. Salt Lake City: Signature, 1993.

Metcalfe, Brent Lee. "The Priority of Mosiah: A Prelude to Book of Mormon Exegesis." In Metcalfe, *New Approaches to the Book of Mormon*, 395–444.

Methodist Magazine, The, for the Year of Our Lord 1818. Vol. 1. New York: J. Soule and T. Mason, 1818.

Mettinger, Tryggve N. D. *A Farewell to the Servant Songs: A Critical Examination of an Exegetical Axiom*. Lund, Sweden: C. W. K. Gleerup, 1983.

Midgley, Louis. "No Middle Ground: The Debate over the Authenticity of the Book of Mormon." In *Historicity and the Latter-day Saint Scriptures*, edited by Paul Y. Hoskisson, 149–70. Provo, UT: Brigham Young University Religious Studies Center, 2001.

Miller, Adam S. *Speculative Grace: Bruno Latour and Object-Oriented Theology*. New York: Fordham University Press, 2013.

Miller, William. *Evidence from Scripture and History of the Second Coming of Christ, about the Year 1843; Exhibited in a Course of Lectures*. Boston: Joshua V. Himes, 1842.

Moench Charles, Melodie. "Book of Mormon Christology." In Metcalfe, *New Approaches to the Book of Mormon*, 81–114.

Moorhead, James H. "Apocalypticism in Mainstream Protestantism, 1800 to the Present." In *The Encyclopedia of Apocalypticism*. Vol. 3, *Apocalypticism in the Modern Period and the Contemporary Age*, edited by Stephen J. Stein, 72–107. New York: Continuum, 2000.

Moorhead, James H. "Between Progress and Apocalypse: A Reassessment of Millennialism in American Religious Thought, 1800–1880." *Journal of American History* 71, no. 3 (December 1984): 524–42.

Morris, Larry E. *A Documentary History of the Book of Mormon*. New York: Oxford University Press, 2019.

Motyer, J. Alec. *The Prophecy of Isaiah: An Introduction and Commentary*. Downers Grove, IL: IVP Academic, 1993.

Moyise, Steve, and Maarten J. J. Menken, eds. *Isaiah in the New Testament*. New York: T and T Clark International, 2005.

N. "Observations on Isa. liii.8." *Missionary Magazine* 7 (1802): 496–98.

Neubauer, Ad. *The Fifty-Third Chapter of Isaiah according to the Jewish Interpreters*. 2 vols. Translated by S. R. Driver and Ad. Neubauer. New York: Ktav, 1969.

Neusner, Jacob. *Isaiah in Talmud and Midrash*. 2 vols. New York: University Press of America, 2007.

Nibley, Hugh W. *An Approach to the Book of Mormon*. Vol. 6 in *Collected Works of Hugh Nibley*. 3rd ed. Edited by John W. Welch. Salt Lake City: Deseret; Provo, UT: FARMS, 1988.

Nibley, Hugh W. *Teachings of the Book of Mormon: Transcripts of Lectures Presented to an Honors Book of Mormon Class at Brigham Young University, 1988–1990*. 4 vols. Provo, UT: FARMS, 1992.

Nickerson, Matthew. "Nephi's Psalm: 2 Nephi 4:16–35 in the Light of Form-Critical Analysis." *Journal of Book of Mormon Studies* 6, no. 2 (1997): 26–42.

Noll, Mark A. *America's God: From Jonathan Edwards to Abraham Lincoln*. New York: Oxford University Press, 2002.

Noll, Mark A. *A History of Christianity in the United States and Canada*. Grand Rapids, MI: Eerdmans, 1992.

Noll, Mark A. *In the Beginning Was the Word: The Bible in American Public Life, 1492–1783*. New York: Oxford University Press, 2016.

Nyman, Monte S. *"Great Are the Words of Isaiah."* Salt Lake City: Bookcraft, 1980.

Nyman, Monte S. *I Nephi Wrote This Record: Book of Mormon Commentary*. Orem, UT: Granite, 2004.

Nyman, Monte S., ed. *Second Nephi, the Doctrinal Structure*. Provo, UT: BYU Religious Studies Center, 1989.

Nyman, Monte S., and Charles D. Tate, eds. *First Nephi, the Doctrinal Foundation*. Provo, UT: BYU Religious Studies Center, 1989.

Oaks, Dallin H. "The Historicity of the Book of Mormon." In *Historicity and the Latter-day Saint Scriptures*, edited by Paul Y. Hoskisson, 237–48. Provo, UT: BYU Religious Studies Center, 2001.

O'Dea, Thomas F. *The Mormons*. Chicago: University of Chicago Press, 1964.

"On the Sonship of Jesus Christ." *Connecticut Evangelical Magazine and Religious Intelligencer* 5, no. 4 (October 1804): 129–37.

Ostler, Blake Thomas. "The Throne-Theophany and Prophetic Commission in 1 Nephi: A Form-Critical Analysis." *BYU Studies* 26, no. 4 (1986): 67–95.

Oswalt, John N. *The Book of Isaiah*. 2 vols. Grand Rapids, MI: Eerdmans, 1998.

Oxford English Dictionary. Online ed. Oxford: Oxford University Press. https://www.oed.com.

Park, Benjamin E. "The Book of Mormon and Early America's Political and Intellectual Tradition." *Journal of Book of Mormon Studies* 23 (2014): 167–75.

Parry, Donald W. *Exploring the Isaiah Scrolls and Their Textual Variants*. Leiden, Neth.: Brill, 2019.

Parry, Donald W. *Harmonizing Isaiah: Combining Ancient Sources*. Provo, UT: FARMS, 2001.

Parry, Donald W. review of *The Book of Isaiah: A New Translation with Interpretive Keys from the Book of Mormon*, by Avraham Gileadi. *Review of Books on the Book of Mormon* 4, no. 1 (1992): 52–62.

Parry, Donald W., Jay A. Parry, and Tina M. Peterson. *Understanding Isaiah*. Salt Lake City: Deseret, 1998.

Parry, Donald W., Daniel C. Peterson, and John W. Welch, eds. *Echoes and Evidences of the Book of Mormon*. Provo, UT: FARMS, 2002.

Parry, Donald W., and John W. Welch, eds. *Isaiah in the Book of Mormon*. Provo, UT: FARMS, 1998.

Pascal, Blaise. *The Provincial Letters / Pensées / Scientific Treatises*. Translated by Thomas M'Crie, W. F. Trotter, and Richard Scofield. Chicago: Encyclopaedia Britannica, 1952.

Patrick, Symon, William Lowth, Richard Arnald, Daniel Whitby, and Moses Lowman. *A Critical Commentary and Paraphrase on the Old and New Testament and the Apocrypha*. Corrected by J. R. Pitman. 6 vols. London: Richard Priestley, 1822.

Perry, Seth. *Bible Culture and Authority in the Early United States*. Princeton, NJ: Princeton University Press, 2018.

Persuitte, David. *Joseph Smith and the Origins of "The Book of Mormon."* Jefferson, NC: McFarland, 1985.

Pfisterer Darr, Katheryn. *Isaiah's Vision and the Family of God*. Louisville, KY: Westminster John Knox, 1994.

Pike, Dana M. "'How Beautiful upon the Mountains': The Imagery of Isaiah 52:7–10 and Its Occurrences in the Book of Mormon." In Parry and Welch, *Isaiah in the Book of Mormon*, 249–91.

Poole, Matthew. *Annotations upon the Holy Bible: Wherein the Sacred Text Is Inserted, and Various Reading Annexed, Together with the Parallel Scriptures*. 3 vols. New York: Robert Carter and Brothers, 1853.

Porterfield, Amanda. *Conceived in Doubt: Religion and Politics in the New American Nation*. Chicago: University of Chicago Press, 2012.

Pratt, Orson. *Reply to a Pamphlet Printed at Glasgow, with the "Approbation of Clergymen of Different Denominations" Entitled "Remarks on Mormonism."* Liverpool, UK: R. James, 1849.

Rendtorff, Rolf. "The Book of Isaiah: A Complex Unity: Synchronic and Diachronic Reading." In *New Visions of Isaiah*, edited by Roy F. Melugin and Marvin A. Sweeney, 32–49. Sheffield, UK: Sheffield Academic, 1996.

Rendtorff, Rolf. *Canon and Theology: Overtures to an Old Testament Theology*. Edinburgh: T and T Clark, 1994.

Reynolds, George, and Janne M. Sjodahl. *Commentary on the Book of Mormon*. 7 vols. Salt Lake City: Deseret, 1955.

Reynolds, Noel B. "Chiastic Structuring of Large Texts: 2 Nephi as a Case Study." *BYU Studies Quarterly* 59 Supp (2020): 177–92.

Reynolds, Noel B. "Nephi's Outline." In *Book of Mormon Authorship: New Light on Ancient Origins*, edited by Noel B. Reynolds, 53–74. Provo, UT: FARMS, 1982.

Reynolds, Noel B. "Nephite Kingship Reconsidered." In *Mormons, Scripture, and the Ancient World: Studies in Honor of John L. Sorenson*, edited by Davis Bitton, 151–89. Provo, UT: FARMS, 1998.

Reynolds, Noel B. "On Doubting Nephi's Break between 1 and 2 Nephi: A Critique of Joseph Spencer's *An Other Testament: On Typology*." *Interpreter* 25 (2017): 85–102.

Reynolds, Noel B. "The Political Dimension in Nephi's Small Plates." *BYU Studies* 27, no. 4 (Fall 1987): 15–37.

Richards, LeGrand. *A Marvelous Work and a Wonder*. Salt Lake City: Deseret, 1990.

Ricks, Eldin. *Book of Mormon Commentary*. Vol. 1, *Comprising the Complete Text of the First Book of Nephi with Explanatory Notes*. Salt Lake City: Deseret News Press, 1953.

Ridderbos, J. *Isaiah*. Translated by John Vriend. Grand Rapids, MI: Zondervan, 1985.

Riley, William L. "A Comparison of Passages from Isaiah and Other Old Testament Prophets in Ethan Smith's *View of the Hebrews* and the Book of Mormon." M.A. thesis, Brigham Young University, 1971.

Roberts, B. H. *New Witnesses for God*. 3 vols. Salt Lake City: Deseret News, 1909.

Roberts, J. J. M. *First Isaiah*. Minneapolis: Fortress, 2015.

Rust, Richard Dilworth. *Feasting on the Word: The Literary Testimony of the Book of Mormon*. Salt Lake City: Deseret; Provo, UT: FARMS, 1997.

Sawyer, John F. A. *The Fifth Gospel: Isaiah in the History of Christianity*. New York: Cambridge University Press, 1996.

Sawyer, John F. A. *Isaiah through the Centuries*. Hoboken, NJ: Wiley Blackwell, 2018.

Schwain, Kristin. "The Bible and Art." In *The Oxford Handbook of the Bible in America*, edited by Paul C. Gutjahr, 407–23. New York: Oxford University Press, 2017.

Scott, Thomas. *The Holy Bible Containing the Old and New Testaments, According to the Authorized Version: With Explanatory Notes, Practical Observations, and Copious Marginal References*. New ed. 5 vols. London: L. and G. Seeley et al., 1839.

Seifrid, Mark A. "Romans." In Beale and Carson, *Commentary on the New Testament Use of the Old Testament*, 607–94.

Seitz, Christopher R. *Isaiah 1–39*. Interpretation: A Bible Commentary for Teaching and Preaching. Louisville, KY: John Knox Press, 1993.

Seitz, Christopher R. *Zion's Final Destiny: The Development of the Book of Isaiah*. Minneapolis: Fortress, 1991.

Shalev, Eran. *American Zion: The Old Testament as a Political Text from the Revolution to the Civil War*. New Haven, CT: Yale University Press, 2013.

Sharkansky, Ira. *Governing Jerusalem: Again on the World's Agenda*. Detroit, MI: Wayne State University Press, 1996.

Shipps, Jan. *Mormonism: The Story of a New Religious Tradition*. Urbana: University of Illinois Press, 1985.

Silva, Moisés. "Galatians." In Beale and Carson, *Commentary on the New Testament Use of the Old Testament*, 785–812.

Simpson, Thomas W. *American Universities and the Birth of Modern Mormonism, 1867–1940*. Chapel Hill: University of North Carolina Press, 2016.

Skinner, Andrew C. *Third Nephi: The Fifth Gospel*. Springville, UT: CFI, 2012.

Skousen, Royal. *Analysis of Textual Variants of the Book of Mormon*. 6 parts. 2nd ed. Provo, UT: FARMS and BYU Studies, 2017.

Skousen, Royal, ed. *The Book of Mormon: The Earliest Text*. New Haven, CT: Yale University Press, 2009.

Skousen, Royal. *The History of the Text of the Book of Mormon*. Parts 1 and 2, *Grammatical Variation*. Provo, UT: FARMS and BYU Studies, 2016.

Skousen, W. Cleon. *Isaiah Speaks to Modern Times*. Salt Lake City: Ensign, 1984.

Smith, Ethan. *A Dissertation on the Prophecies Relative to Antichrist and the Last Times; Exhibiting the Rise, Character, and Overthrow of That Terrible Power: And a Treatise on the Seven Apocalyptic Vials*. Charlestown, MA: Samuel T. Armstrong, 1811.

Smith, Ethan. *View of the Hebrews*. 2nd ed. Edited by Charles D. Tate Jr. Provo, UT: Brigham Young University Religious Studies Center, 1996.

Smith, Gary V. *Isaiah 1–39*. The New American Commentary: An Exegetical and Theological Exposition of Holy Scripture. Nashville, TN: B and H, 2007.

Smith, Gary V. *Isaiah 40–66*. The New American Commentary: An Exegetical and Theological Exposition of Holy Scripture. Nashville, TN: B and H, 2009.

Smith, Joseph. *The Book of Mormon*. Palmyra, NY: E. B. Grandin, 1830. Repr., Independence, MO: Herald, 1970.

Smith, Joseph. "Joseph Smith—History." *Pearl of Great Price*. Salt Lake City: Church of Jesus Christ of Latter-day Saints, 2013. https://www.churchofjesuschrist.org/study/scriptures/pgp/title-page?lang=eng. Last updated March 24, 2015.

Smith, Wilfred Cantwell. *What Is Scripture? A Comparative Approach*. Minneapolis: Fortress, 1993.

Sommer, Benjamin D. *A Prophet Reads Scripture: Allusion in Isaiah 40–66*. Stanford, CA: Stanford University Press, 1998.

Sondrup, Steven P. "The Psalm of Nephi: A Lyric Reading." *BYU Studies* 21, no. 3 (1981): 357–72.

Sorenson, John L. *Mormon's Map*. Provo, UT: FARMS, 2000.

Southcott, Joanna. *The Strange Effects of Faith, with Remarkable Prophecies (made in 1792, &c) of Things Which Are to Come: Also Some Account of My Life, Part 1*. London: Galabin and Marchant, 1801.

Spencer, Joseph M. *The Anatomy of Book of Mormon Theology*. 2 vols. Salt Lake City: Greg Kofford, 2021.

Spencer, Joseph M. *1st Nephi: A Brief Theological Introduction*. Provo, UT: Neal A. Maxwell Institute, 2020.

Spencer, Joseph M. "A Moderate Millenarianism: Apocalypticism in the Church of Jesus Christ of Latter-day Saints." *Religions* 10, no. 5 (2019): 339.

Spencer, Joseph M. *An Other Testament: On Typology*. 2nd ed. Provo, UT: Maxwell Institute, 2016.

Spencer, Joseph M. "Performative Prophecy." In *God Himself Shall Come Down: Reading Mosiah 15*. Edited by Andrew C. Smith and Joseph M. Spencer, 1–26. N.p.: Proceedings of the Mormon Theology Seminar, 2023.

Spencer, Joseph M. *The Vision of All: Twenty-Five Lectures on Isaiah in Nephi's Record.* Salt Lake City: Greg Kofford, 2016.

Spencer, Joseph M., and Jenny Webb, eds. *Reading Nephi Reading Isaiah: 2 Nephi 26–27.* 2nd ed. Provo, UT: Neal A. Maxwell Institute, 2016.

Sperry, Sidney B. *Answers to Book of Mormon Questions.* Salt Lake City: Bookcraft, 1967.

Sperry, Sidney B. *Book of Mormon Chronology: The Dating of Book of Mormon People and Events.* Salt Lake City: Deseret, 1970.

Sperry, Sidney B. *Book of Mormon Compendium.* Salt Lake City: Bookcraft, 1968.

Sperry, Sidney B. *The Book of Mormon Testifies.* Salt Lake City: Bookcraft, 1952.

Sperry, Sidney B. "The 'Isaiah Problem' in the Book of Mormon." *Improvement Era* 42 (September 1939): 524–25, 564–69; (October 1939): 594, 634, 636–37.

Sperry, Sidney B. *Our Book of Mormon.* Salt Lake City: Bookcraft, 1950.

Sperry, Sidney B. "The Text of Isaiah in the Book of Mormon." MA thesis, University of Chicago, 1926.

Sperry, Sidney B., and Merrill Y. Van Wagoner. "The Inspired Revision of the Bible." *Improvement Era* 43 (April 1940): 206–7, 251–53; (May 1940): 270–71; (June 1940): 336–37, 376–77; (July 1940): 408–9; (August 1940): 472–73, 488 (September 1940): 536–37, 568.

Stein, Stephen J. "Apocalypticism outside the Mainstream in the United States," in *The Encyclopedia of Apocalypticism.* Vol. 3, *Apocalypticism in the Modern Period and the Contemporary Age,* edited by Stephen J. Stein, 108–39. New York: Continuum, 2000.

Stein, Stephen J. *The Shaker Experience in America: A History of the United Society of Believers.* New Haven, CT: Yale University Press, 1992.

Stein, Stephen J. "Signs of the Times: The Theological Foundations of Early Mormon Apocalyptic." *Sunstone Magazine* 8, nos. 1–2 (January–March 1983): 59–65.

Steinberg, Avi. *The Lost Book of Mormon: A Journey through the Mythic Lands of Nephi, Zarahemla, and Kansas City, Missouri.* New York: Doubleday, 2014.

Stendahl, Krister. *Paul among Jews and Gentiles: And Other Essays.* Minneapolis: Fortress, 1976.

Stendahl, Krister. "The Sermon on the Mount and Third Nephi." In *Reflections on Mormonism, Judaeo-Christian Parallels: Papers Delivered at the Religious Studies Center Symposium, Brigham Young University, March 10–11, 1978,* edited by Truman G. Madsen, 139–54. Provo, UT: Brigham Young University Religious Studies Center, 1978.

Stewart, Philemon. *A Holy, Sacred and Divine Roll and Book; from the Lord God of Heaven, to the Inhabitants of Earth: Revealed in the United Society at New Lebanon, County of Columbia, State of New-York, United States of America.* 2 vols. Canterbury, NH: United Society, 1843.

Stout, Harry S. *The New England Soul: Preaching and Religious Culture in Colonial New England.* New York: Oxford University Press, 2012.

Strathearn, Gaye, and Jacob Moody. "Christ's Interpretation of Isaiah 52's 'My Servant' in 3 Nephi." In *Third Nephi: An Incomparable Scripture,* edited by Andrew C. Skinner and Gaye Strathearn, 175–90. Salt Lake City: Deseret; Provo, UT: Neal A. Maxwell Institute, 2012.

Stromberg, Jacob. *An Introduction to the Study of Isaiah.* New York: T and T Clark, 2011.

Sturgess, Gary L. "The Book of Mosiah: Thoughts about Its Structure, Purposes, Themes, and Authorship." *Journal of Book of Mormon Studies* 4, no. 2 (1995): 107–35.

Swedenborg, Emanuel. *Arcana Coelestia; or, Heavenly Mysteries Contained in the Sacred Scriptures, or Word of the Lord, Manifested and Laid Open; Beginning with the Book of Genesis, Interspersed with Relations of Wonderful Things Seen in the World of Spirits and the Heaven of Angels.* 2 vols. London: J. and E. Hodson, 1802.

Sweeney, Marvin A. *Isaiah 1–39, with an Introduction to Prophetic Literature.* Grand Rapids, MI: Eerdmans, 1996.

Swint, Mark. *Compare Isaiah: Understanding Biblical Scriptures in the Book of Mormon.* Springville, UT: Horizon, 2009.

Tatham, David. "Edward Hicks, Elias Hicks, and John Comly: Perspectives on the Peaceable Kingdom Theme." *American Art Journal* 13, no. 2 (Spring 1981): 36–50.

Taysom, Stephen C. *Shakers, Mormons, and Religious Worlds: Conflicting Visions, Contested Boundaries.* Bloomington: Indiana University Press, 2011.

Thomas, John Christopher. *A Pentecostal Reads the Book of Mormon: A Literary and Theological Introduction.* Cleveland, TN: CPT, 2016.

Thomas, Mark D. *Digging in Cumorah: Reclaiming Book of Mormon Narratives.* Salt Lake City: Signature, 1999.

Thomasson, Gordon C. "Mosiah: The Complex Symbolism and Symbolic Complex of Kingship in the Book of Mormon." *Journal of Book of Mormon Studies* 2, no. 1 (1993): 21–38.

Thompson, John S., and Eric Smith. "Isaiah and the Latter-day Saints: A Bibliographic Survey." In Parry and Welch, *Isaiah in the Book of Mormon*, 445–509.

Townsend, Colby. "'Behold, Other Scriptures I Would That Ye Should Write': Malachi in the Book of Mormon." *Dialogue* 51, no. 2 (Summer 2018): 103–38.

Townsend, Colby. "'The Robe of Righteousness': Exilic and Post-Exilic Isaiah in *The Book of Mormon*." *Dialogue* 55, no. 3 (Fall 2022): 75–106.

Tull Willey, Patricia. *Remember the Former Things: The Recollection of Previous Texts in Second Isaiah.* Atlanta: Society of Biblical Literature, 1997.

Turley, Richard E. Jr., and William W. Slaughter. *How We Got the Book of Mormon.* Salt Lake City: Deseret, 2011.

Tvedtnes, John A. "'Fulness of the Gospel' and 'Familiar Spirit.'" *Journal of Book of Mormon Studies* 7, no. 1 (1998): 74.

Tvedtnes, John A. "The Isaiah Variants in the Book of Mormon." Published typescript. Provo, UT: FARMS, 1981.

Twain, Mark. *The Innocents Abroad / Roughing It.* New York: Library of America, 1984.

Uhlig, Torsten. *The Theme of Hardening in the Book of Isaiah: An Analysis of Communicative Action.* Tübingen, Ger.: Mohr Siebeck, 2009.

Ulrich, Eugene, and Peter W. Flint. *Qumran Cave 1.* Vol.2, *The Isaiah Scrolls.* 2 vols. New York: Oxford University Press, 2010.

Underwood, Grant. *The Millenarian World of Early Mormonism.* Urbana: University of Illinois Press, 1993.

Van Dyke, Blair G., and David B. Galbraith. "The Jerusalem Center for Near Eastern Studies: Reflections of a Modern Pioneer." *Religious Educator* 9, no. 1 (2008): 29–38.

Vermeylen, Jacques. "L'unité du livre d'Isaïe." In *The Book of Isaiah/Le livre d'Isaïe: Les oracles et leurs relectures: Unité et complexité de l'ouvrage*, edited by Jacques Vermeylen, 11–53. Leuven, Belg.: Leuven University Press, 1989.

Vest, H. Grant. "The Problem of Isaiah in the Book of Mormon." MS thesis, Brigham Young University, 1938.

Vitringa, Campegius. *Commentarius in Librum Prophetiarum Jesaiae*. 2 vols. Johan Nicolai Andreas, 1722.

Vogel, Dan, ed. *Early Mormon Documents*. 5 vols. Salt Lake City: Signature, 1996–2003.

Vogel, Dan. *Joseph Smith: The Making of a Prophet*. Salt Lake City: Signature, 2004.

Von Rad, Gerhard. *Old Testament Theology*. 2 vols. Translated by D. M. G. Stalker. New York: Harper and Row, 1965.

Wagner, J. Ross. *Heralds of the Good News: Isaiah and Paul in Concert in the Letter to the Romans*. Leiden, Neth.: Brill, 2002.

Wagner, J. Ross. "Isaiah in Romans and Galatians." In *Isaiah in the New Testament*, Edited by Steve Moyise and Maarten J. Menken, 117–32. New York: T and T Clark, 2005.

Walters, Wesley P. "The Use of the Old Testament in the Book of Mormon." ThM thesis, Covenant Theological Seminary, Creve Coeur, MO, 1981.

Watson, Richard. *A Biblical and Theological Dictionary: Explanatory of the History, Manners, and Customs of the Jews, and Neighbouring Nations. With an Account of the Most Remarkable Places and Persons Mentioned in Sacred Scripture; An Exposition of the Principal Doctrines of Christianity; and Notices of Jewish and Christian Sects and Heresies*. New York: B. Waugh and T. Mason, 1832.

Wayment, Thomas A., and Haley Wilson-Lemmon. "A Recovered Resource: The Use of Adam Clarke's Bible Commentary in Joseph Smith's Bible Translation." In *Producing Ancient Scripture: Joseph Smith's Translation Projects in the Development of Mormon Christianity*, edited by Michael Hubbard MacKay, Mark Ashurst-McGee, and Brian M. Hauglid, 262–84. Salt Lake City: University of Utah Press, 2020.

Webb, Jenny. "Slumbering Voices: Death and Textuality in Second Nephi." In Spencer and Webb, *Reading Nephi Reading Isaiah*, 59–74.

Weeks, William R. "Mistakes of Millerism." *New York Evangelist* 14, no. 7 (February 16, 1843): 41–44; 14, no. 9 (March 2, 1843): 65–66; 14, no. 11 (March 16, 1843): 81–82; 14, no. 13 (March 30, 1843): 49; 14, no. 15 (April 13, 1843): 57–58.

Welch, John W. "Chiasmus in the Book of Mormon." In *Chiasmus in Antiquity*, edited by John W. Welch, 198–210. Provo, UT: FARMS, 1981.

Welch, John W. *The Legal Cases in the Book of Mormon*. Provo, UT: Brigham Young University Press and Neal A. Maxwell Institute Press, 2008.

Welch, John W. *The Sermon at the Temple and the Sermon on the Mount: A Latter-day Saint Approach*. Salt Lake City: Deseret; Provo, UT: FARMS, 1990.

Wesley, John. *Wesley's Notes on the Bible*. Grand Rapids, MI: Francis Asbury, 1987.

Westermann, Claus. *Isaiah 40–66: A Commentary*. Translated by David M. G. Stalker. Philadelphia: Westminster, 1969.

Wildberger, Hans. *Isaiah 1–12: A Commentary*. Translated by Thomas H. Trapp. Minneapolis: Augsburg Fortress, 1991.

Wildberger, Hans. *Isaiah 13–27: A Continental Commentary*. Translated by Thomas H. Trapp. Minneapolis: Fortress, 1997.

Wildberger, Hans. *Isaiah 28–39: A Continental Commentary*. Translated by Thomas H. Trapp. Minneapolis: Fortress, 2002.

Wilk, Florian. "Isaiah in 1 and 2 Corinthians." In *Isaiah in the New Testament*, edited by Steve Moyise and Maarten J. Menken, 133–58. New York: T and T Clark, 2005.

Wilken, Robert Louis, ed. *Isaiah Interpreted by Early Christian and Medieval Commentators*. Translated by Robert Louis Wilken, Angela Russell Christman, and Michael J. Hollerich. Grand Rapids, MI: Eerdmans, 2007.

Williams, R. John. "The Ghost and the Machine: Plates and Paratext in the Book of Mormon." In Fenton and Hickman, *Americanist Approaches*, 45–82.

Williamson, H. G. M. *The Book Called Isaiah: Deutero-Isaiah's Role in Composition and Redaction*. New York: Oxford University Press, 1994.

Williamson, H. G. M. *A Critical and Exegetical Commentary on Isaiah 1–27*. Vol. 2, *Isaiah 6–12*. New York: T and T Clark International, 2018.

Williamson, H. G. M. "Recent Issues in the Study of Isaiah." In *Interpreting Isaiah: Issues and Approaches*, edited by David G. Firth and H. G. M. Williamson, 21–39. Downers Grove, IL: InterVarsity, 2009.

Williamson, H. G. M. *Variations on a Theme: King, Messiah and Servant in the Book of Isaiah*. The Didsbury Lectures 1997. Carlisle, UK: Paternoster, 1998.

Wimbush, Vincent L., ed. *Theorizing Scriptures: New Critical Orientations to a Cultural Phenomenon*. New Brunswick, NJ: Rutgers University Press, 2008.

Winchester, Elhanan. *A Course of Lectures, on the Prophecies That Remain to Be Fulfilled. Delivered in the Borough of Southwark, as also, at the Chapel in Glasshouse-Yard, in the Year 1789*. 2 vols. London: I. Garner, 1789.

Wittgenstein, Ludwig. *Tractatus Logico-Philosophicus*. Translated by D. F. Pears and B. F. McGuinness. New York: Routledge, 1974.

Woodward, Robert. *A System of Christian Theology: Containing an Explanation of the Doctrines, Duties, and Precepts of the Christian Religion*. Northampton, UK: T. Dicey, 1791.

Wright, David P. "'In Plain Terms That We May Understand': Joseph Smith's Transformation of Hebrews in Alma 12–13." In Metcalfe, *New Approaches to the Book of Mormon*, 165–229.

Wright, David P. "Isaiah in the Book of Mormon: Or Joseph Smith in Isaiah." In *American Apocrypha: Essays on the Book of Mormon*, edited by Dan Vogel and Brent Lee Metcalfe, 157–234. Salt Lake City: Signature, 2002.

Wright, David P. "Joseph Smith's Interpretation of Isaiah in the Book of Mormon." *Dialogue* 31, no. 4 (1998): 181–206.

Wright, N. T. *The New Testament and the People of God*. Minneapolis: Fortress, 1992.

Wunderli, Earl M. *An Imperfect Book: What the Book of Mormon Tells Us about Itself*. Salt Lake City: Signature, 2013.

Wunderli, Earl M. "Critique of Alma 36 as an Extended Chiasm." *Dialogue* 38, no. 4 (2005): 97–110.

Young, Edward J. *The Book of Isaiah*. 3 vols. Grand Rapids, MI: Eerdmans, 1965.

Index

Abinadi: Abinadite Church, 70–72; asked to interpret Isaiah to accuse him, 13, 30, 33; in Book of Mormon/Isaiah arc, 13–15, 26, 29–31; couples "to redeem" with "his people," 50; deflationary interpretation of Christ, 76, 120; and dynasty, 71–72, 75; esoteric interpretation of Isaiah, 42–45, 48, 51, 55, 60–62, 65, 67, 77; explains Isaiah 52:7, 33–34, 48, 54; eye-to eye-interpretation, 33, 36, 49, 82, 118; foretells Christian era, 47–49; Hebrew prophet to Christian interpreter, 30–31; martyrdom, 33, 38, 44, 70, 75; and Nephi's Isaiah exegesis, 74; and Nephite tradition, 69–76; as polemic, 61, 65; post-Isaiah 53 commentary, 62–69; and pre-Christian anticipation of Christ, 64; as protagonist, 51–52, 68; quaint Christology, 54–55, 60, 62, 64, 101; typology, 63, 65
Adventism, 103, 109–16
Alma (former priest of Noah), 16, 44–45, 70–71
angels, 75, 87, 115, 136–37, 161–62, 212–13
Anglicans, 58, 104–5, 108–9, 188, 217
Anthon, Charles, 212–13
anti-Christ, 113, 142, 179
apocalypticism: Christ and, 139, 196; Isaiah in the mainstream, 102–7; at the margins, 107–17; Nephi's approaches to Isaiah, 139, 160, 192, 198, 214; in Third Isaiah, 7
apostate/apostasy, 37, 67, 169, 202
apostles: in the Book of Mormon, 47, 169; Christian commentators on, 48, 50, 62–63, 67, 104–6, 115, 142, 213; Isaiah as, 54; Latter-day Saint, 153, 158, 202, 208
Arius (Arian), 57
Asbury, Francis, 104
Assyria: campaign, 6, 187, 203, 207; collapse, 34, 132; imperial power, 9, 206; and the remnant, 170, 183
Athanasius, 56–57
atonement, 13, 40, 78
Augustine, 56, 167
Axelgard, Frederick, 154–56

Babylon (Babylonian): collapse, 9, 34–35, 178, 183–84, 187; exile, 8, 36, 104, 106, 121, 186, 195, 199; mystical, 145; Neo-Babylonian, 6, 170; and Nephi, 203; and redemption, 37, 188, 194; and the remnant, 164–65, 170–71, 179
baptism (baptize), 15–16, 85, 87, 94, 165
Baptists, 104, 106, 109, 141
believers, 21, 26, 67, 142, 144, 177, 189, 211–12, 221: unbelievers, 78

Index

Benjamin (Book of Mormon king), 17, 32, 66, 75
Bible: biblicization of America, 61; "inspired version," 200–201; and the Book of Mormon, 2–5, 17, 21–24, 53, 81, 83, 92, 164, 202, 240, 208–10; Seventh Day Adventist, 116; and Sidney Sperry, 199–200; Shaker, 113; wording, 70, 82, 130, 180, 199
Blenkinsopp, Joseph, 39, 215
Book of Mormon: 3 Nephi as apex, 77; antebellum readers of, 2, 55, 102, 105, 108–10, 113, 116, 140–41, 148, 193–94, 198, 204–5; author's positionality (believer), 21; critics, 121, 143, 211; dictation, 3, 17–23, 97, 12–27, 158–59, 166, 177, 197, 200; first edition (1830), 12, 17, 60, 102, 140; and frontier, 198, 220; gold plates, 17, 204, 206, 209–13; historicity, 20–24, 62, 104, 106, 122, 219–21; the "Isaiah chapters," 176–79; millenarianism, 102, 110, 116, 145, 189, 193–96; peoples, 2–5, 15; programmatic reading of Isaiah, 7–12; remains sealed, 214–21; rhetorical approach, 219; Samoan, 1; Twain on, 2, 167; versification and chapter breaks, 158–60, 164–66. *See also Scripture Index*
Book of Mormon, translation: and the Book of Lehi, 18, 124; Martin Harris and, 18, 204; and Mary Whitmer, 213; for modern audience, 20; and necromancy, 209–12
Bradish, Luther, 212
brass plates, 129, 138, 140, 160–62, 166, 168, 199–202
Brodie, Fawn McKay, 2, 179
Brown, Kent, 154
Brown, Raymond, 93
Brown, Samuel, 210
Brueggeman, Walter, 36, 182, 191
Bushman, Claudia, 167, 177
Bushman, Richard, 212

Calvin, John (Calvinism), 58, 63, 217
Campbell, Alexander, 67
celibacy, 113
Charles, Melodie Moench, 43
Chiasmus, 154
Childs, Brevard, 54, 130, 205

Christology: in 3 Nephi, 78, 82, 101, 117–19; Abinadi's, 39–46, 62, 67–70, 74–77, 117–19; early Christian, 53–57; Johannine, 5, 89, 99; and Nephi, 198
Clarke, Adam, 59, 63, 104–9, 142
Cloward, Robert, 203–4
Community of Christ (Reorganized Church of Jesus Christ of Latter Day Saints), 200, 202
Congregationalists, 108, 143
Conrad, Edgar, 170
covenant: and Christians, 114, 142; covenantal history, 81–83, 138, 173, 195; and Israel, 79–83, 91–99, 117, 120–22, 176, 178, 180, 187, 195; Nephi and, 128, 130, 138–39, 163–65, 173, 183–84, 205; sermons, 84–87

Dabney, J.P., 60
Dead Sea Scrolls, 204
devil, 97–98, 184
Disciples of Christ, 67, 109
disputations, 15–16, 94

Edwards, Jonathan, 60, 140
Eisenman, Robert, 204
Epiphany, 140–41, 149
Episcopalians, 108–9
"Epistle of the Apostles," 106
eschatology (eschaton): in 3 Nephi, 97–100, 105; and Abinadi, 68; American Christians on, 141–47; and commentaries on Isaiah, 106–7; gathering, 113, 186; Jews conversion to Christianity and, 103; Johannine, 120; latter-day, 203; and Mormon, 79; and Nephi, 149–50, 193, 197–98; prophecies, 128; and redemption, 133, 136, 139–40, 188–89; and the sealed book, 216; signs of, 139, 195–96. *See also* Miller, William; restoration; Shakers
Eusebius of Caesarea, 104
evangelicals, 59–60, 104, 110
evangelist, 54
Evans, John, 142
exegesis, 31, 144, 149
exile: Babylonian: 8, 97, 133, 178, 183, 186, 195, 199; and Jerusalem, 131; Judah, 35–

37; Lehites in, 2, 169–71; post-exile Israel, 22, 104, 164; pre-exile text, 220
Eyre, Joseph, 142–43

Faber, George Stanley, 108
First Isaiah, 6–9, 35, 127, 176, 184
Frederick, Nicholas, 85

Gardner, Brant, 153, 204
gathering, the: Christian commentators on, 141; of Gentiles, 169; to Israel (land), 105; and Israel's covenant, 79–83; of Nephites, 45, 87; prophecies concerning, 91–92, 96, 98, 113–18, 131, 137, 145, 147, 185–88, 195
generations (Isianic term), 42–51, 55–60, 66–67, 70–73
Gentiles: American, 147–48; in commentaries, 114; European, 169, 171; Isaiah's prophecies and, 98, 105–6, 117, 131–36, 139–41, 169–70, 213; nations, 36–37; and Nephi, 165, 169, 188, 191, 196, 198, 206; skepticism, 218; Ethan Smith and, 146–47; unrepentant, 82–83
Gethsemane, 78, 87–91
Gileadi, Avraham, 203
God: Abinadi's claims concerns, 41; and the Book of Mormon, 25; coming of, 31, 36, 54, 65–66; enfleshed, 42–45, 59, 118, 140, 150; Israel as servant of, 8; marriage of God to people, 111–12; nature of, 15–16, 44, 118; one with Christ, 92–94; paternity metaphor, 43–44; postexilic restoration, 164; and prophetic mission, 61, 182; and redemption, 34–38, 49–50, 130–34, 145, 163–65, 182–89; self-revelation of, 30; strangeness of work, 205; submission of, 13; wrath of, 192
Godhead, 15, 43
Goldingay, John, 34–35
Gorton, Clay, 202
gospels, 8, 84–91, 99; synoptic, 84–91, 99
grace, 12, 64, 140

Hann, R., 217–18
Hardy, Grant, 78, 153, 167, 169, 204
Hardy, Heather, 204
Harris, Martin, 18, 204, 211–12

Hartshorn, Charles, 202
Hebrew/Hebrews: and Abinadi, 30–31, 118–19; language in Isaiah, 186–87, 208–9; prophets, 11, 51, 53, 79. *See also* Jews/Jewish; Old Testament (Hebrew Bible)
Henry, Matthew, 58, 63–64, 104, 106, 141–42, 187–88, 191
heresy (heretical), 65, 68, 106
hermeneutics: Abinadi's, 14, 40–41, 46, 51–53, 62, 65–70, 73–75, 119–22; American Christian, 114, 144, 148–49; and the Book of Mormon writ large, 17, 220–21; Christian, 31; of Christ in the Book of Mormon, 98–99, 101, 110, 116–19; Christological, 82; early Christian, 55, 57, 59, 62, 216; Jacob's, 186; Nephi's, 11–13, 20, 73, 125, 128, 136–40, 150–52, 168, 172–74, 193–98, 205–14; Old Testament, 83
heterodoxy, 43, 62, 65, 68, 116, 148
Hezekiah, 9
Hicks, Edward, 190–93
Holy Ghost or Spirit: and baptism, 87, 94, 153; and the Bible, 81; doctrine of, 15, 165; in early Christianity, 59; familiar spirits, 9, 207–29; gifts of, 4; in godhead, 43; and the Lord's Supper, 89; of prophesying, 31, 40–46, 51, 60–61, 64–68, 159, 173
Horsley, Samuel, 108
Howard, Richard, 202

ideal listener, defined, 22–24
inclusio, 150
intertextuality, 85
Irenaeus, 106
Isaiah: disappears in Book of Mormon, 69; divine plan for history, 184; as fifth gospel, 54, 78, 111; foundation for the Book of Mormon, 5, 11; House of Israel, 80, 87, 91, 98, 121, 128, 130–37, 169–72, 185–86; neighbors, 9, 184; and proof texting, 144–45, 185–86; scattering of, 79, 99, 107, 111, 114, 130, 130–36, 144–49, 154, 186–89, 194, 196; second redemption of, 169; theological difficulty, 183; violent language of, 190–92; warnings, 115, 183
Israel, ten tribes of, 105, 131–32, 144–48

Jacob (Book of Mormon): and the future, 152; hermeneutics, 12, 132–36, 150; humility, 149; and knowledge of Christ, 66; and likening, 203; and Old World, 133, 139; pet formulas, 134; prophecies of, 173; and redemption, 175–77, 185–88, 193–94; and Ethan Smith, 143; witness, 157–58, 166–68

Jacob (Old Testament): covenant, 81; and God, 130; house of, 79, 83, 180–84; tribes of, 131

Jacob, House of, 79, 83, 180–83, 205

Jerome, 54, 56, 104

Jesus Christ: and Abinadi, 117–22; Bread of Life sermon, 90; commandment to read Isaiah, 16, 66, 77, 98, 138–39; first day discourses, 80–83, 87–91; as hen, 80; incarnation, 41–43, 56–57, 60; intercessory prayer, 88; and Isaiah in Third Nehi, 91–99; and Israel's covenant, 79–84; Lord and "Father," 93; as mighty one of Israel, 136; second day discourses, 81–83, 86–88, 91, 97; Sermon on the Mount, 4–5, 78, 84–86, 138

Jews/Jewish: in 1 Nephi, 160; in 2 Nephi, 163; American Christians on, 141–47; Book of Mormon references to, 2; conversion to Christianity, 91–92, 95–96, 99, 103–7; Deuteronomists, 216; Jewish history, 13, 139; Judaism, 68, 216; Noah's priests as, 31, 54, 61; post-Jewish Christians, 68; and prophecy, 132–34, 147–49, 173, 186, 188; restoration of, 107, 110, 137, 143, 171, 194; scriptures, 30, 161, 202; and the sealed book, 216–17; secular, 1; and signs, 111; and supersessionism, 114. *See also* gathering; Old Testament (Hebrew Bible)

Johannine, 84–86, 89–98: non-Johannine, 93, 118

Johnston, Philip, 208

Judah: Assyria and, 203; in exile, 8, 34–37; fate of, 180; kingdom of, 170; lands of, 6; restoration, 164; scattered, 145, 147; sticks of, 144; wickedness, 182

judgment, 6, 22, 48–51, 114, 117–18, 183, 191, 205

justice, 189, 191; injustice, 29

Justin Martyr, 41, 56, 104, 106

Kim, Hyun Chul Paul, 183

Laman, 10, 14, 163

Lamanites: addressed by Christ, 78–85; and Christian gospel before Christ, 66; and land, 31–32, 71–73; in latter-days, 163, 166–73; and race, 10; and redemption, 130, 206, 209; and war against, 35–38, 82

land of promise. *See* promised land

Law, Mosaic, 31, 38, 40, 66–68, 81, 84–85

Lehi, 7, 10, 18, 50, 76, 81, 136–37, 153, 157–63, 166–70

Lemuel, 163

likening: and Abinadi, 75; Nephi, 128–34, 136–39, 143, 148–52, 171–76, 185, 189, 193–98, 203–7, 210–11, 214; Noah's priests, 37; and Zeniffites, 73–74

literal/literalist: Christ's interpretation of Isaiah, 101; commentary on Isaiah, 104–5, 111, 114, 141–44, 147–48; covenant, 80–82; fulfillment of prophecy, 185–87, 203–7; Nephi's record, 128–29, 133–36, 149–50, 193–94, 198; seed, 64–65

literature: apocalyptic, 216; Book of Mormon as, 4, 221; on the Book of Mormon, 20–21; divisions, 6–8; genre, 3; in Isaiah, 34, 69, 140, 170, 205; on Isaiah in the Book of Mormon, 75, 90, 219, 221; Mormon's, 100, 120, 154; of Nephi's record, 131, 152–55, 159, 171, 178; Pauline, 9; pseudobiblical, 61; resistant availability of, xi; structure, 71; study orientation to, 24

liturgy, 140–41, 149

Lowth, Robert, 58–60

Lowth, William, 104–7, 188

Ludlow, Victor, 202

Luther, Martin, 57–58, 63, 217

McConkie, Bruce R., 153, 202

McConkie, Joseph Fielding, 202, 209

McDonald, John, 108

Medes, 37

mercy, 78–79, 142, 184

Messiah (messianic): Abinadi's teachings on, 39–48, 51, 54, 71, 98, 119; Christian commentators on, 63, 111; and Israel's branches, 164–65, 178–79, 182, 184; and Israel's covenant, 81; Jarom on, 66; in John, 93; Mormon on, 100; and Mosaic

Index

Law, 84; prophecies concerning, 132–35, 176, 187–90. *See also* Song of the Suffering Servant
Methodists, 58–59, 63,104, 106, 109, 141–42, 192
Miller, Adam, xi
Miller, William, 103, 109–16
Millet, Robert, 202, 209
Mitchill, Samuel, 212
Mormon (Book of Mormon prophet): abridger, 19–20, 25, 123–24, 136; continuity and discontinuity in record, 136–40; four sequential phases, 25–26; spiritualizing of national hopes, 79–80
Moroni (angel), 16, 121–22, 206
Moses (Lawgiver), 31, 40, 66, 68, 85, 123
music, 190, 204

Native Americans, 108, 116, 144, 171, 212
necromancy, 208–13
Nephi: clarifies Isaiah's meaning for his brothers, 162; close readings, 151, 155; delimits audience, 194; feel and flow, 158; how 1 and 2 Nephi work together, 166–67; Isaiah as beating heart of record, 151; Isaiah as second witness, 157; land of, 31–36, 49, 71–75; large plates, 156; and the "learned," 211–21; lens of prophecy, 152; long quotations of Isaiah, 122, 129, 167, 195; Nephi's project, 20, 124–27, 137–40, 151–52, 172–75, 186, 195; never uses Isaiah's name, 197; novel hermeneutic, 205–14; on "more sacred things," 156–57, 163–65, 172–79, 188; oral tradition, 73, 166; pet formulas, 134; picture of disaster, 207; small plates, 136, 155–56, 159, 185; structure of writings, 20, 151–68, 173, 176, 178; systematicity, 125, 138, 151; three favored Isaiah passages, 148, 177, 196; two revelatory sources, 161–62, 168; underdog son, 129; views Isaiah positively, 151, 176; young man, 151, 167
Nephite: Christ speaks to, 77–83, 85, 88; church, 15, 26, 45; colony, 10, 31–37, 45, 48–50, 54, 70–74, 168–69; defined, 10; divide from Lamanites, 163, 206; dynasties, 71–72, 75; history, 18–20, 167, 173; and Isaiah, 12, 53, 66, 69–76, 120, 181; judges, 26; in Lehi's dream, 168, 170; monarchy, 26, 73; prophecy, 172; prophets, 2, 179; proto-, 130; speak from dust, 208–9
New World: history, 139; and Isaiah, 2–3; Israel in, 143, 148, 205; Jesus Christ in, 5, 10, 16, 76–93; Mormon and, 25; Nephi and, 123–24, 130, 134, 155, 160, 198; prophecies concerning, 161, 168–72, 207
Noah (Book of Mormon king), priests of: Abinadi's show trial, 13–14, 30–31, 53–55, 128, 150; authority, 40; context of, 31–38, 69, 72–75; hermeneutic, 14, 77, 82, 98–99, 117; and the Lord's bared arm, 46–52; and the song of the suffering servant, 38–46; not straw men, 68
Noah (king), wickedness, 12, 29
Non-Conformist, 58, 104, 141, 187
nursing mothers and fathers, 131, 134–35, 140–50
Nyman, Monte, 153, 202, 209

obsession-withdrawal-return, 17
Old Testament (Hebrew Bible): American Christians and, 61, 111, 141; and the Book of Mormon, 3–4, 66, 79; branch image in, 178; Christ addresses in Book of Mormon, 83–84; as cipher, 65; generation within, 59; Isaiah as theological high water mark, xvii; and Jerusalem, 1; Johannine image, 90; narrative style, 29–30; and rabbinic tradition, 216; prophets in, 35, 49; Joseph Smith and, 201
Old World: Jesus Christ in, 5, 10, 81, 84, 88–89; Nephi and, 133–36, 139, 148, 161, 171, 186
olive tree, allegory of, 185
original chapter breaks, 158–64
orthodoxy, 43, 57, 106, 112, 120–21, 201–2

parable, 62, 66, 180, 210
Parry, Donald, 201–3
patristics, 55–63, 216
Paul, Pauline, 4–5, 9, 54, 63, 67, 103–5, 110
peace: Christian commentators on, 54; and Christ's seed, 64; eschatological, 26, 102, 164, 169–71, 184; the peaceable kingdom, 113–14, 189–96; publishers of, 33–35, 38, 46–49, 62, 69, 96, 137
Persians, 6, 8, 37

poetry/poem, 38–42, 51, 58–59, 97, 104, 159, 190, 215
polemics, 8, 57, 60–65, 101–2, 106, 117, 121, 208
Poole, Matthew, 58, 141, 187–88
Pratt, Orson, 158–60, 208
pre-Christian: Abinadi's teachings on Christ, 40, 44–51, 62–70, 77, 99, 101, 118, 120, 122; Nephi's teachings on, 193
Presbyterians, 59, 108
promised land, 1, 97, 117, 139, 145, 147, 153, 170–71, 184
Protestants, 58–64, 102, 108, 110, 191, 217
Puritans, 141

Quakers, 190

reception: of the Bible, xii; and the Book of Mormon, 111, 139, 206; of Isaiah, 23–24, 41, 99, 151, 190, 214–18
redemption: future, 73, 83, 85, 127, 129–33, 176–83; of gentiles, 170; of Israel, 98, 139, 184; of Jerusalem, 33, 36–37, 49, 92, 96, 137; Jewish, 142–43, 149, 163, 194; Lehites, 147–48, 166, 169, 195–96; and the Messiah, 41, 44–50, 62, 68, 176; second redemption, 185–89; in Second and Third Isaiah, 6; of Zion, 95
reform, moral, 110
Reformation/Reformers, 57–60, 101, 217
remnant, of Israel: Abinadi discusses, 14; Christ discusses in 3 Nephi, 79–83, 87; and gentiles, 134; Lehites, 78, 135, 139, 148–49, 164–65, 169–72, 176–84, 187–88, 193, 196, 198; Nephi discusses, 13–14; prophecies concerning, 14
Reorganized Church of Jesus Christ of Latter Day Saints. See Community of Christ
restoration: Christian commentators on, 142–47; of Jerusalem, 36, 104–7; of land, 117, 136, 184; of Lehites, 37, 163–64, 186–89,1 95; Miller does not discuss, 114; prophecies of, 6, 79, 82, 91–92, 98, 130–31, 137, 175; and soteriological redemption, 47, 58
resurrection: Abinadi and, 39–47, 64, 66; Christian commentaries on, 57, 62–63, 112–13; Jacob and, 163; witnesses to, 213; and world history, 148

Revelation (Book), 4–5, 110–12, 216–17
revelation (prophecy): and Gentiles, 36–37; God's self-revelation as Christ, 30, 50; of Nephi, 123, 153, 161; sealed, 216–17; and Shakers, 113; of Joseph Smith, 97
Reynolds, George, 203
Reynolds, Noel, 153–54
ritual, 15–16, 129
Roman Catholic, 60–63, 111
Rome, 203, 217

Sacrament of the Lord's Supper, 89–90
salvation: earth shall see, 33, 36, 38, 50, 92; and gentiles, 131; history, 98, 102, 117, 119, 195, 218; and the law, 40; published, 33–34, 46–49, 62, 95–96
Scott, Thomas, 59, 105, 107–8
Second Great Awakening, 113
Second Isaiah, 6–9, 27, 34–37, 111, 127–30, 140, 175–76, 187, 199, 220
sects, 109, 216
secularism (secular), 1, 61, 213, 218
seed: of Jacob, 79; of Joseph, 79; Lehites', 83, 134, 169, 188, 206; and the Messiah, 42–48, 51, 62–66, 71, 118; spiritual, 58
seer stone, 210
Seventh Day Adventism. See Adventism
sex, 13
Shakers, 113–16
Sjodahl, Janne, 203
Skousen, Cleon, 208
Smith, Emma, 18
Smith, Ethan, 108, 143–49
Smith, Joseph: Bible revisions, 200–202; Fawn Brodie on, 2, 179; early history, xii–xiv; First Vision, 109; and the Godhead, 43; and the lost Book of Mormon manuscript, 97–98; translation process, 17–23
Sommer, Benjamin, 174
Song of the Suffering Servant, 38–46, 50–51, 57, 77, 98, 181
Southcott, Joanna, 217–18
Sperry, Sidney B., 154, 199–203, 219: Isaiah problem, 199
spirits (ghosts), 208–10
Steinberg, Avi, 1
Stendahl, Krister, 5, 84–90
Stewart, Philemon, 113

Index

Tate, Charles, 153
temple, 36, 50, 109, 112, 170
Ten Commandments, 4–5
theology: in 3 Nephi, 78–80, 86; Abinadite, 42, 50, 57–60, 65–68, 75–77, 101, 116–21; difficult, 183; Johannine, 86, 89–98; Latter-day Saint, 111; of Nephi, 124–29, 152, 173, 184, 210, 213–14; Nephite, 15–16; questions related to the Book of Mormon, 21, 24
Third Isaiah, 6–8, 111
Tritheism, 43
Tvedtnes, John A., 208

Universalism, 142

Vest, Grant, 199
View of the Hebrews, 143–49

Walters, Wesley, 202
war, 37–38, 49, 54, 102, 109–10, 171, 192, 206
Welch, John, 154
Wesley, John, 58
Whitmer, Mary, 213
wilderness, 111, 117, 149, 153
Williamson, Hugh, 170
Winchester, Elhanan, 142
witnesses: to Book of Mormon, 213; first witness, 157; of Isaiah, 177; mutual, 93, 95; Nephi, 157–58, 163–65, 172–73; prophets as, 35; second witness, 157, 176; third witness, 157
Wright, David, 203
Wright, N.T., 65

Zarahemla, 31–34, 72–75
Zeniff, 32–37, 72–74: Zeniffite colony, 36, 54, 70, 74

Scripture Index

***Old Testament
(Hebrew Bible)***
Genesis
22   91
22:18   83

Exodus
20:1–17   4

Deuteronomy
18   91
18:15   83
18:18–19   83

2 Kings
16:2   182

Song of Songs
2:8   34

Isaiah
1–12   8
2   9, 181
2–4   179–80
2–5   177–83
2–12   184
2–14   7, 173, 176–77, 185–86, 194, 197
2–55   170

2:2   180
2:2–4   180
2:5   180–81
2:5–4:1   170, 180
2:6   181
3:15   191
4:2   180
4:2–6   180
5   179–80
5:1   180
5:1–30   180
6:1   182
6:10   183
6–12   177, 182–83, 187
7   183
7:1   182
7:14   114
8   183
8:16   183
8:16–18   216
8:17   183
9   183
10:13–14   135
11   107, 135, 144–48, 177, 179, 184–93
11:4   191–92
11:4–5   192
11:4–9   189, 191
11:6–9   190, 192

11:10   xiv, 107
11:11   135, 177, 186–88
11:11–12   127, 143, 145–46, 176–77, 185–88
11–12   182
13–14   177, 184
13–27   8
14:1   184
14:4   184
14:32   191
15–27   9
18   108, 146–47
22:10   112
24:32   191
28:17   112
28–35   8–9
28–39   9
29   9, 21, 135, 197–207, 213–20
29:1–24   205
29:3   206
29:3–4   206–7
29:3–7   200–1
29:4   206–9
29:8   201
29:8–24   200–201
29:11   170, 204, 210–11
29:11–12   214–18
29:11–14   127, 195–96, 210

Scripture Index

Isaiah (*continued*)
29:14   134, 199
30:27–33   192
30:30   112
35:1–2   111
36–39   8
40–47   8
40–48   8, 130
40–55   6, 175
40–66   111
40:2   35
48   8, 130–31, 134
48–49   129–32, 160, 172
48–51   7
48–54   7–8
49   112, 127–37, 140–49, 172, 175, 193
49–55   8, 130
49:6   131, 140
49:7   140
49:14–26   142
49:15   140
49:16   140
49:18–22   145
49:18–23   141, 146
49:19–20   143
49:20   141
49:21   131, 145
49:22   37, 134–35, 146, 170
49:22–23   8, 111, 127–28, 131–37, 142–43, 146–48, 164, 175, 185
49:23   133, 135, 140–41
50:4   xi–xii
52   7, 95–99, 104–7, 119, 121, 137, 139, 148
52–53   38, 53, 62–67
52:1   95
52:1–2   121
52:1–3   94–96, 105
52:1–6   104
52:1–12   97, 104
52:6   95
52:6–7   94
52:7   34, 46–48, 54, 62, 64, 69–70, 95, 104, 137, 170
52:7–10   13–14, 30, 33, 37–40, 45–47, 51–52, 55, 62, 64, 69, 74, 77, 103, 117–20, 131, 136
52:8   49, 104
52:8–10   47–48, 82–83, 91–95, 104
52:10   37, 51, 104, 128, 170
52:10–12   97
52:11   121
52:11–12   94–97, 104–5
52:11–15   94
52:13–15   97–98
52:14   97
53   38–47, 51, 54, 62, 77, 97–98, 118, 181
53:1   38, 50
53:1–3   114
53:1–12   51
53:4   70
53:6   181
53:7   41
53:8   42–43, 46, 48, 55–64
53:10   41–42, 45–48, 62–64
54   7, 83, 98, 105–7, 121, 148
54:1–3   106
54:2   121
54:4   121
54:5   111
60   8, 141
60:3   146
60:3   141
60:6   141
60:18   111
61:1–3   8
62:11–12   112
65:12   112
66:15–16   111

Ezekiel
37:15–28   144

Daniel
5:25–26   112
8:13–14   112

Micah
5:8–15   83

Nahum
1:15   34

Malachi
3–4   4, 83

New Testament
Matthew
3:17   85
5–7   4, 84
8:17   70
17:1   86
26:41   89

Luke
4:16–23   8
22:19–20   89
22:29–46   87
22:43   87
22:44   87

John
4   84
10:16   81, 84, 86
10:18   94
10:24   93
10:30   93
12:28   86
17   84, 88
20:27   86

Romans
9–11   63
11   146
11:11–26   146
11:16–25   185

Galatians
4   105–6

Revelation
12   111
20:6   112

Book of Mormon
1 Nephi
1–5   138, 153, 159–60
1–9   12, 155, 158
1:1   73
1:9   159
1:11–12   159
1:16–17   154–55, 160
1:18   159

2:21   169
5:1   159
5:10   159
5:17   159
6–9   159–60
6:1–6   156, 159
7   153
8   153
8:3   169
8:4   168
8:17–18   169
8:21   168
9:2–6   156, 159
10   153
10–14   159–60
10–15   12
10–22   155
10:1   155, 160
10:4–10   129
11–14   153, 185, 197
12:22   169
13:1–9   169
13:10–19   169
13:20–29   169
13:23–29   202
13:30–41   169
13:35   210
13:36   136
13:37   137
13:39   169
14:15   192
14:18–28   5
15   159–160
15–18   153
15   138
15:14   166
15:20   129, 137, 162
16:1–19:21   159–60
19   153, 156
19–22   12
19:1–2   156
19:1–5   155–56
19:3   150, 156
19:5   175
19:14   132
19:22–21:26   159–60
19:23   171
19:23–24   152
19:24   130, 134

22   131–32, 138, 147, 153, 159–60
22:2–28   162
22:4   147
22:8   152, 172
22:12   136
22:23   191

2 Nephi
1   153
1–5   157–58, 163
2–3   153
5   153, 156
5:27–29   156
5:28–34   151, 156
5:30–32   156
6   132, 156, 186
6–8   163
6–10   12, 157–58, 175, 185
6–30   156–58
6:3   185
6:4   133
6:5   152, 172
6:6–7   134
6:11   132
6:13   133
6:14   185
6:14–15   135
7:4   221
9   153
10:10   134
11   157, 176–77
11–15   176
11–24   12, 179, 185–86
11:1   157, 176
11:2   172, 176
11:2–3   157
11:2   52
11:8   52, 172, 189
12   157, 176
12–15   177
12–24   157, 176
12:5   181
12:6   181
14:1   184
14:2   165, 179
14:2–3   164, 178
14:4   184
14:19   184

15:1   180
16:13   164
16–22   164, 176–77, 182
20:22   164, 178
21   189
21:1   179
23–24   164, 176–77, 184
24:19   165, 179
24:21   164, 178
24:32   191
25   186
25–27   165, 197, 199, 204–5
25–30   12, 157–58, 172–73, 194
25   186
25:1   173
25:1–8   165
25:2   134
25:4   152, 173, 194
25:5   2
25:7   152, 173, 195
25:8   194, 205
25:16–17   186
25:24–25   66
26–27   202–3
26:15   221
26:16   207–10
26:20   191
26:20–33   165
27   199–202, 212
27:3   200
27:3–35   201
27:7–8   210
27:12   213
27:13   211, 213
27:15–18   211
27:16   213
27:23   213, 219
27:25   214
27:26   221
27:26–27   214
27:27   221
28–29   61, 165
28–30   165
28–32   153
29   186
29:1   186
29:2   135
29:5   132

2 Nephi (continued)
29:12–13   148
30   156, 192–93
30:3   188
30:4   188
30:7   188
30:8   188–89
30:9–15   189
30:10   189
30:15   193
30:18   156
31   165
31–33   157–58
31:1   156
31:4–21   15
31:21   15
32   165
32:7   215
33   165

Jacob
4:4   66
6:1–2   185
7:26   2

Jarom
1:11   66

Omni
1:12   72
1:12–13   73
1:13   31, 73
1:27   32

Words of Mormon
1:18   32

Mosiah
1–6   13
1:19   32
1:27   72
3   75
7:1   32
8:7–8   32
9:1   31–32, 73
9:1–2   73
9:2   72
9:3   72
9:8   36
11:1   32
11:2   13, 29
11:3   13, 29
11:4–5   29
11:7   13, 29
11:8–13   29
11:10   36
11:16–19   29
11:18–19   35
11:19   13, 37
11:20   13, 29
11:21   30
12:3   30
12:11   30
12:16   33
12:19   13, 30, 33
12:20   13, 32
12:21–24   33
12:25   31, 40, 45–46, 60, 67
12:25–27   43
12:27–28   40
12:28   31
13:1   33
13:25   42
13:28   40
13:30–31   65
13:33   40, 76
13:34   41
13:34–35   41
13:35   41
14:1   38
14:1–2   50
14:2   39
14:3   39
14:4   39
14:5   39
14:6   39
14:7   41
14:8   39
14:9   39
14:10   39
14:11   39
14:12   39
14:32   191
15:1   43, 45, 50
15:1–9   15, 43
15:2–3   41
15:3–4   49
15:4   81
15:5   44
15:6   81
15:7   44
15:7–8   81
15:8   44
15:10   42–43, 46
15:11   43–44
15:11–16:3   81
15:12   81
15:11–20   43
15:13   44
15:14   46
15:17   47
15:18   47
15:19   47
15:21   47
15:22   44
15:24   47–48
15:26   45, 47
15:28   48–49
15:29   118
15:29–31   48
16:1   48–49, 118
16:4   50
16:6   47, 66, 76
16:14–15   67
17:2   80
17:4   44
17:8   31
18:1   15, 71
18:1–2   71
18:1–17   15
18:9   44
18:19   71
27:37   69

Alma
7:11   70
39:17   66

Helaman
8:20   70

3 Nephi
1:14   118–19
5:20–21   79

5:23–25 79
8:20 80
9:15 80
9:15–18 85
10:5–7 80
11:7 85
11:14 86
11:22 15, 94
11:25 94
11:27 94
11:28 15
12–14 84
15–16 81
15:1 5
15:1–9 84
15:4 81
15:6 81
15:7–8 81
15:11–16:3 81
15:12 81
16:4 50, 81
16:4–5 83
16:5–15 82
16:6–7 83
16:11 83
16:13–15 83
16:16–20 80
16:17 82
16:17–20 91
16:18 82
17:1–20:9 81
17:2 80–82, 91
17:11 87
17:14 87
17:15 87

17:17 87
17:24 87
18 84
18:7 89
18:11 89
19 84, 88–91
19:13 87
19:14 87
19:15 88
19:19 88
19:25 88
19:27 88
19:28 88
19:31 88
19:34 88
19:35 88
20–21 105
20:6–7 105
20:8 90
20:10 91
20:10–23:5 81
20:10–26:5 81
20:11–12 91, 105
20:13 83
20:16 83
20:16–19 83
20:23–27 83
20:29 137, 139
20:31 91
20:32–35 92–93
20:32–45 83
20:33 91, 118
20:35 93
20:36 95, 105
20:40 95, 105

20:41 95, 105
20:46 94–95, 139
21:1 138–39, 195
21:5 83
21:10 97
21:11 83
21:12–21 83
21:22–25 83
21:26 98
21:27–28 98
21:28 105
22:1 98, 105
23:1 16, 77, 98
23:2 98
23:6 4
24–25 83

Mormon
4:5 192
8–9 61
8:5 16–17
8:12 17
8:23 17

Ether
4:13–17 5

Moroni
10:30 121
10:31 121

Doctrine and Covenants
10:43 97–98

JOSEPH M. SPENCER is an associate professor of ancient scripture at Brigham Young University.

The University of Illinois Press
is a founding member of the
Association of University Presses.

University of Illinois Press
1325 South Oak Street
Champaign, IL 61820–6903
www.press.uillinois.edu